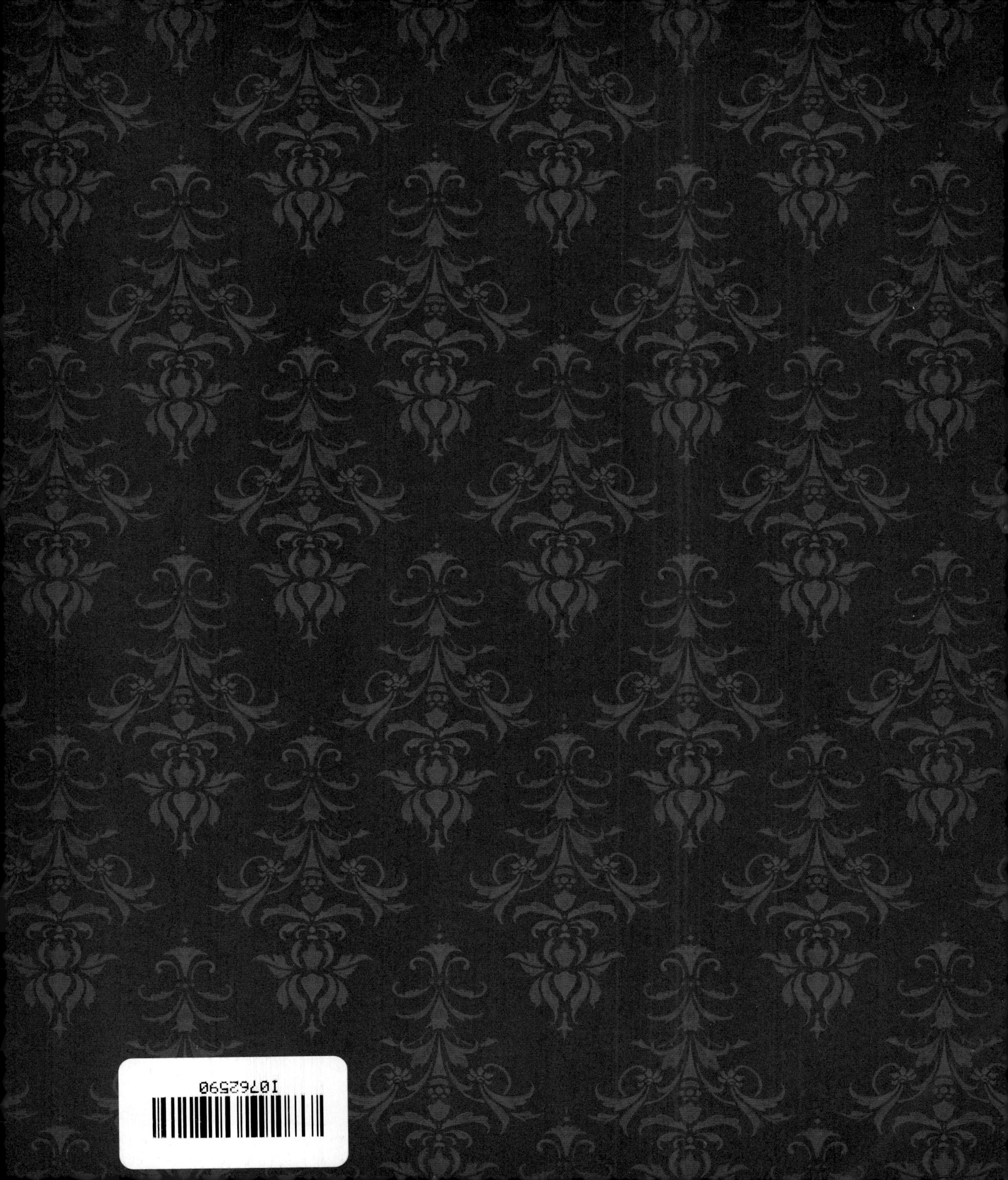

Prism

The Art Journey of Cosmic Spectrum

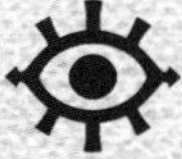

3dtotal Publishing

Correspondence: publishing@3dtotal.com
Website: www.3dtotal.com

First published in the United Kingdom, 2023, by 3dtotal Publishing.

Address: 3dtotal.com Ltd,
29 Foregate Street, Worcester
WR1 1DS, United Kingdom.

Hard cover ISBN: 978-1-912843-56-5

Printed and bound in China by
C&C Offset Printing Co., Ltd

Visit www.3dtotalpublishing.com for a complete list of available book titles.

Managing Director: Tom Greenway
Studio Manager: Simon Morse
Lead Editor: Samantha Rigby
Lead Designer: Joseph Cartwright
Editor: Jenny Fox-Proverbs

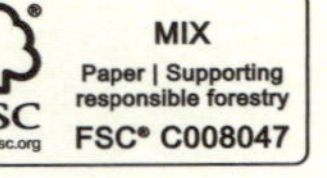

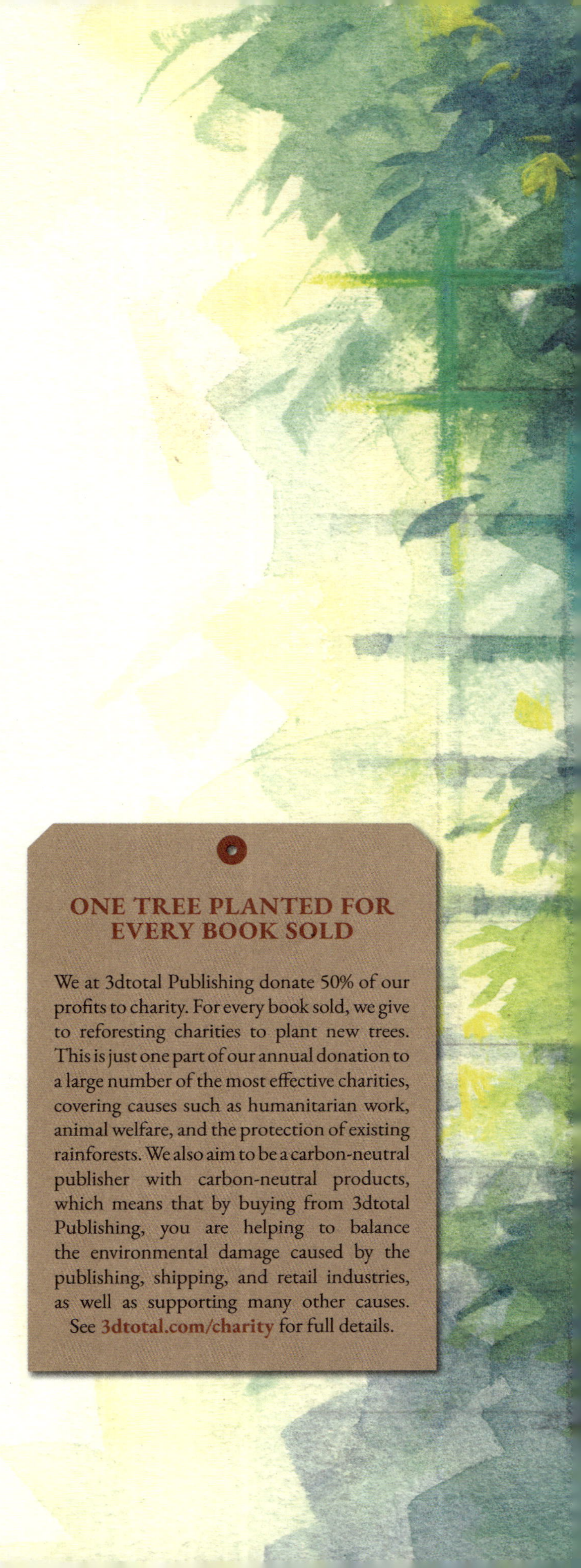

ONE TREE PLANTED FOR EVERY BOOK SOLD

We at 3dtotal Publishing donate 50% of our profits to charity. For every book sold, we give to reforesting charities to plant new trees. This is just one part of our annual donation to a large number of the most effective charities, covering causes such as humanitarian work, animal welfare, and the protection of existing rainforests. We also aim to be a carbon-neutral publisher with carbon-neutral products, which means that by buying from 3dtotal Publishing, you are helping to balance the environmental damage caused by the publishing, shipping, and retail industries, as well as supporting many other causes. See **3dtotal.com/charity** for full details.

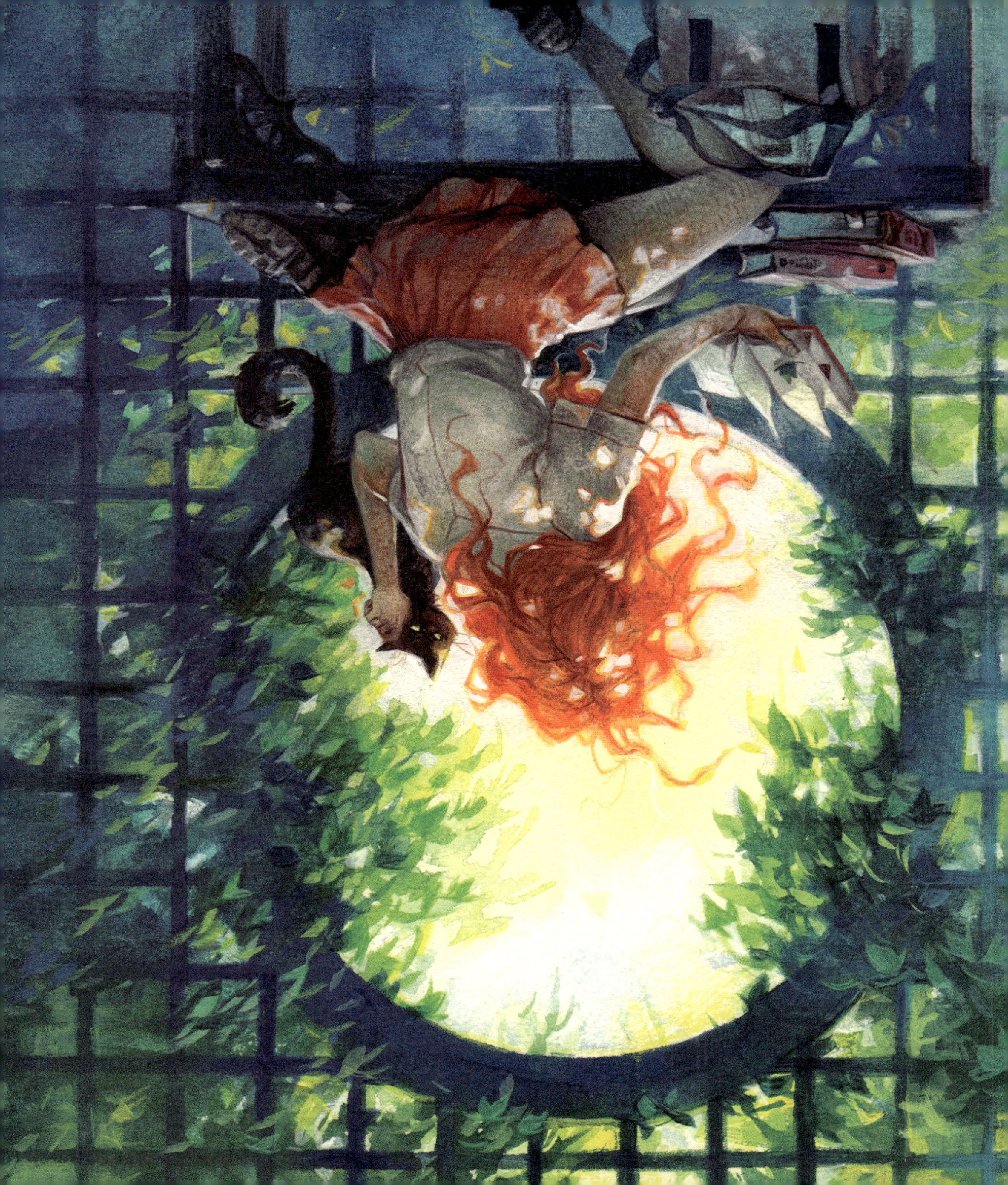

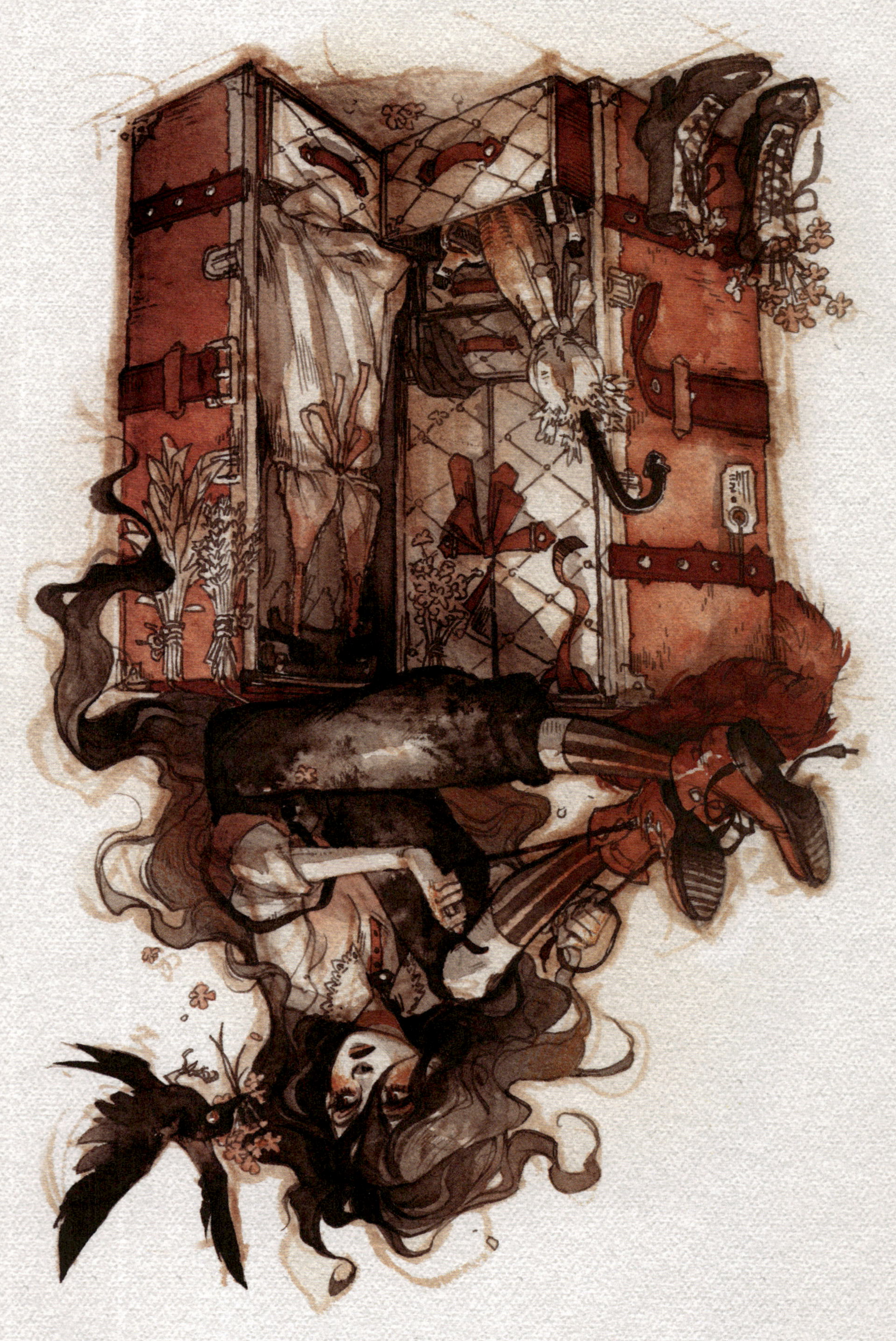

Contents

Foreword

My exposure to Yana's art dates back to the beginning of my online career in 2013, when I created an Instagram account to post my doodles. Although we had never spoken to each other, she was certainly one of the very first artists I followed there and I have admired silently ever since. I recall being captivated by her gorgeous, expressive characters. You could tell, even then, that she was this new breed of artist, of eclectic influences with a very strong sense of personality and style. As time passed, her work became more and more intricate. I saw how those characters started to become something else, now surrounded by moody spaces and deeper, richer color palettes.

Yana's art is very meaningful and that's something that makes her stand out. She's passionate about the characters she creates and the stories she wants to tell. That passion shines through in whatever she's creating, whether it is a simple sketch, a whole illustration, or even a YouTube video. I firmly believe that the kind of genuine, deep-burning love I see in her is a core element needed to grow and evolve as an artist.

As someone who loves playing around with different mediums, I have always admired the outstanding control Yana has over both traditional and digital tools. What makes her work so unique is the way she's capable of adapting her art so naturally and effortlessly without losing its essence. That's definitely not easy to achieve, and only shows how much work and effort she has poured in to get where she is today. It's been delightful seeing her explore, grow, and change to become better as time goes by, not only artistically but also by overcoming the pitfalls of this field and taking the reins of her own work. Yana will inspire you, as she inspires me, to become the sole author of your own work and to tell the world the stories you've always wanted to tell.

I'm beyond honored to introduce Yana's book to you. The creative journey within these pages will encourage those who are looking to find their footing in the field of art, and enrich those who are already part of it. Enjoy the ride! ❤

Gretel Lusky
Illustrator & Comic Artist
www.gretlusky.com
Instagram: @gretlusky

Ocean © Gretel Lusky

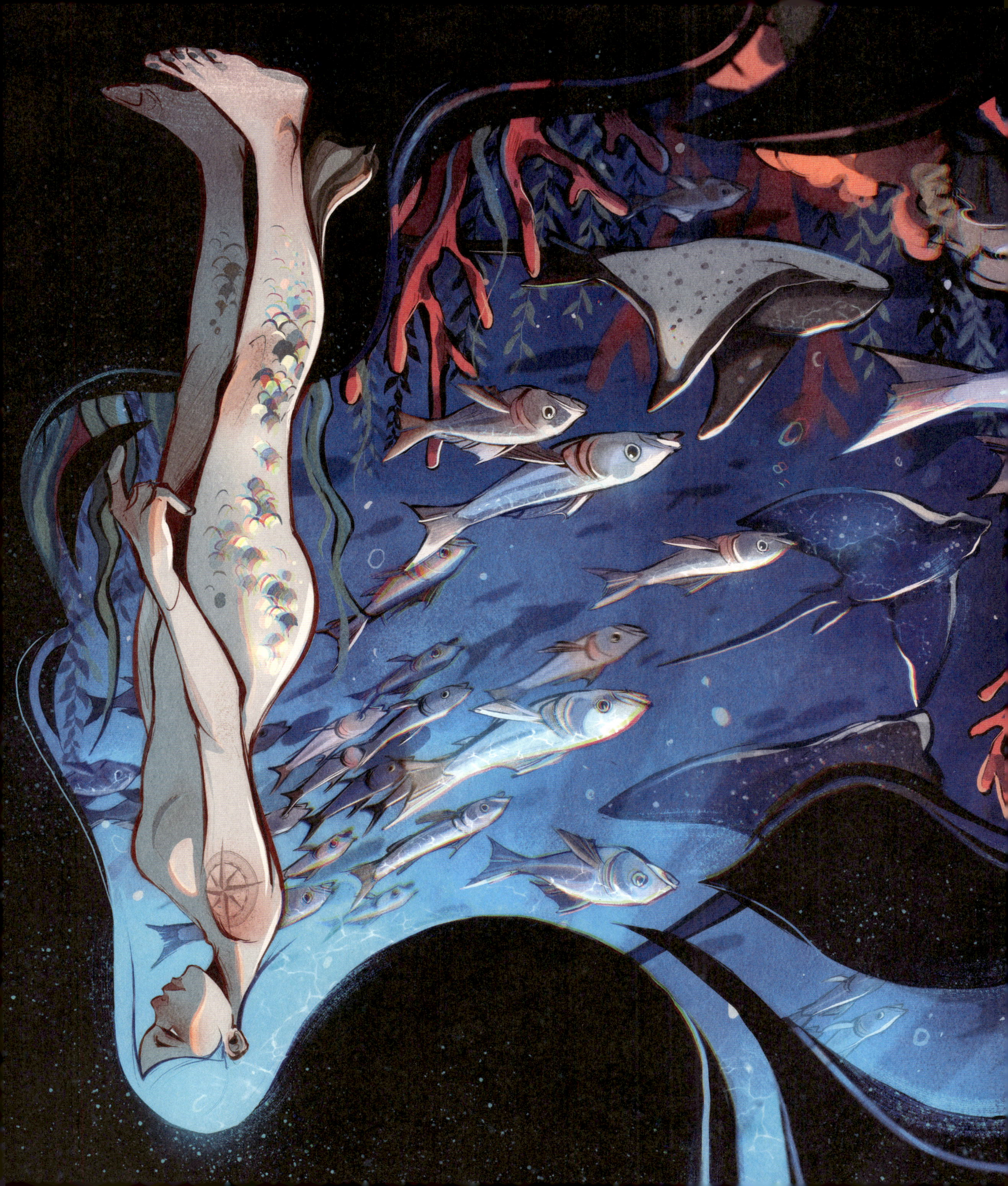

Introduction

Dear reader,

I adore art books and you probably do too. These glittering, beautiful things were my first coveted material possessions – I spent months saving up for them as soon as I had access to money. When I was thirteen, a friend's older sister showed me a small collection of art books (she was an amazing artist herself). It was one of my very first experiences of intense inspiration and awe – an encounter that lit a fire in my heart. The books were by emerging Korean artists in the comics and games industries, and I had never seen anything like them before. I was dazzled by every aspect – so much care was put into the graphic design, layouts, cover materials, and presentation. And of course, the beautiful artwork... each book was truly a labor of love. It was like a little window into the artists' soul. From that moment onward, I hoped to make such books myself one day.

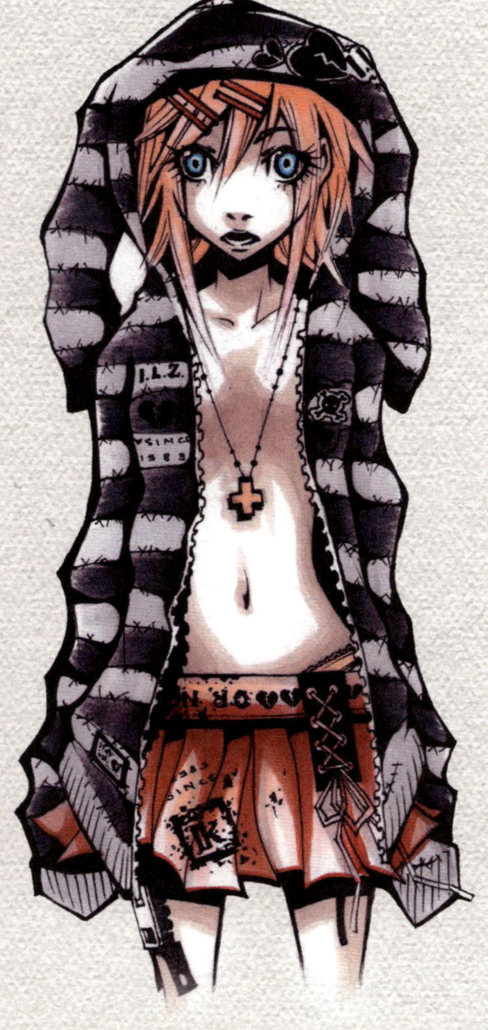

I'm happy to say that I've managed to produce a few art books of my own at this point, but none of them are quite like *Prism*. This book is the biggest window into my world because it's full of artwork I produced after I managed to solve most of my pressing internal struggles. More importantly, it's full of my insights and thoughts about being an artist. My relationship with art has shifted many times in life – I've used it as a distraction from the real world, a coping mechanism for persistent depression, a way to shut people out, and a way to self-examine. The pivoting point was sharing my art with people by posting it online. It was a big change. From then, art became my way of reconnecting with the world, a tool for self-expression, a path towards friends and communities of like-minded people, and eventually my way to earn a living. It's not always a straight-forward path and it can be very difficult to expose yourself to the world this way. But one thing I know for sure is that when you make something truly personal, it has a way of resonating.

I thought it would be apt to start this book with a recent recreation of a very old drawing of mine, a microcosm of my art journey! I will admit that Kima (the girl pictured here) started out as a shameless self-insert character. I was only twelve when I made her... how quickly the years flew by. Since then, she has developed a unique personality and a convoluted plot-line of her own, and has finally taken her rightful place on the cover of this book, right beside HaeJin.

My ultimate intent is to give something tangible and valuable to my supportive audience, many of whom have been following my work for over a decade. After all, I always crave an art book from artists I admire, and feel a great sadness when they do not have one available. I aspire for my art to have that effect on somebody – it would be a privilege and would truly make all my efforts worthwhile. I hope you find this book to be an endless well of inspiration that will urge you to create art of your own, and I hope it lights a fire in your heart the way art books do for me.

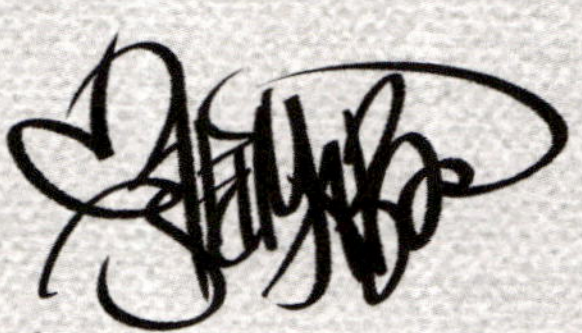

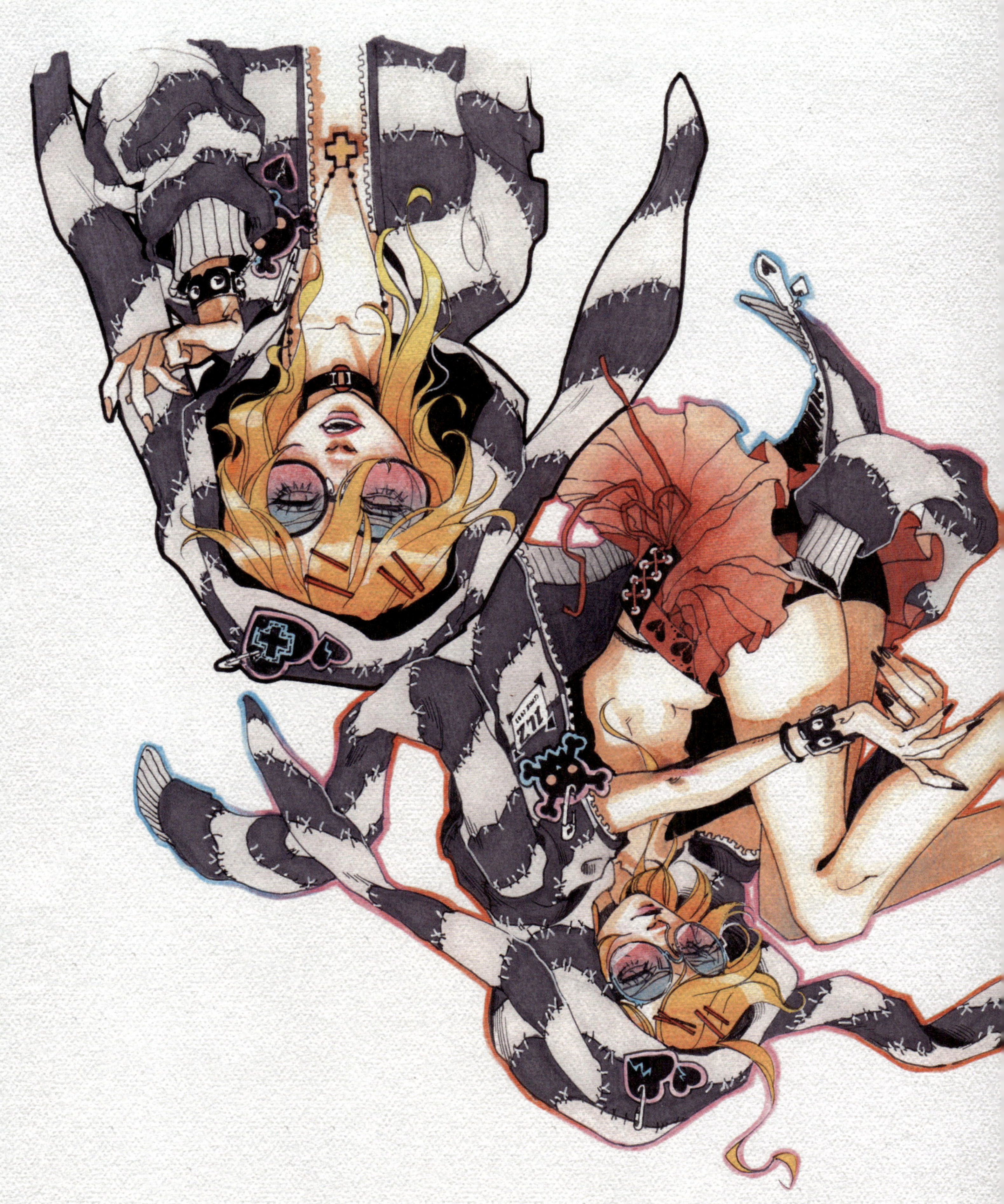

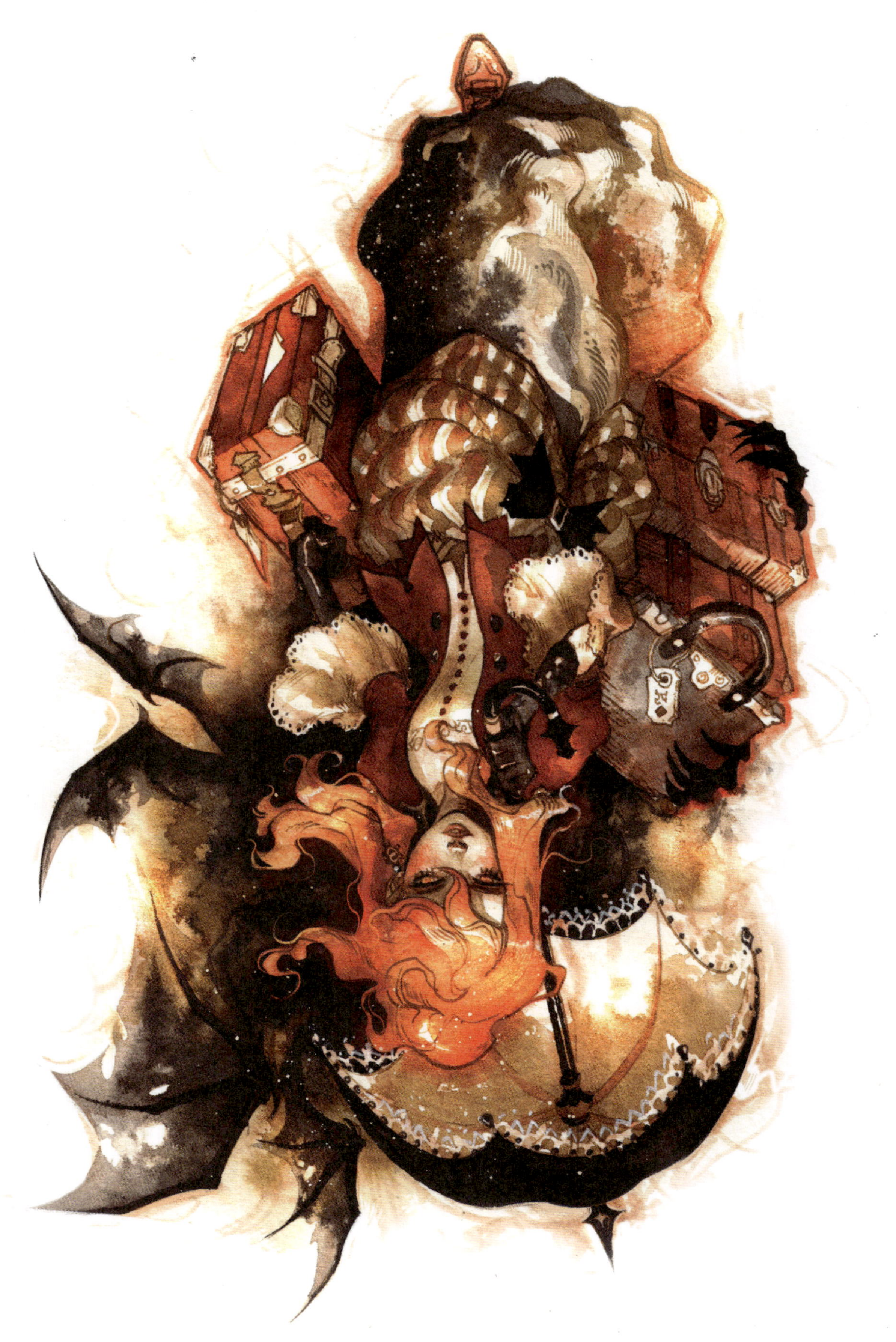

My relationship with art

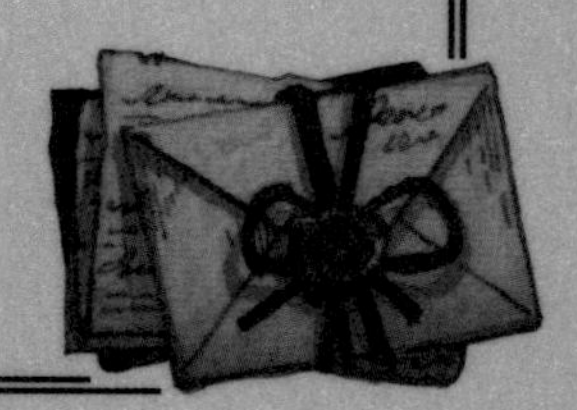

My relationship with art

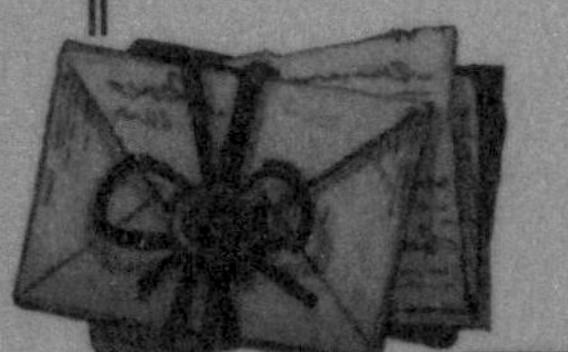

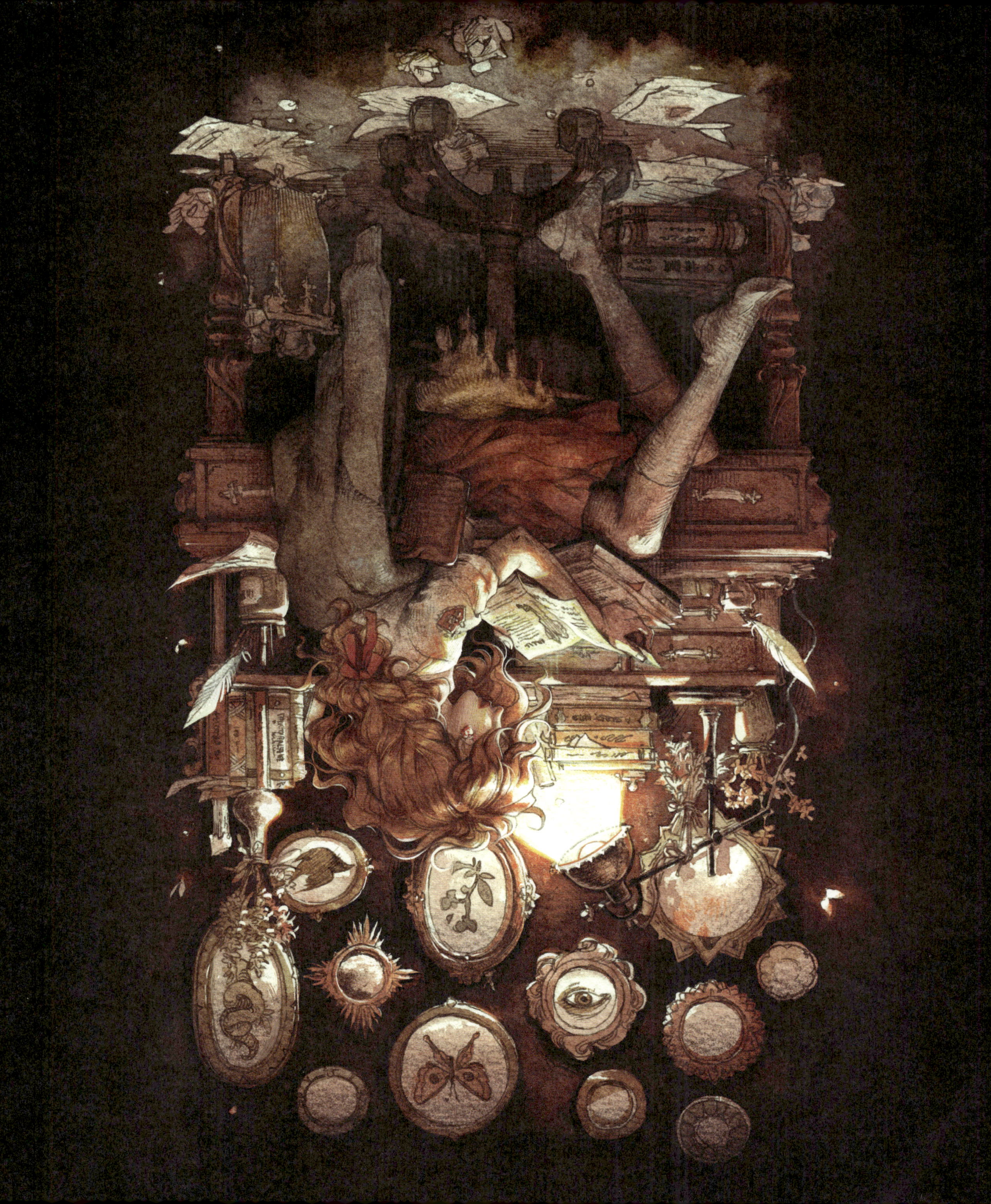

Early connections

I don't remember a time in my life when drawing wasn't my favorite activity, aside from endless summer days spent exploring the neighborhood as a child. I think I've always gravitated toward drawing characters too – I remember drawing a lot of cartoon animals, especially Bugs Bunny, when I was little.

This may be strange to say, but I don't think I ever had a specific inspirational moment or a key influence in my life that pushed me toward a career in art. It was always my favorite thing to do, but what really cemented my relationship with art was my family's immigration to Canada when I was eleven years old, which I liked to call "the move." It took me years to realize that this was actually a somewhat traumatic experience. For a very long time, I viewed my life as split into the hazy dreamlike filtered memories of "before the move," and the sharp dragging confusion of "after the move," with some sort of inexplicable dark abyss that stretched on for miles in between.

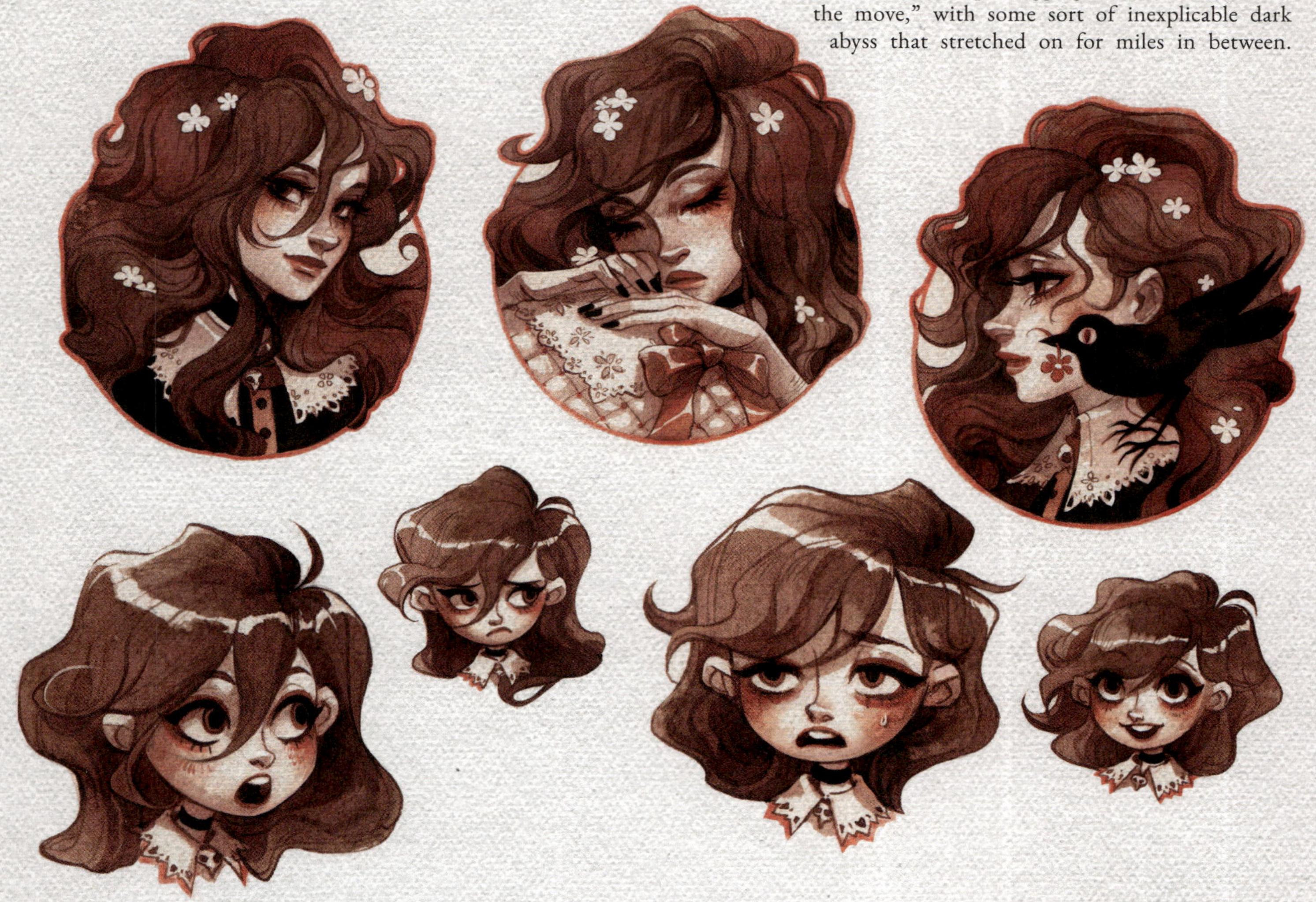

After the move, art became my therapeutic outlet – it was my coping mechanism. It felt like a private relationship with something, a place to go that felt comforting. Art was my constant – something I could always go back to and rely on regardless of ever-changing life circumstances. It was something that couldn't be taken away from me and something I couldn't lose. Given the intensity with which I clung to art, the prospect of having to pursue a career doing something other than drawing has never even entered my mind. Also, I think I am lucky in the sense that I never doubted my ability to make a career out of drawing; it always just felt like the one thing I was meant to do.

In recent years, my beliefs about the nature of reality have shifted toward something more mysterious and enigmatic than materialistic, hard-science theories. I don't really believe in coincidences anymore and I like to think that everyone's life has a clear thread running through it, whether they can see it or not.

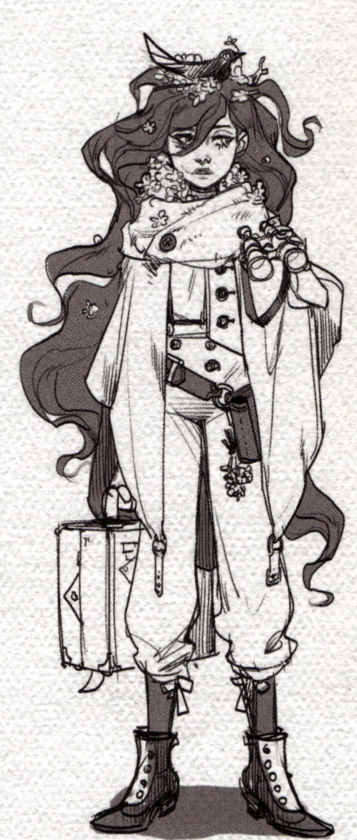

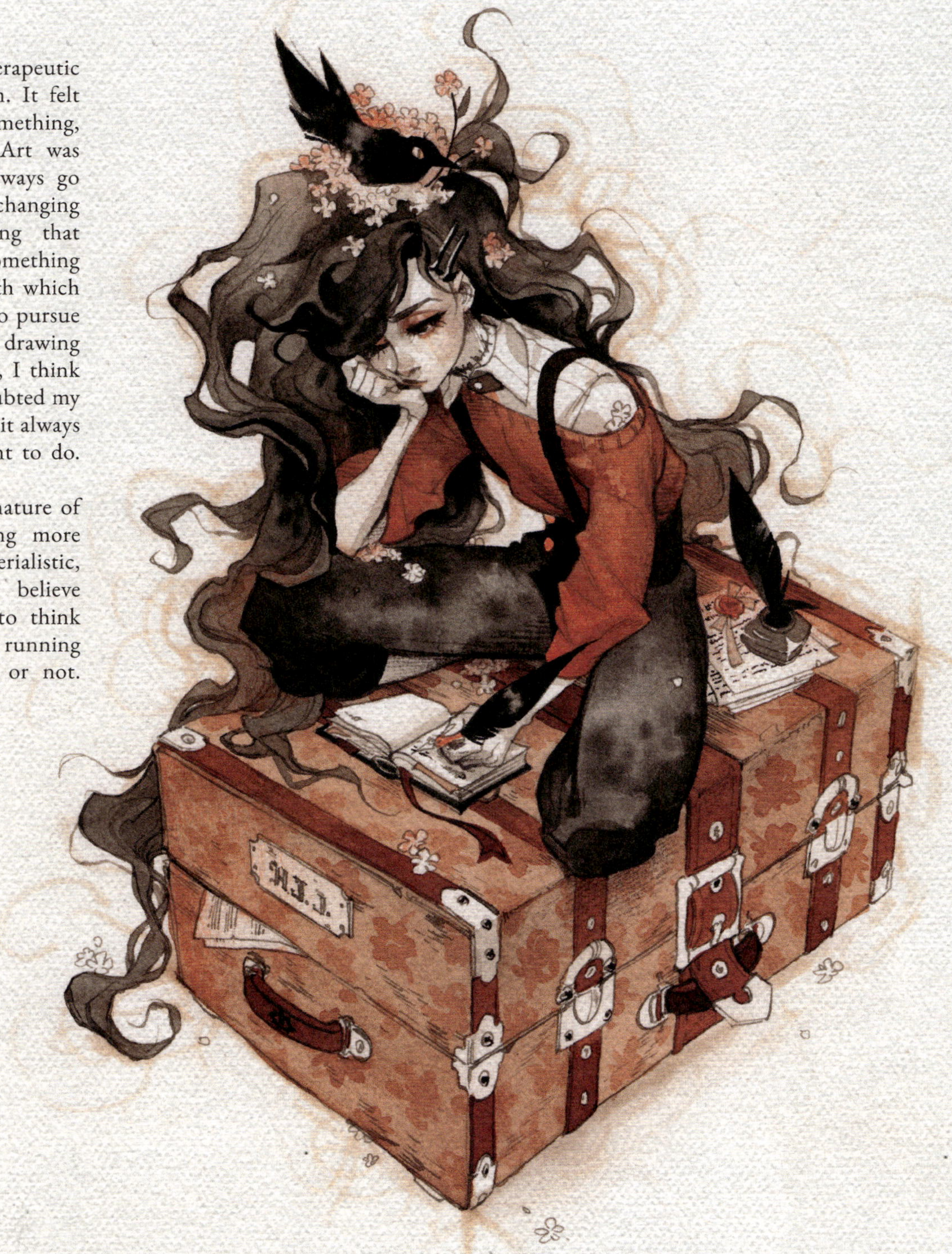

"I was lucky in the sense that I never doubted my ability to make a career out of drawing"

Formal studies

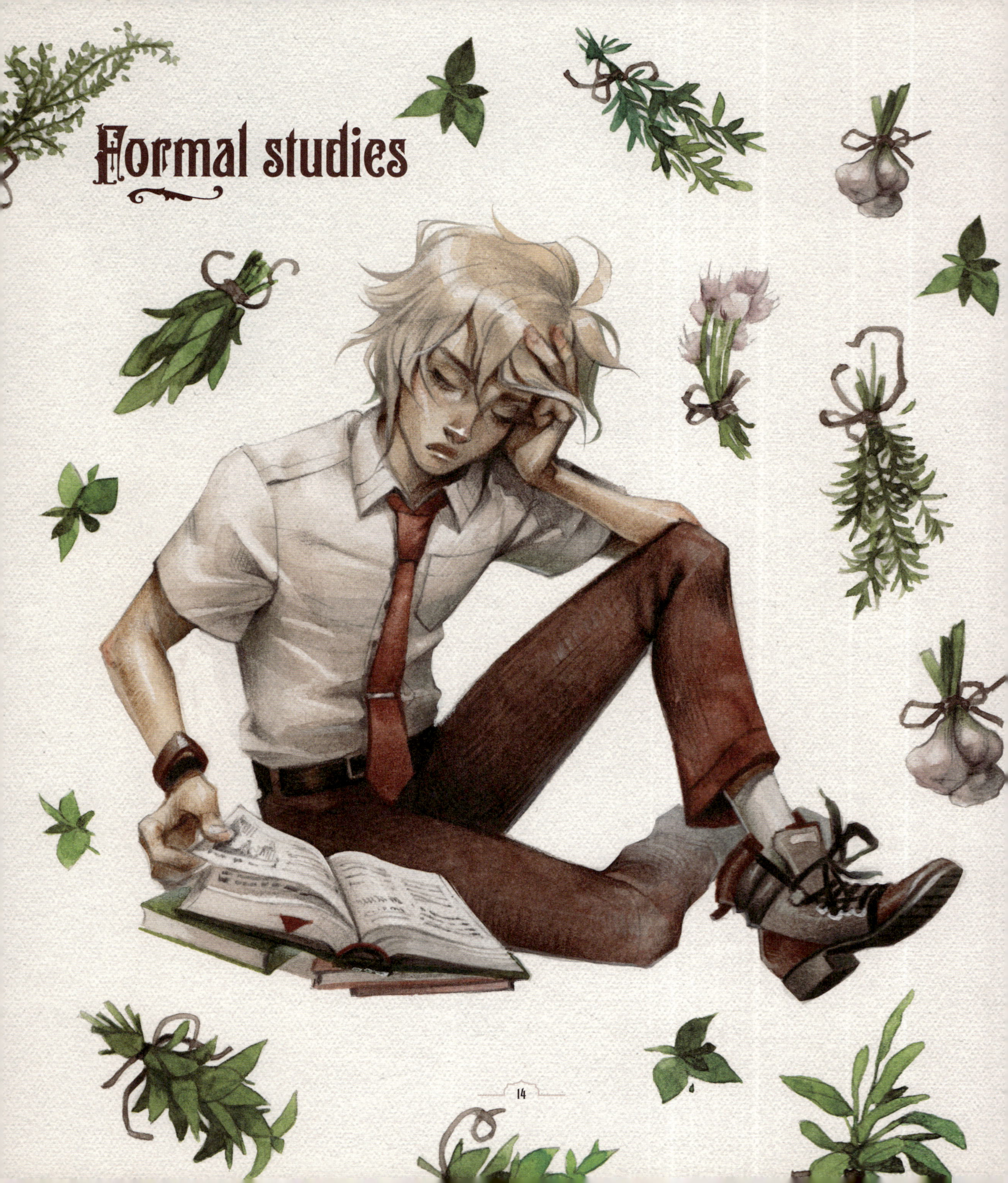

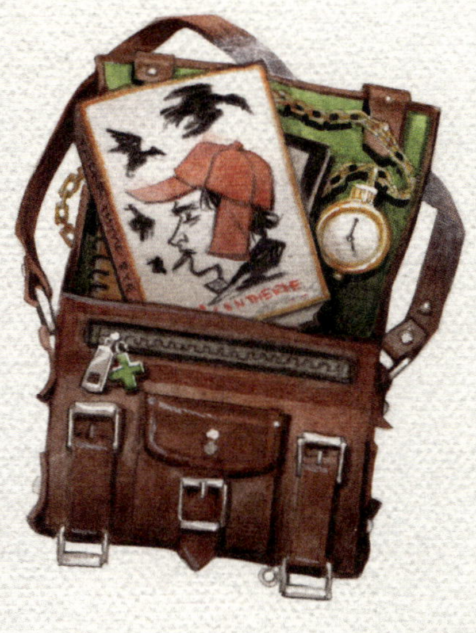

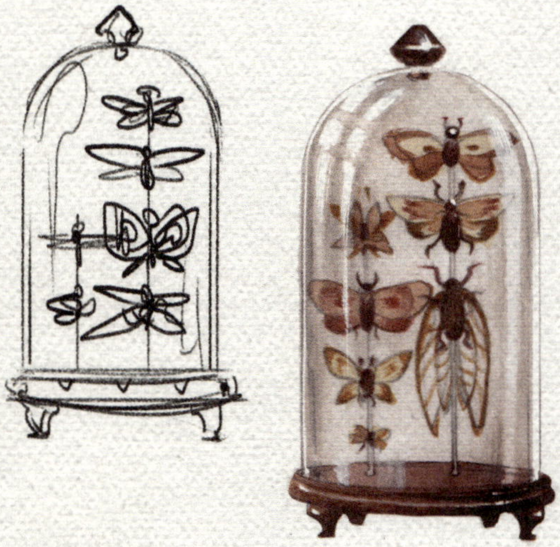

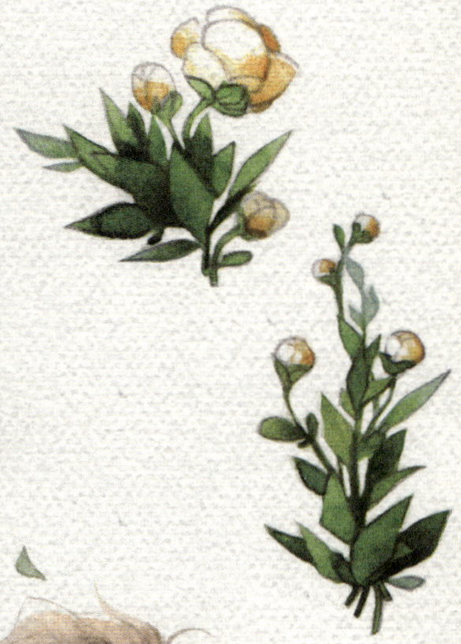

I went to an art-focused high school, where I majored in art and minored (begrudgingly) in music – for some reason my parents wanted me to be a violin teacher! That just wasn't on the cards for me.

My teenage years were spent in quiet desperation, and I took time off after high school to decide what I should do next. There were many reasons why I considered not going to university or college at all, but alas, my parents insisted that it was necessary. I decided to take the most broad and generic art-related program I could think of at The Ontario College of Art and Design University (OCAD U): Graphic Design.

After a year in Graphic Design, it was clear to me that I should pick something more specific, so I switched to Illustration for my second year, simultaneously deciding to focus on improving my fundamental art skills above all else. Unfortunately, the curriculum did not prove to be helpful for achieving my goals, so I went to study Traditional Animation at Sheridan College instead. I didn't have much of an interest in the animation industry to be honest, but after touring the campus and seeing the work of animation students on the walls, it was clear that it was the program to take if I wanted to improve and expand my skills.

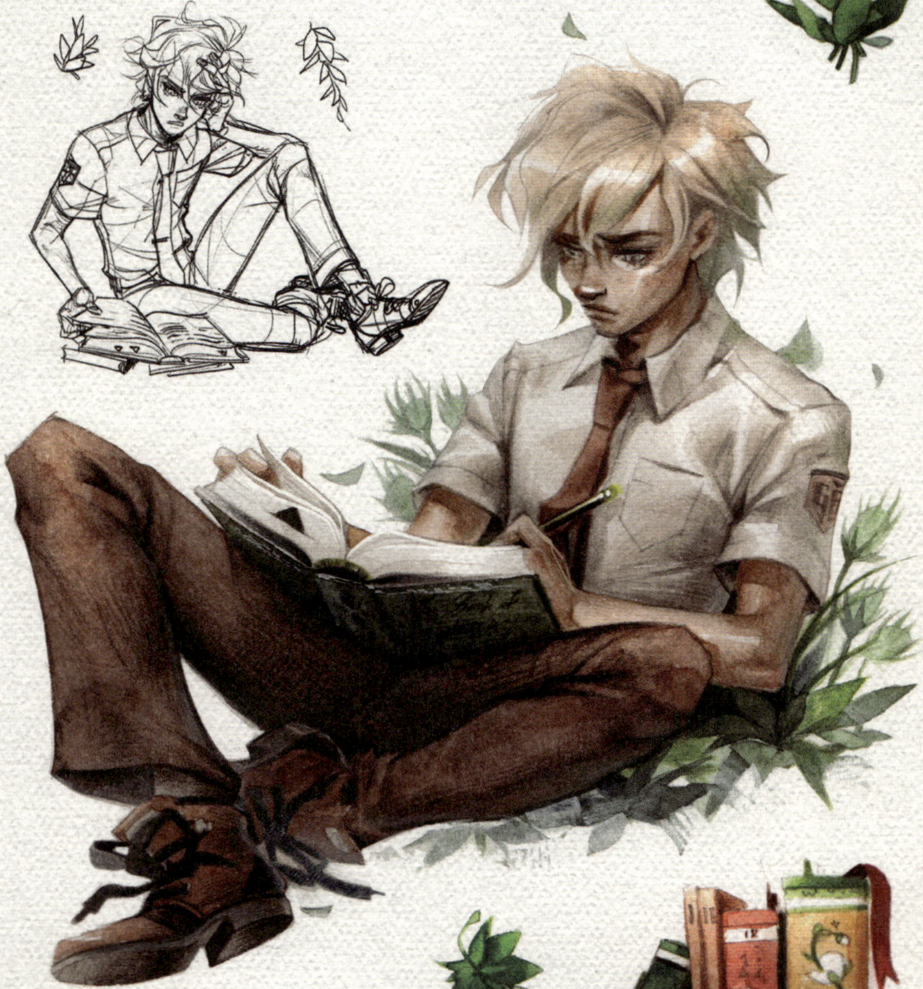

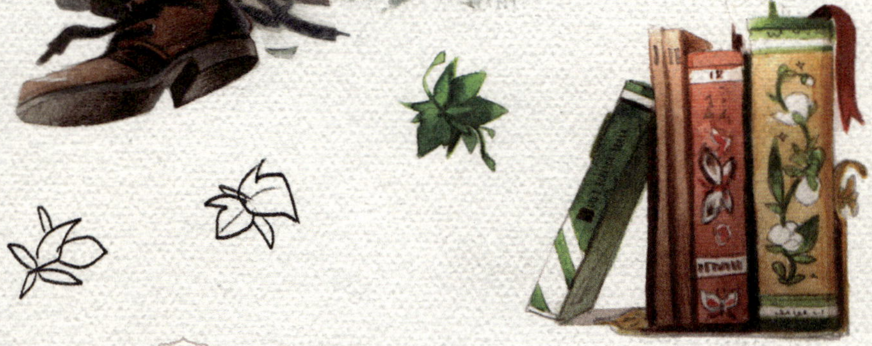

It may sound like I had a solid plan in mind for my career at this point, but the truth is I still had absolutely no idea what I was going to do post-graduation. Although I had technically been freelancing on a small scale for many years already, I was still under the impression that I'd have to get a permanent studio job once I graduated (this was the only path discussed in both OCAD U and Sheridan College – not a single mention was made of freelancing or an independent career, from what I can remember).

However, the future just wasn't something I thought about – I was too busy battling with depression, and was more concerned about finding the will to get out of bed the next morning. (I know it sounds very sad, but eventually I won! More on that later.) I just figured that logically, gaining technical skills was a solid base that would benefit me no matter what I chose to do in the future, so that's what I did. Every step I took post-high-school graduation added something valuable to my skill-set, but I am haunted by the feeling that I always sidelined my true passion, treating it as a carrot on a stick to drive me through the things I mistakenly thought were the "proper path." In some ways though, maybe I needed that carrot on a stick?

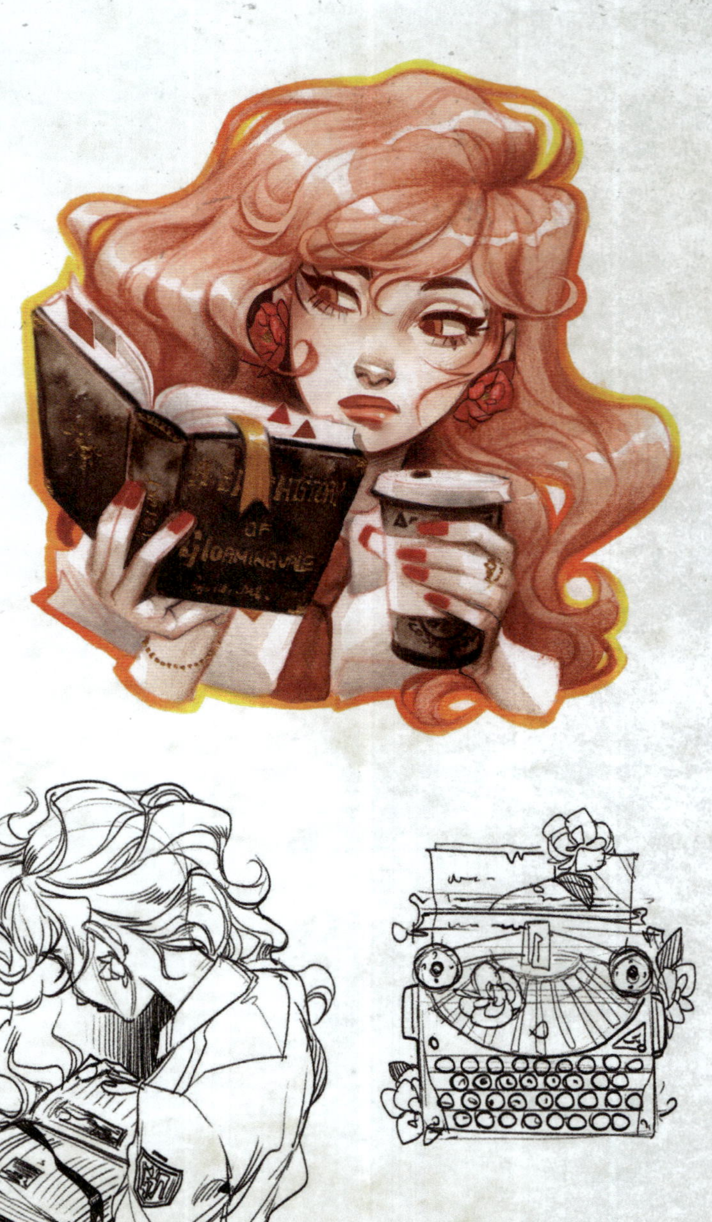

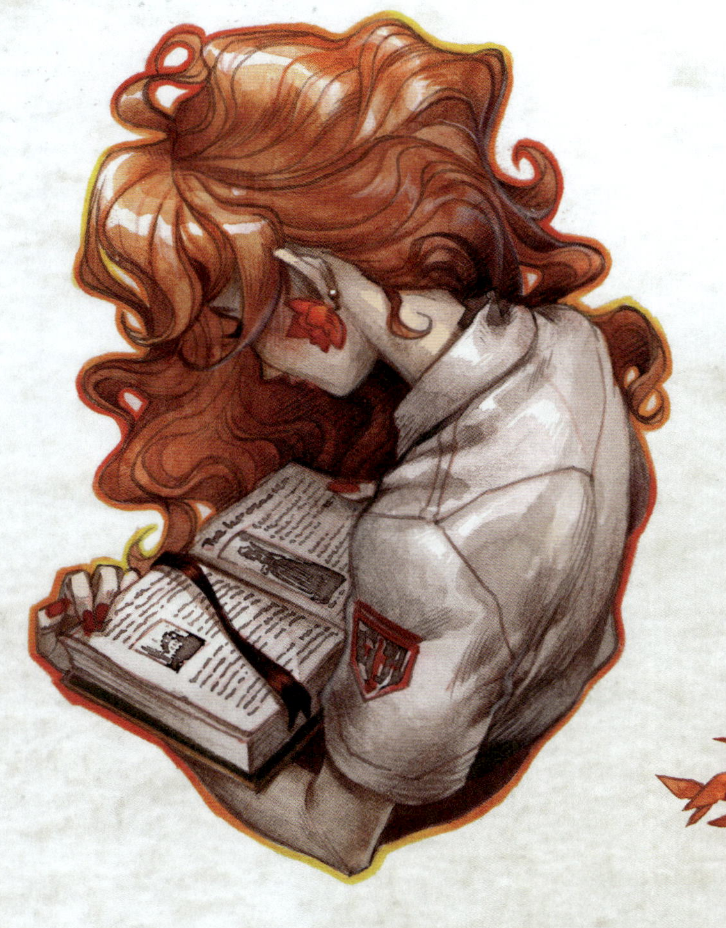

The Scholar

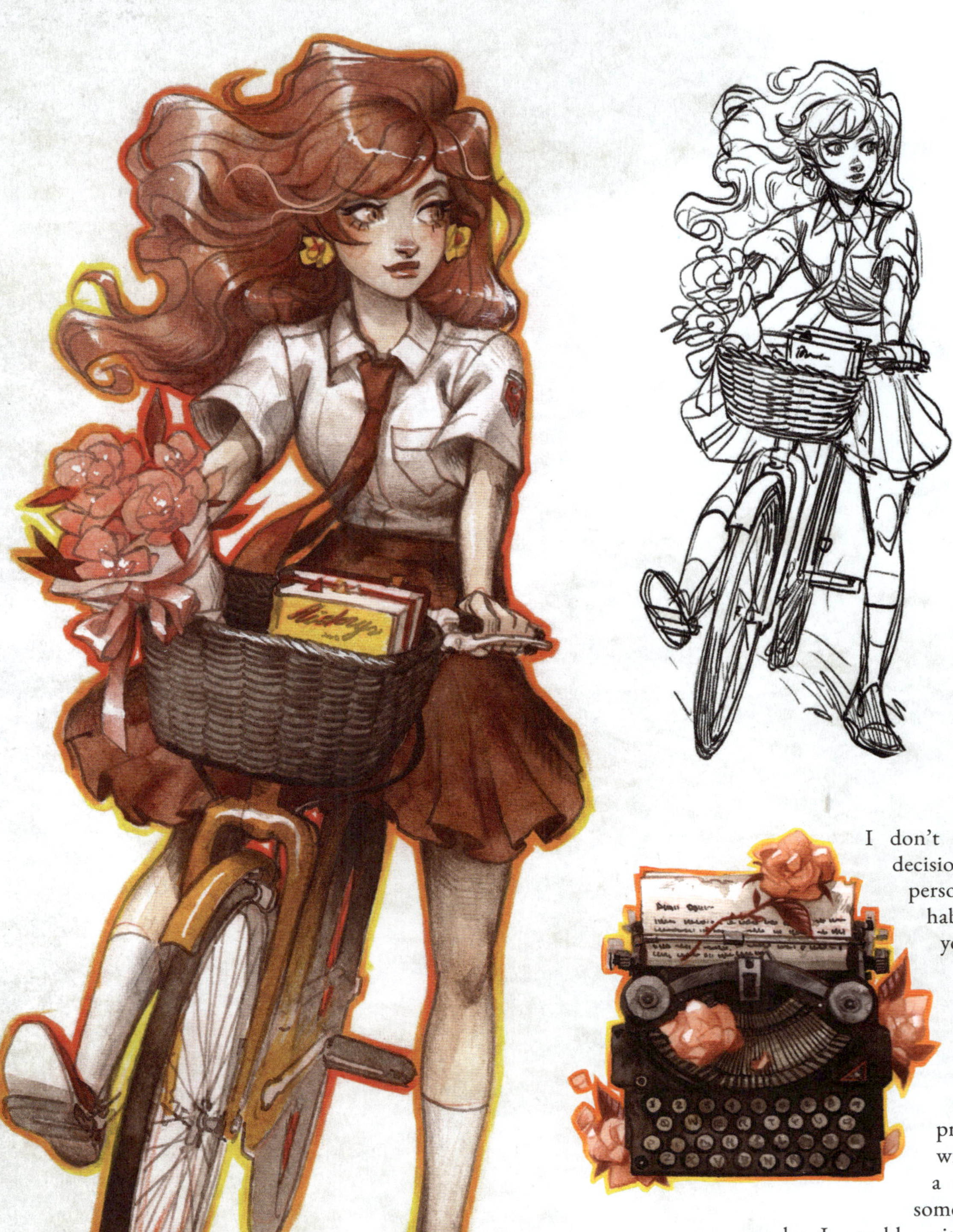

I don't like to regret my past decisions. Being a regretful person can become a poisonous habit – all it does is corrode your soul and waste your time. That being said, if I could do things all over again, I think I'd make two different choices. First, I would bet on myself pursuing personal projects right off the bat without bothering with a studio job or illustrating somebody else's work. And maybe I would quit Sheridan College after my second year. I remained in college because I thought sticking it out till graduation was the right thing to do. Right by whom, though? My parents? The completionist in me? The belief that quitting would have made me a failure, a loser in the eyes of others? My biggest enemy always seems to be self-doubt, even now just as it was back then, but thankfully to a lesser degree.

Choosing an independent career

There's a notion that carving your own entrepreneurial path is this huge gamble, whereas taking the standard full-time job route is a safer, more stable option. But how true is that, really?

I think going your own way (career-wise) may be a financial gamble, but to me, taking the standard day-job was just a different kind of gamble. A gamble on how well my mental health would hold up on a long-term scale. Maybe my complete intolerance for existential crises was the secret blessing in disguise all along! In some ways, this is about the avoidance of pain. Financial instability is painful, yes, but the slow descent into meaninglessness is even more painful. It's hard for me to talk about these things without sounding dramatic, but the truth is that there was never much of a distinction between my "life" and my "work."

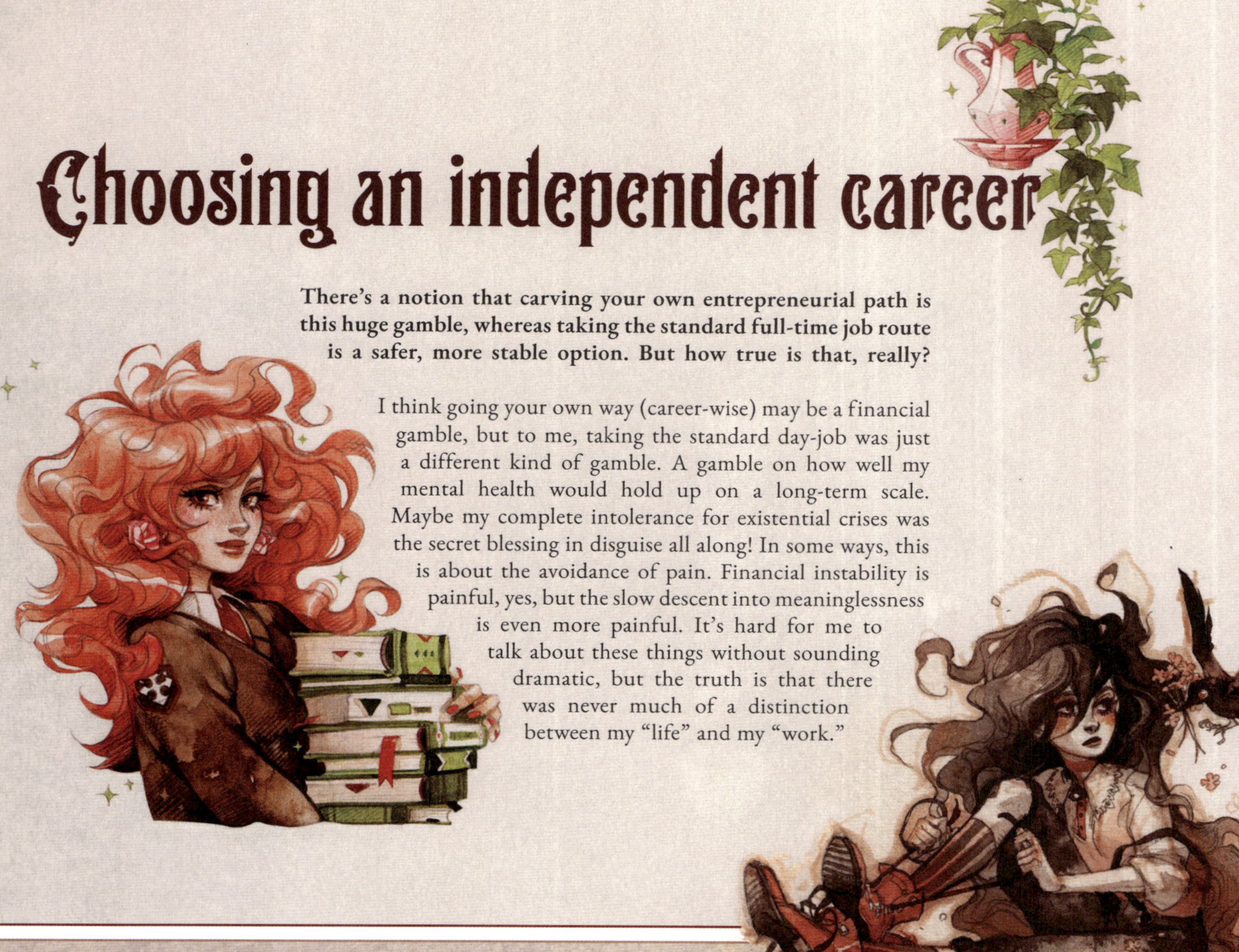

Know yourself

My advice on choosing a career would be this: aim for the highest good, know yourself, and adjust accordingly. Put the emphasis on *know yourself*. Over the years, I've realized that I don't work well in groups, preferring to have complete control of all aspects of my projects, and thrive when left to my own devices. Maybe you thrive in a group environment and find meaning in being part of a team. Maybe you lack self-discipline, or you're too stoic and dutiful, tolerating unnecessary discomfort. The less you understand yourself, the more likely you are to make grave mistakes in life; knowing yourself is probably the most important thing there is, and not just in the context of an artistic career. I chose to be an independent artist because it's the best fit for me, and I've never regretted it.

Ever since my early teens, all I ever wanted to do was write stories and share them with the world in the form of comics. This was the constant in my life, and everything else felt like background noise. Somehow, studying art and working in art was always part of this background noise, even though I knew that it obviously helped me gain the skills necessary to create the kind of comics I wanted to. It's tough to explain why I do this, but to this day my life seems to revolve around crossing a million tasks off an infinite list, at the end of which I will be working on my comic. Eighty percent of my time is spent doing everything other than what I truly want to do. Permanently residing in the background noise of my life. I sure hope that lease runs out soon, haha!

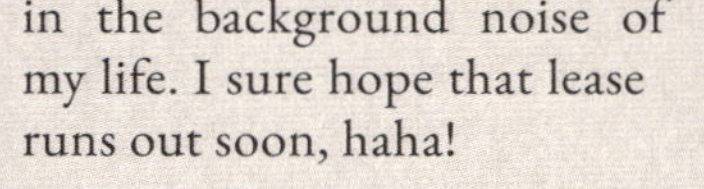

Milestone moments

I tend to collapse my life into an insufficient microcosm of extremes. In reality, I've worked on a few projects that I am quite happy with (definitely not background noise)! These are my most cherished milestones thus far:

- Crowdfunding and self-publishing my first chaotic attempt at a comic: *IDFracture* volume 1.
- My self-published sketch collection: *Carousel*.
- My self-published art books: *In Absentia* and *Milk of Melancholy*.
- A major accomplishment is *Grimoire Noir*, a graphic novel I illustrated in partnership with the writer Vera Greentea. I discuss the experience further in the chapter *Case Study: Grimoire Noir*.

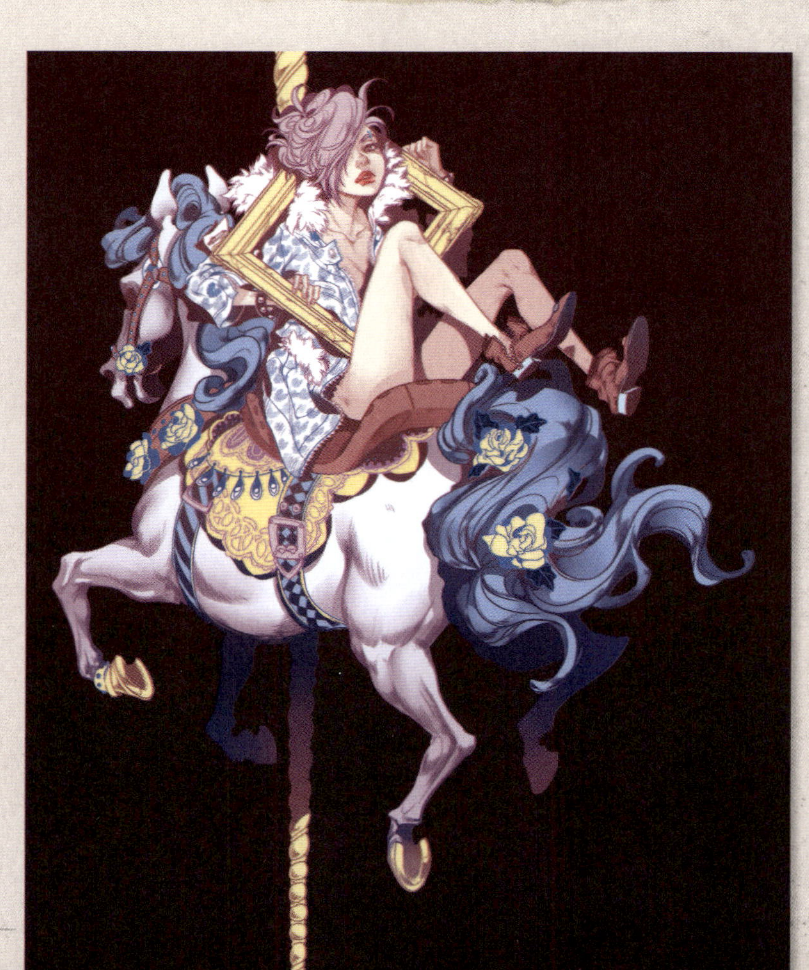

Making a living as an artist

I've had an independent entrepreneurial streak from a young age, and made my first attempts at earning money from art early on in life. I started accepting commissions when I was about fifteen or sixteen (for actual money, that is – previously, it was make-believe online forum currency). Since then, it has been a steady process of trial and error. I have definitely experienced my fair share of ups and downs, but I think overall it was steady growth.

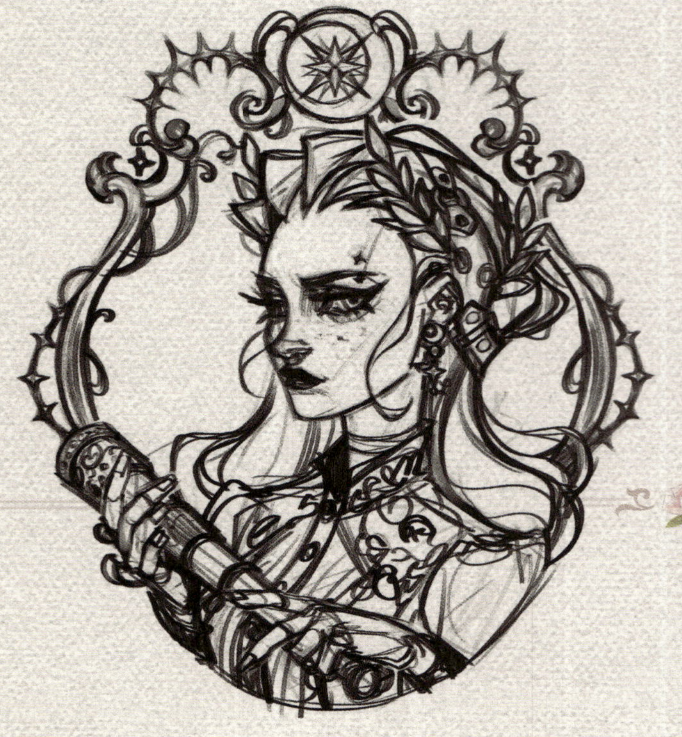

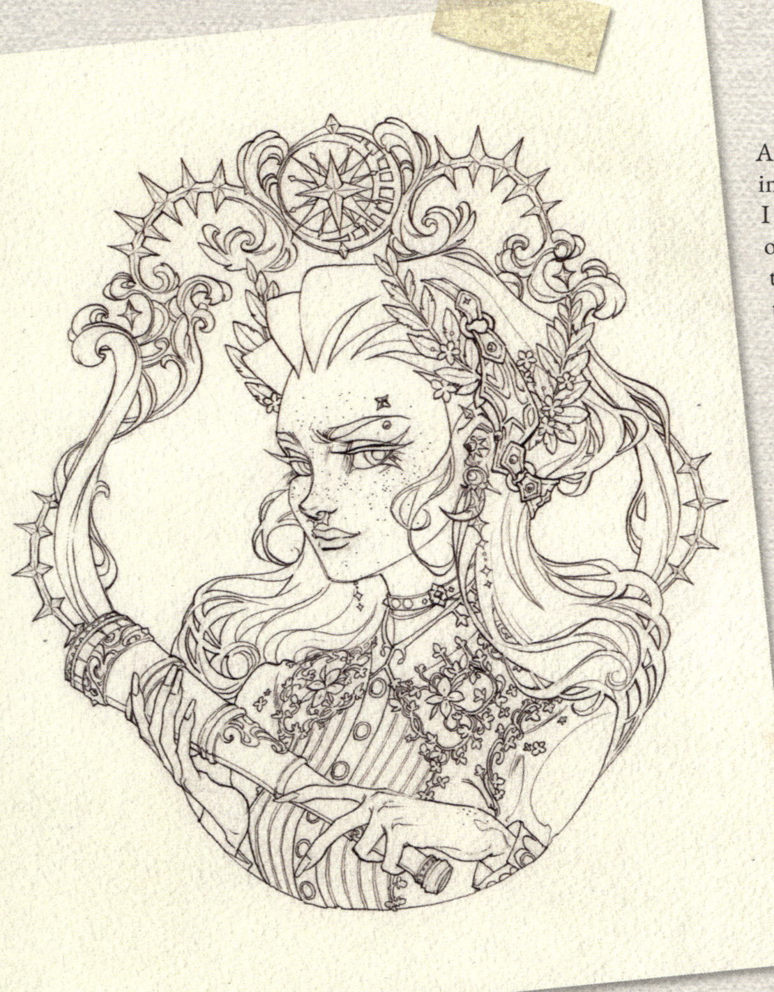

Aside from being the classic perpetually broke art student, the biggest dip in income resulted from working on *Grimoire Noir*, the graphic novel I was contracted to illustrate from 2015 until the end of 2017. My lack of real-world experience meant that I couldn't anticipate just how much time I would need to put into the project, and the true value of that time. In a nutshell, I learned the importance of valuing my own time and efforts, and adjusting my expectations in many ways. The bizarre thing is that I always thought of myself as someone who understands the value of my work. It was shocking to discover that I clearly did not! One of the many shocking discoveries I made about myself around that time.

I have to admit that it's still difficult to think of it as a blessing in disguise, but I try my best to see this and all other negative experiences that way. The miraculous thing is that after re-calibrating my expectations and adjusting the way I operate with client work, my art career has taken off dramatically and has been reliably growing since 2018, which I am immensely grateful for.

Currently, I'm slowly moving away from occasional freelance work toward full independence, with the goal of working on my comic series and personal art only. That's the glittering dream. Thanks to the internet and social media, this actually seems possible and I'm very excited for what the future holds!

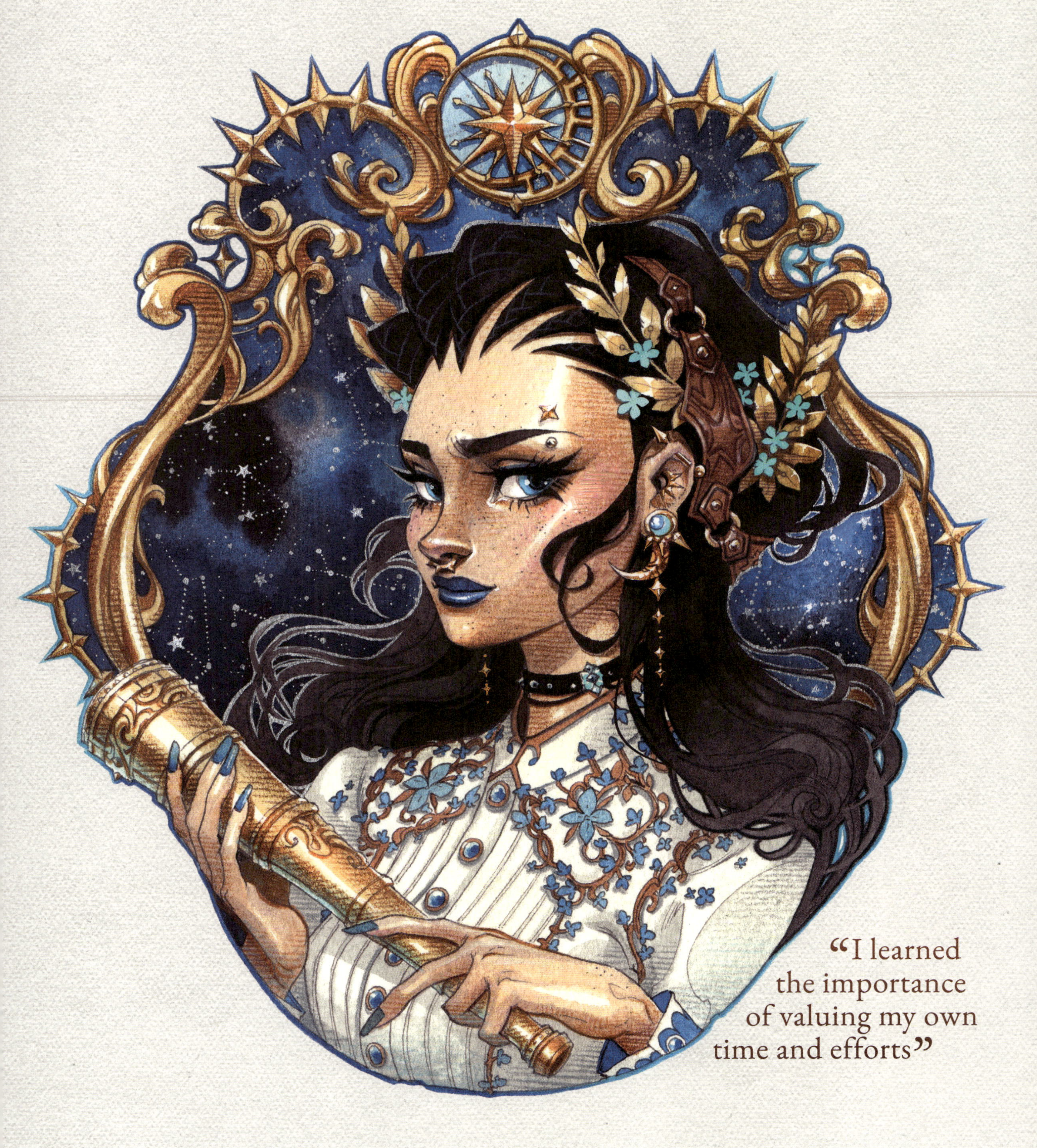

"I learned
the importance
of valuing my own
time and efforts"

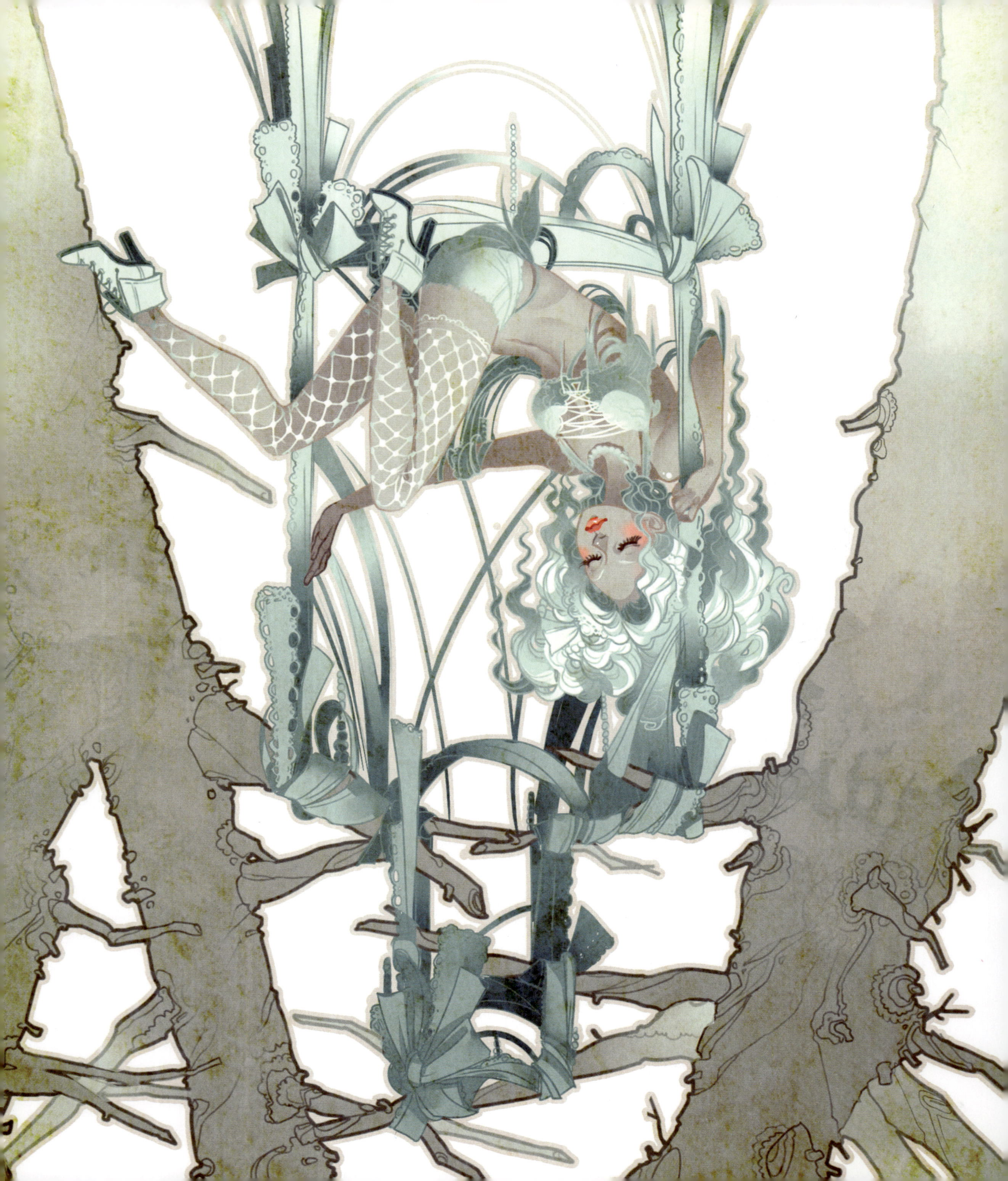

Stylistic influences: A timeline

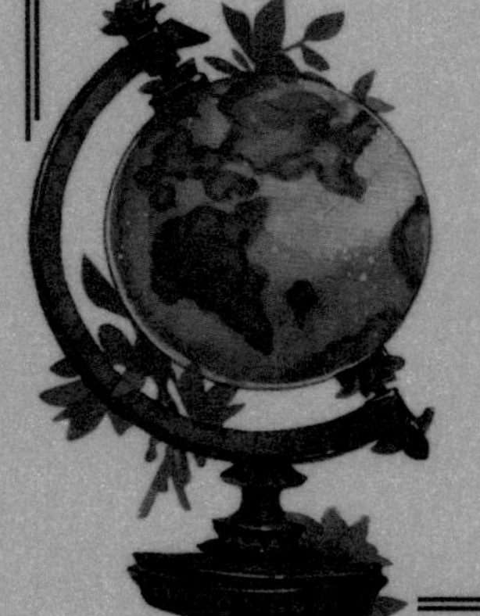

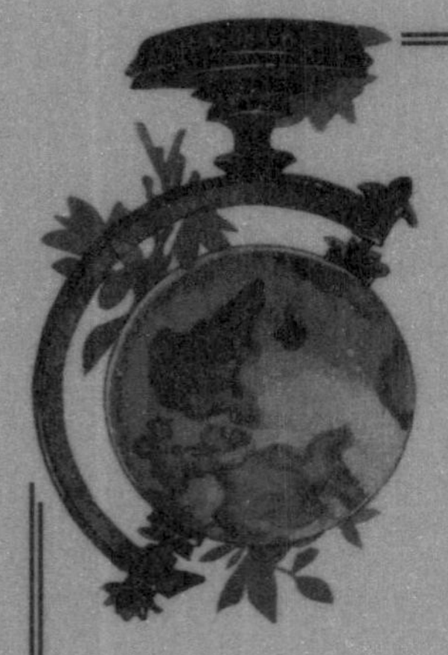

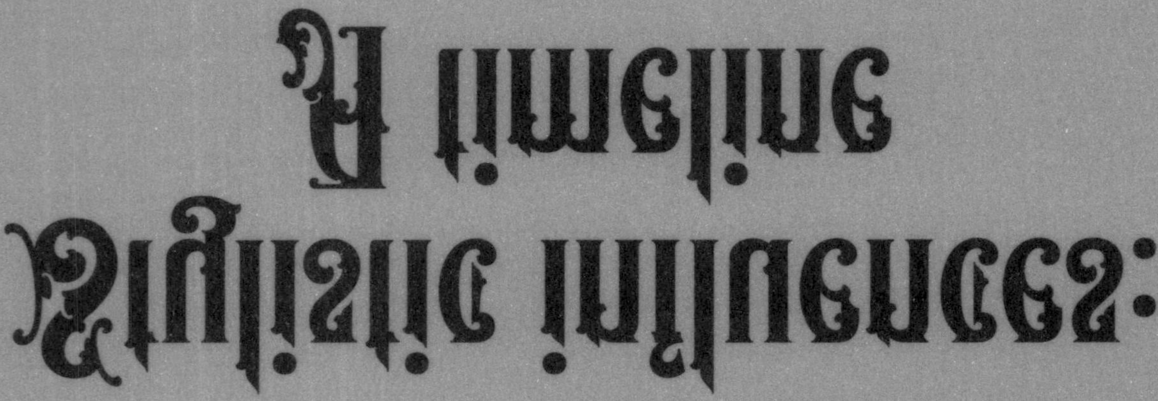

Stylistic influences: A timeline

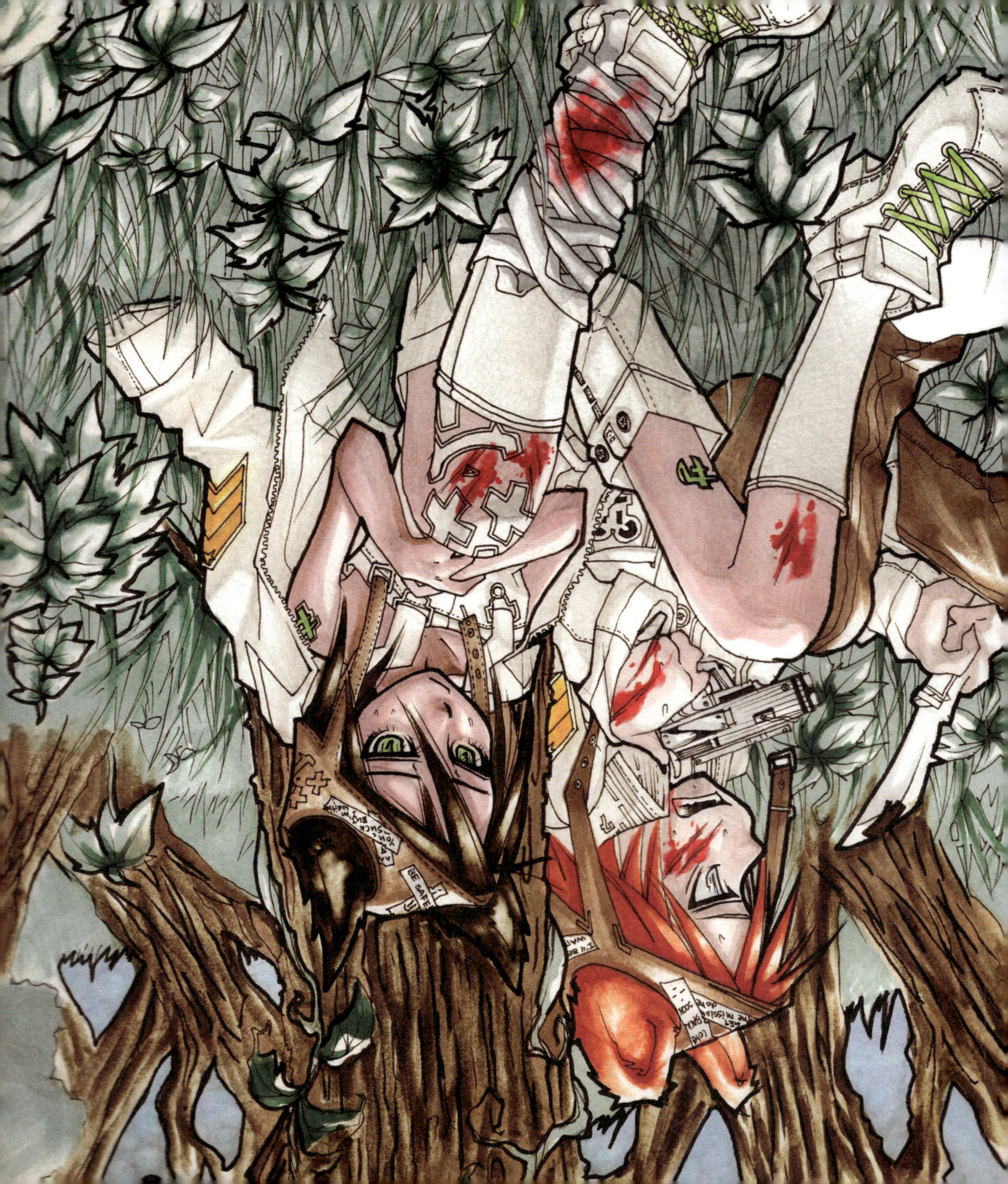

The evolution of my art

I am thrilled to share my art journey (which at the time of writing spans two decades) with you across these pages. This is something I've always wanted to do, but never managed to fit into my other self-published art books. I absolutely love seeing how the work of other artists evolves over a long period of time, and I hope you'll find the same enjoyment as I guide you through my artistic progress and influences.

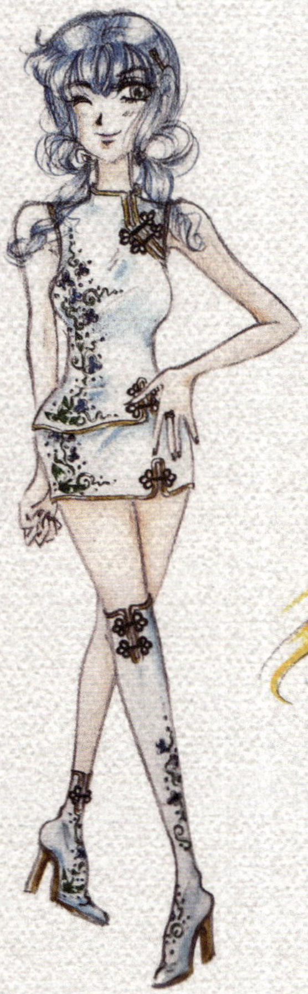

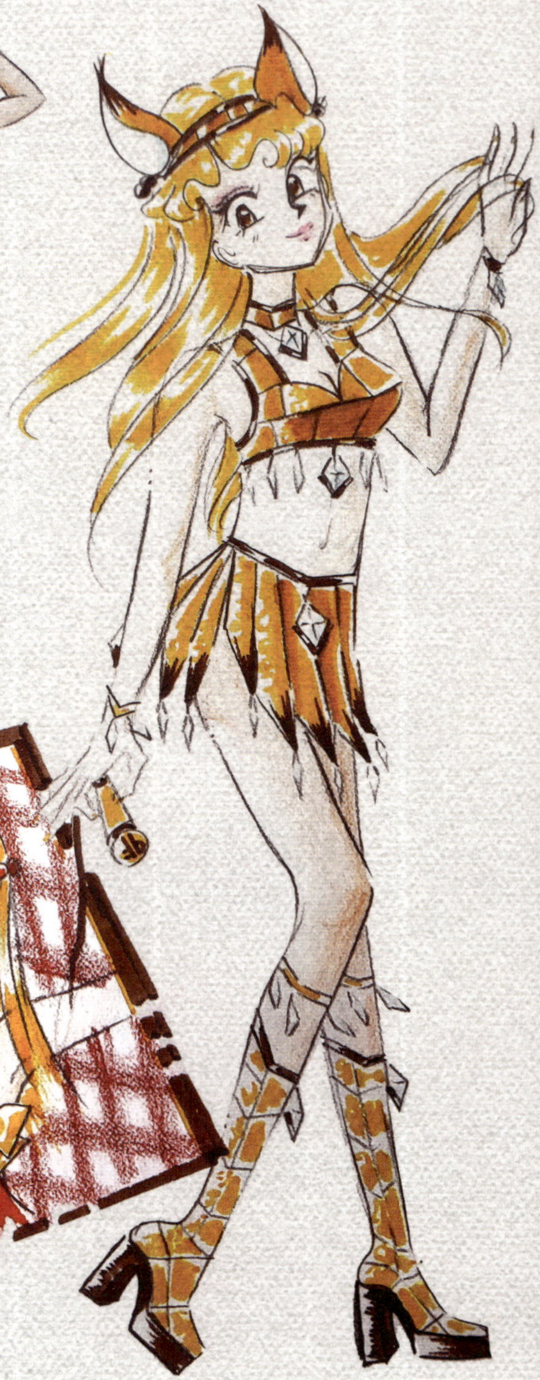

10–12 years old

My journey begins

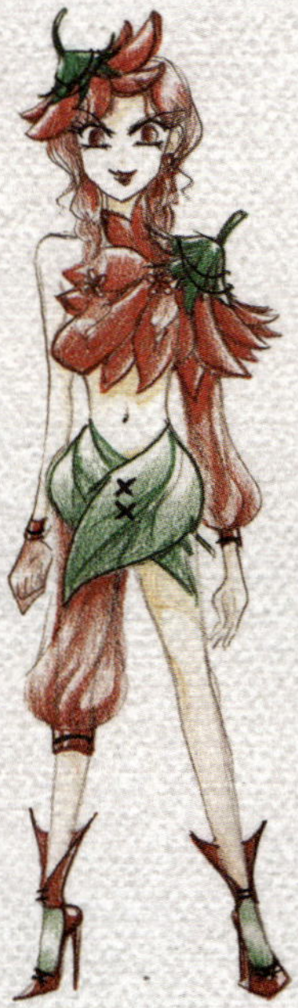

I was eleven years old when my family emigrated from the far east of Russia to Canada. Upon arriving, my excitement slowly melted into an absence of belonging, though this hit me much harder a few years down the road in my early teens. Since I didn't know much English and I'm introverted by nature, I drew in my notebook margins to pass the time.

Early influences

Before leaving Russia, a friend gave me a couple of VHS tapes full of dubbed *Sailor Moon* episodes – I was instantly captivated. Any access I had to the internet was spent staring in awe at the show's image galleries. They featured illustrations by Naoko Takeuchi and snippets of the manga. During those years, my only goal in life was to learn how to make beautiful and stylish drawings like Naoko's. It was a lofty goal, but a perfect escape from reality.

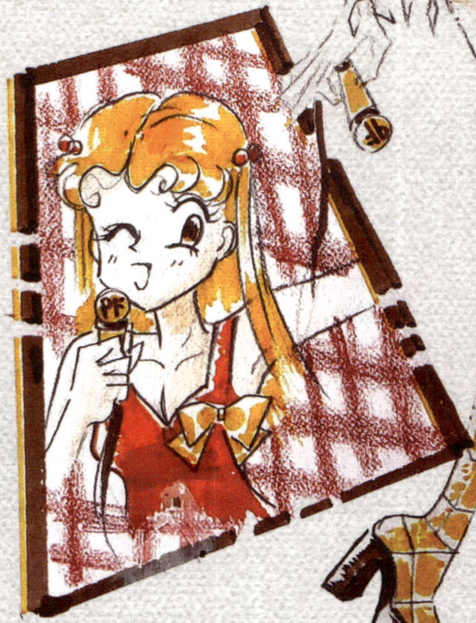

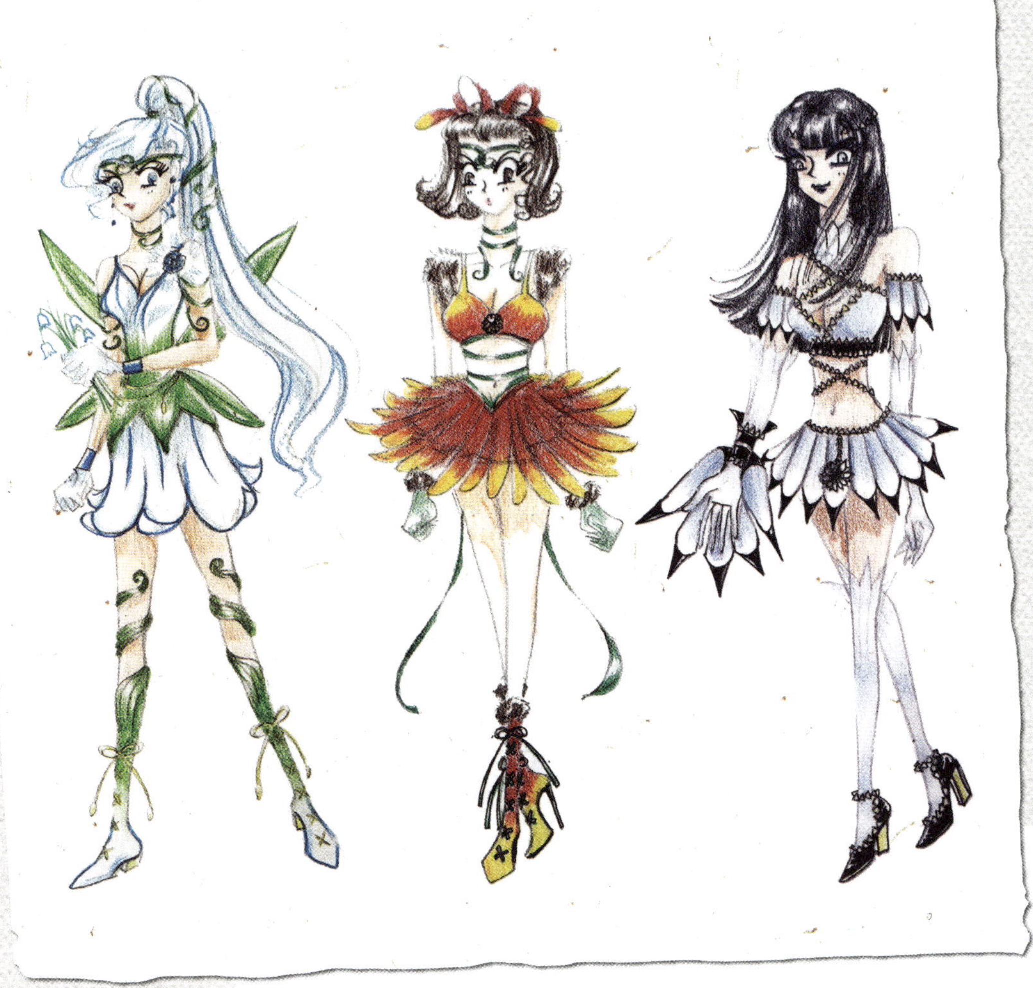

Focus on the aesthetic

Although I wasn't entirely aware of it at the time, I can see now that fashion was the most attractive aspect of *Sailor Moon* for me, aside from the mysterious, ethereal, and romantic atmosphere. I viewed the characters as simple, magic-wielding girls in a good-versus-evil story premise, but didn't really focus on their individual narratives. I just loved their aesthetic, and emulating it for my own character outfits.

Around this time, I used graphite and colored pencils for most of my drawings, relying on my trusty set of Prismacolor pencils. It wasn't until my late teens that I used wet media – for now, I preferred to work with tools that were sharp and precise, without the need for water.

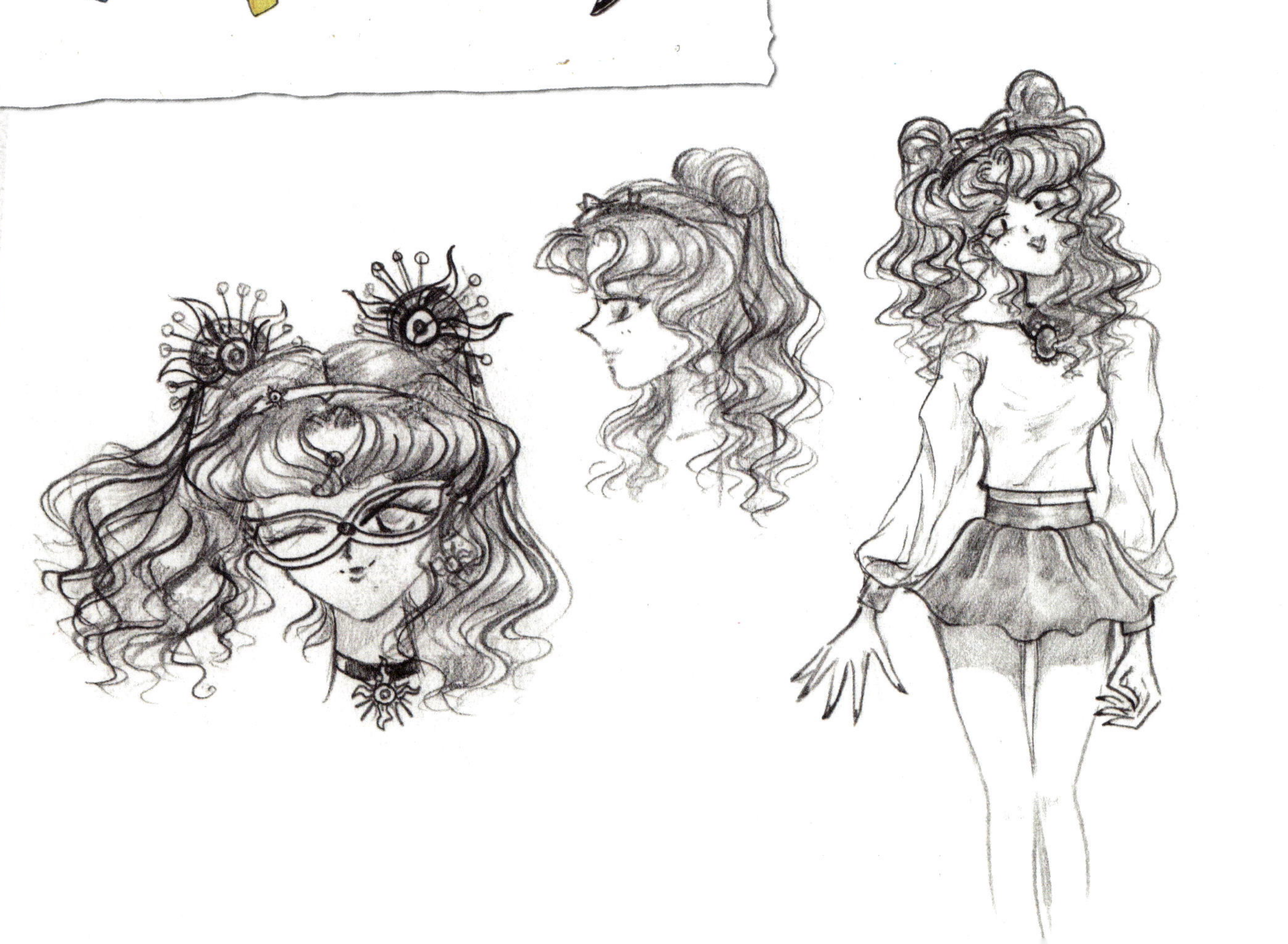

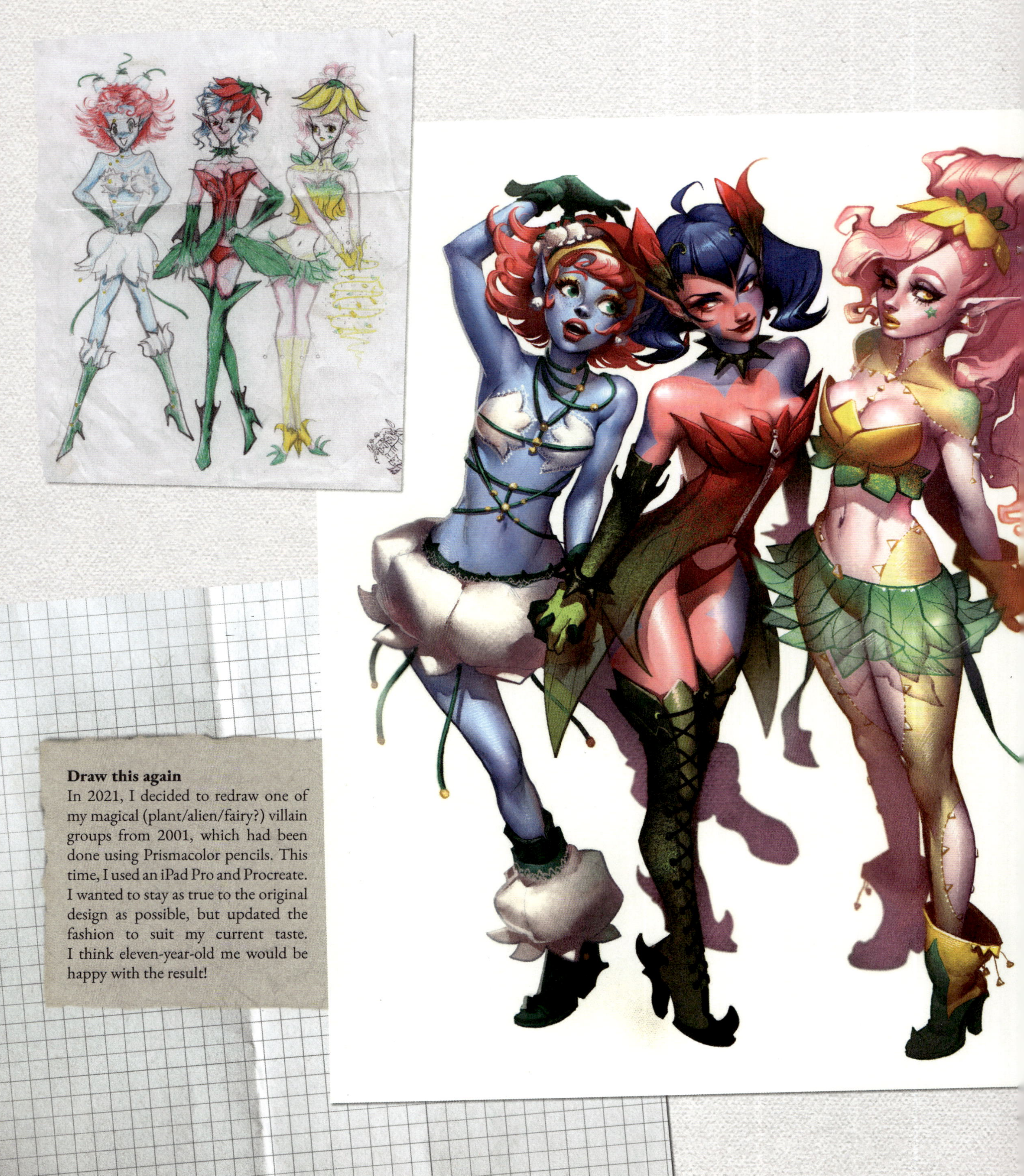

Draw this again

In 2021, I decided to redraw one of my magical (plant/alien/fairy?) villain groups from 2001, which had been done using Prismacolor pencils. This time, I used an iPad Pro and Procreate. I wanted to stay as true to the original design as possible, but updated the fashion to suit my current taste. I think eleven-year-old me would be happy with the result!

13–15 years old

Discovering Japanese and Korean comic artists

Between seventh and eighth grade, I met a friend who introduced me to many comic artists through her older sister's art-book collection. This was an intense blast of inspiration, and just like that, I was completely whisked away from my *Sailor Moon* phase.

Style experiments

In particular, I was taken by the illustrations of Hyung-tae Kim, a popular Korean video-game character designer. The stylistic departure was quite drastic, but this is basically where I started experimenting with different styles in an effort to achieve certain rendering looks with my limited art supplies and abilities. One technique I was quite proud of at the time was using a textured surface underneath the paper when filling an area with a colored or graphite pencil, which retained the texture. I used this method to add interest to my character art for the next few years.

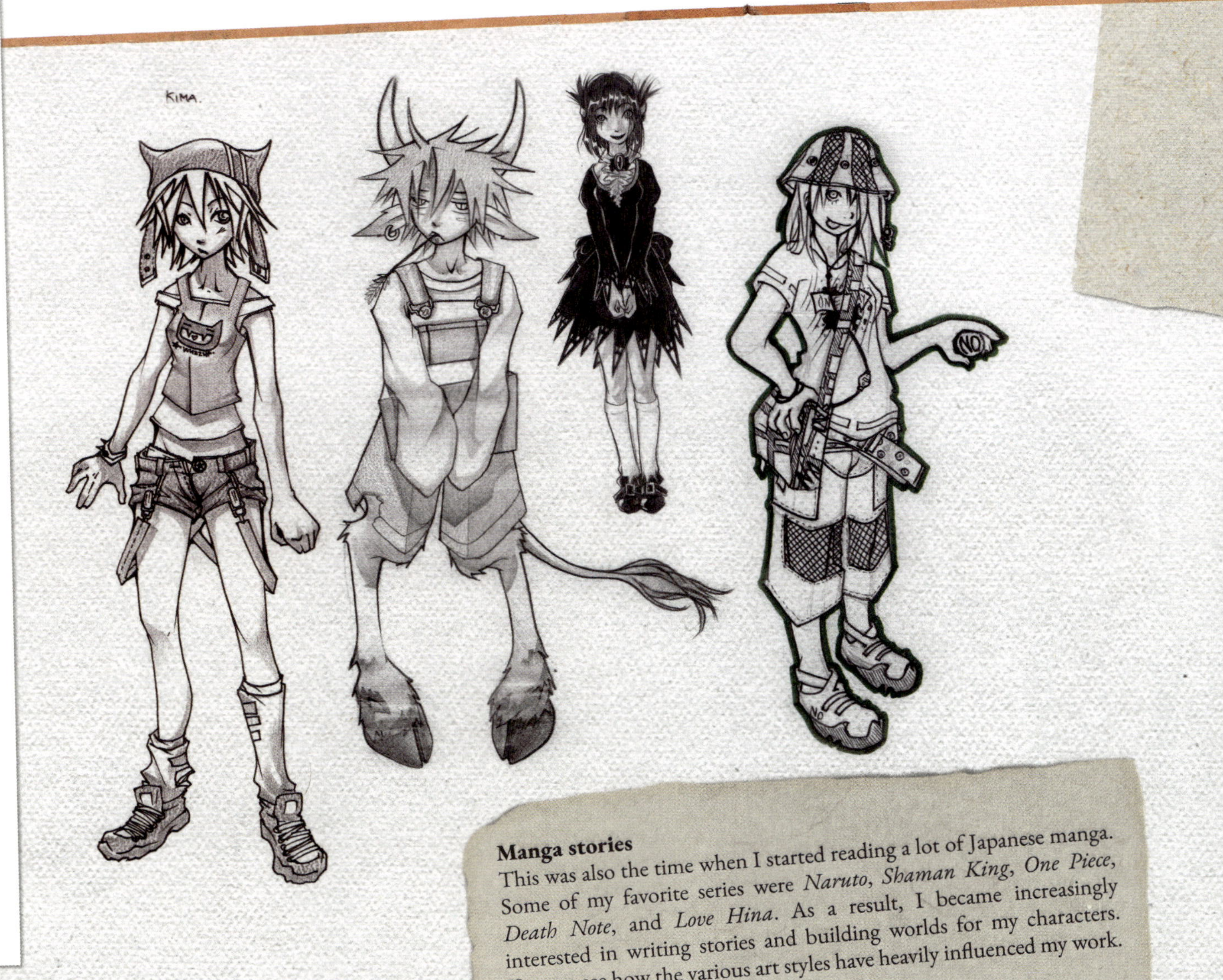

Manga stories

This was also the time when I started reading a lot of Japanese manga. Some of my favorite series were *Naruto*, *Shaman King*, *One Piece*, *Death Note*, and *Love Hina*. As a result, I became increasingly interested in writing stories and building worlds for my characters. You can see how the various art styles have heavily influenced my work.

Pens and markers

I started using a wider range of art materials, adding fineliners (Sakura Pigma Microns), ballpoint pens, and Prismacolor alcohol sketch markers to my process, leaving colored pencils behind. My older brother was an industrial-design student at the time and left his markers and fineliners lying around everywhere, which is how I got my hands on them. This meant an extremely limited color choice, but I made it work. This is probably why I feel very overwhelmed with too many options and prefer to work within color limitations.

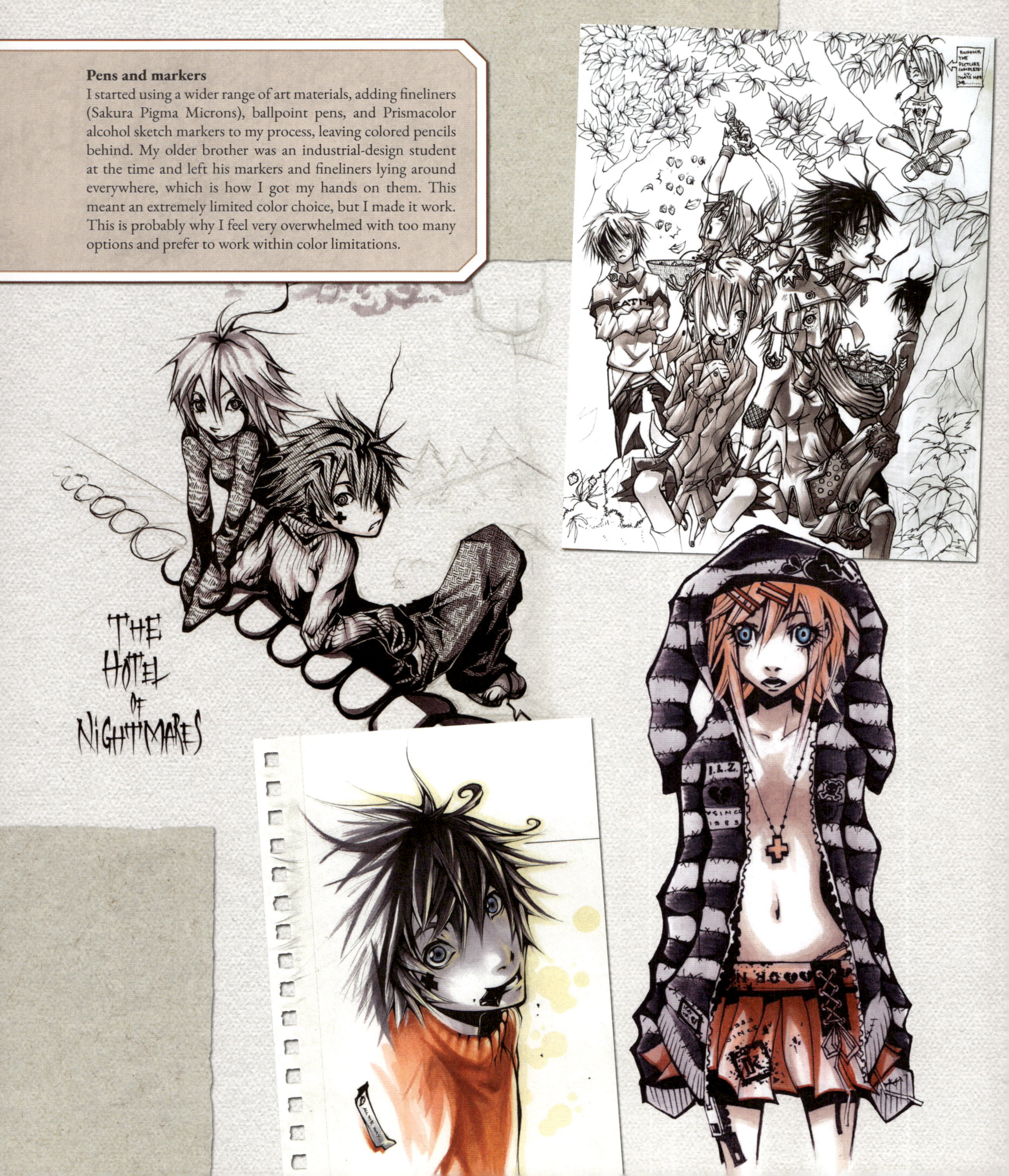

Inking and line work

When I was fifteen years old, I tried Japanese screen-tone stickers for the first time and thought they were incredibly fun! Unfortunately, they are also very expensive and tedious to handle, so as soon as I used up what I had, I never tried them again.

At the same age, I fell in love with inking and line work. Line work has turned into a lifelong obsession and my favorite part of the process. There's something so satisfying about transforming a loose sketch into a clean, crisp drawing. High contrast, line weight, and shape polishing are the elements I've always found the most pleasing about my process.

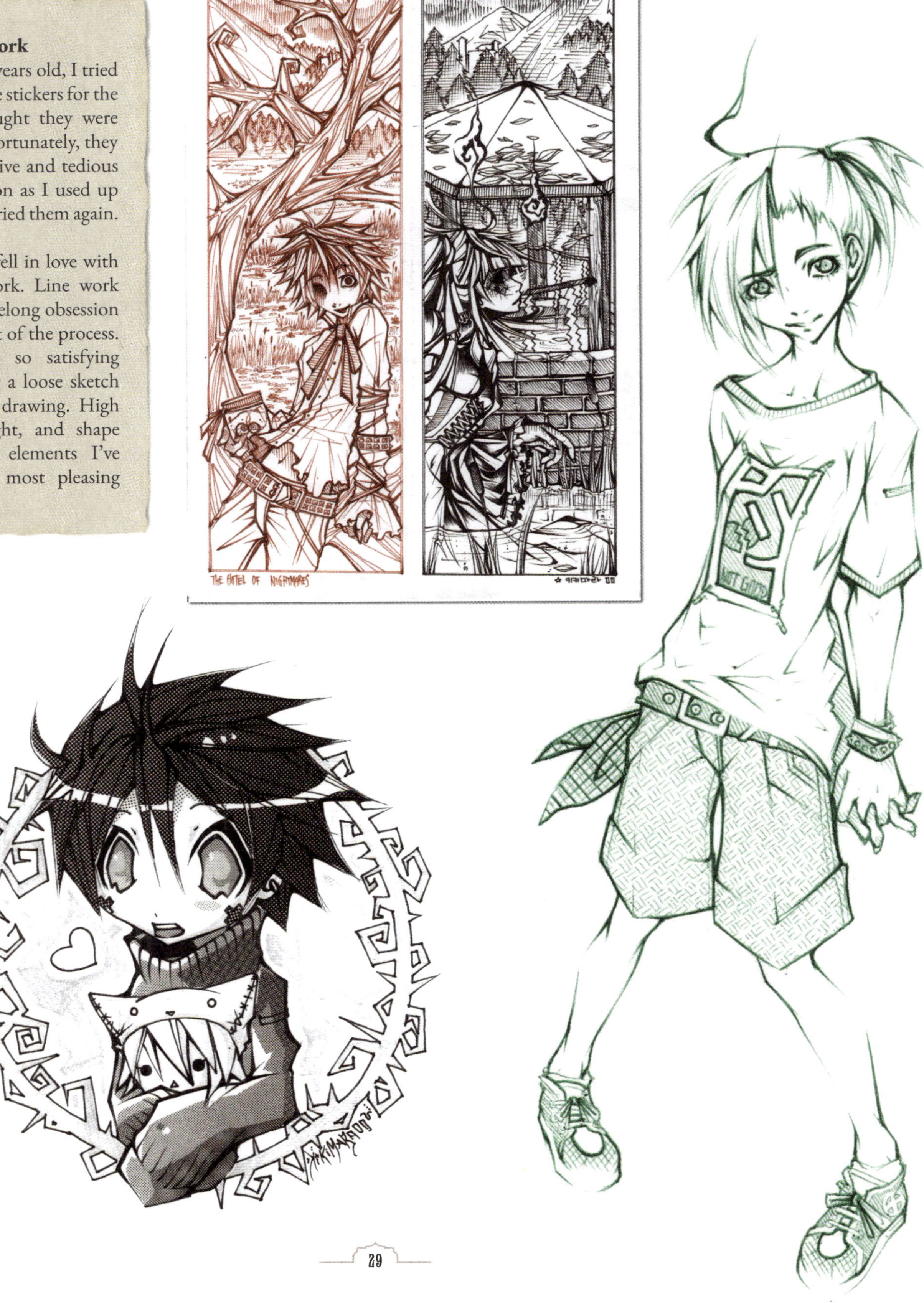

16–18 years old

Starting a webcomic and experimenting with digital art

At this point, I'd been preoccupied with worldbuilding and doodling characters, but it wasn't until the age of sixteen that I managed to move past drawing only a few sequential comic pages for an original story. I had a "comic" project for one of my art classes and had to draw ten pages to fulfill the assignment. It started off as a joke with a simple, silly premise, but after completing the assignment, I realized that this comic had the most consecutive pages I'd drawn in my life! I wasn't going to let this dedicated effort go to waste.

The origin of *IDFracture*

I found myself excited about the fresh characters I'd created, so I quickly expanded the story, working on it, off and on, for the next four years. This was the haphazard beginning of *IDFracture* (initially titled *Fiona*), my first attempt at an online comic. Who knew I would still be rewriting the same story fifteen years later!

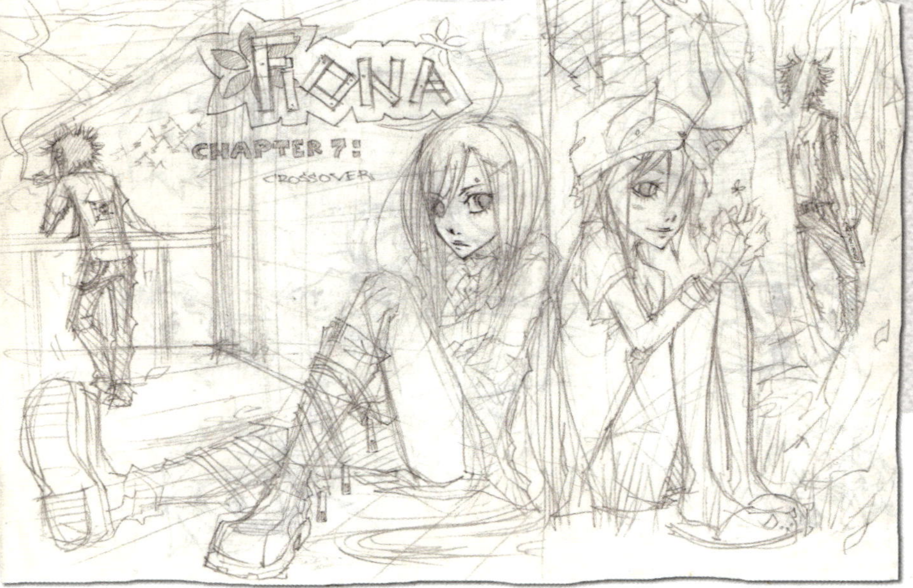

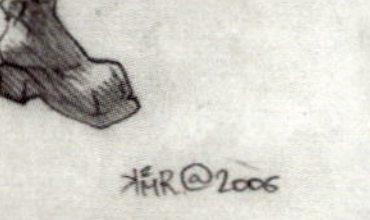

Merging narratives

The more time I spent trying to weave a new plot into an existing story, the more it started to bleed into another narrative I'd created: *Hotel of Nightmares* (*H.o.N.*). I considered *H.o.N.* to be my ultimate escape, spending almost every day doodling the characters, including Kima, Neino, Pells, Hell, and Leanne. I had placed the *IDFracture* characters within the general world of *H.o.N.* and distinctly remember doodling a sketch for a future chapter where there would be a small crossover. I had no idea that ten years later I'd merge these two stories entirely. It's so mysterious how certain ideas came to me in visual form, carrying almost no meaning at the time, only to suddenly take on an entirely different context all these years later.

Transplanted characters

When I wasn't busy working on schoolwork or the *IDFracture* comic, I created yet another window of escape. To satisfy my then-current obsession with post-apocalyptic settings and gangs of delinquents, I simply took my existing *H.o.N.* characters and placed them into a new setting, forming an alternative universe. I called this project *Single Displacement*, and had the time of my life doodling scenes, designing new outfits, and writing snippets of story.

You may have noticed that I had a strong preference for heavy line art back then. It was more fun to draw, but also much easier to cover up mistakes. Around this time, I slowly moved toward thinner lines, and more precise, deliberate shadow areas.

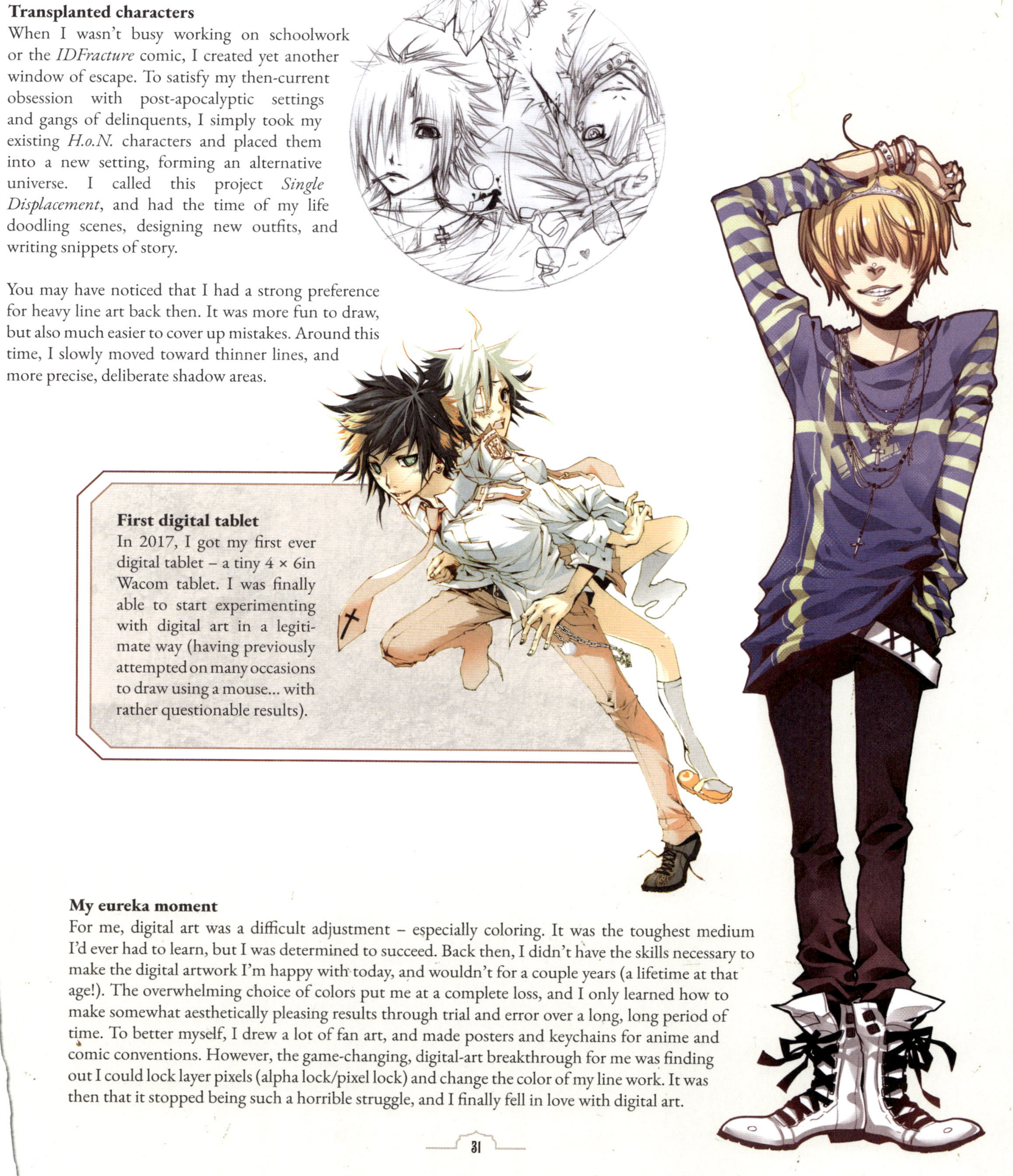

First digital tablet

In 2017, I got my first ever digital tablet – a tiny 4 × 6in Wacom tablet. I was finally able to start experimenting with digital art in a legitimate way (having previously attempted on many occasions to draw using a mouse... with rather questionable results).

My eureka moment

For me, digital art was a difficult adjustment – especially coloring. It was the toughest medium I'd ever had to learn, but I was determined to succeed. Back then, I didn't have the skills necessary to make the digital artwork I'm happy with today, and wouldn't for a couple years (a lifetime at that age!). The overwhelming choice of colors put me at a complete loss, and I only learned how to make somewhat aesthetically pleasing results through trial and error over a long, long period of time. To better myself, I drew a lot of fan art, and made posters and keychains for anime and comic conventions. However, the game-changing, digital-art breakthrough for me was finding out I could lock layer pixels (alpha lock/pixel lock) and change the color of my line work. It was then that it stopped being such a horrible struggle, and I finally fell in love with digital art.

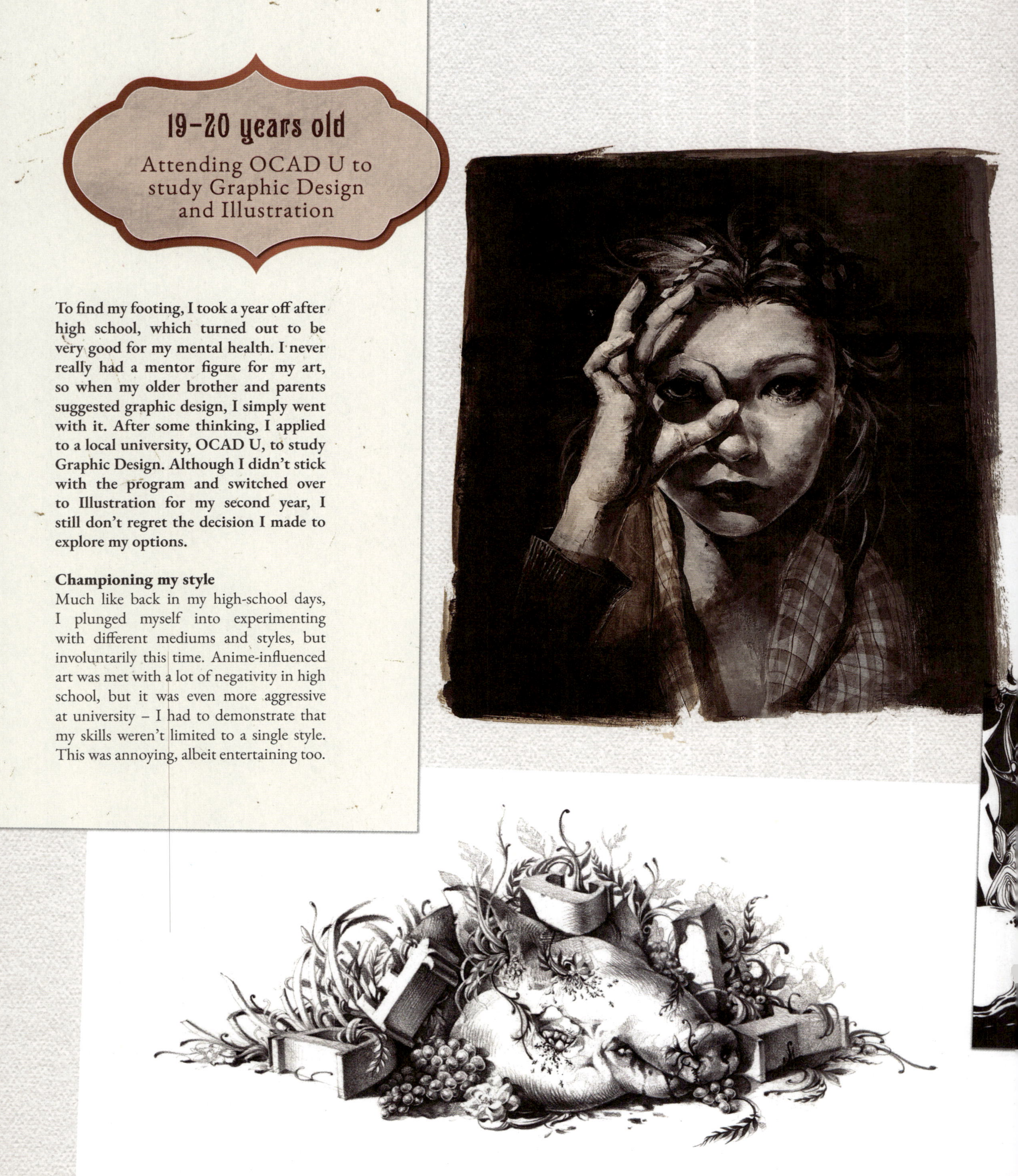

19–20 years old

Attending OCAD U to study Graphic Design and Illustration

To find my footing, I took a year off after high school, which turned out to be very good for my mental health. I never really had a mentor figure for my art, so when my older brother and parents suggested graphic design, I simply went with it. After some thinking, I applied to a local university, OCAD U, to study Graphic Design. Although I didn't stick with the program and switched over to Illustration for my second year, I still don't regret the decision I made to explore my options.

Championing my style

Much like back in my high-school days, I plunged myself into experimenting with different mediums and styles, but involuntarily this time. Anime-influenced art was met with a lot of negativity in high school, but it was even more aggressive at university – I had to demonstrate that my skills weren't limited to a single style. This was annoying, albeit entertaining too.

Switching it up

During those years, I think it was my streak of absurd confidence in my artistic abilities that saved me from feeling demoralized by the condescending criticism from authority figures. I rolled my eyes at their disparaging remarks about my "anime art." After all, I wasn't drawing my little anime pictures in a vacuum. The online art community was my safe haven – my artwork was appreciated there, and sticking to it paved the way for my successful career. Even after I switched majors, I still felt out of place, as if I wasn't getting the most out of my studies. So, I switched to Sheridan College, enrolling on their Traditional Animation program.

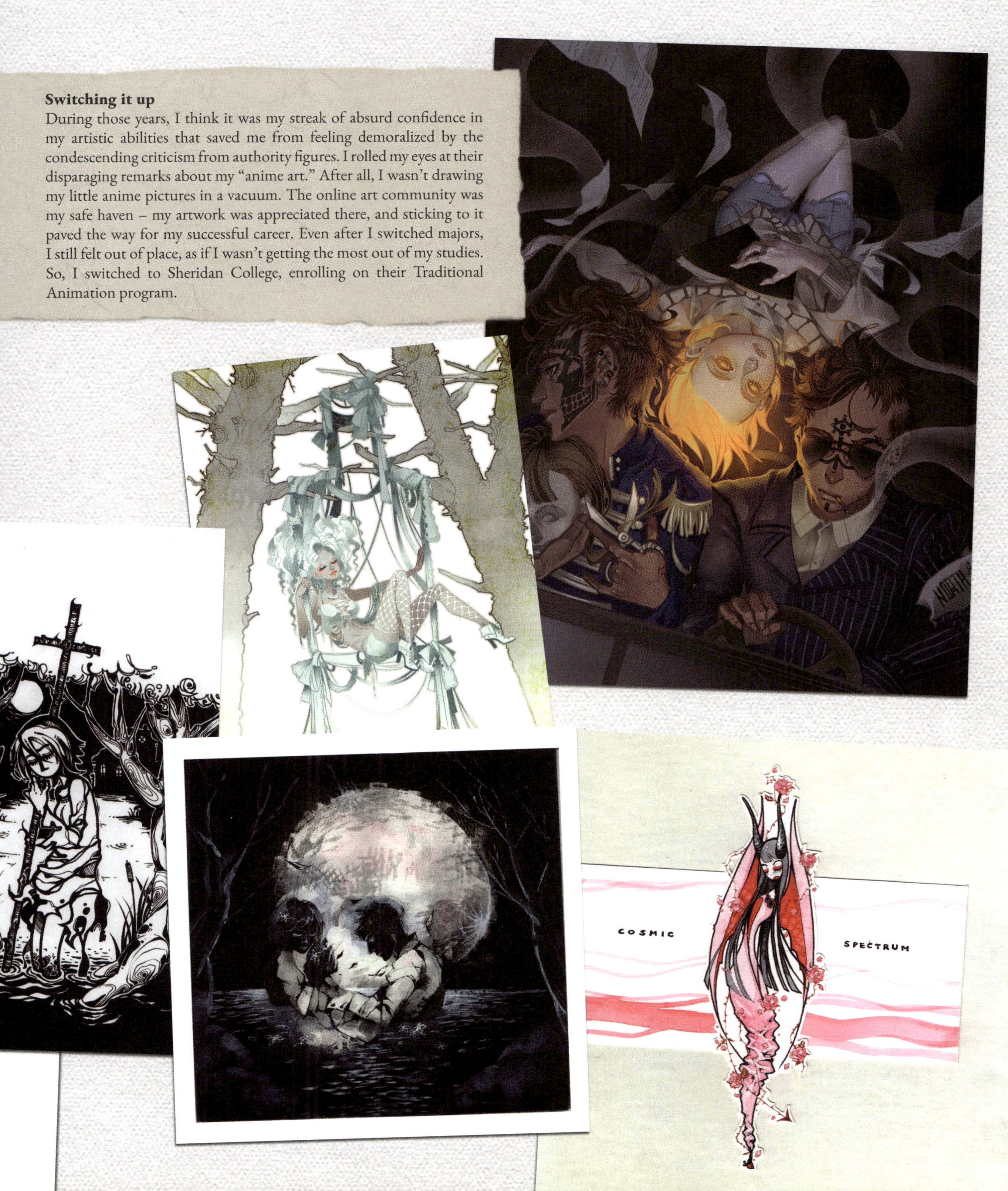

21–25 years old

Self-publishing and attending Sheridan College to study animation

The summer before I started at Sheridan College, I decided to self-publish my *IDFracture* comic pages – a lifelong dream that became a reality with the help of Kickstarter. It was a very small campaign, but I think the book turned out relatively well, considering I had no prior experience with such things. Soon after, I made a small print run of my very first collection of sketches, titled *Carousel*.

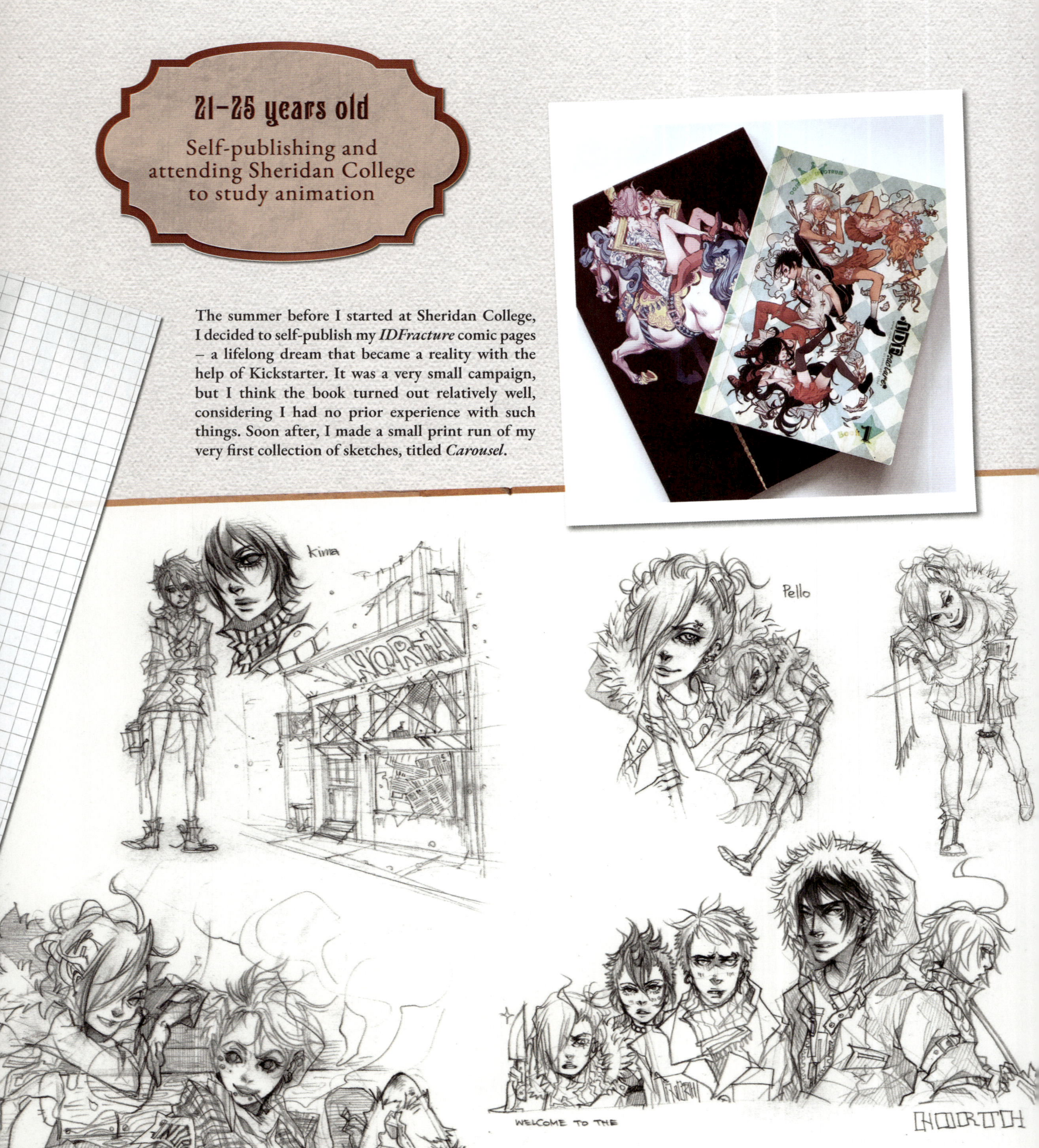

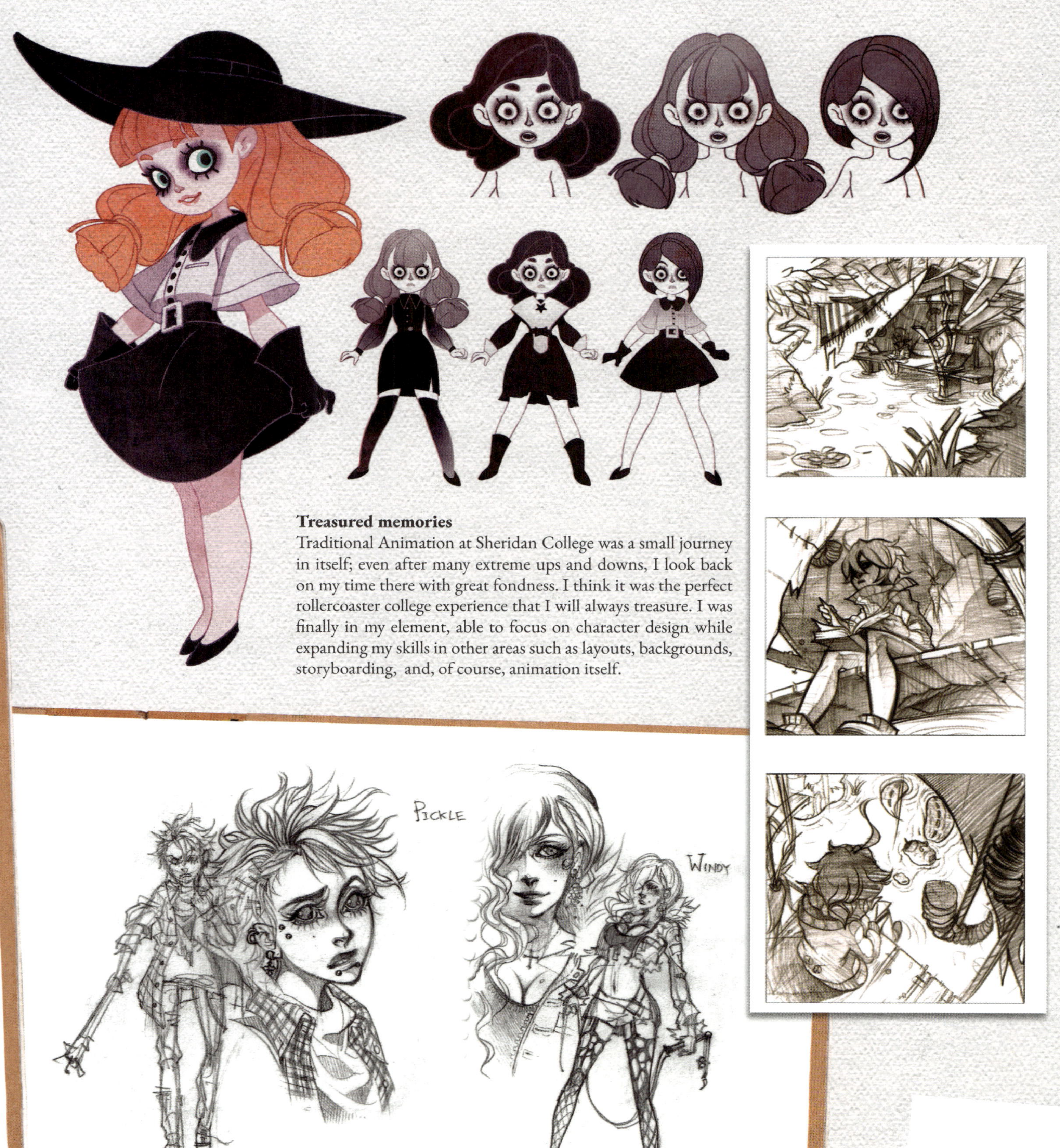

Treasured memories

Traditional Animation at Sheridan College was a small journey in itself; even after many extreme ups and downs, I look back on my time there with great fondness. I think it was the perfect rollercoaster college experience that I will always treasure. I was finally in my element, able to focus on character design while expanding my skills in other areas such as layouts, backgrounds, storyboarding, and, of course, animation itself.

Focus on characters

Although I couldn't get away with doing it all the time, I took every opportunity to weave my characters into an assignment. This made me absolutely love school work and I got to try out new stylistic approaches. The obsession with my characters kept growing stronger, and I spent most of my free time drawing them.

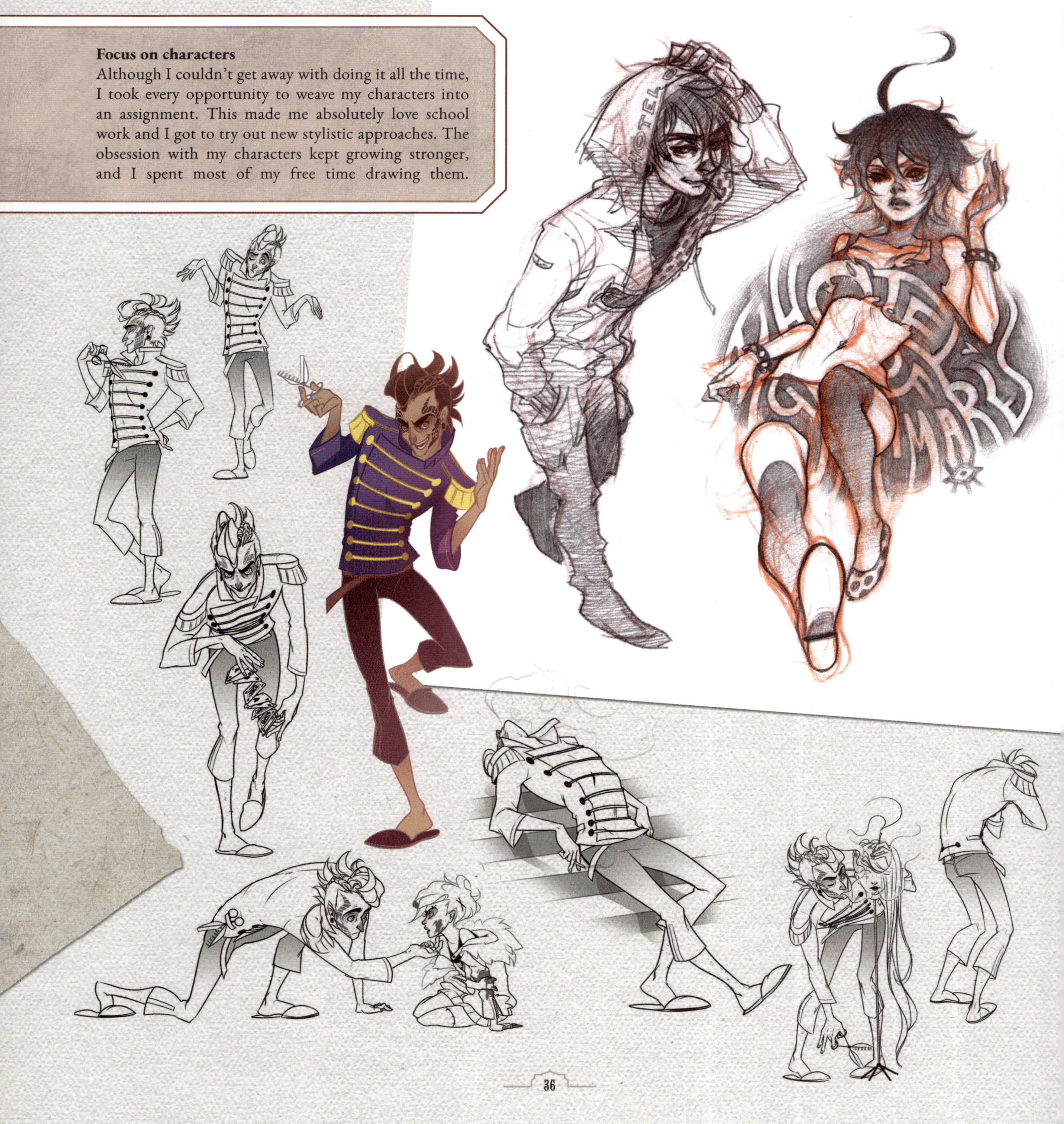

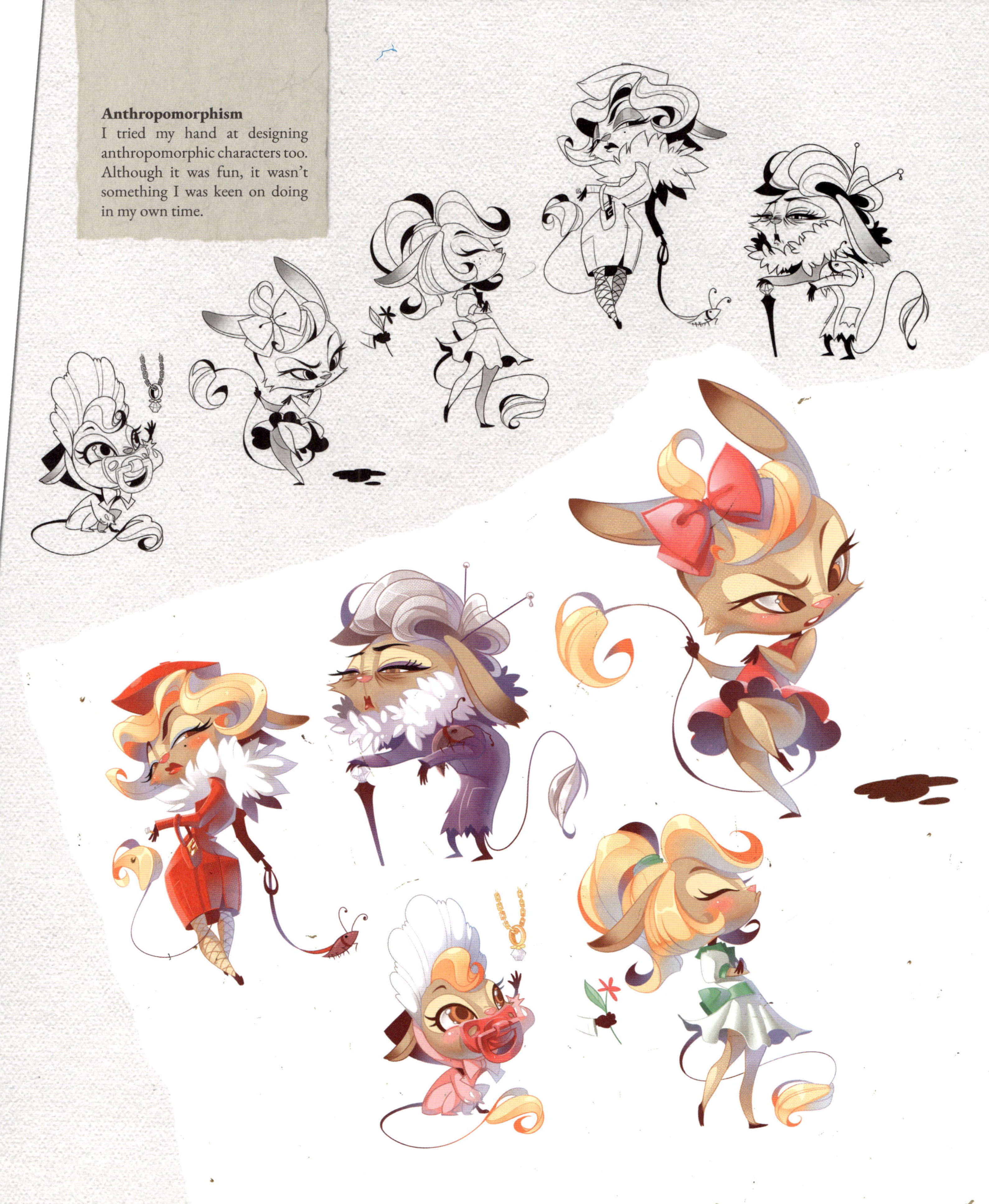

Anthropomorphism

I tried my hand at designing anthropomorphic characters too. Although it was fun, it wasn't something I was keen on doing in my own time.

Juggling study with work

My financial situation as a student on a government loan wasn't great, so I did quite a bit of freelance work and private commissions on the side. Trying to juggle work with school was very tough, and I often felt extremely burned out as a result. Unfortunately, this was the only way for me to pay my rent, and I do think I gained a lot of valuable experience by persevering through difficult circumstances.

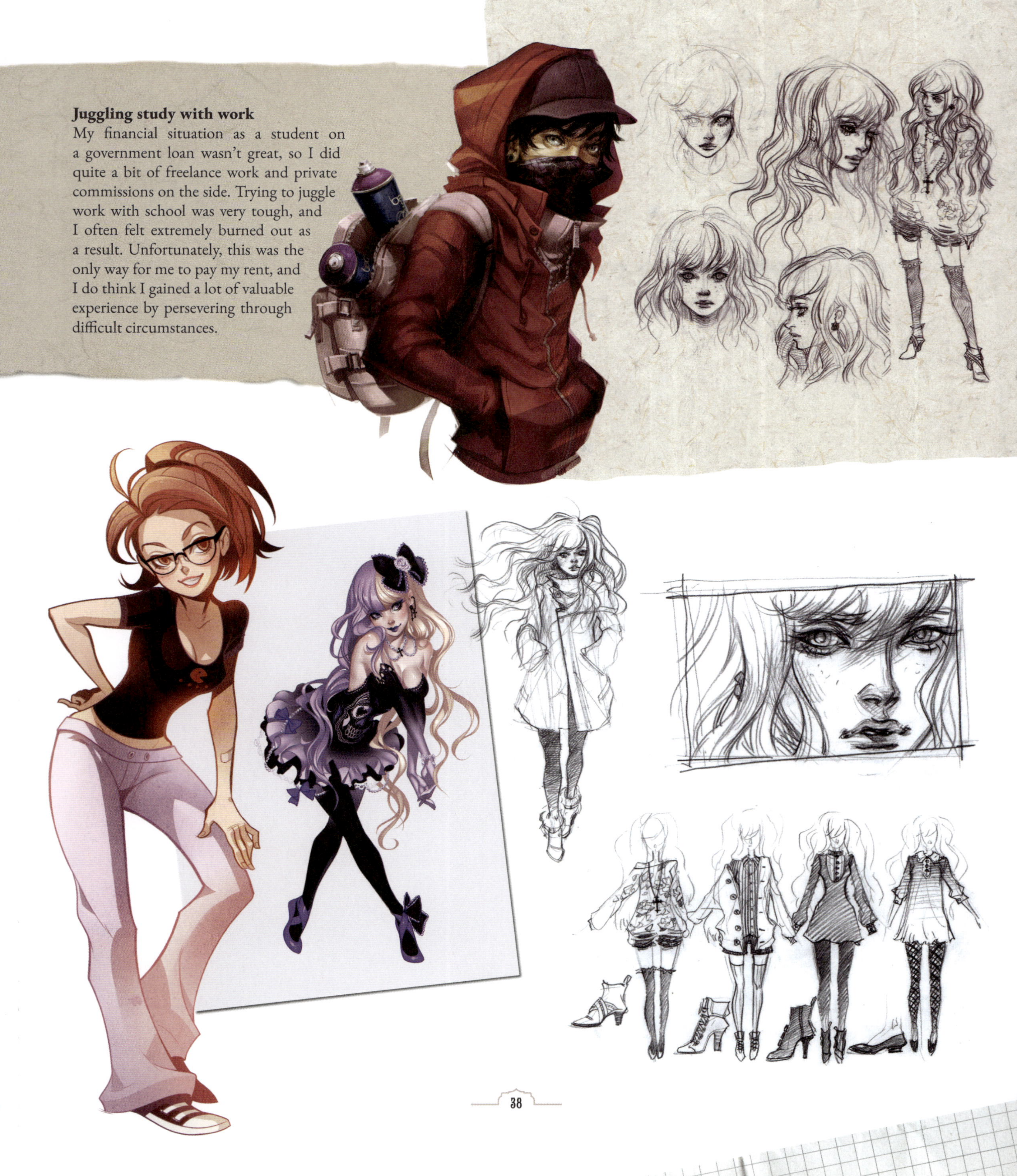

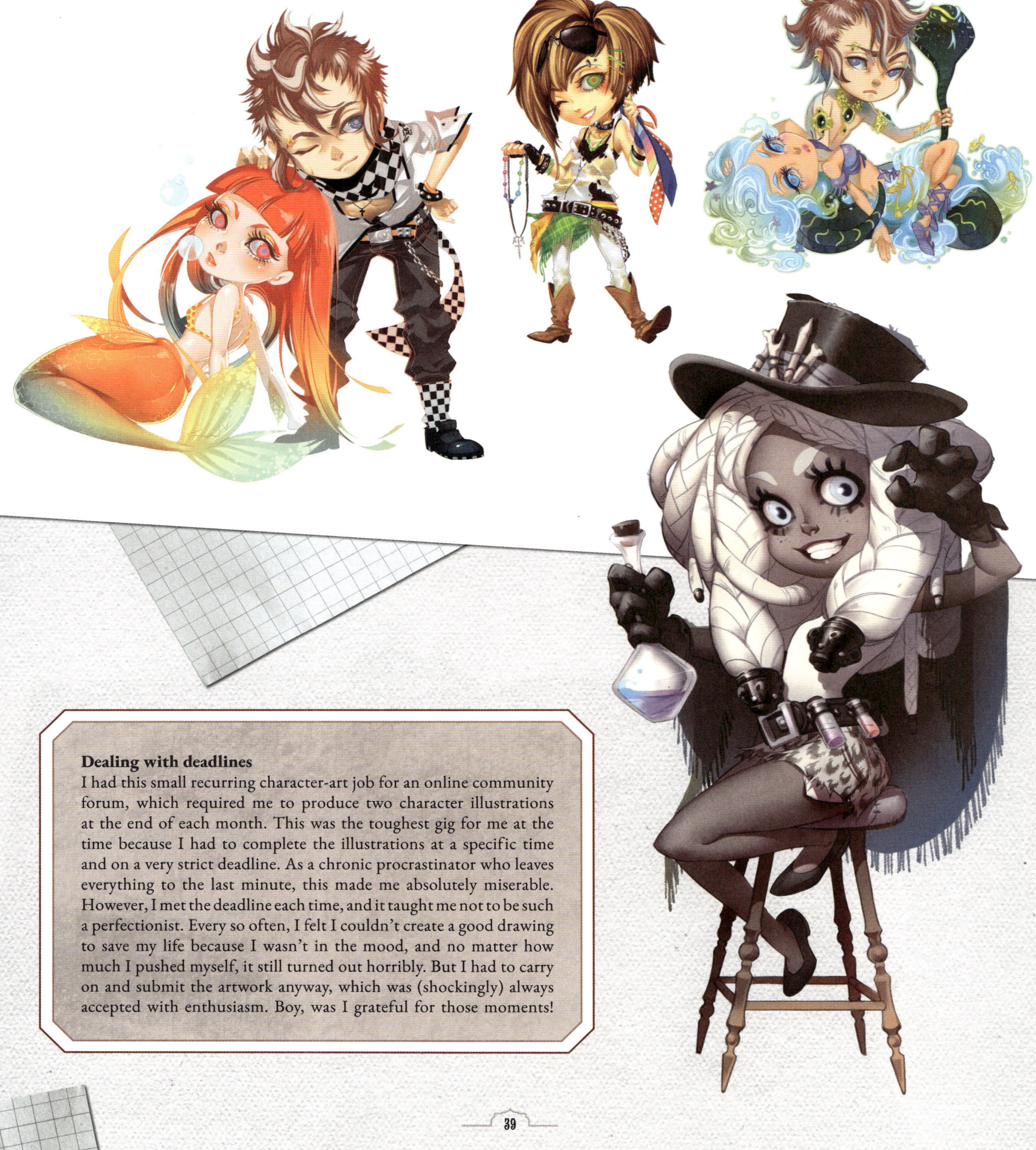

Dealing with deadlines

I had this small recurring character-art job for an online community forum, which required me to produce two character illustrations at the end of each month. This was the toughest gig for me at the time because I had to complete the illustrations at a specific time and on a very strict deadline. As a chronic procrastinator who leaves everything to the last minute, this made me absolutely miserable. However, I met the deadline each time, and it taught me not to be such a perfectionist. Every so often, I felt I couldn't create a good drawing to save my life because I wasn't in the mood, and no matter how much I pushed myself, it still turned out horribly. But I had to carry on and submit the artwork anyway, which was (shockingly) always accepted with enthusiasm. Boy, was I grateful for those moments!

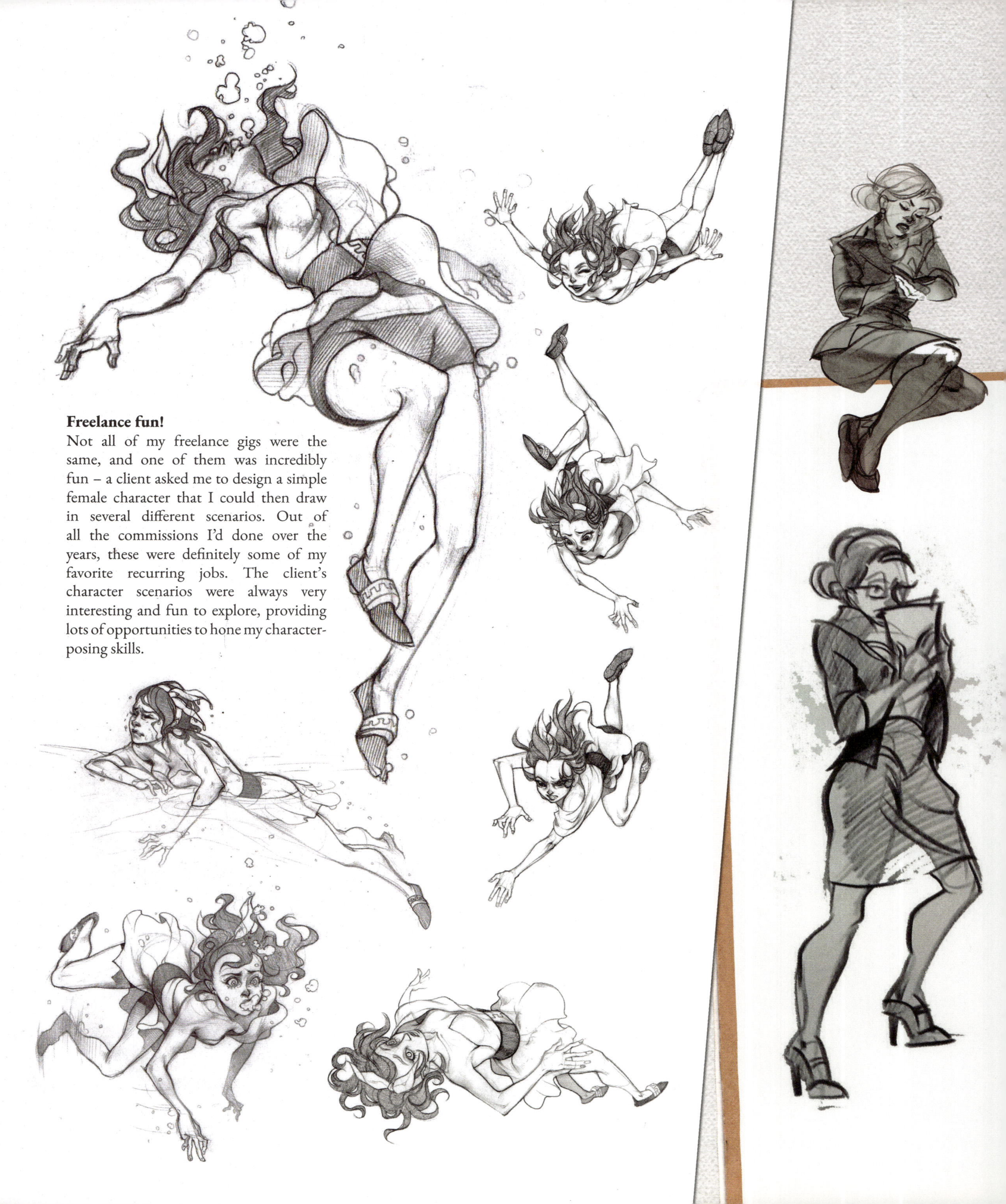

Freelance fun!

Not all of my freelance gigs were the same, and one of them was incredibly fun – a client asked me to design a simple female character that I could then draw in several different scenarios. Out of all the commissions I'd done over the years, these were definitely some of my favorite recurring jobs. The client's character scenarios were always very interesting and fun to explore, providing lots of opportunities to hone my character-posing skills.

Figure drawings and costumes

One of my favorite components of studying Traditional Animation was the focus on figure drawing – especially the costumed sessions. Up until Sheridan College, my experience with figure drawing was relatively limited, and my knowledge of anatomy even more so. Studying anatomy in conjunction with lots of figure-drawing practice each week massively elevated my overall skills. Here is a selection of costumed figure drawings done while at Sheridan College.

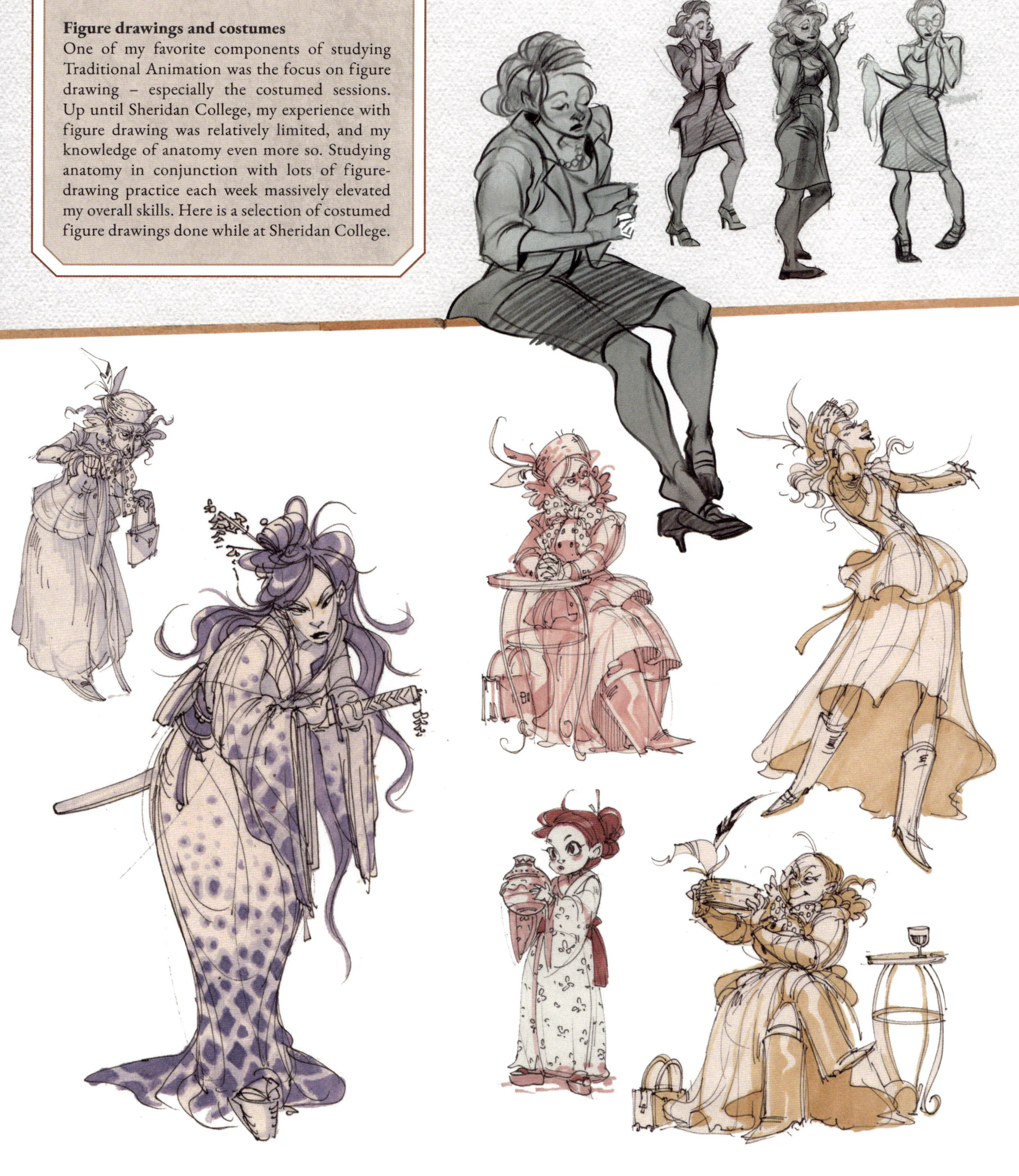

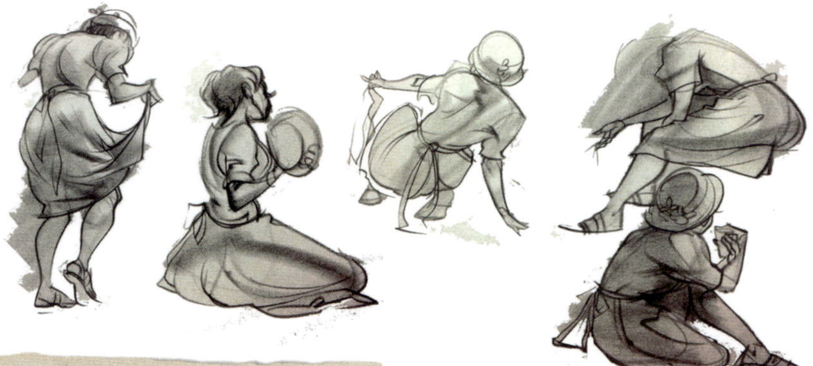

Visual communication

The storytelling aspect makes costumed figure drawing so fun. Each pose the model takes tells a mini story, and I think having that component makes drawing a lot easier and more enjoyable for me. For this reason, I absolutely love creating comics, and I can't even begin to explain the level of engagement I feel when my task is to visually communicate a series of actions and moods.

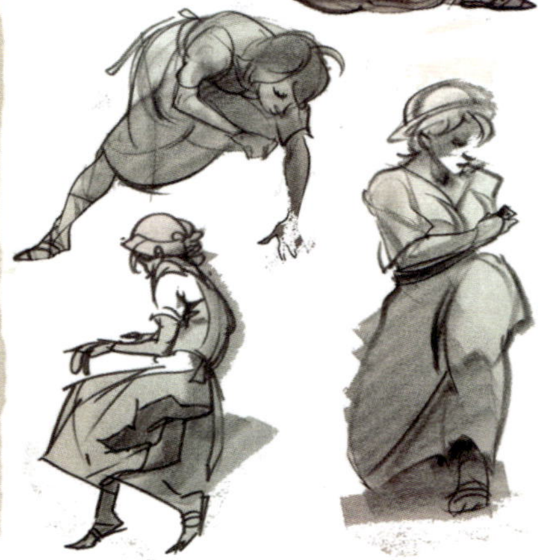

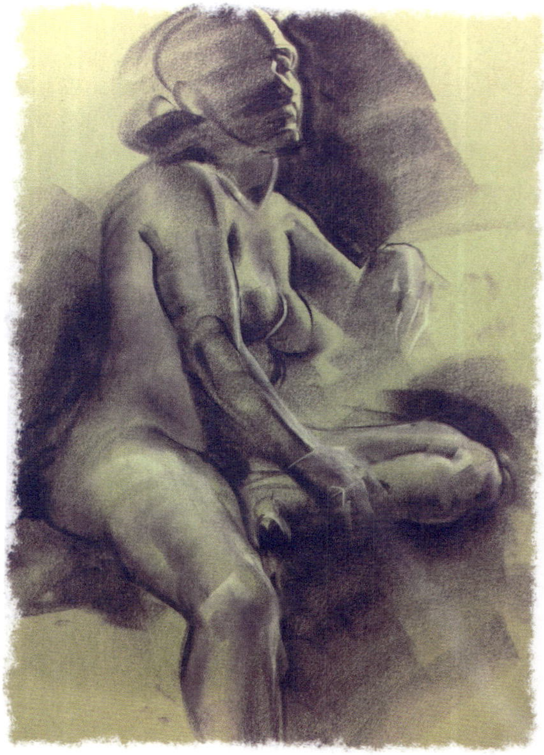

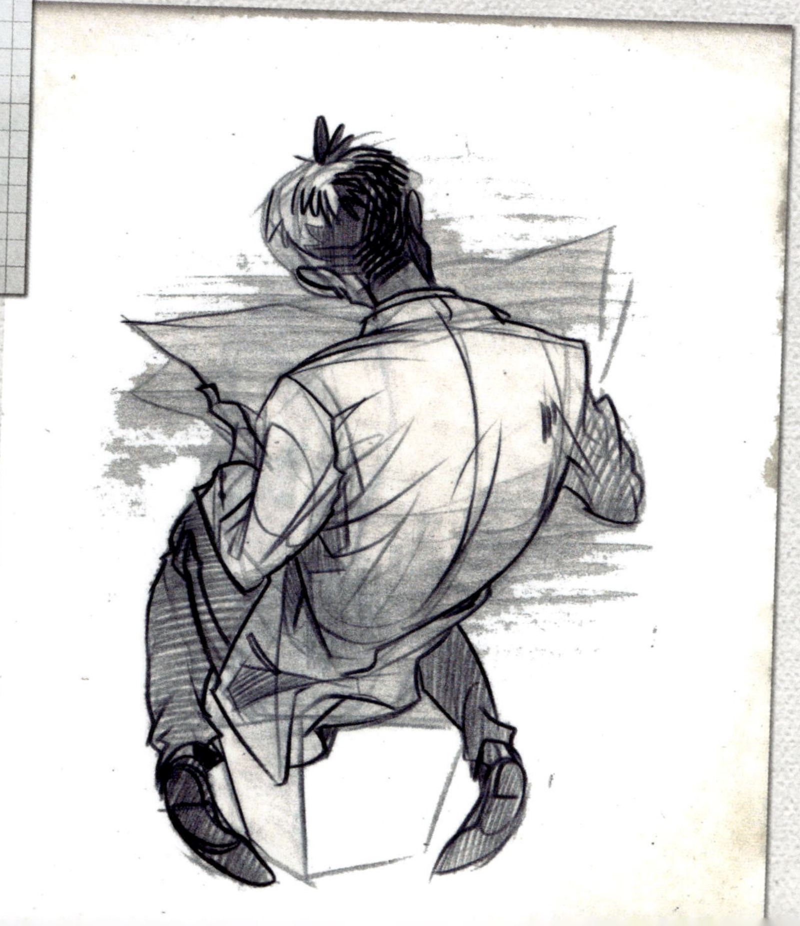

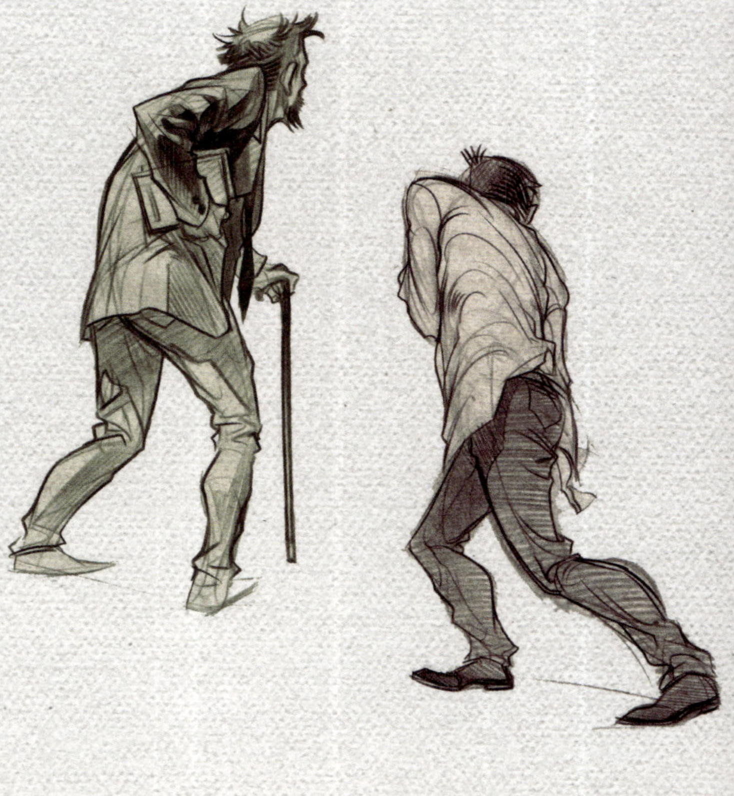

Graduation, independence, and back to the present

I don't think I can pinpoint any specific year of my life as the starting point to my art career. Was it the first time I posted my art on social media? My first paid commission, or my first sale of an original piece? Who knows! One thing I know for sure is that things changed drastically when I graduated from college and began forging my own path forward. It felt like a fresh start, and I was super excited to explore my career options!

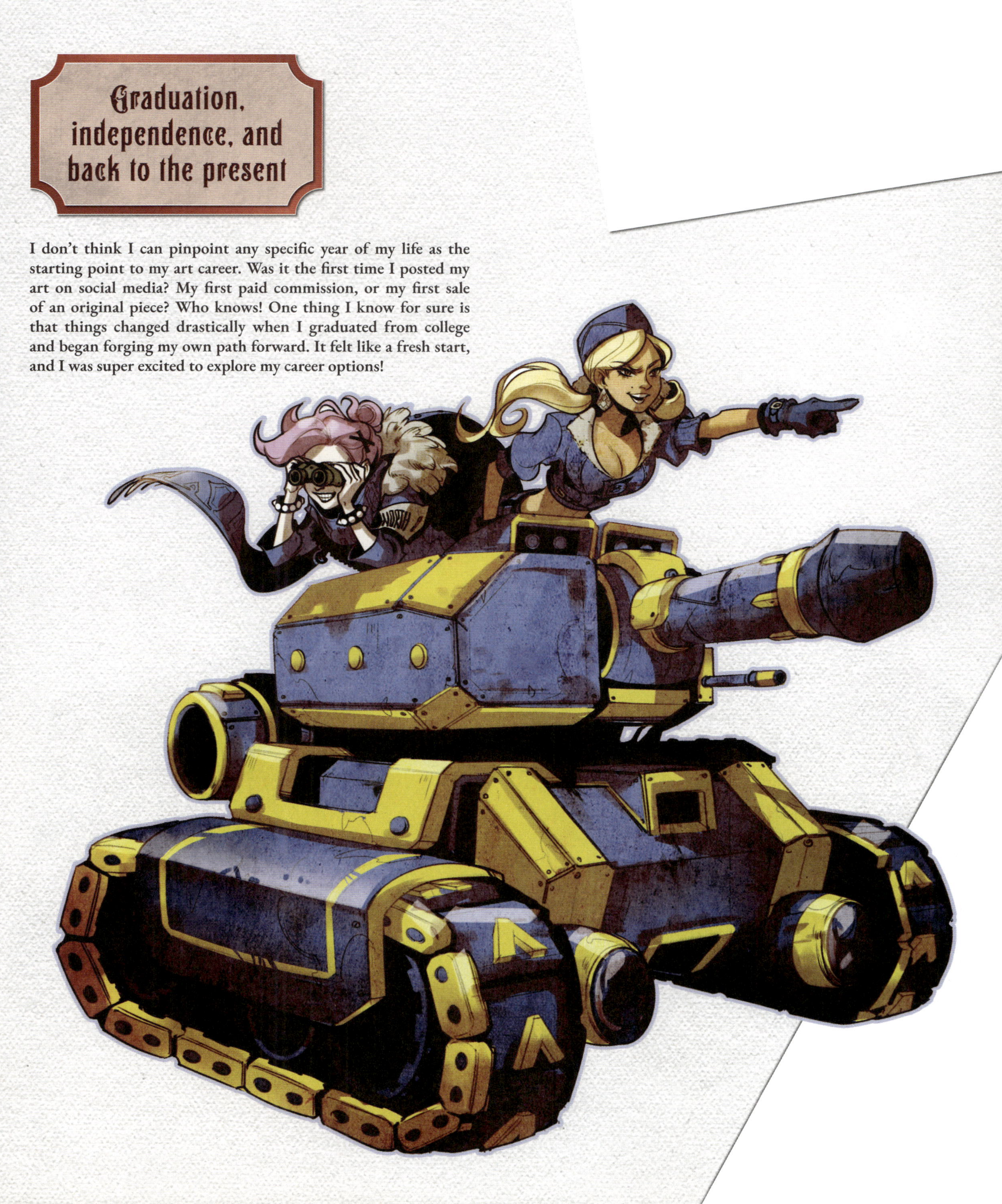

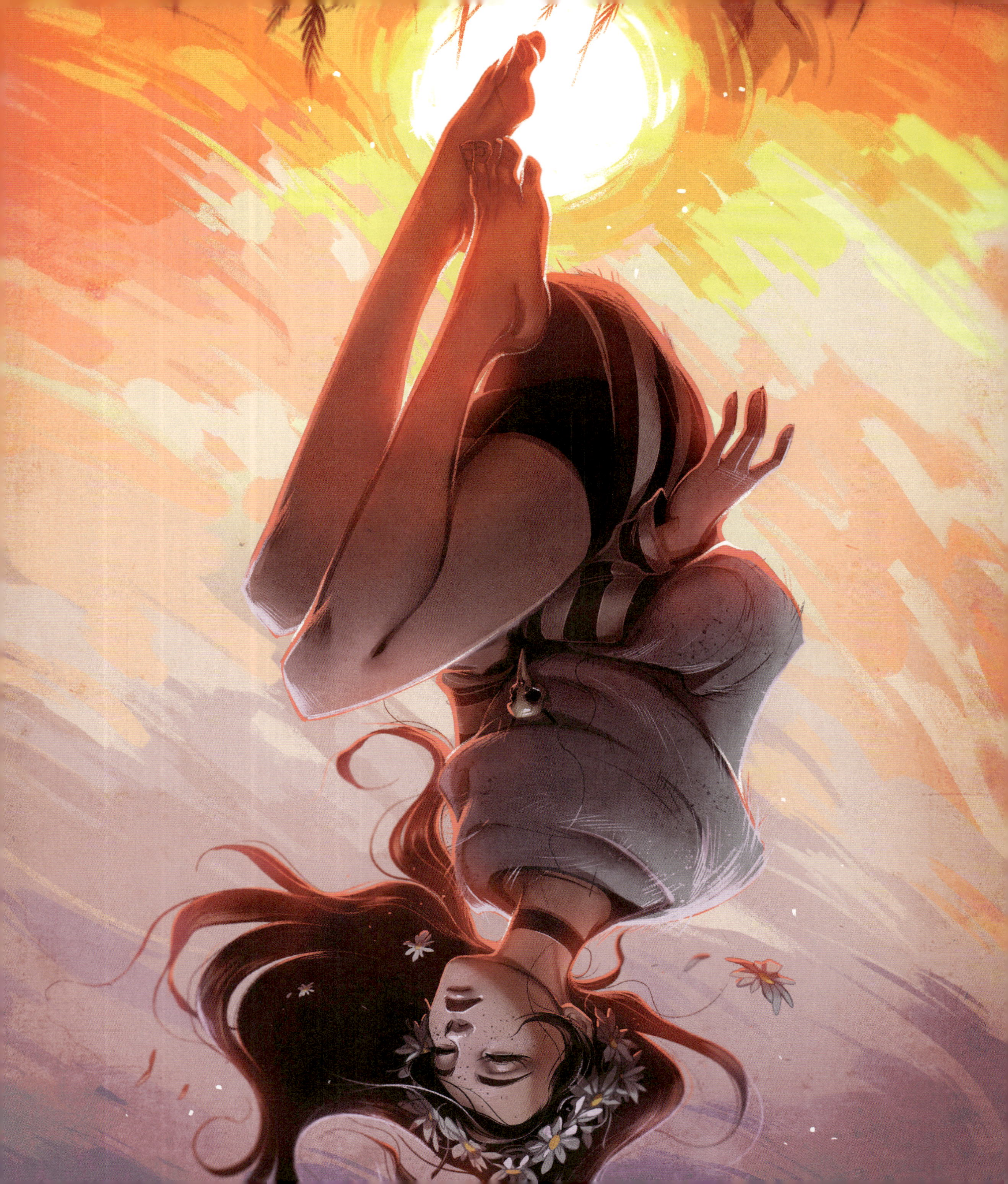

Case study: Grimoire Noir

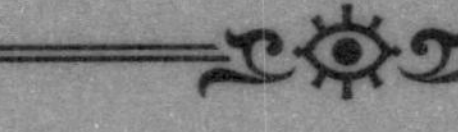

Case study: Grimoire Noir

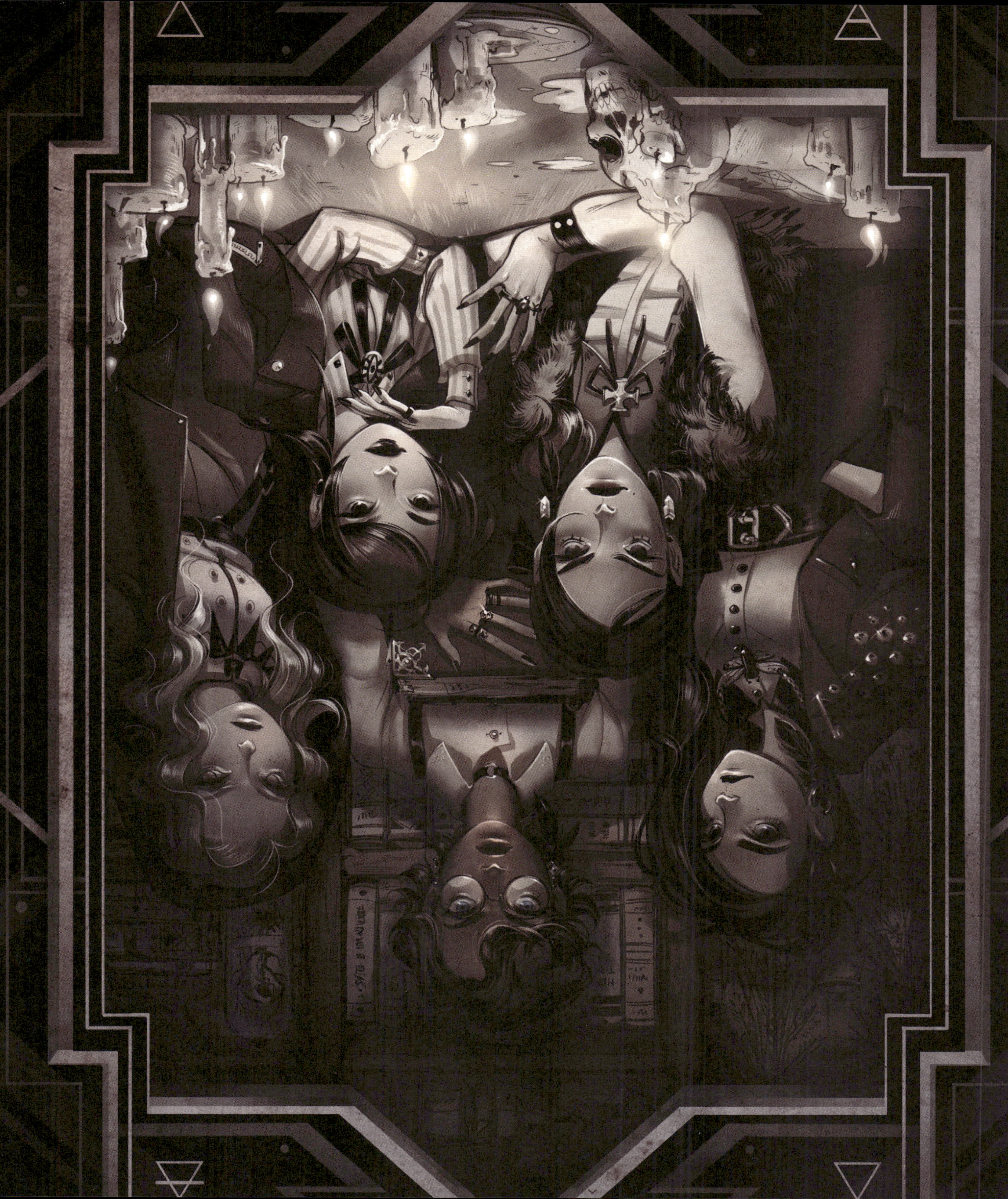

Prologue

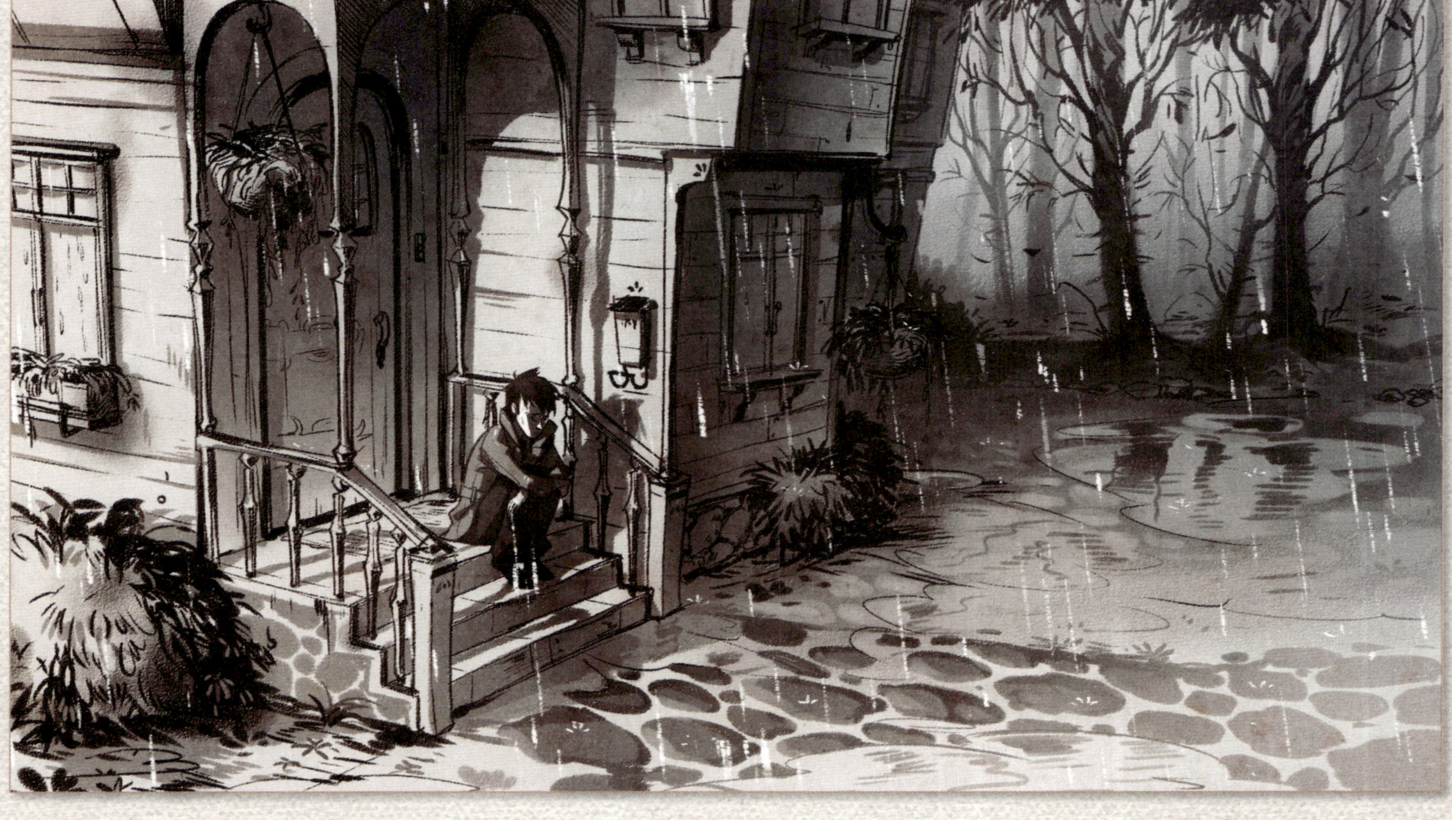

As one of the very first style tests for *Grimoire Noir*, this drawing helped me narrow down the workflow and layer division.

***Grimoire Noir* is a 250-page graphic novel written by Vera Greentea and published by First Second. I worked on it from 2016 to 2018, and to this day it is by far the biggest and most gruelling project I have completed in my career as an illustrator, teaching me many valuable lessons about being a freelance artist.**

The opportunity arose about two months after I started my first full-time 2D-artist position at a mobile game studio. I honestly found myself completely out of place in a game-studio environment. I enjoyed the occasional exchange with fellow artists in the workplace, but just did not care enough for the world of mobile games to be able to get any meaningful satisfaction out of the content I produced. Since my lifelong goal and dream was to eventually work on my own comic series, I decided that illustrating a graphic novel would at least be a step in the right direction, even if it wasn't written by me and meant a reduction in income. Looking back on the decision to suddenly quit my job, I understand why my family was concerned and repeatedly tried to talk me out of it. In retrospect, this was a major step toward learning how to find success as a freelance artist, even if it was an extremely challenging one too!

Once I accepted the job and was greenlit to start work, one of the first things I did was go to the local library and read as many graphic novels as I could fine, especially those from the same publisher. This allowed me to scope out what was already in print, and pinpoint the direction for my art. I wanted to do something new, something different. I decided to attempt a highly detailed and polished cinematic approach to this project – something I didn't see much in American young-adult graphic novels. Also, I personally felt I could use a lot of improvement in this style.

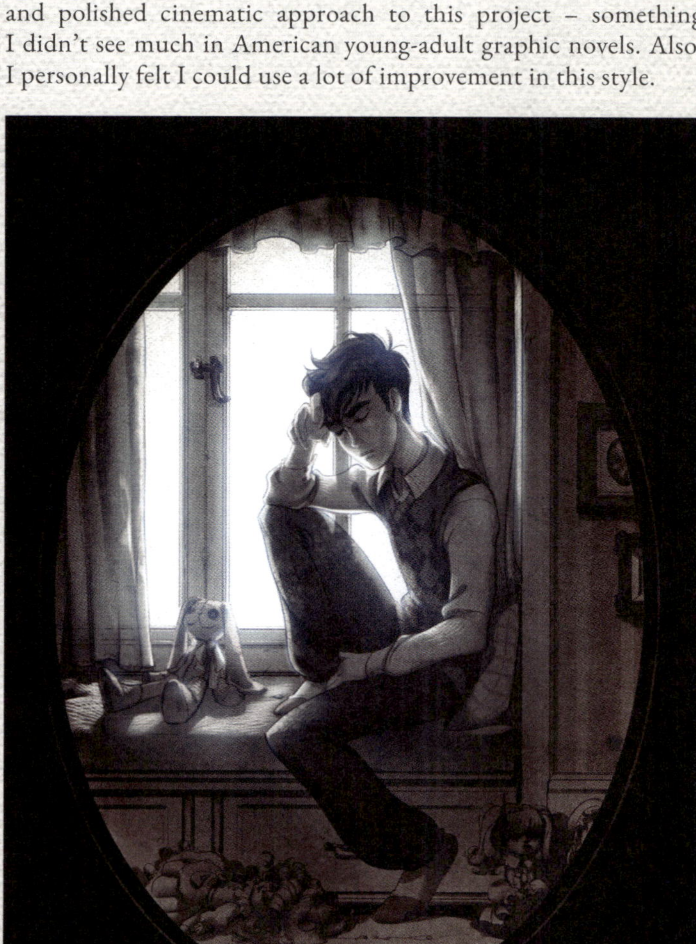

In this illustration, I aimed to make a sunny morning look cold and lonely. I really enjoy showing strong emotions in a setting not commonly used to depict that particular feeling.

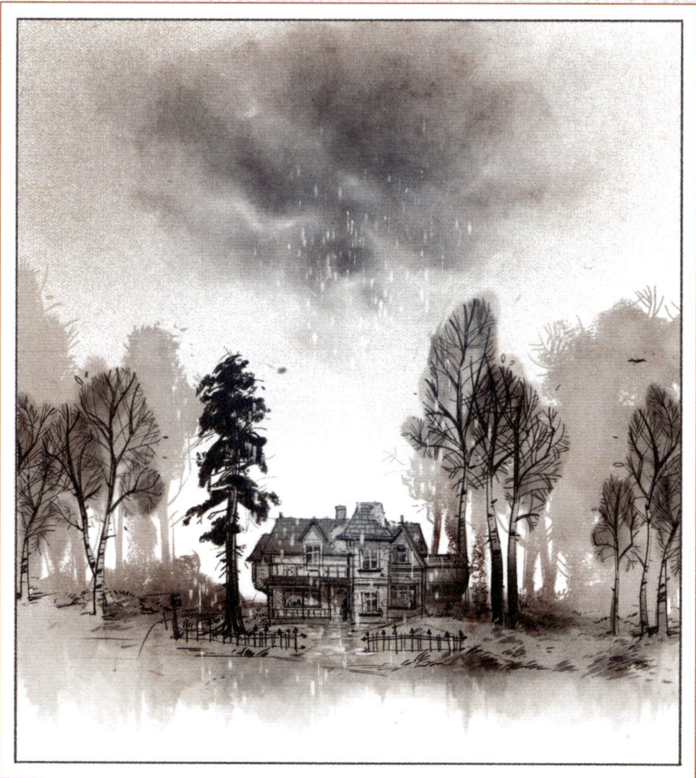

I wanted to give the opening pages of *Grimoire Noir* a dreamlike quality. The result is a setting that seems a bit removed from "regular" reality. It is a magical town, after all.

One of the most important goals in much of my artwork has consistently been to communicate a distinct and engrossing atmosphere. Some of my most vivid childhood memories are those of emotional engagement from watching a movie or reading a book. It was always the atmosphere that stayed with me more than anything else... I could forget the plot, but would always remember the characters, and the distinctive color and flavor of their unique world. This is the kind of effect I set out to create on the pages of *Grimoire Noir*. I think that at the very least, I achieved that particular goal and am so incredibly happy that I had the perseverance to care about every single page and panel equally throughout the whole book, despite my frustrations with some parts of the project.

In this chapter I will share behind-the-scenes sketches and preliminary drawings for the first time, as well as take you through the process of how I established a consistent digital workflow for the pages of this lengthy comic project.

Preliminary character design

After establishing the art direction with these two test pages, I set out to design the main characters, tackling one chapter at a time.

My typical approach to each chapter was to first give it a thorough read, noting every first character appearance and description, every unique location, and every object of importance. Afterward, I would make lists and do the necessary research to gather references to be able to create convincing background imagery and give the characters a believable setting.

What follows are some of the initial character concepts...

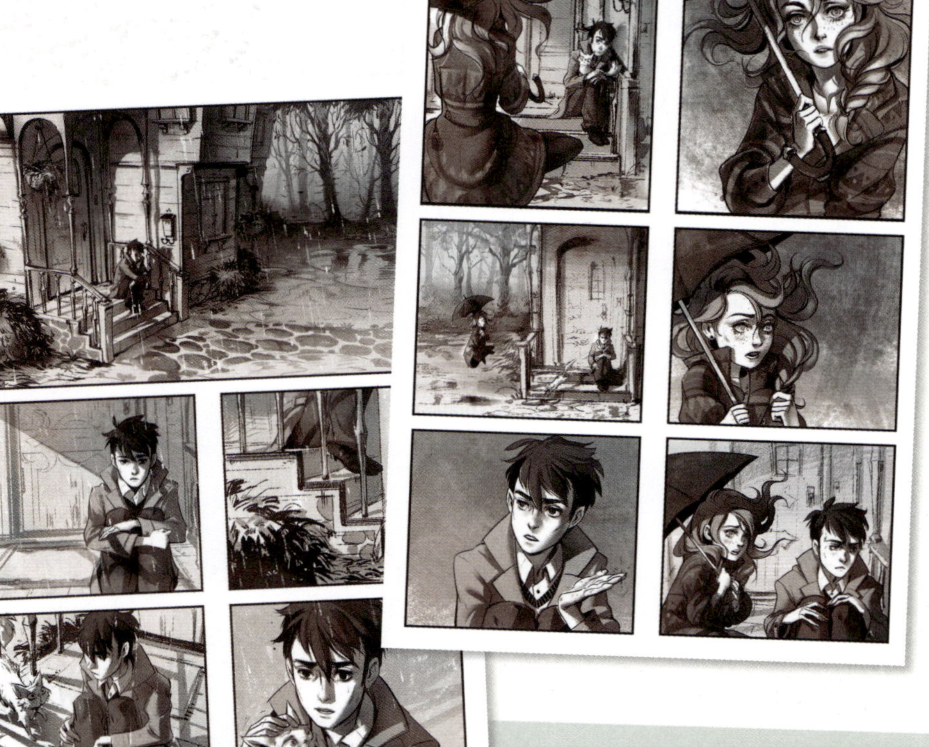

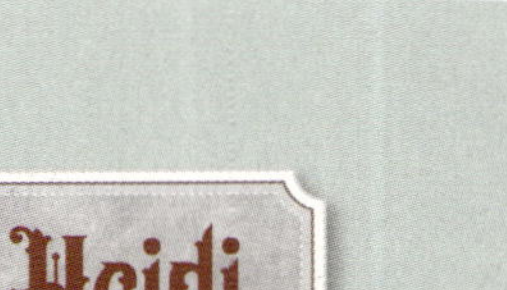

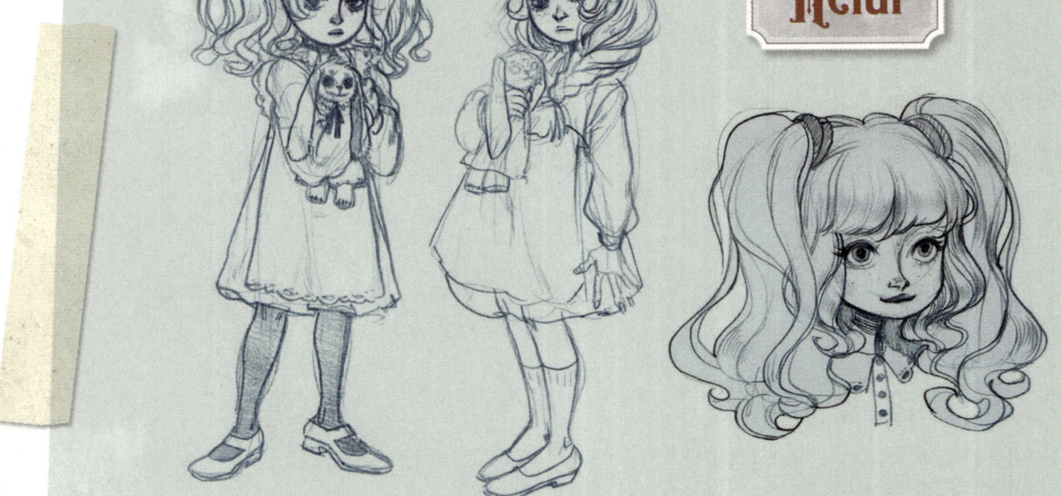

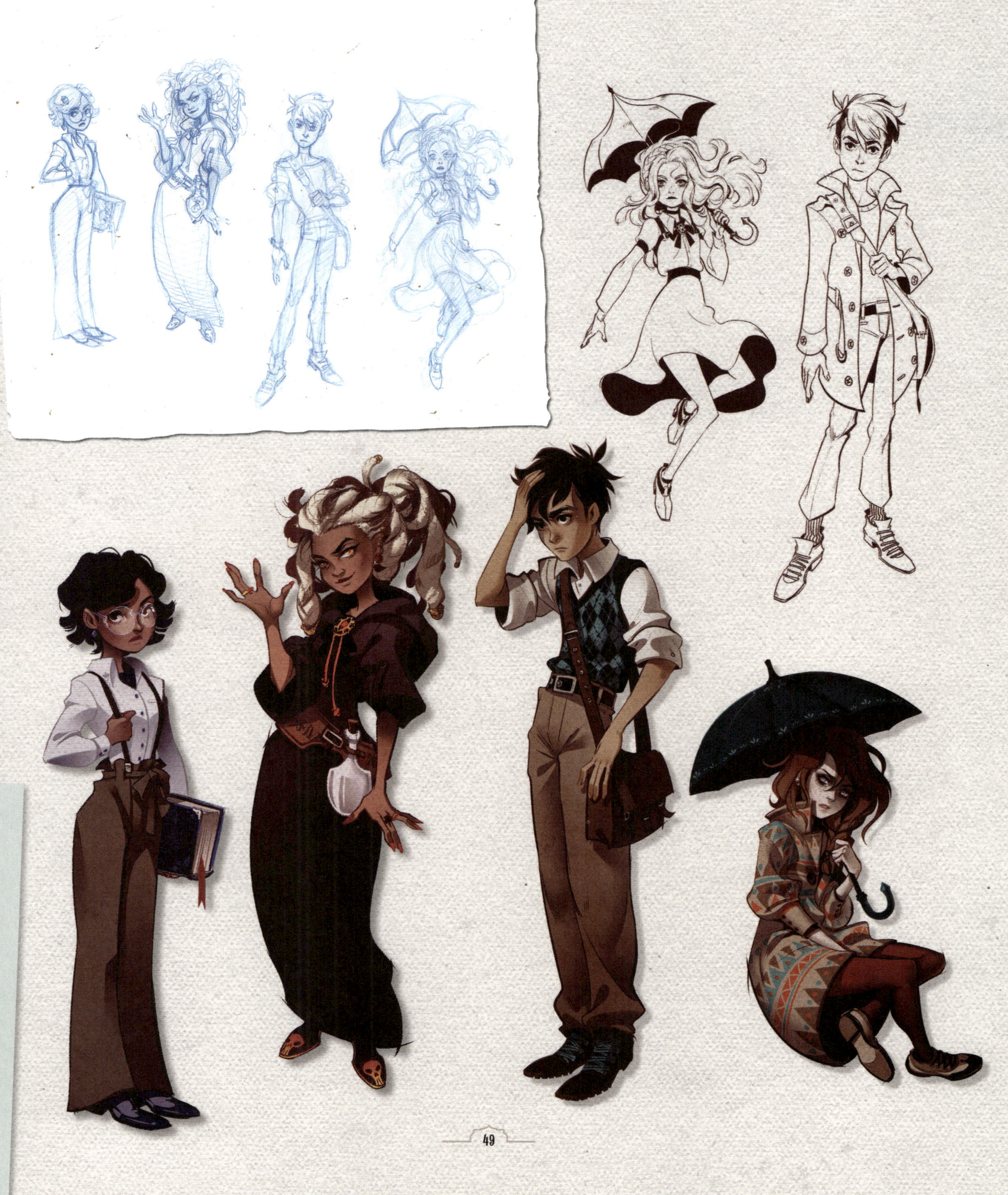

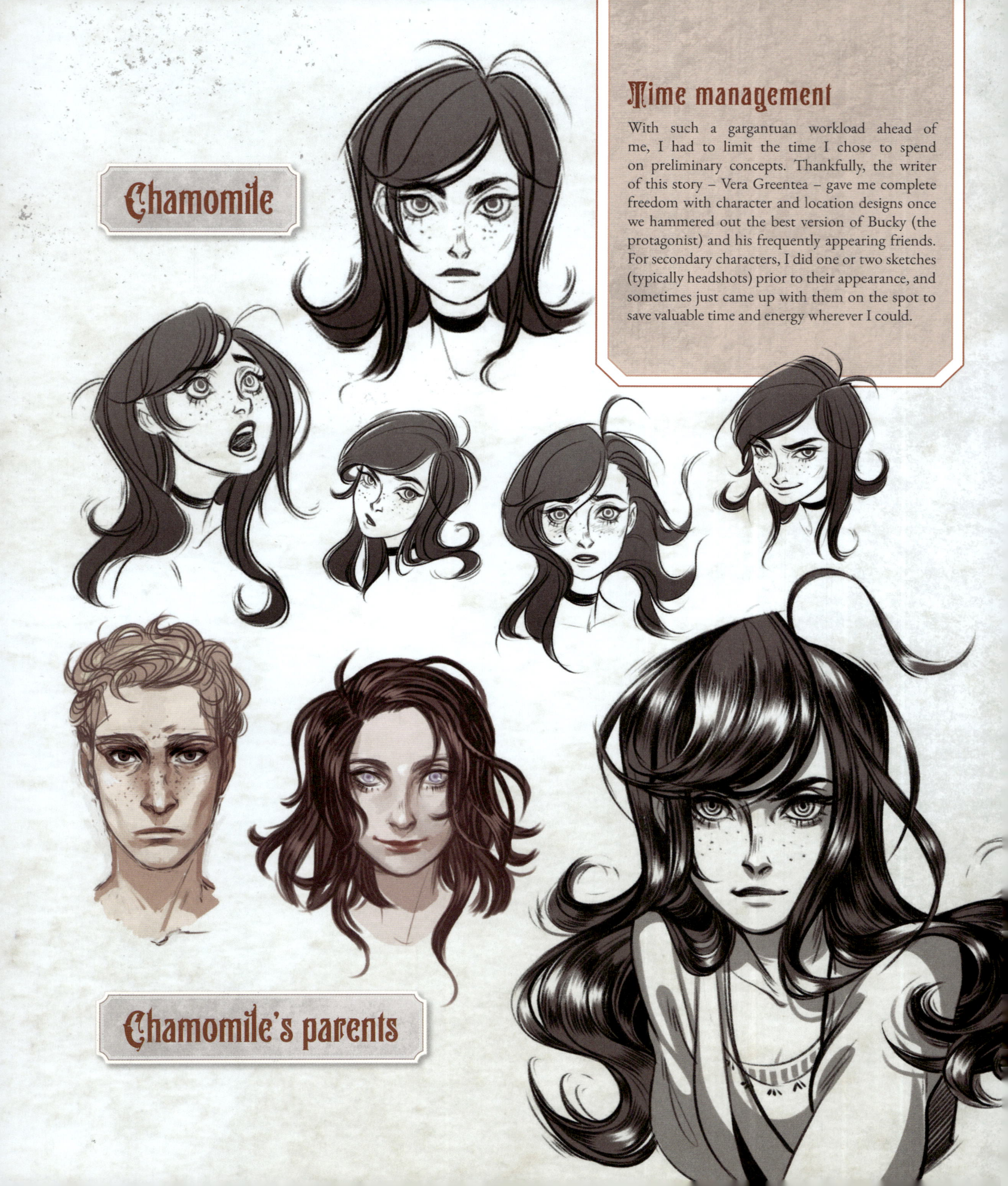

Time management

With such a gargantuan workload ahead of me, I had to limit the time I chose to spend on preliminary concepts. Thankfully, the writer of this story – Vera Greentea – gave me complete freedom with character and location designs once we hammered out the best version of Bucky (the protagonist) and his frequently appearing friends. For secondary characters, I did one or two sketches (typically headshots) prior to their appearance, and sometimes just came up with them on the spot to save valuable time and energy wherever I could.

Chamomile

Chamomile's parents

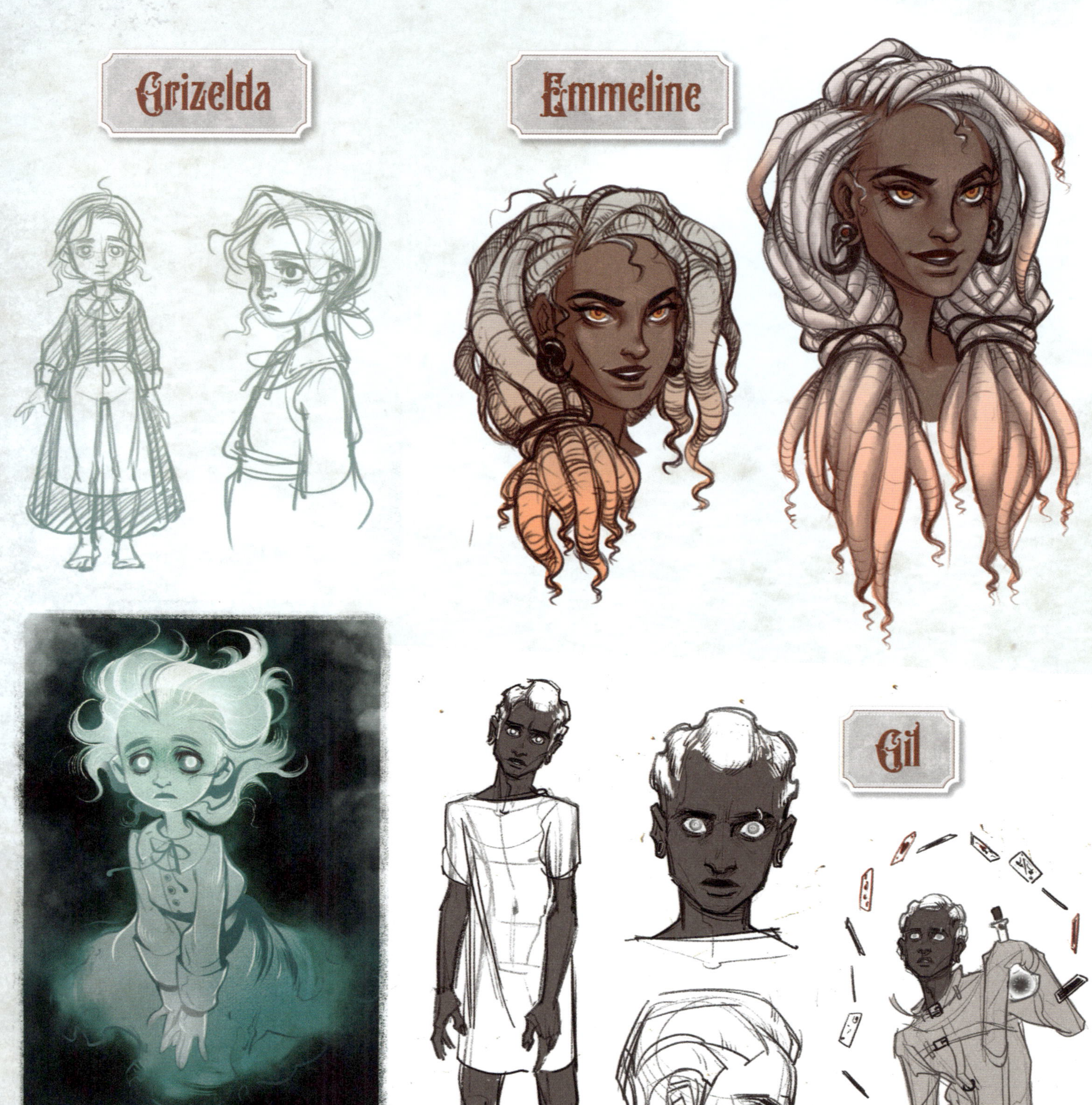
Grizelda
Emmeline
Gil

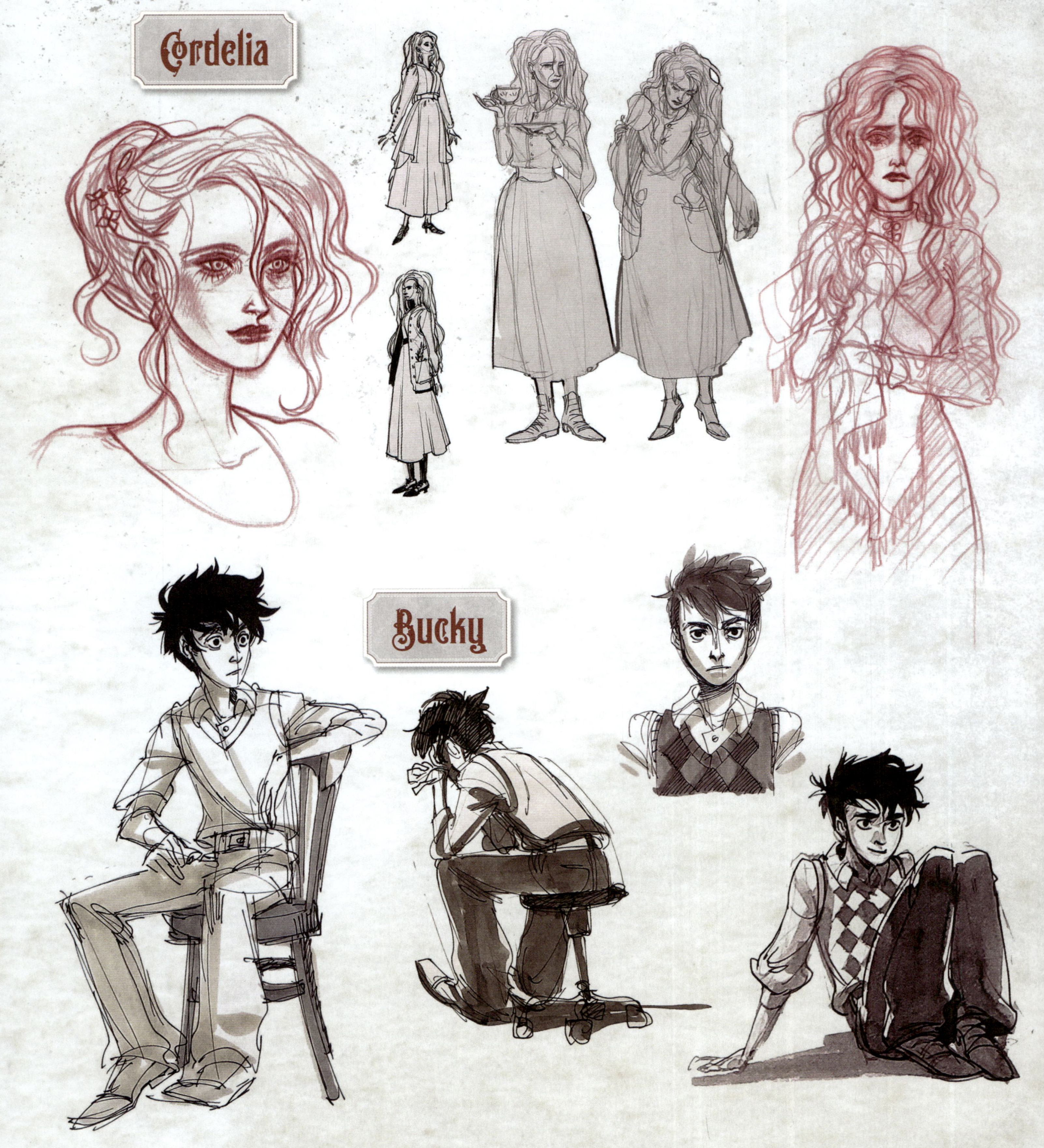
Cordelia
Bucky

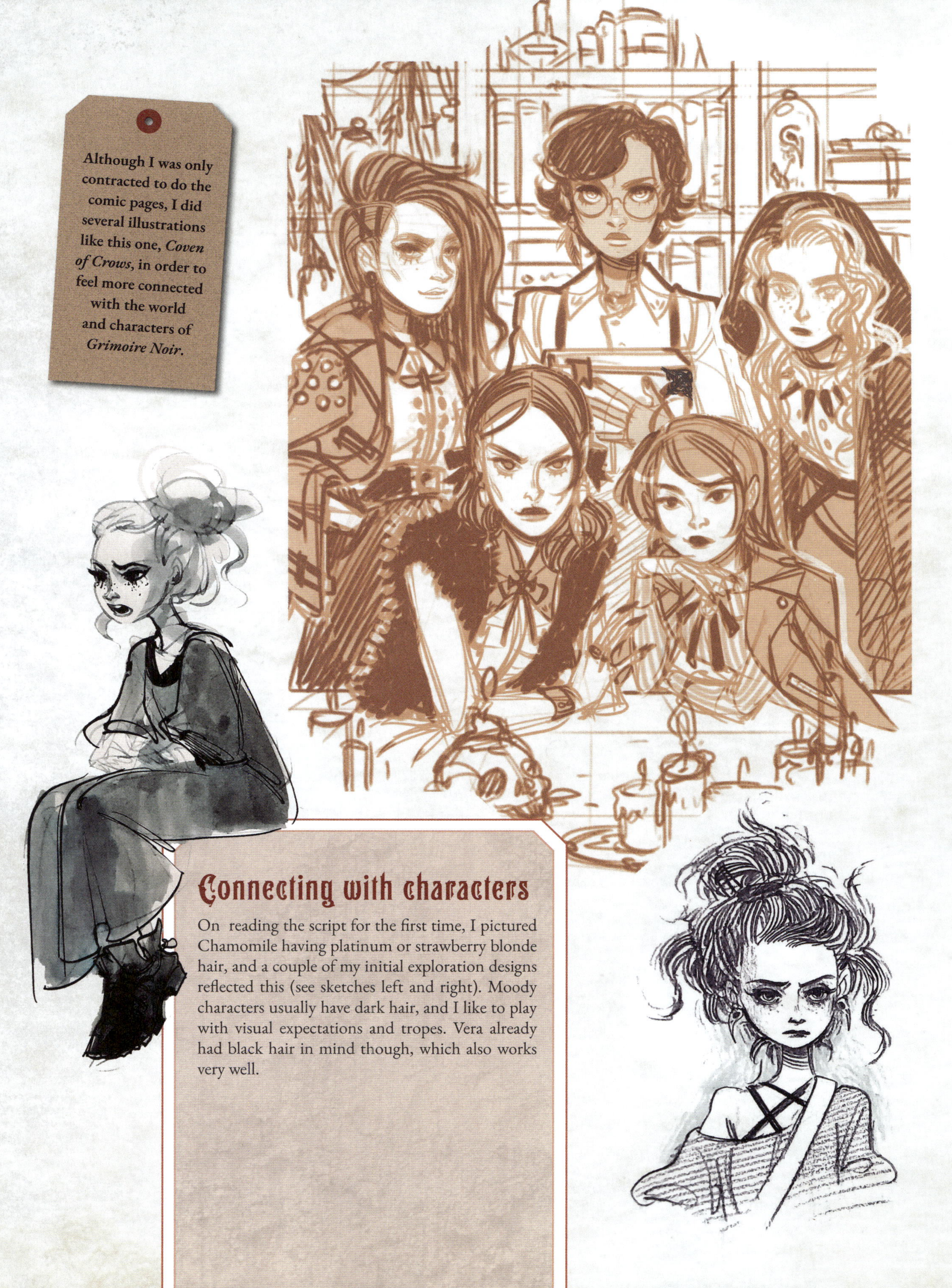

Although I was only contracted to do the comic pages, I did several illustrations like this one, *Coven of Crows*, in order to feel more connected with the world and characters of *Grimoire Noir*.

Connecting with characters

On reading the script for the first time, I pictured Chamomile having platinum or strawberry blonde hair, and a couple of my initial exploration designs reflected this (see sketches left and right). Moody characters usually have dark hair, and I like to play with visual expectations and tropes. Vera already had black hair in mind though, which also works very well.

Costume drama

The part of pre-production where I spared no proverbial expense was the costume department. I've always been very keen on fashion. I absolutely adore coming up with outfits for my characters, and so went the extra mile to put together unique and detailed outfits for all characters (even ones that don't appear all that much). I think fashion is a major tool of personal expression, and speaks volumes about a character. Therefore it always strikes me as a huge shame to sacrifice fashion detailing in order to simplify the design and its execution. I believe that if the character's fashion is approached in a detail-oriented manner, it can help to make them feel like a real person with their own life away from the pages of the comic. Thankfully my love for drawing clothing details carried me through the hard work! Here are some examples of costume designs for Chamomile, and some quick sketches of other characters...

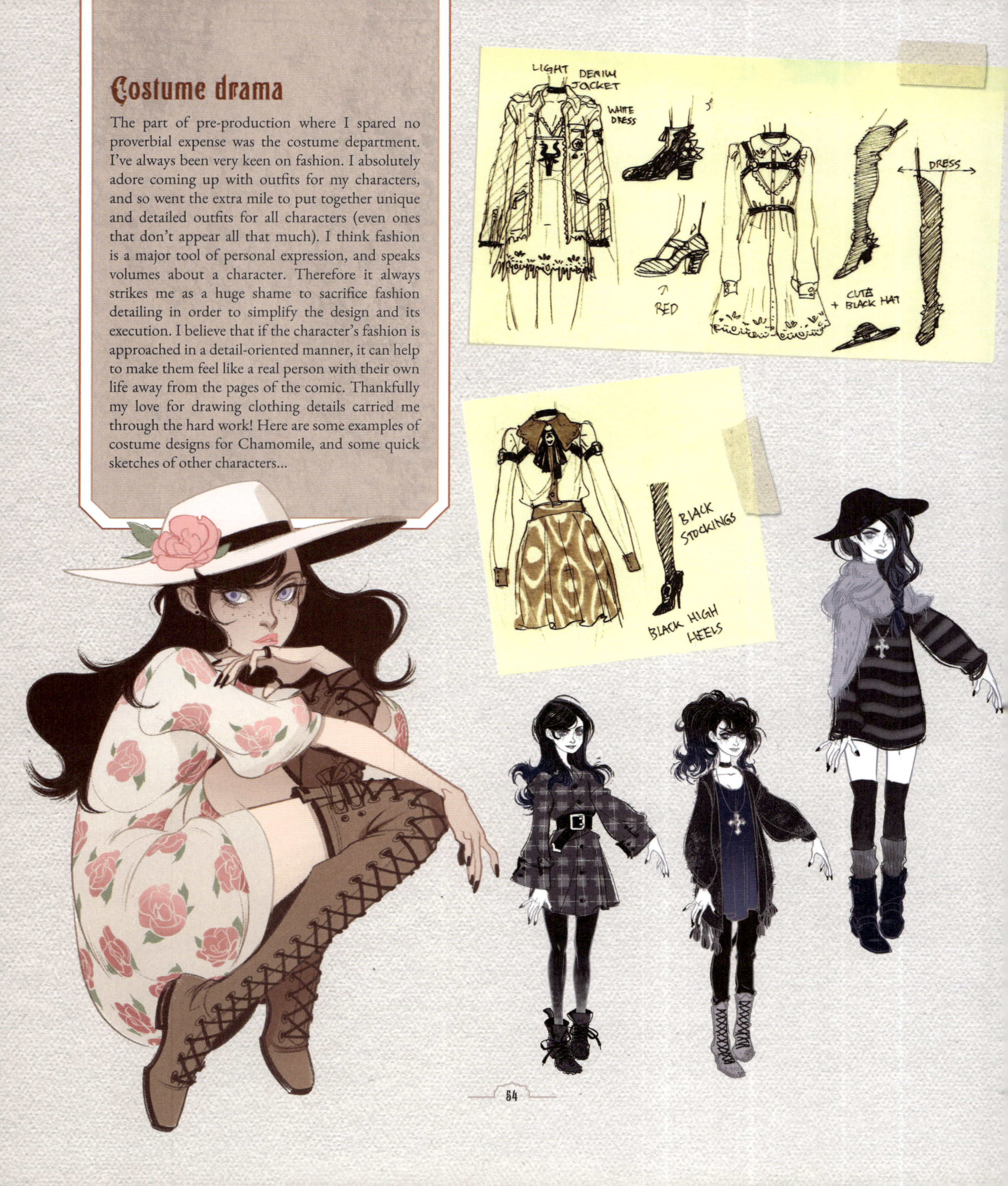

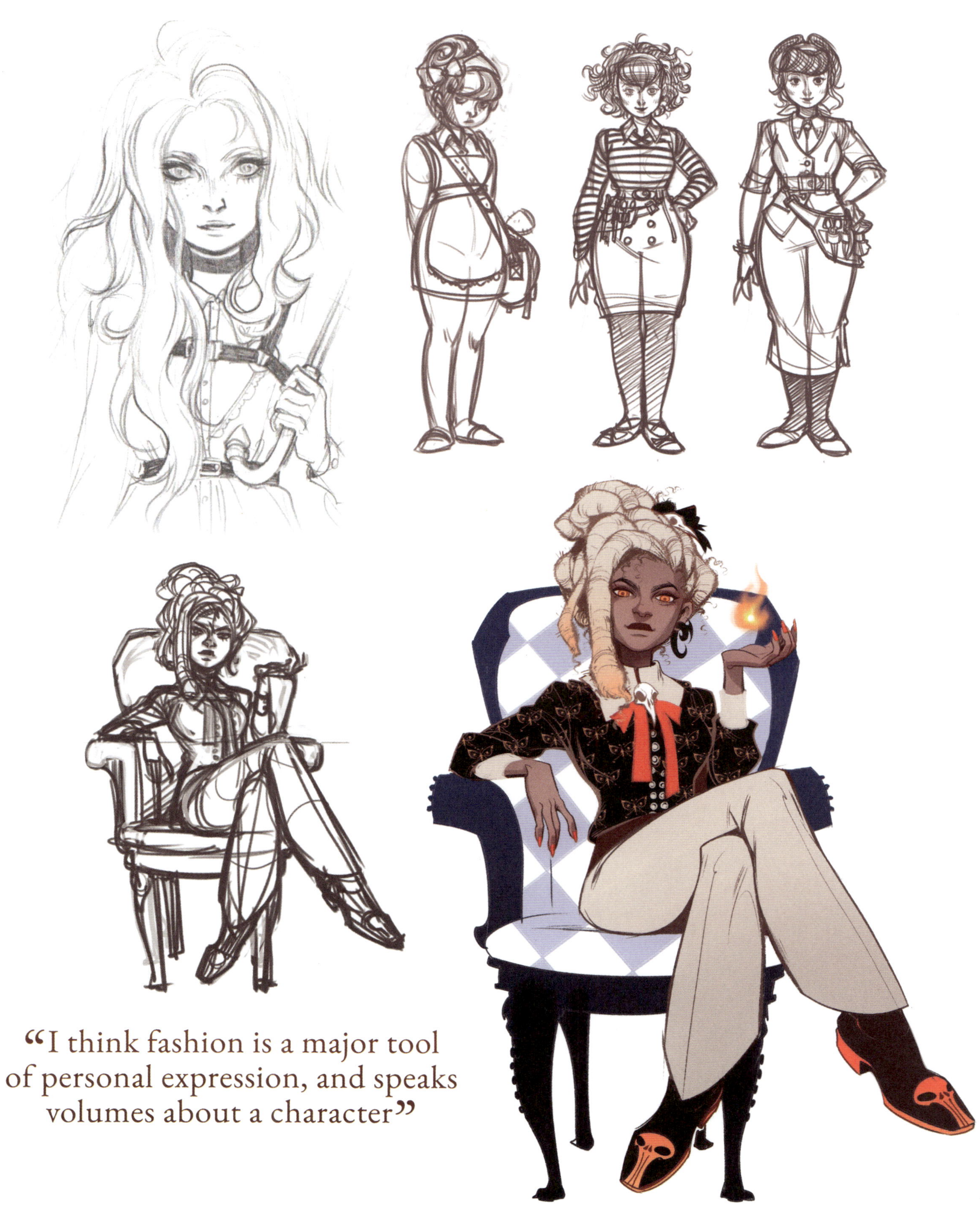

"I think fashion is a major tool of personal expression, and speaks volumes about a character"

Thumbnails

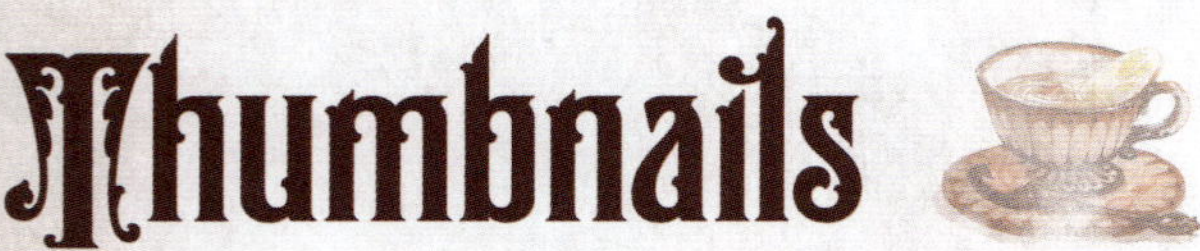

Here are selected thumbnails from various chapters of *Grimoire Noir*. As mentioned before, after doing initial design work and gathering references, I jumped straight into thumbnailing the whole chapter. Having had little experience with comics prior to this project, there was a fair amount of trial and error involved. I bounced back and forth between a super-detailed and a bare-bones approach, eventually finding a happy medium that worked best for me.

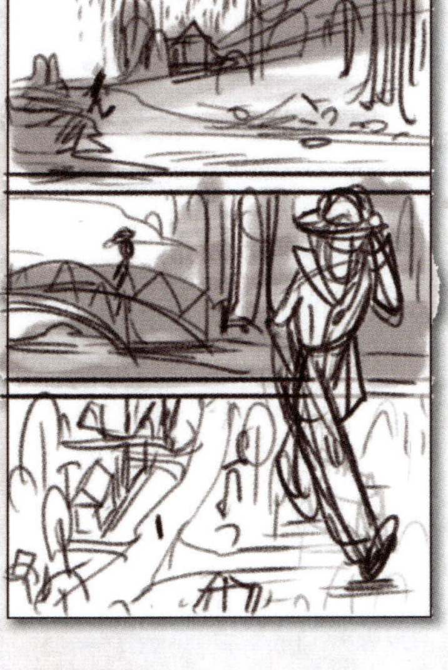

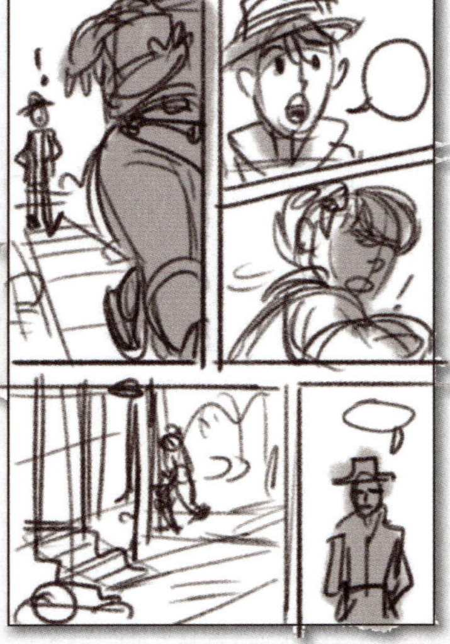

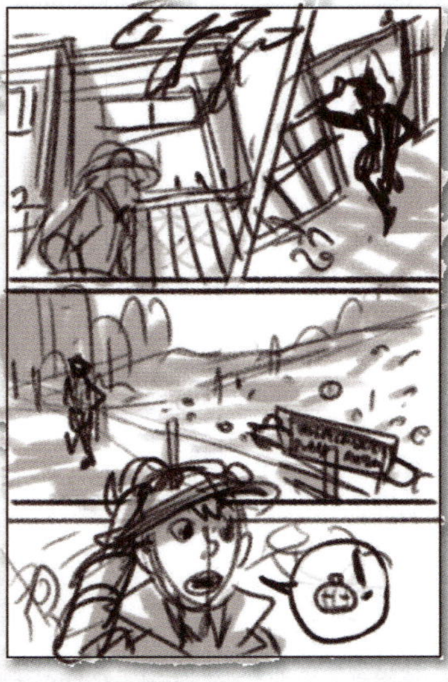

This trio of thumbnails shows the first few pages of Chapter 2, done digitally.

Pages 27–29 from *Grimoire Noir*

Keeping it digital

Even though I decided early on that the graphic novel would be executed digitally, for some reason I did the thumbnails for the first chapter in my sketchbook. I swiftly realized that this was a big mistake – not only did I fail to match the correct proportions of the pages, but I also had to erase elements multiple times and had no ability to copy/paste. The whole thing just took much longer than it should have. I quickly created a digital template for future chapter thumbnails and never attempted to do this in my sketchbook again.

As you can see, my thumbnails get more detailed after switching to Adobe Photoshop (my drawing app of choice), but for the last few chapters I stopped incorporating tonal information as seen on pages 27–29 and pages 163–165 of *Grimoire Noir*. Pages 126–128 use a more bare-bones approach, which was slightly faster, but I found that the time I saved on the thumbnails migrated to the layout step anyway. Pages 229–231 are the happy medium, containing just enough detail and proportional accuracy to facilitate a super-quick sketching process for the final layouts before inking.

The key purpose of thumbnails:

- To establish a clear angle and perspective of the shot.
- To figure out the optimal placement for characters to aid the visual story-telling.
- To ensure that the actions are clear.

Quiet time

For me, thumbnailing is the most mentally straining and difficult part of the process, but also the most fun and engaging. Sadly, it's something I have to do in silence without any interruptions, unlike any other part of the production. I typically love listening to audiobooks, podcasts, YouTube videos, or music while working, but thumbnailing is a special task that requires one-hundred-percent attention. However, while working on *Grimoire Noir*, I did like to throw on the sound of stormy weather in the background, which certainly helped set the mood!

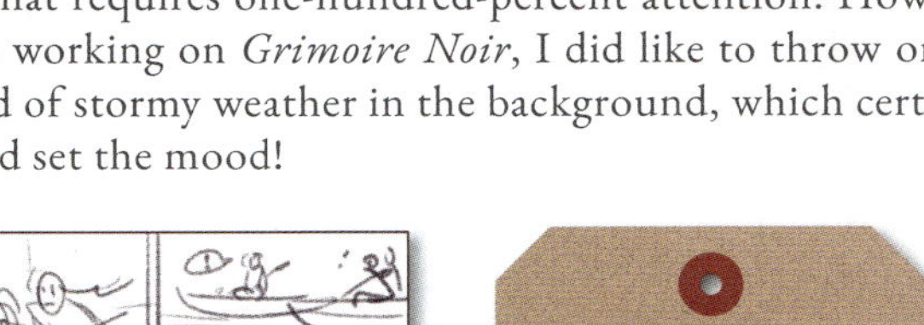

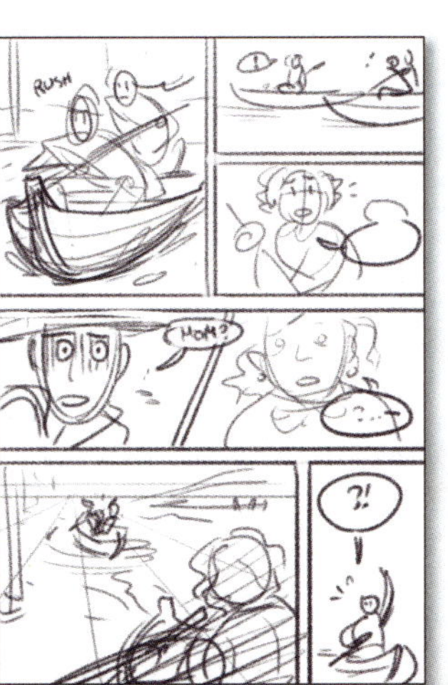

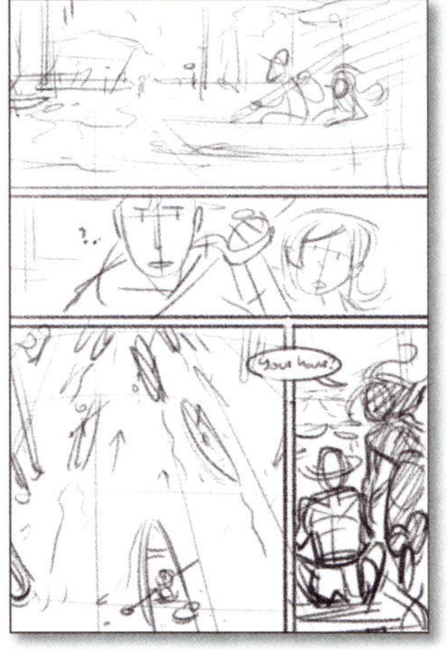

These thumbnails did the job but were too bare bones for my liking, so I incorporated more details going forward.

Pages 126–128 from *Grimoire Noir*

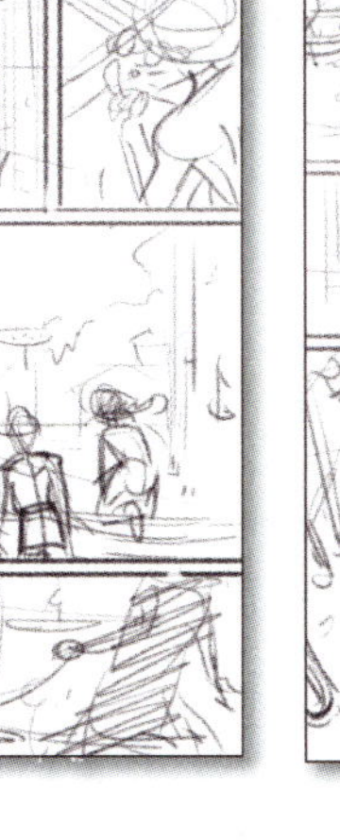

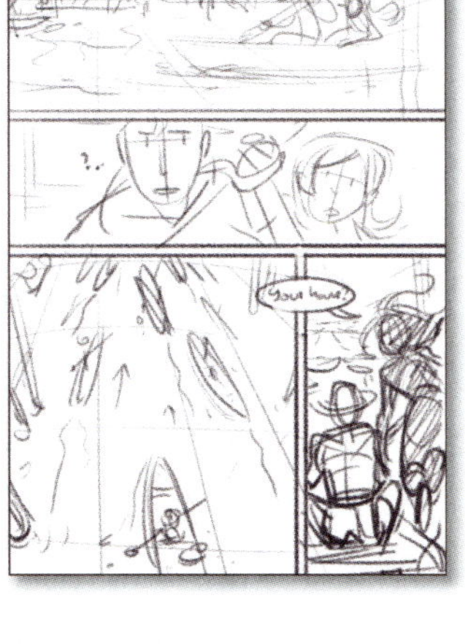

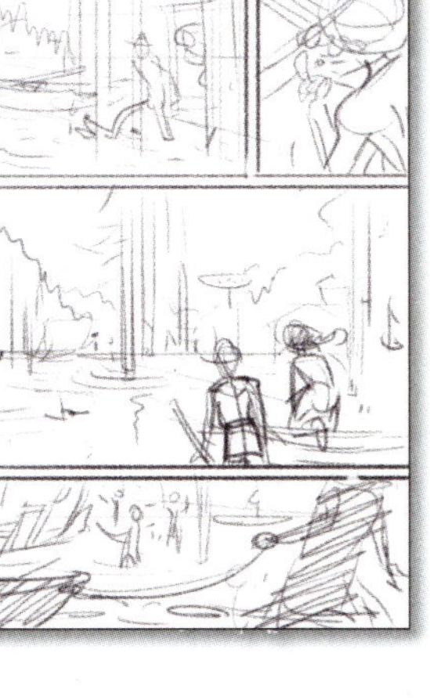

This more detailed approach turned out to be redundant and time-consuming, so I pulled back and dropped the tonal information.

Pages 163–165 from *Grimoire Noir*

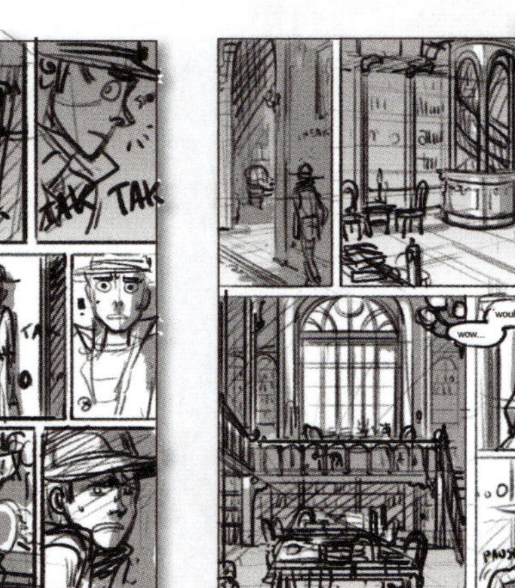

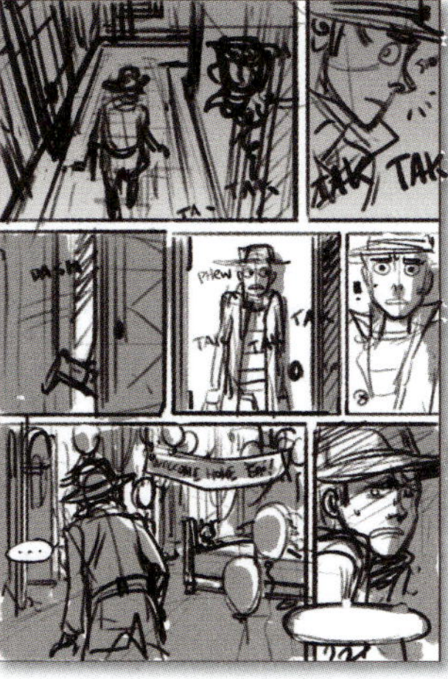

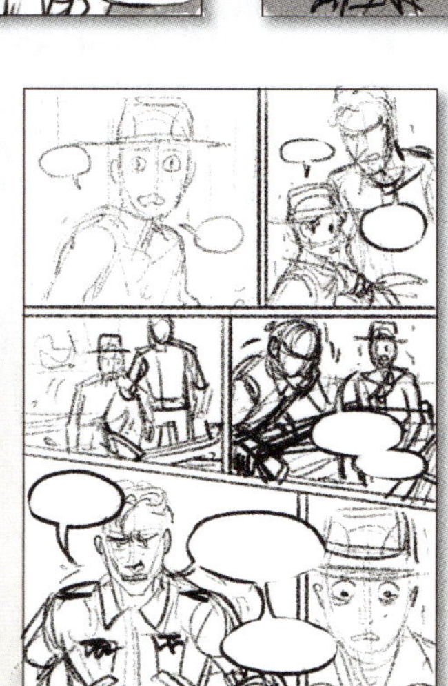

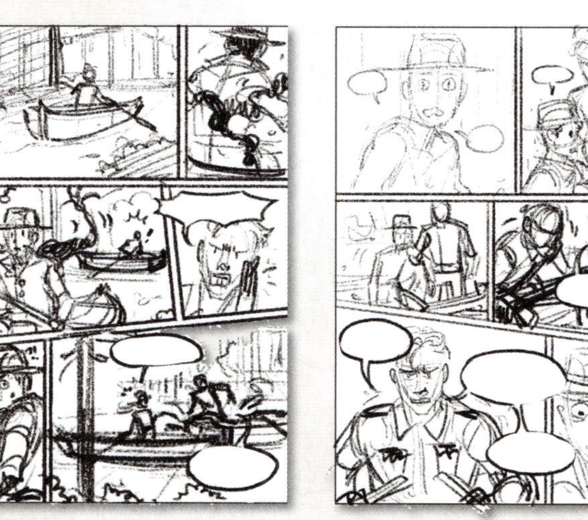

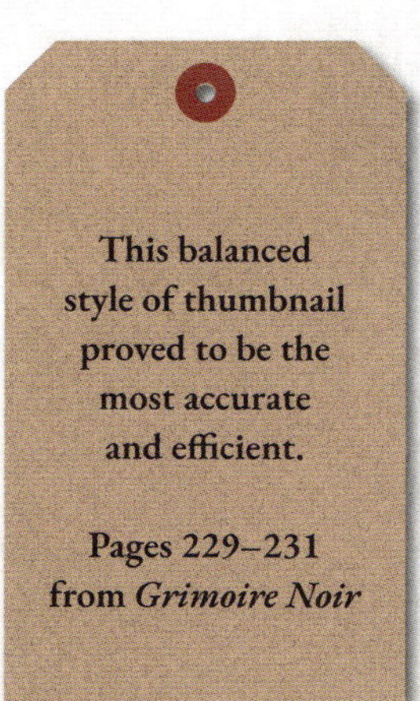

This balanced style of thumbnail proved to be the most accurate and efficient.

Pages 229–231 from *Grimoire Noir*

Workflow

To keep the process running smoothly and waste as little time as possible, I developed a clear process for taking a single page from thumbnail to finished product. I think this was one of the best decisions I made early on – it helped me keep the whole novel very consistent and cohesive.

After thumbnailing a full chapter, I jumped straight into layouts, which I drew directly over a blown-up image of the thumbnail. I established something like a factory process, doing certain steps in bulk, such as creating every PSD file for each page of the chapter, pasting in the thumbnails as a sketch base-layer and setting it to 10% opacity, then cleaning up the panel frames for every page.

When this setup was complete, I drew in all the characters for the entire chapter, and any prop they were interacting with. Finally, I went back and sketched in all the backgrounds. This was created entirely using Photoshop CC on a PC desktop, using a Wacom Cintiq 22HD drawing monitor.

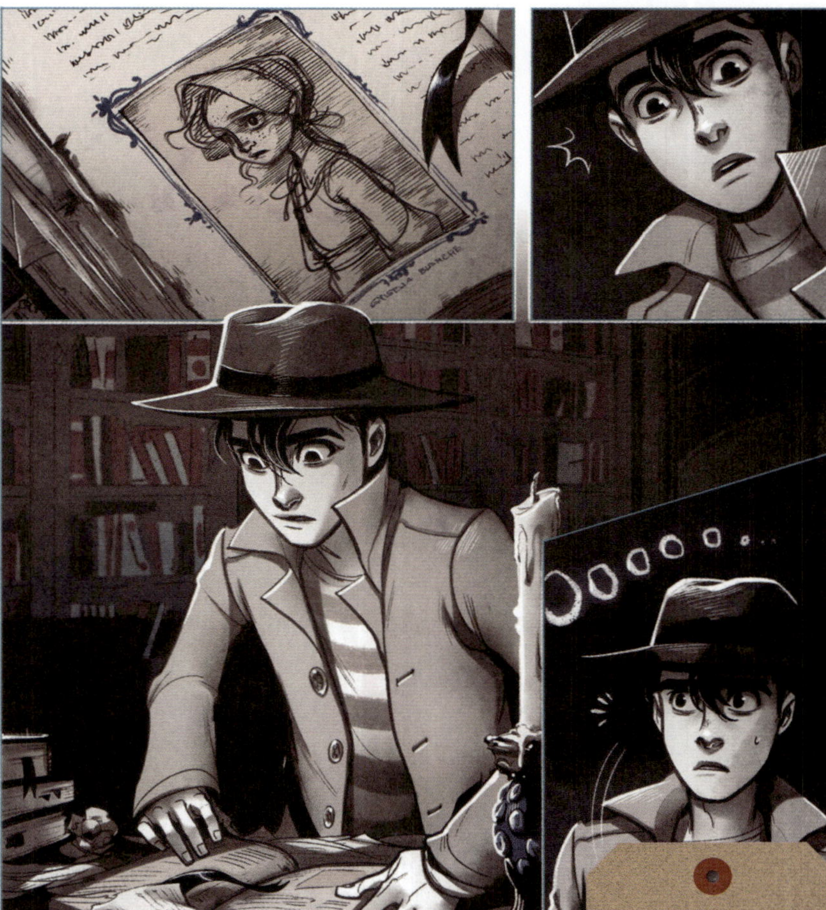

I use this page throughout the case study because it's balanced, using background-heavy panels and simpler character-only panels as well.

Page 167 from *Grimoire Noir*

Mind over matter

It may seem strange to break up the process so much, but I found that it was easier on me mentally. Small steps meant that I was constantly under the illusion of getting things done quickly and moving rapidly through the pages. It was one of the many mind-trickery strategies I had to come up with in order to stay in control under the pressure of an immense workload.

LAYER BY LAYER

Here is the basic breakdown of layers from top to bottom in a Photoshop file, illustrated by one of my favorite pages, which appears around halfway through the book.

I decided it was important to show the layers in this way because their order has a huge impact on the result, and it is something that's seldom covered in other tutorials I've seen. The first and last layers are created first, and the others added in a way that doesn't match the actual end state of the PSD file, so I hope this will provide clarity in terms of where to place certain layers.

(Note: I have slightly simplified the layers for the sake of cohesion; sometimes I break down certain layers further to make them easier to work with, but this is the typical structure. Layers 1–8 are eventually collapsed into a folder I label "raw layers", and are hidden from view in the final art.)

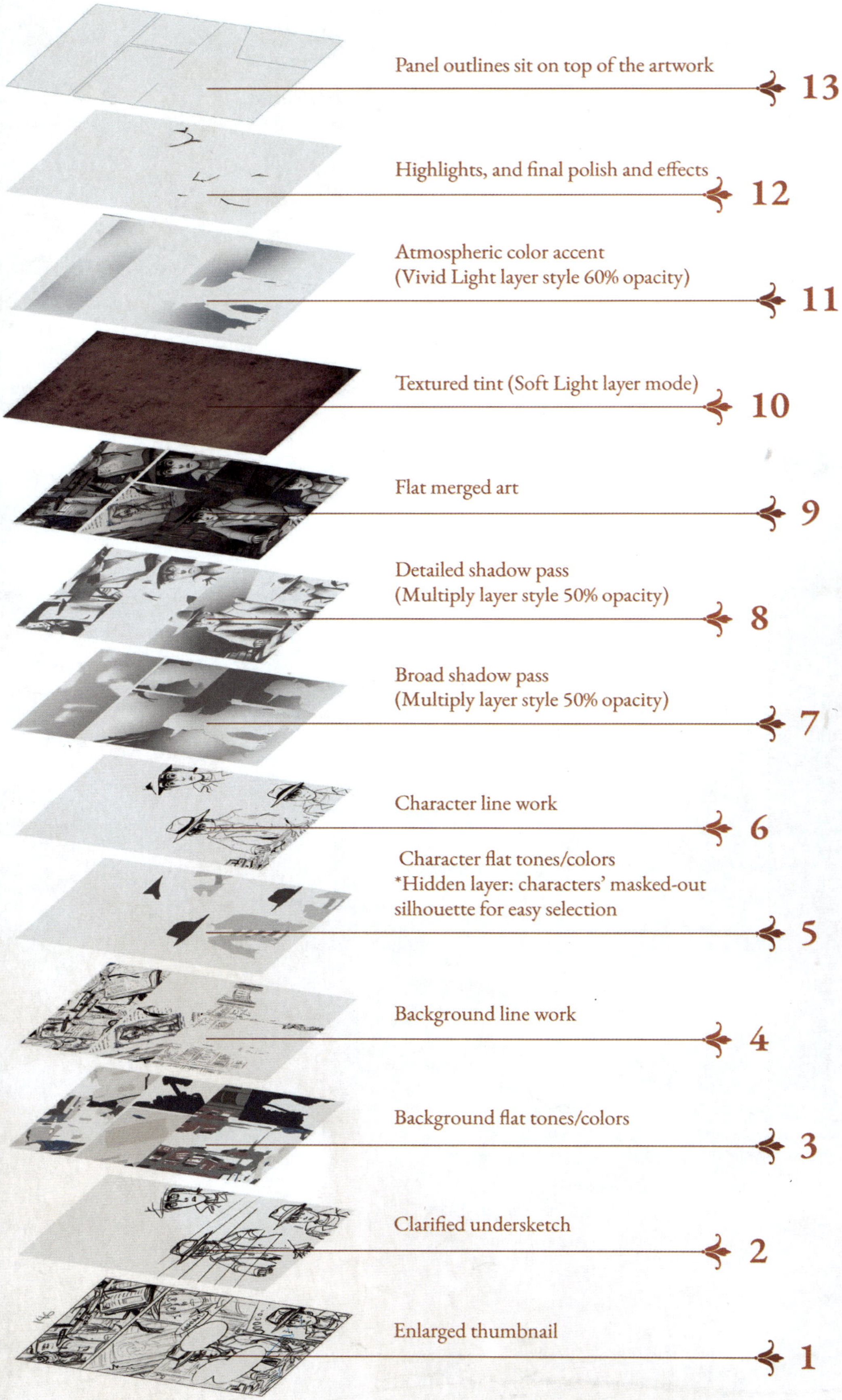

13 Panel outlines sit on top of the artwork

12 Highlights, and final polish and effects

11 Atmospheric color accent
(Vivid Light layer style 60% opacity)

10 Textured tint (Soft Light layer mode)

9 Flat merged art

8 Detailed shadow pass
(Multiply layer style 50% opacity)

7 Broad shadow pass
(Multiply layer style 50% opacity)

6 Character line work

5 Character flat tones/colors
*Hidden layer: characters' masked-out silhouette for easy selection

4 Background line work

3 Background flat tones/colors

2 Clarified undersketch

1 Enlarged thumbnail

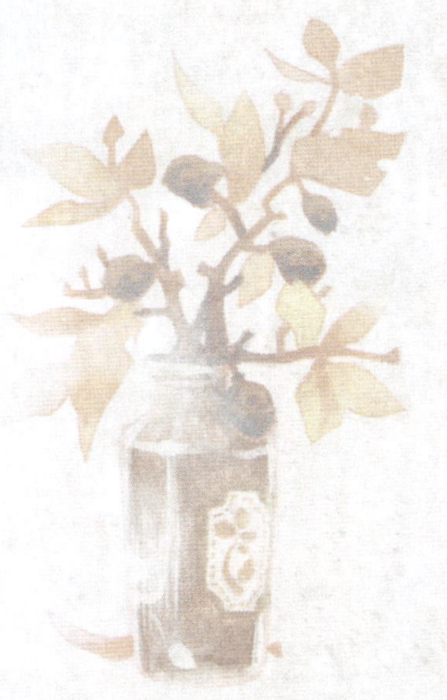

Bringing layers to life

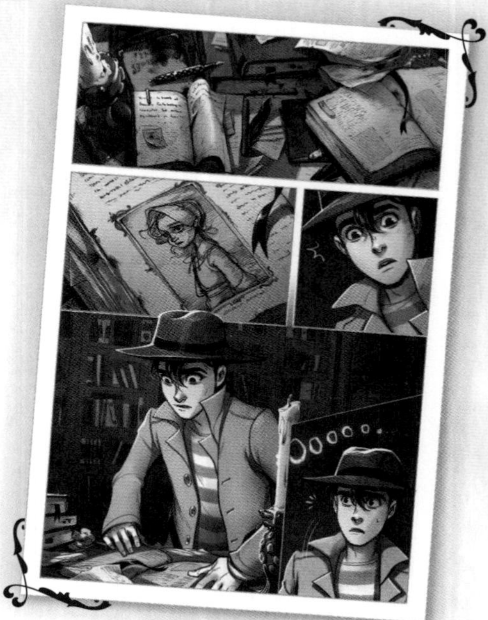

This case study provides an overview of the process I used to create cinematic comic pages for *Grimoire Noir*. It took a lot of experimenting to zero in on this specific method, and once I was done, I made note of the specific layer styles and opacity percentages for future reference. Finding a coherent workflow is essential when creating a series of consistent drawings, whether sequential art or illustrations. As mentioned, *Grimoire Noir* was created entirely in Photoshop CC on a PC desktop, using a Wacom Cintiq 22HD drawing monitor, but this method could be adapted to any software.

1 Layout sketch

I sketch the page layout directly over the thumbnail; often the thumbnail is already detailed enough that I don't need to elaborate. I prefer to spend extra time on the thumbnails instead of figuring things out in the layout sketch. On this particular page, I only needed to clarify the character and add perspective lines.

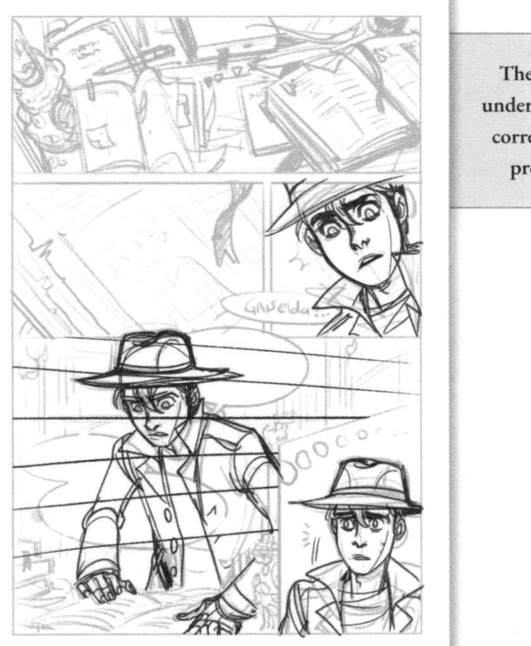

The thumbnail underneath has the correct character proportions.

2 Inking/cleanup

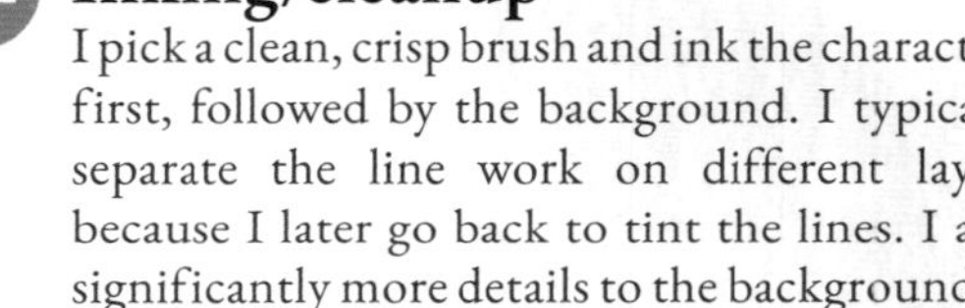

I pick a clean, crisp brush and ink the characters first, followed by the background. I typically separate the line work on different layers because I later go back to tint the lines. I add significantly more details to the background or props if they take up the majority of the frame, or if the frame doesn't feature a character.

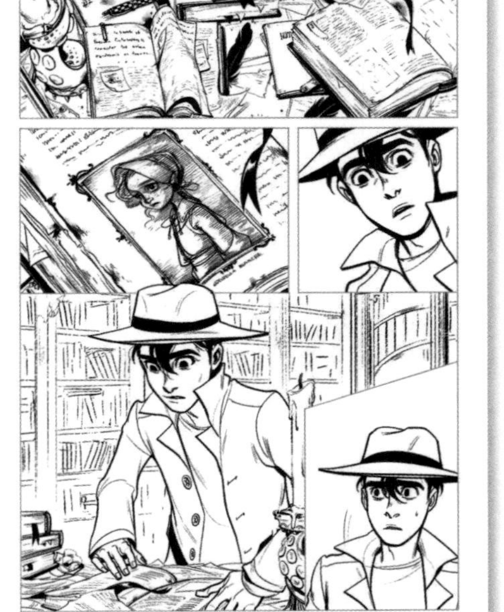

I often use a more sketchy brush for the background to stop me lingering and obsessing over lines. The resulting effect is also more visually interesting.

3 Character mask

Even though it's not visible, this is an important step. I mask out the silhouette of the character in every panel on a separate layer, then make the silhouette white. I ctrl + right-click to select the layer and use that for quick flat colors, and then later for shadow passes. It's useful to have this layer and is definitely worth the extra time it takes. Sometimes I also make a mask for certain elements in the foreground, if I know I will need them later in the process.

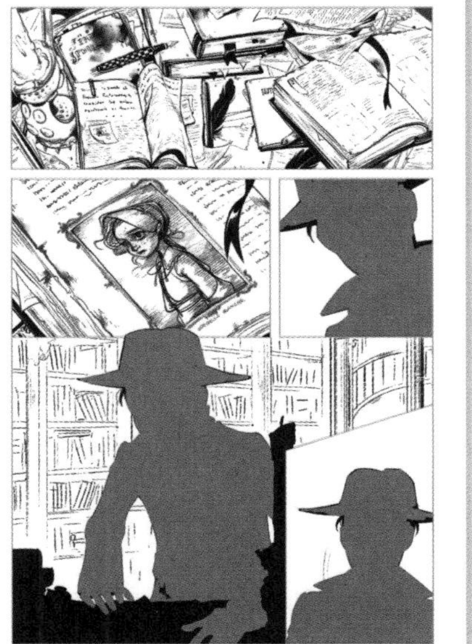

The selection doesn't have to be perfect. I typically make sure it covers all visible areas underneath the lines, then ctrl + shift + click the character line-art layer to add to the mask selection.

4 Flat tones and colors

My approach to *Grimoire Noir* was mostly monochromatic with color accents. In this part of the process, I stick to a predetermined character tonal palette, which I save in a different file for quick reference. Since I approach lighting/shadows on a separate layer, the base tonal palette for the characters is always the same regardless of the lighting scenario, saving time. I deal with the background on a whim, typically picking tones and colors that I feel work to create necessary contrast.

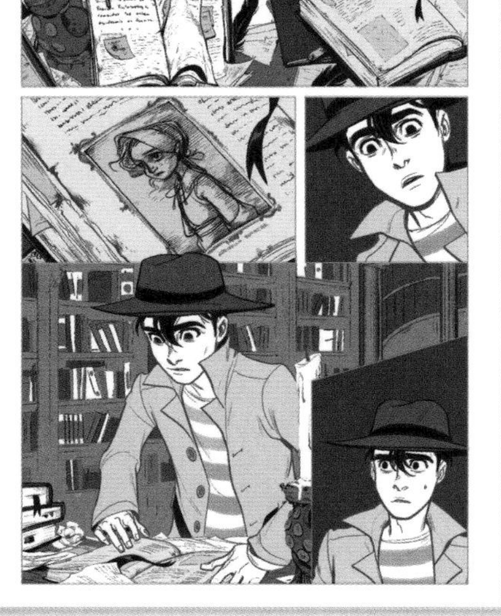

I don't draw the background in every single panel – sometimes a solid color does the job.

5 First shadow pass

I lay down gradients on each panel to determine an approximate light source and further clarify the contrast to make the character pop against the background. I set a layer to Multiply mode and set the opacity to 50%, using black. The character masks I created earlier come in handy during this step, and for the rest of the process. To create a selection of the whole panel minus the character, I simply use the Polygonal or Rectangular Lasso tool to select the frame, then hold ctrl + alt + click on the character mask layer, and the character line-art layer. This set of shortcuts cuts the character(s) out of the selection and I can quickly put down my background gradients in this way.

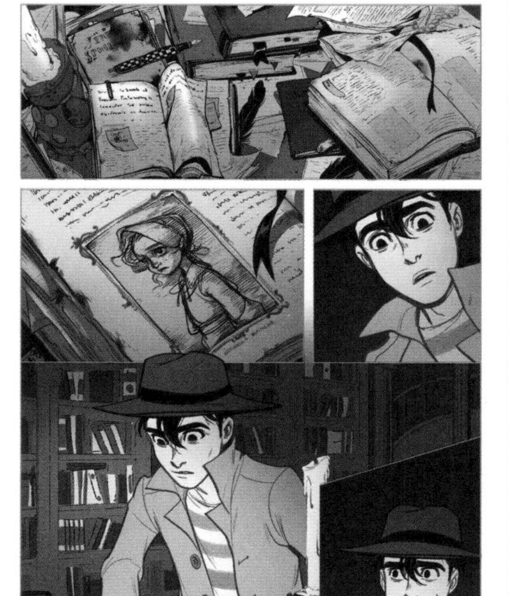

This first shadow pass is a key step for creating atmosphere in the panels.

6 Second shadow pass

I create another layer on top of the first shadow pass, with the same settings: Multiply at 50% opacity. This time, I select the characters first and add more specific shadows, keeping it somewhat simple, but consistent with the level of detail of the rest of the comic. I use a soft eraser tool to smooth out harsh edges where needed, or a smudge tool to blend out.

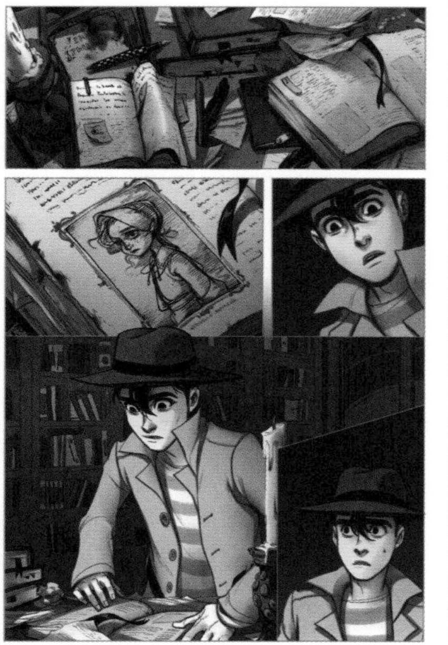

This step makes a big visual difference – the character looked relatively flat up until this point.

7 Textured color tint

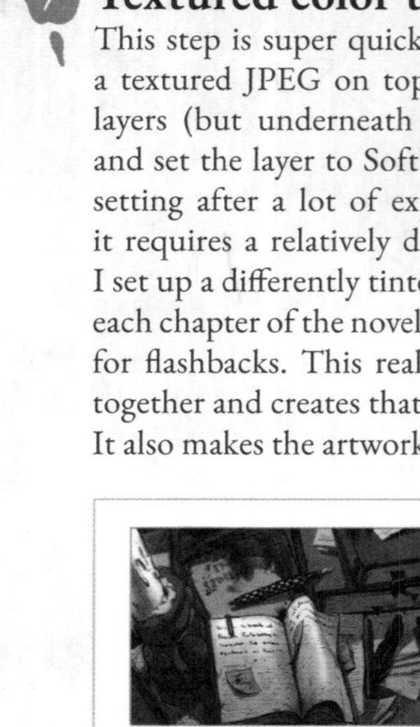

This step is super quick – I simply drag in a textured JPEG on top of all the existing layers (but underneath the panel frames), and set the layer to Soft Light. I found this setting after a lot of experimentation, and it requires a relatively dark-textured image. I set up a differently tinted texture image for each chapter of the novel, and a different tint for flashbacks. This really pulls the images together and creates that vintage look I love. It also makes the artwork look less digital.

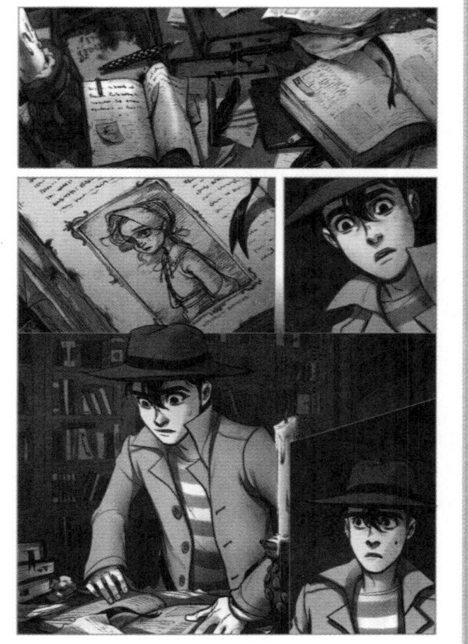

I love the visual interest of the grungy texture – you never know where the scratches are going to end up! I sometimes remove prominent scratches if they're on a character's face.

8 Additional ambient color accent

To take the atmosphere to the next level and create a bit more contrast between the character and the background, I often add soft gradients in the accent color of the current chapter. Here, it's dark, cool blue; I set the layer to 60% opacity and the layer mode to Vivid Light. This creates the desired subtle atmospheric effect. You can see it clearly in the bookshelf backgrounds of the bottom panel.

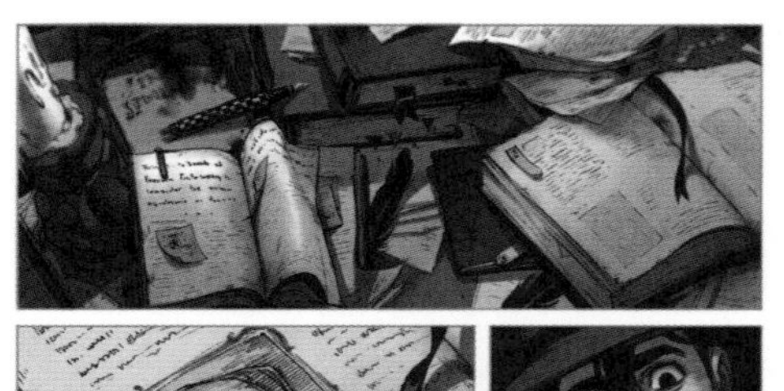

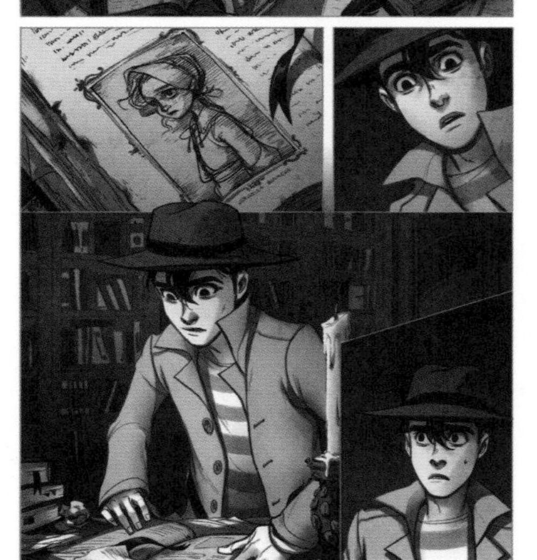

The difference may seem trivial, but the cold tint makes the place look less cozy and inviting, which is appropriate for the story.

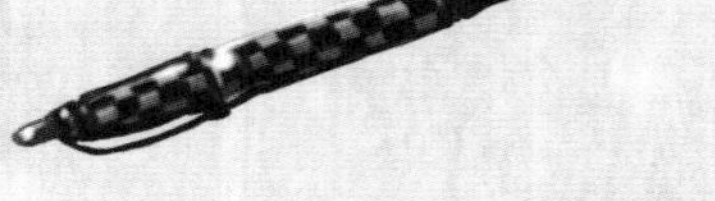

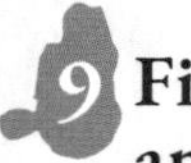
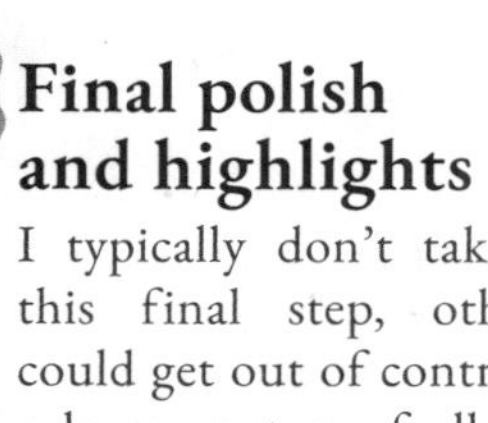

9 Final polish and highlights

I typically don't take long on this final step, otherwise it could get out of control. I make a layer on top of all others to add highlights to the eyes – this breathes life into the character. I mostly use this step to create more contrast and separation between the character and background, or foreground, elements. In previous images, Bucky's hat more or less blends into the background in almost all the panels. One solution is to change the tone of the hat or the background, but the easy solution is to add simple rim lighting. Whether it makes sense or not, it looks nice and serves its purpose of separating the elements! I don't always make decisions based on how "correct" something is. Often, it's just for clarity.

I also occasionally add a slight blur to the background or on the edges, which adds a little extra depth.

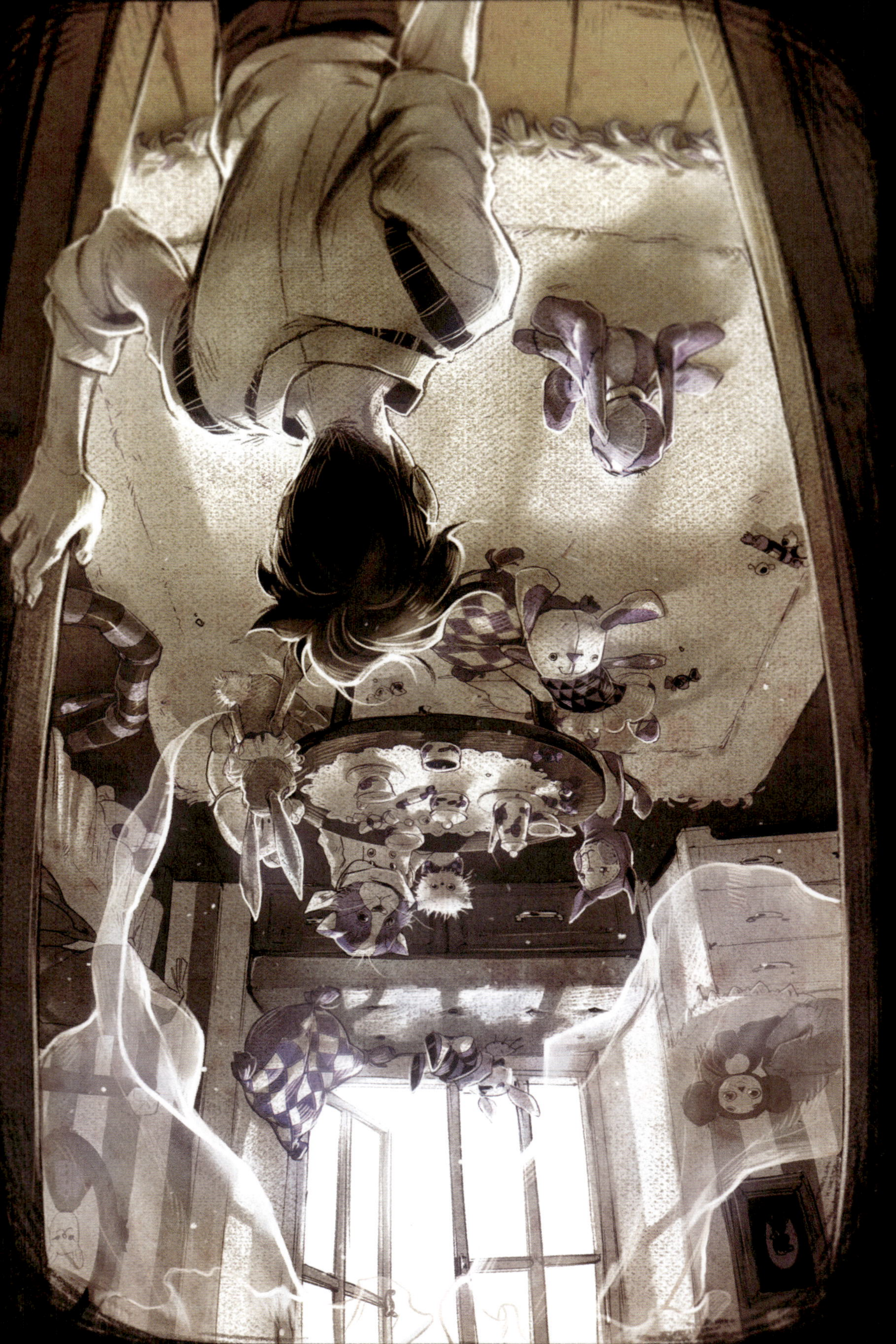

Favorite pages

In addition to the page used for the case study, there are a few other pages I wanted to highlight as personal favorites.

Top left: Page 33 of *Grimoire Noir* was one of the most time-consuming of all, because I really wanted the formal introduction of these girls to be visually impactful.

Top right: One of my favorite moments in the story is shown here on page 123, and I really love Bucky's expression in the last panel.

Bottom left: I love the somber vibe and interesting angles on page 203.

Bottom right: I really like Chamomile's school outfit with a messy bun. She's always floating about, deep in her own thoughts, when alone. Page 209 was a nice opportunity to show that quality.

Opposite page: This was a key moment early on in the story (page 15) that I was super excited to draw. It was my choice to make this panel a full-page illustration for impact. I wanted the open window with blowing curtains to feel ominous despite the sunny day.

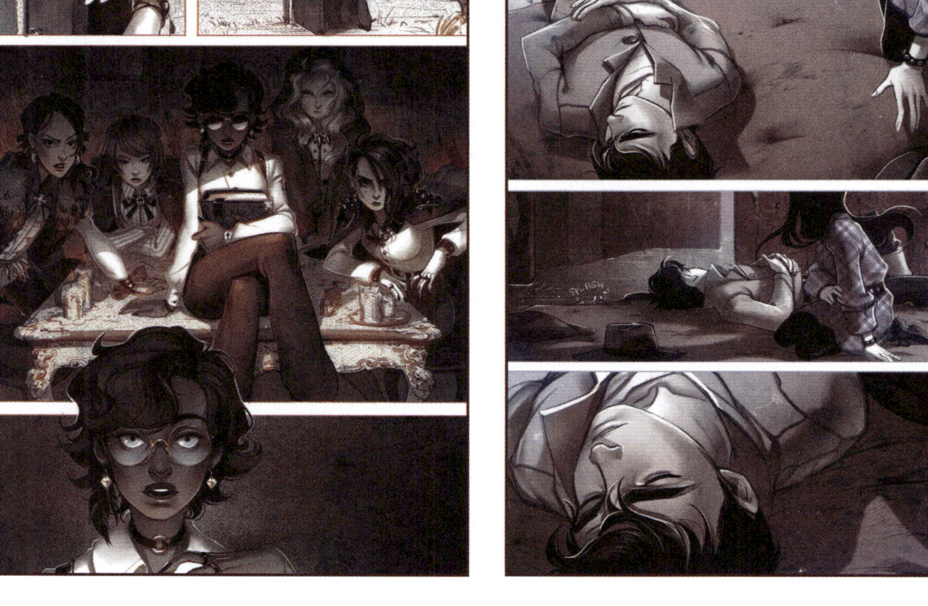

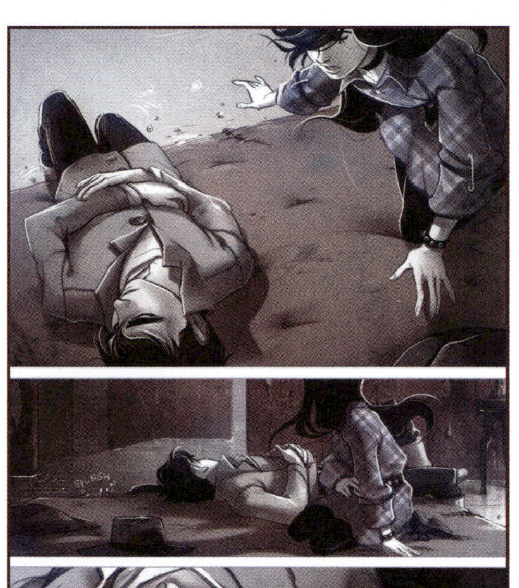

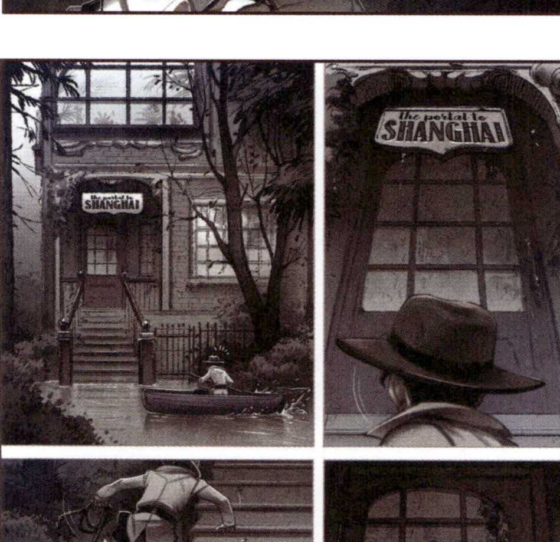

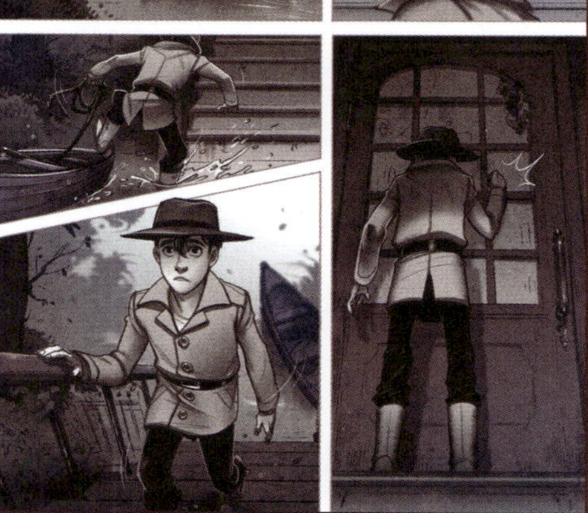

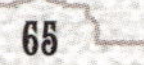

Cover artwork

Before settling on the final image for the cover, I had a few different versions in mind. The chosen cover was the consensus between me and everybody else involved with the final steps of the publishing process, and I am very pleased with how it turned out. In retrospect though, if it had been up to me alone, I would have picked the cover that features a closer look at the main characters.

Initial thumbnails

I initially submitted four thumbnail ideas. I personally lean toward version 2 or 4. I did end up using the back-cover image from version 4 on the final back cover.

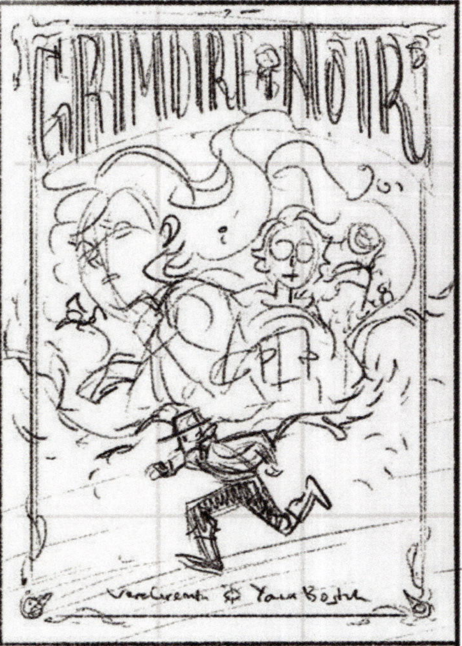

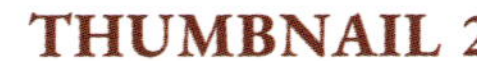

THUMBNAIL 2

THUMBNAIL 3

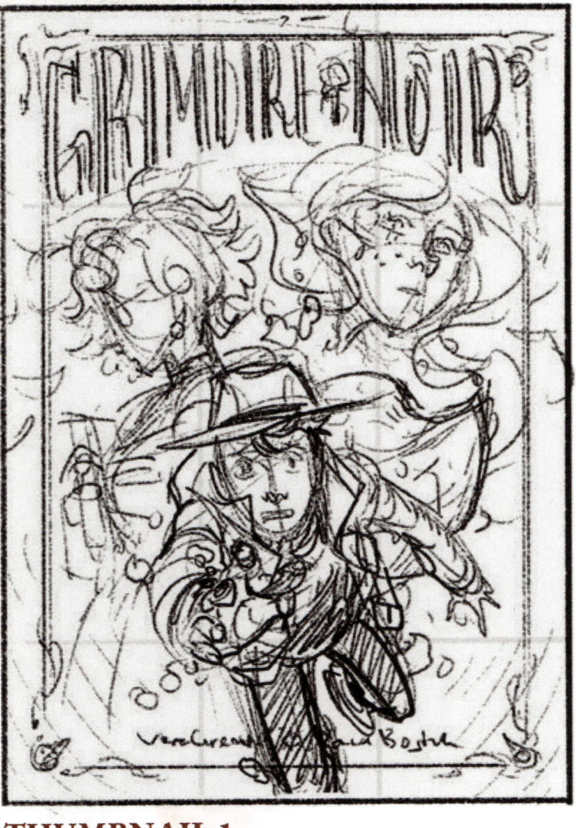

THUMBNAIL 1

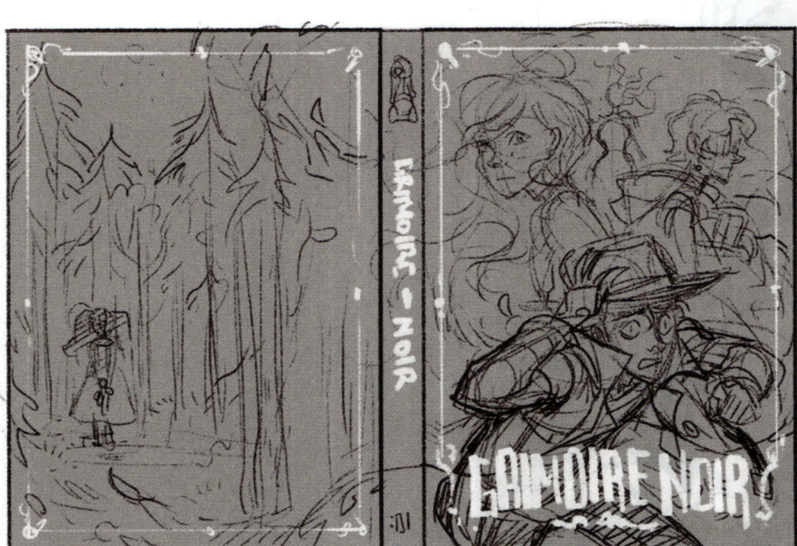

THUMBNAIL 4

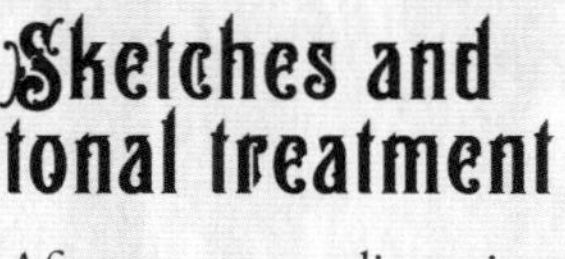

Sketches and tonal treatment

After some discussion with the team, thumbnail versions 1 and 3 were chosen to develop into a more resolved sketch with tonal treatment.

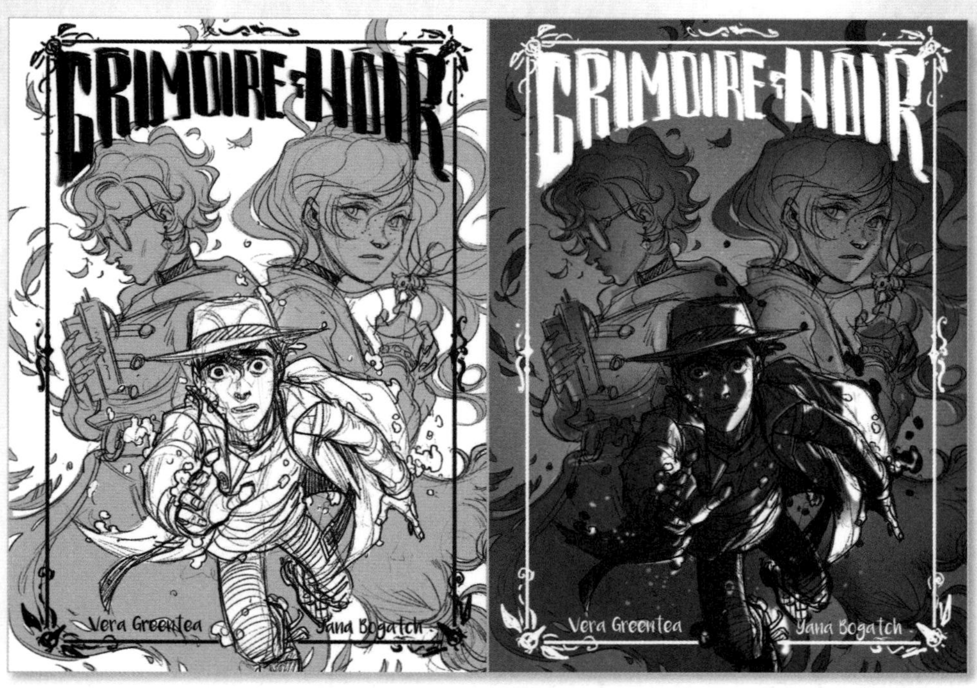

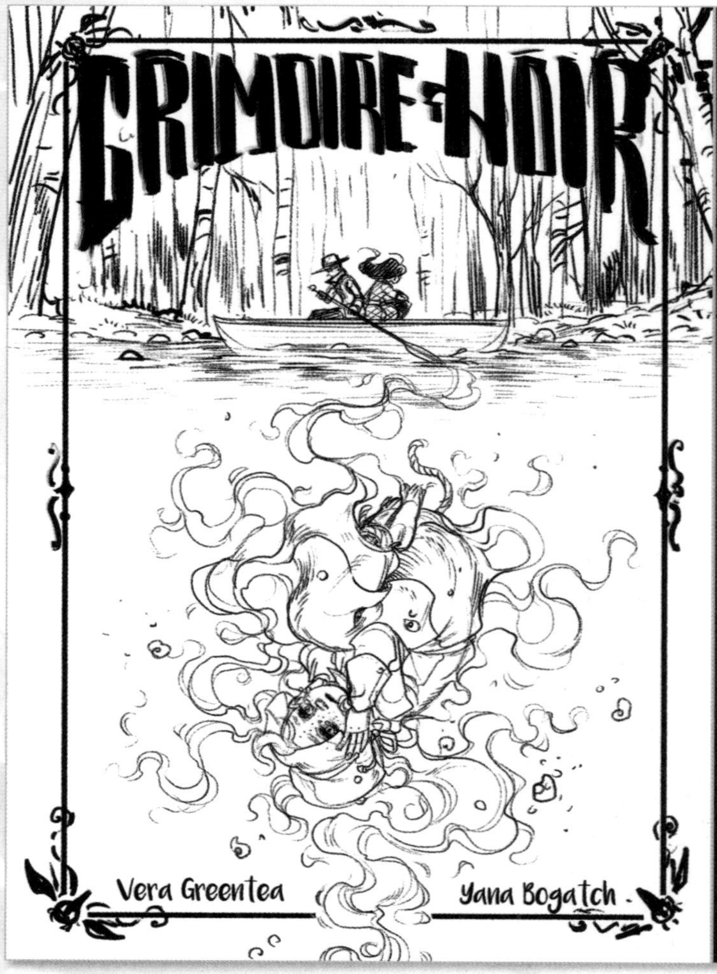

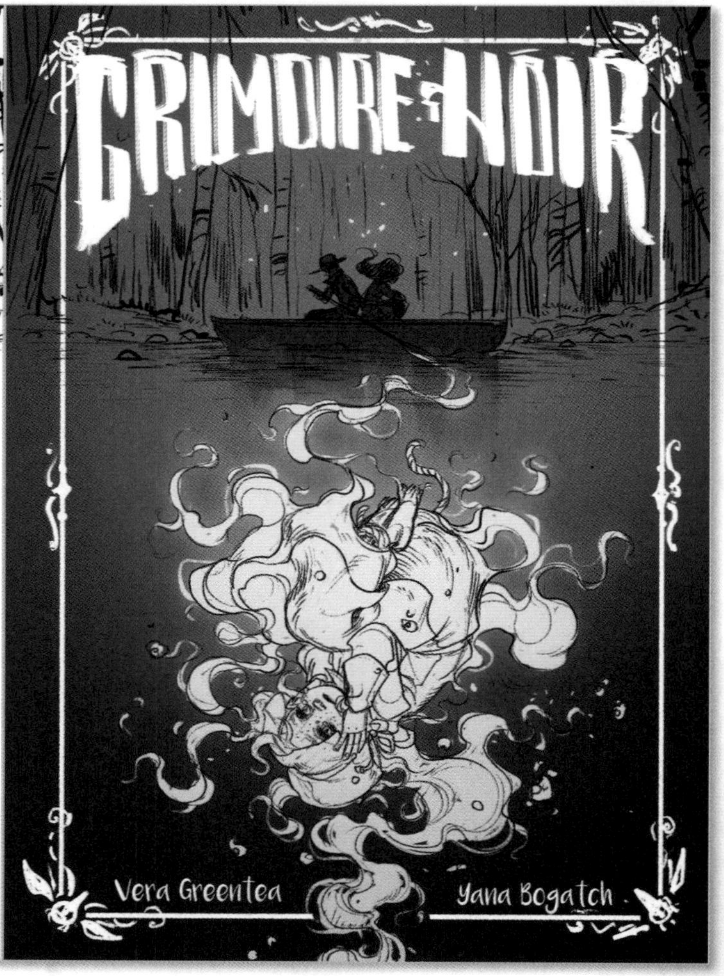

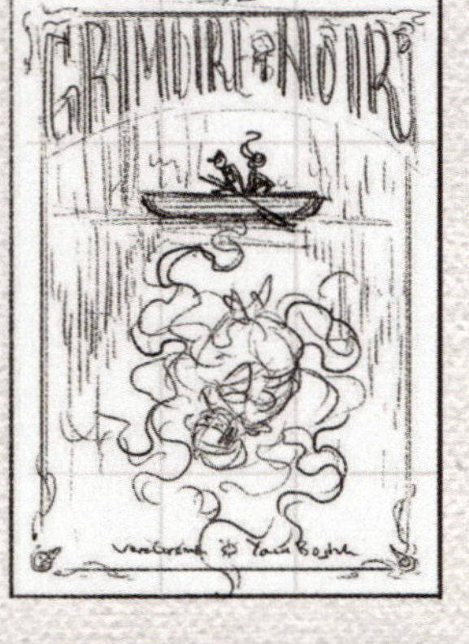

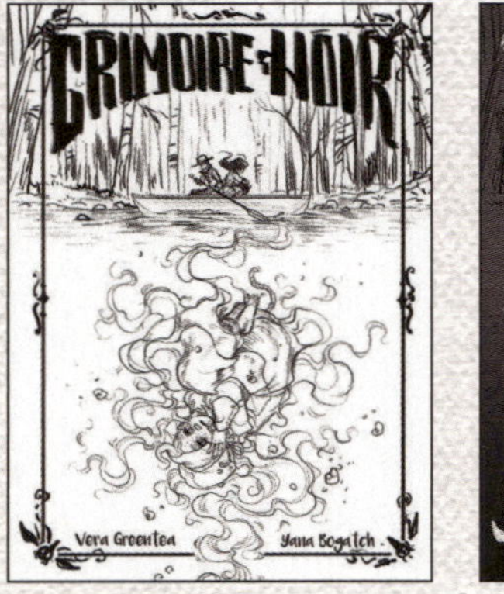

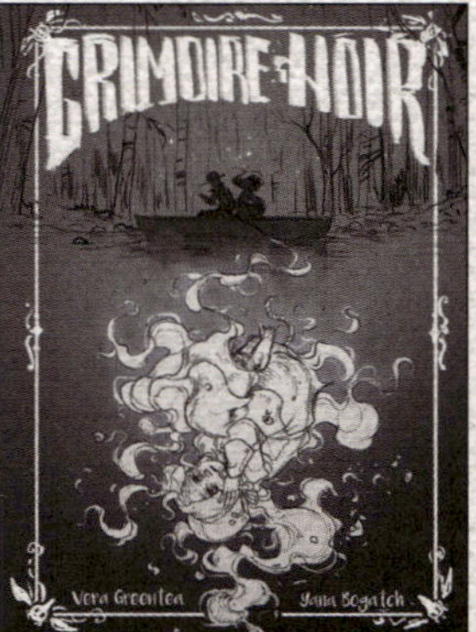

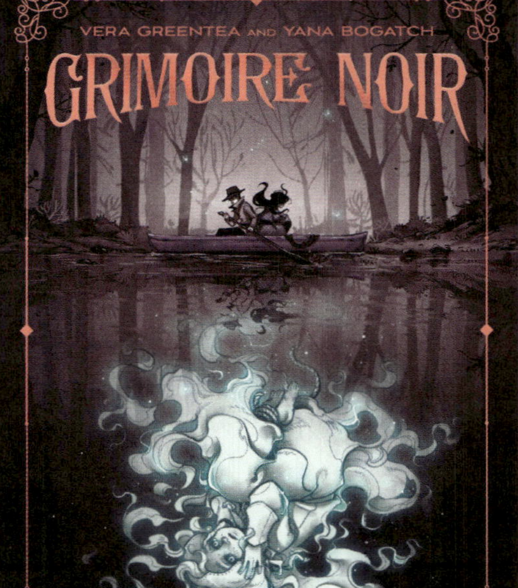

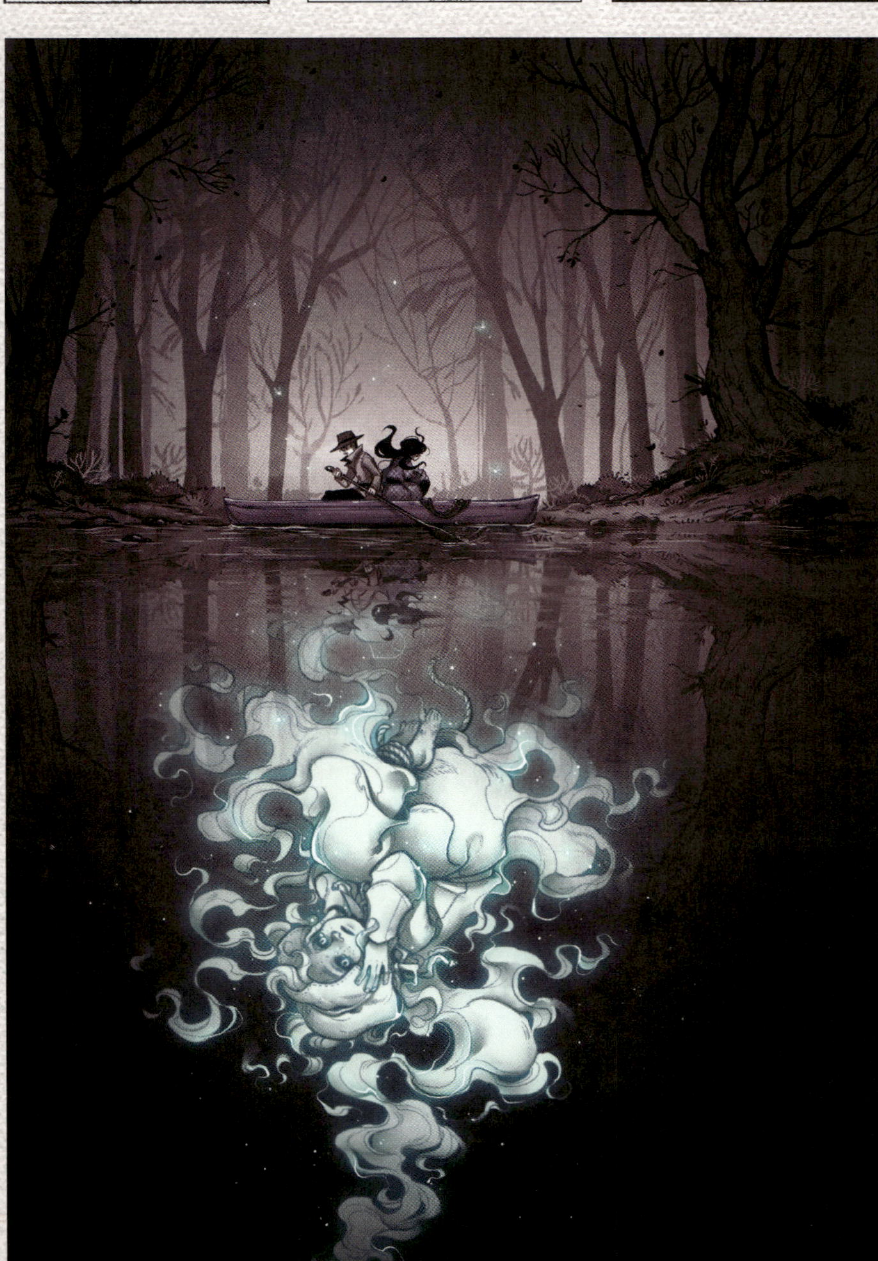

Final cover artwork

The final version has a particularly somber and atmospheric feel, which I do love as it is quite characteristic of my personal artwork. The subject matter and setting of this book are things I love very much: a small mysterious town, dark foggy woods, and troubled teenage protagonists – much like my own comic series that's currently in development.

Epilogue

Going into this project as young artist, I was still very naive about a lot of things: how the comic-adjacent industry works, what it's like to be a freelance artist beyond the context of being a college student, what it's like working with other people, and so on.

Grimoire Noir was a big milestone in my art career thus far, and I really hope that the advice and techniques I shared with you in this chapter are helpful and informative! Even though completing this project was a serious test of endurance, I still poured my heart into it and have a lasting fondness for the characters.

Reflecting on this early experience and its challenges has been very cathartic, and so I'd like to end this chapter with this new illustration, featuring the lead characters of the book, Bucky Orson and Chamomile Hastings. I like to imagine they found a happy ending together somewhere down the road.

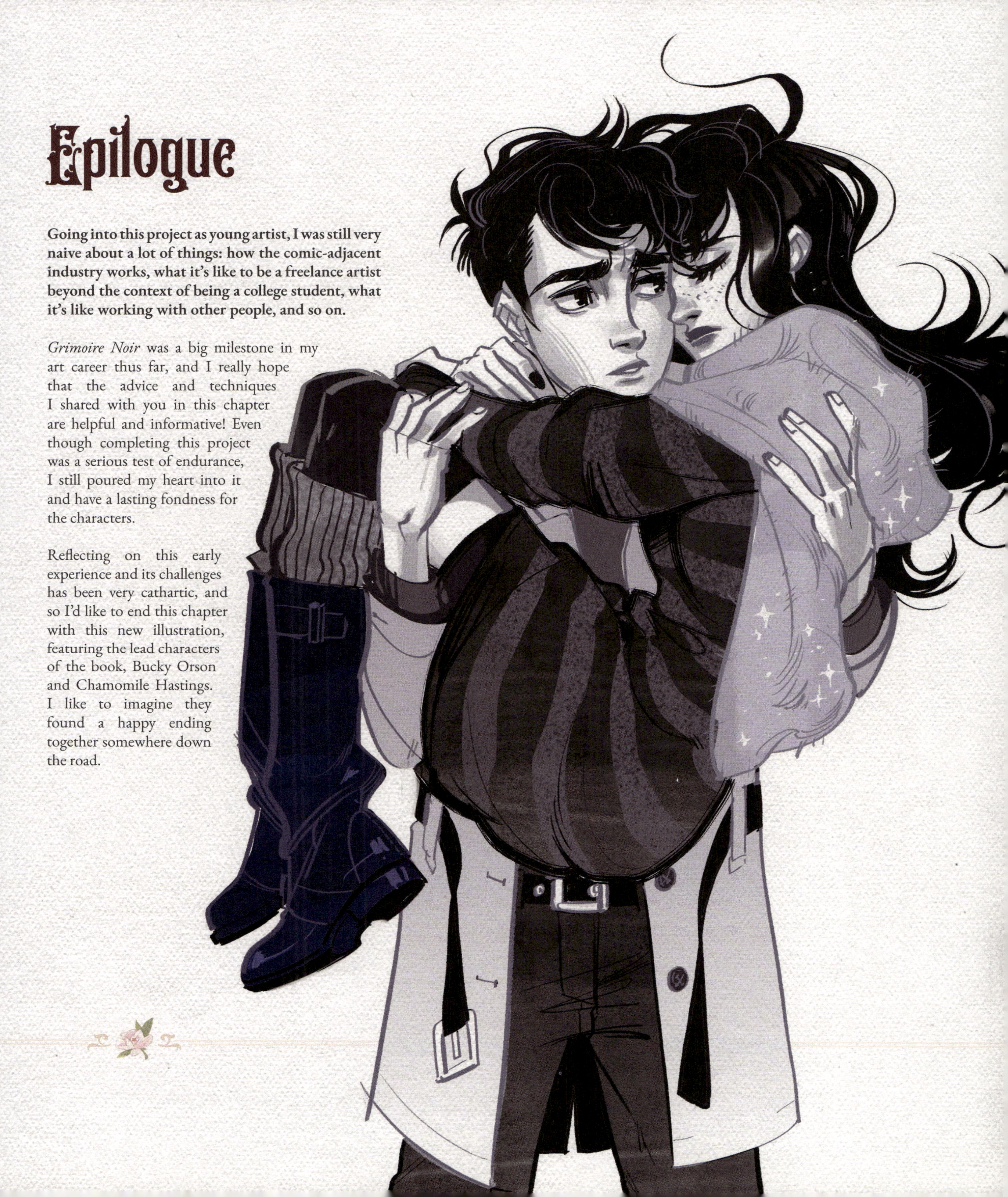

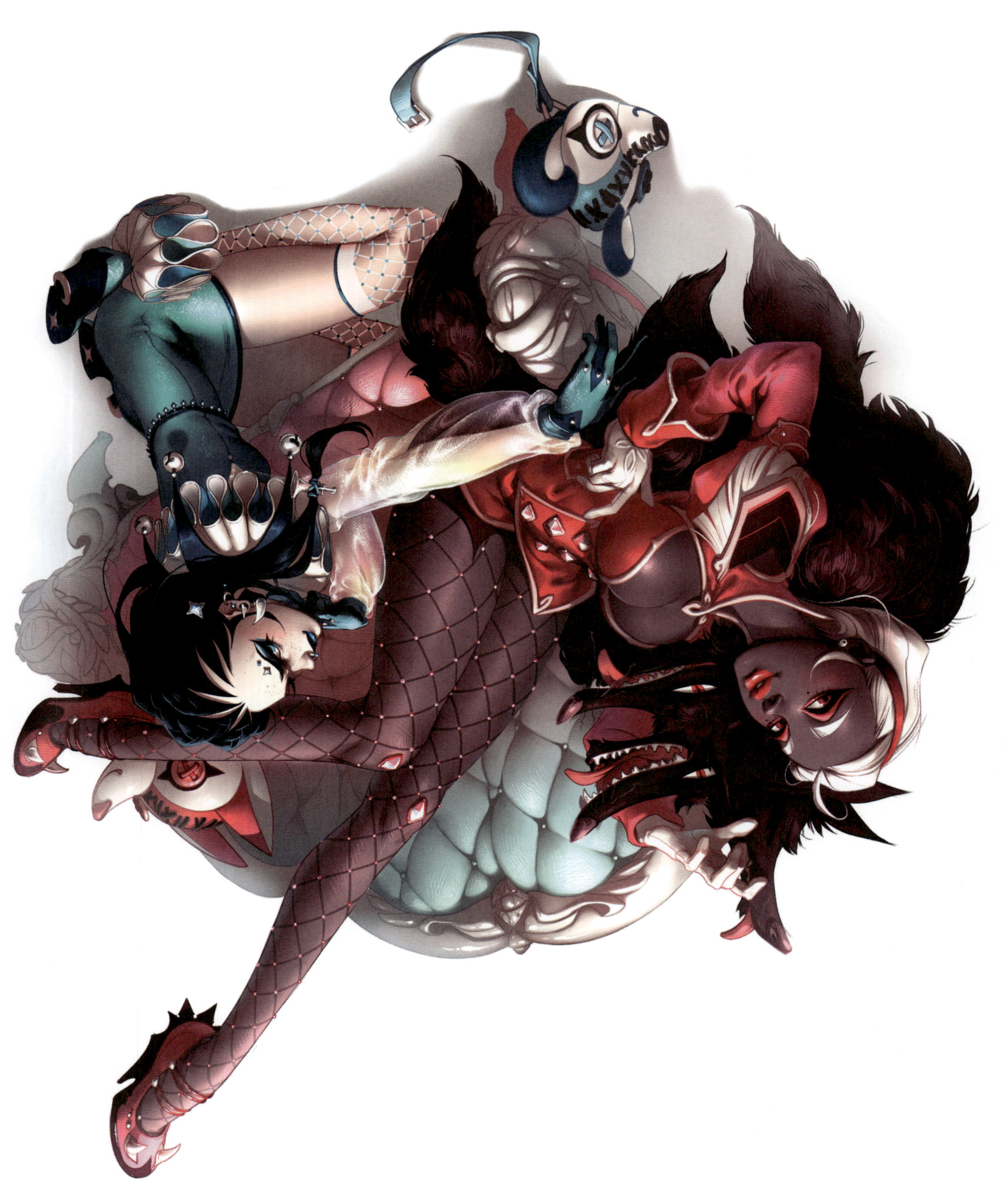

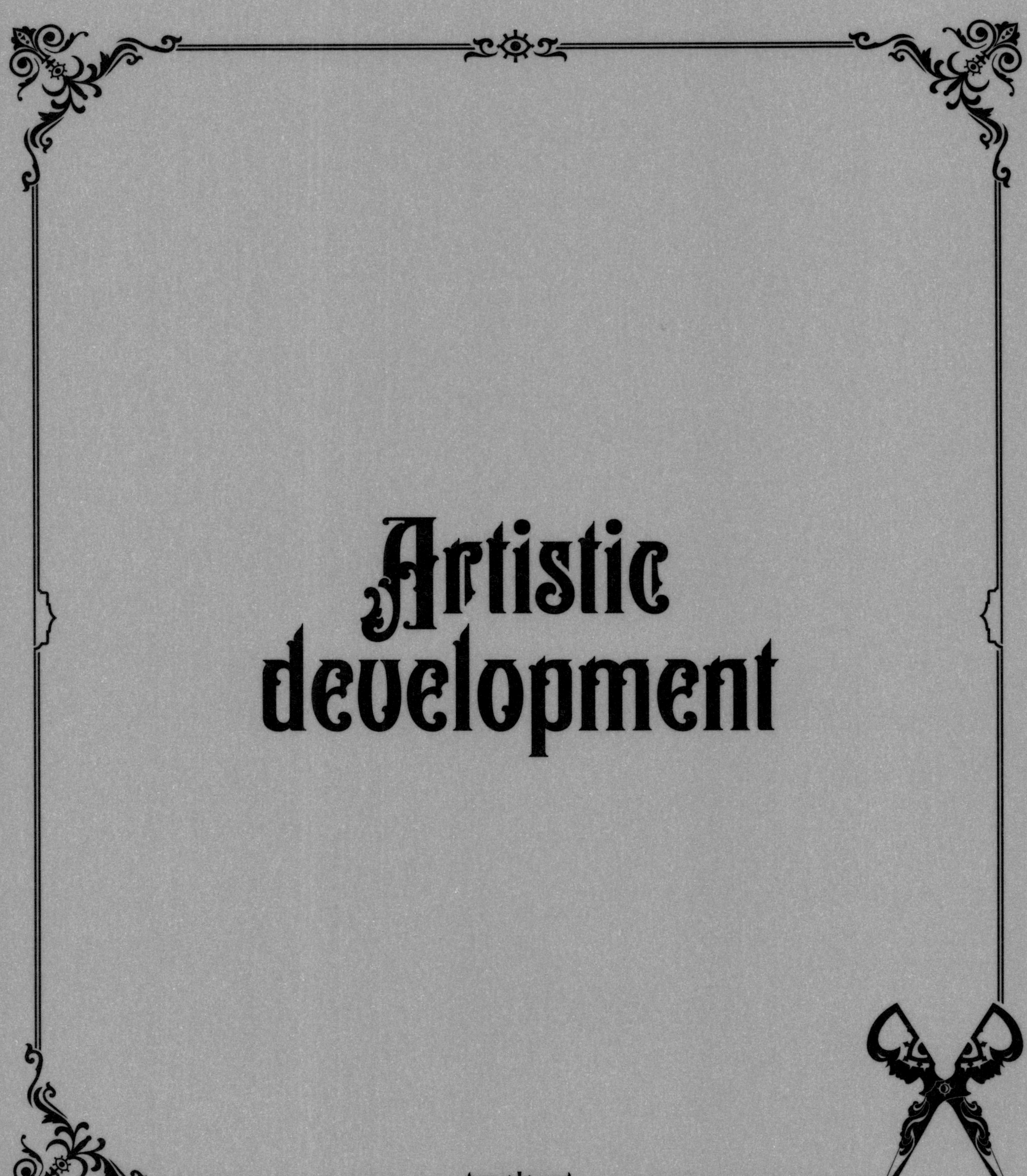

Artistic development

Artistic development

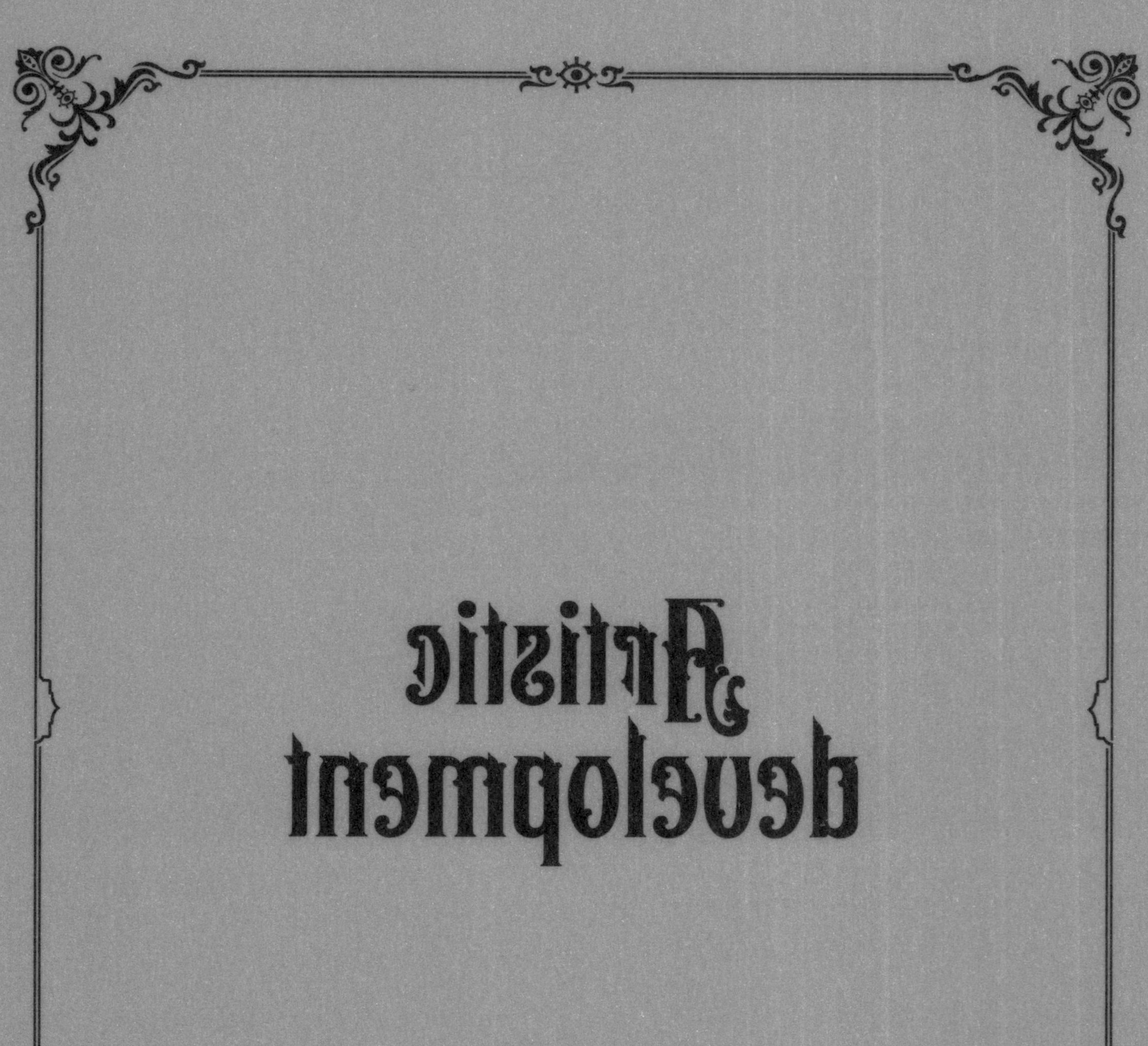

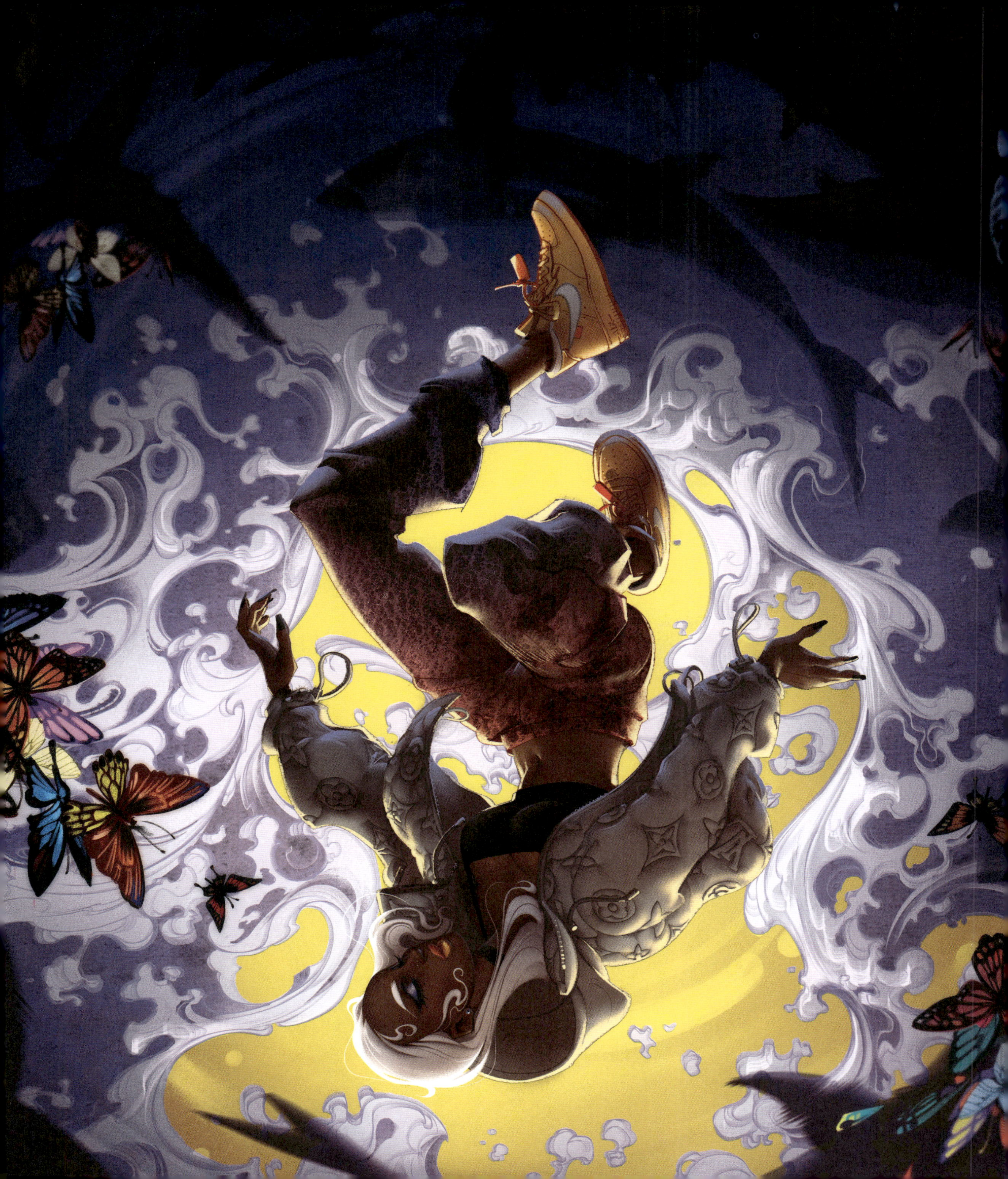

Subject matter

Everything I draw on my own time tends to have something to do with my characters, including their narratives and world. I love to create decorative and fashion-inspired pieces, but they always feature my characters because I like to utilize their existing personalities and designs as a quick-start base for the secondary thematic or decorative concept.

I feel a strong sense of attachment toward my characters because most of them were created many years ago and feel like life-long companions to me. Although their narrative goes through changes, I always enjoy the sense of comfort and familiarity I get from them. It is for this reason that I rarely draw random people, as I find it much less engaging.

I have thought long and hard about what it is I'm hoping to convey through my art, and have concluded that my primary pursuit is beauty. For me, beauty is powerful – it's inspiring and divine. But beauty alone isn't enough, and that's why I always find myself drawn to narrative. I only ever aim to make drawings that are beautiful to me, and find a lot of beauty in the internal struggles and sadness of my characters. This is why my work often has an air of melancholy, which seems to resonate with my audience.

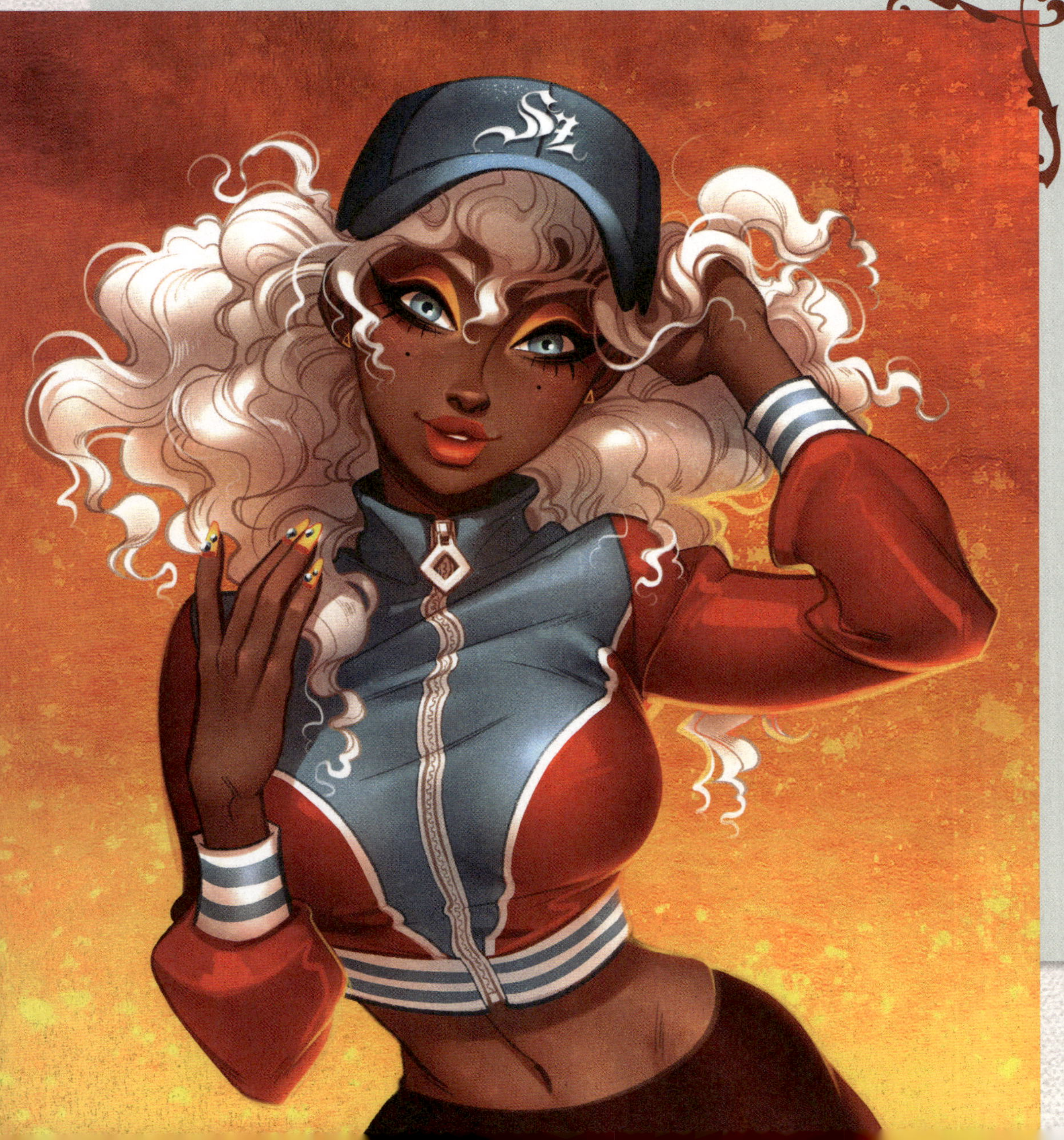

That being said, I think my work is also a bit all over the place since I utilize many different rendering techniques and my style range is quite wide. This is often a point of insecurity for me because I feel like my body of work is incoherent, but I've been told that's just my own perception. In a way, I've always used art as my ultimate self-medication, so it remains to be seen what I manage to say with it from here on, now that I feel sufficiently healed.

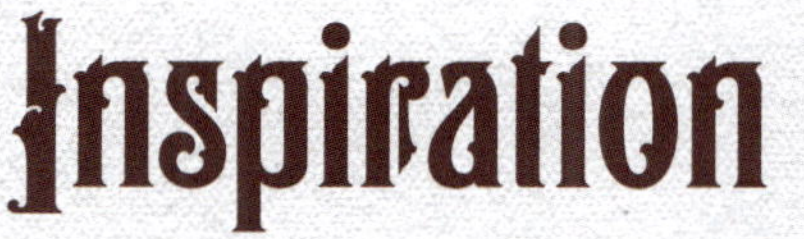

Inspiration

My biggest inspiration is the pursuit of beauty and aesthetics. I have always been a very aesthetically driven person, heavily affected by the visuals in my immediate environment.

For that reason, I take great care when choosing every little object that I surround myself with at home, trying my best to cultivate an overall atmosphere of visual delight wherever I look. This has had a tremendously positive effect on my ability to relax and create at home, which is important as I've always had trouble being creative in an unfamiliar or chaotic environment (such as designated work areas at school). I think beauty has a healing power and I get immense joy from being able to capture harmonious color combinations, the dynamic flow of hair and fabric echoing the movement of waves in the ocean, or the rhythmic shapes of the human body – it's an endlessly exciting pursuit. There's so much beauty in the world, and I think it can be found in the most unlikely places.

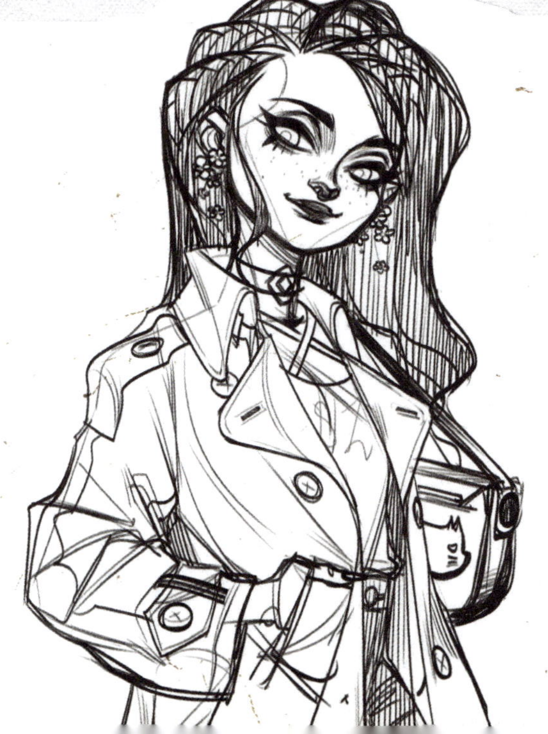

The second biggest source of inspiration for me is music, which plants seeds and ideas for stories and characters in my mind. I have always gravitated toward grand, sometimes dramatic, and often sad music. I think there are a million shades of sadness, and it's incredible how sound can capture indescribable emotions with such intensity. I used to have to take long commutes (two to three hours daily) for many years, and during those times I would just listen to music with my eyes closed and watch the scenes and ideas form in my mind. This is how I come up with key moments that help me weave together narratives for my characters.

Lose the pressure

I don't consciously set out to create work that represents me. I think that focusing on a representational aspect is actually what tends to give me art block, making me feel insecure and inadequate.

It's frightening to think that my artwork is somehow supposed to represent the totality of me as a person, because it doesn't and cannot do that. I like to just focus on things I love or find interesting and appealing in my personal work. When working on freelance commissions, my focus is on making the client happy.

Some years ago, I used to think much more about my work and how it represents me as a person, which always put me in panic mode. But I think my mindset organically shifted after thinking a lot about the nature of creativity – ideas and where they come from. Now I think that what I create comes before me, if that makes any sense. Sometimes a very clear image will appear in my head, and I won't know where that idea has come from or why. Much of the time, I don't make super-conscious decisions when drawing, sort of like being in autopilot mode with no thoughts. I would describe the process as channeling something, a feeling that stops me perceiving the passage of time. This is what makes me feel like I'm just the middleman between something else and the art that I make. This is the idea that inspired me to title this book.

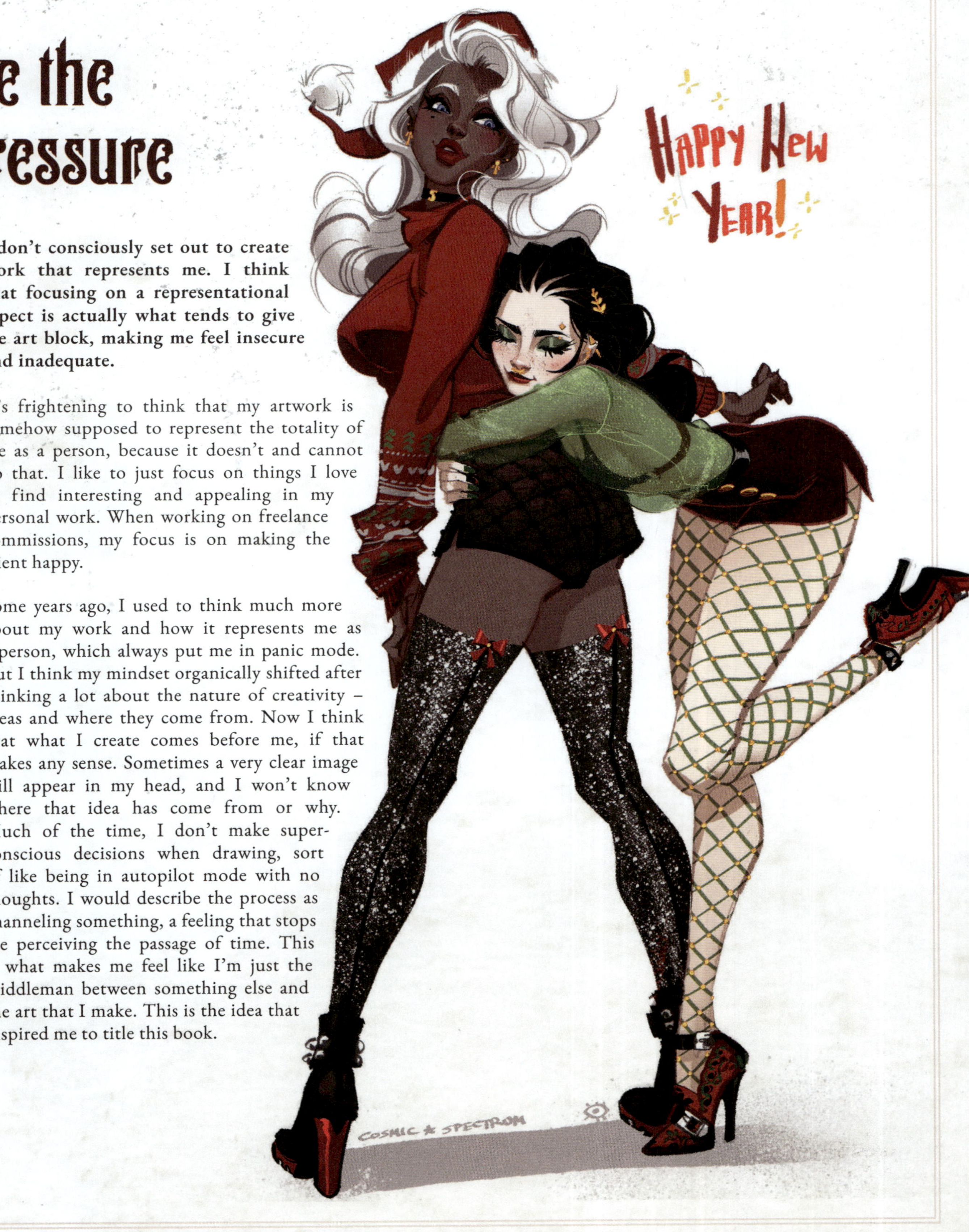

The dangers of a rigid self-concept

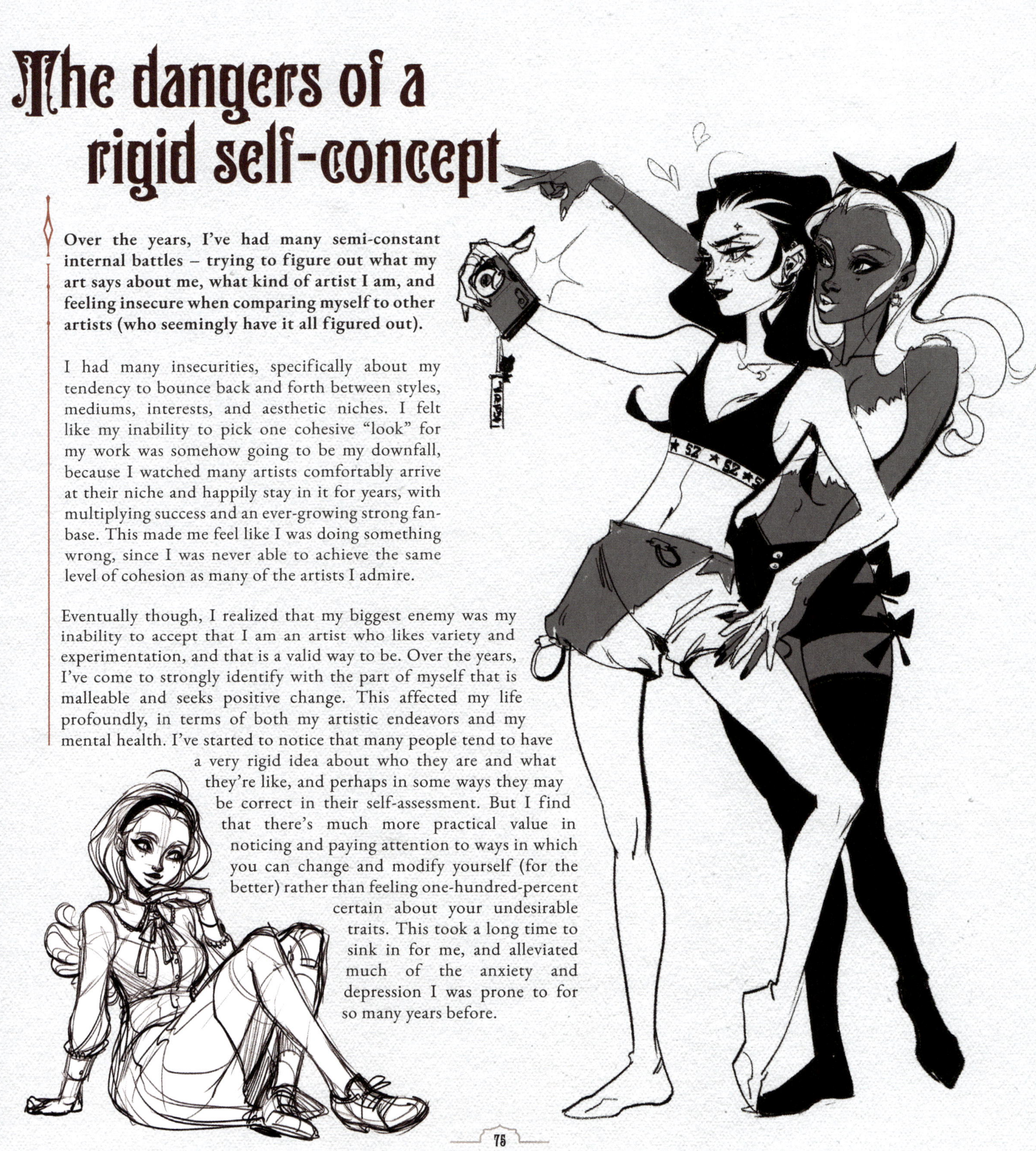

Over the years, I've had many semi-constant internal battles – trying to figure out what my art says about me, what kind of artist I am, and feeling insecure when comparing myself to other artists (who seemingly have it all figured out).

I had many insecurities, specifically about my tendency to bounce back and forth between styles, mediums, interests, and aesthetic niches. I felt like my inability to pick one cohesive "look" for my work was somehow going to be my downfall, because I watched many artists comfortably arrive at their niche and happily stay in it for years, with multiplying success and an ever-growing strong fan-base. This made me feel like I was doing something wrong, since I was never able to achieve the same level of cohesion as many of the artists I admire.

Eventually though, I realized that my biggest enemy was my inability to accept that I am an artist who likes variety and experimentation, and that is a valid way to be. Over the years, I've come to strongly identify with the part of myself that is malleable and seeks positive change. This affected my life profoundly, in terms of both my artistic endeavors and my mental health. I've started to notice that many people tend to have a very rigid idea about who they are and what they're like, and perhaps in some ways they may be correct in their self-assessment. But I find that there's much more practical value in noticing and paying attention to ways in which you can change and modify yourself (for the better) rather than feeling one-hundred-percent certain about your undesirable traits. This took a long time to sink in for me, and alleviated much of the anxiety and depression I was prone to for so many years before.

Artist's block

I think that taking breaks to recharge and refill your pool of inspiration and energy is absolutely vital. I have found myself completely burnt out from work many times before, and sadly it's still something I frequently have to deal with.

One important lesson I learned over the past few years is to stop treating weekends as "extra time to catch up on work." This is exactly the sort of approach that causes burnout, fast. I always try my best to not do any work over the weekend, even if I feel like I should be working (which is honestly something I feel all the time, for better or worse). I notice that my productivity during the week is much higher if I actually take the weekend off, so in the end it's a win/win situation.

Another lesson I've learned – one that is slowly making my life feel more balanced – is the intentional expulsion of guilt for taking random breaks. For instance, if I feel exhausted and want to lie down and read a book for an hour in the middle of a workday, I instantly feel like I'm doing something terribly wrong. The guilt of taking some time to do something that isn't "productive" can be soul crushing, but only for people who think their entire self-worth rests on their productivity. The truth of the matter is that your default mode of being *doesn't* have to be suffering to be meaningful; your worth is inherent and unchanging regardless of what you do or don't do. And so, I tell myself that in the grand scheme of things, I have it together, and everything is generally taken care of. My life won't fall apart if I sit around and read for a couple of hours on a Tuesday afternoon. My point is that it's important to balance your days and not feel guilty about taking breaks – the latter being of utmost importance.

I really enjoy the ebb and flow of consuming and creating, and think it's unhealthy to go too far in either direction. Consuming too much media makes me feel stagnant, and excessive creative output makes me feel depleted and exhausted. Balance is always the key, isn't it?

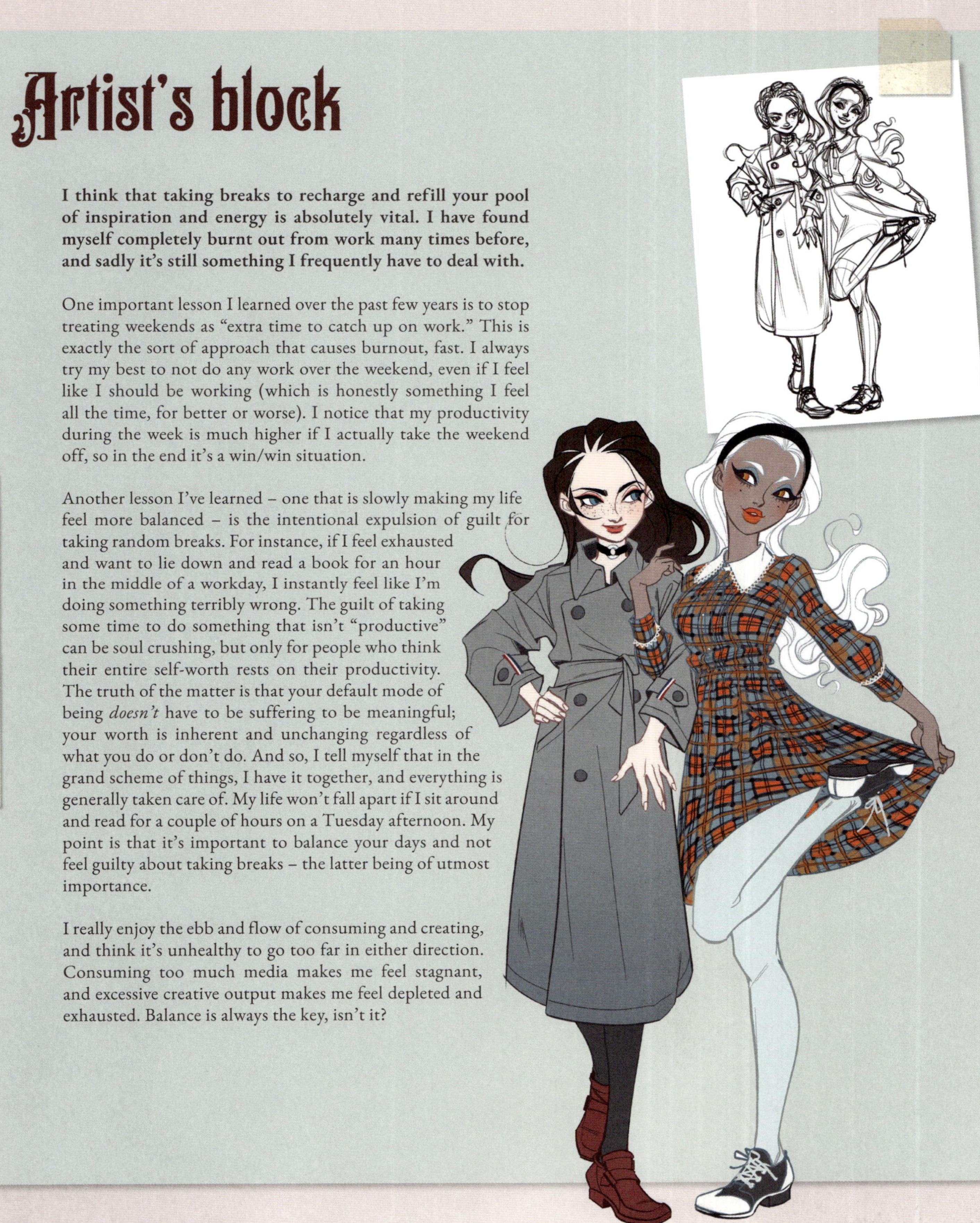

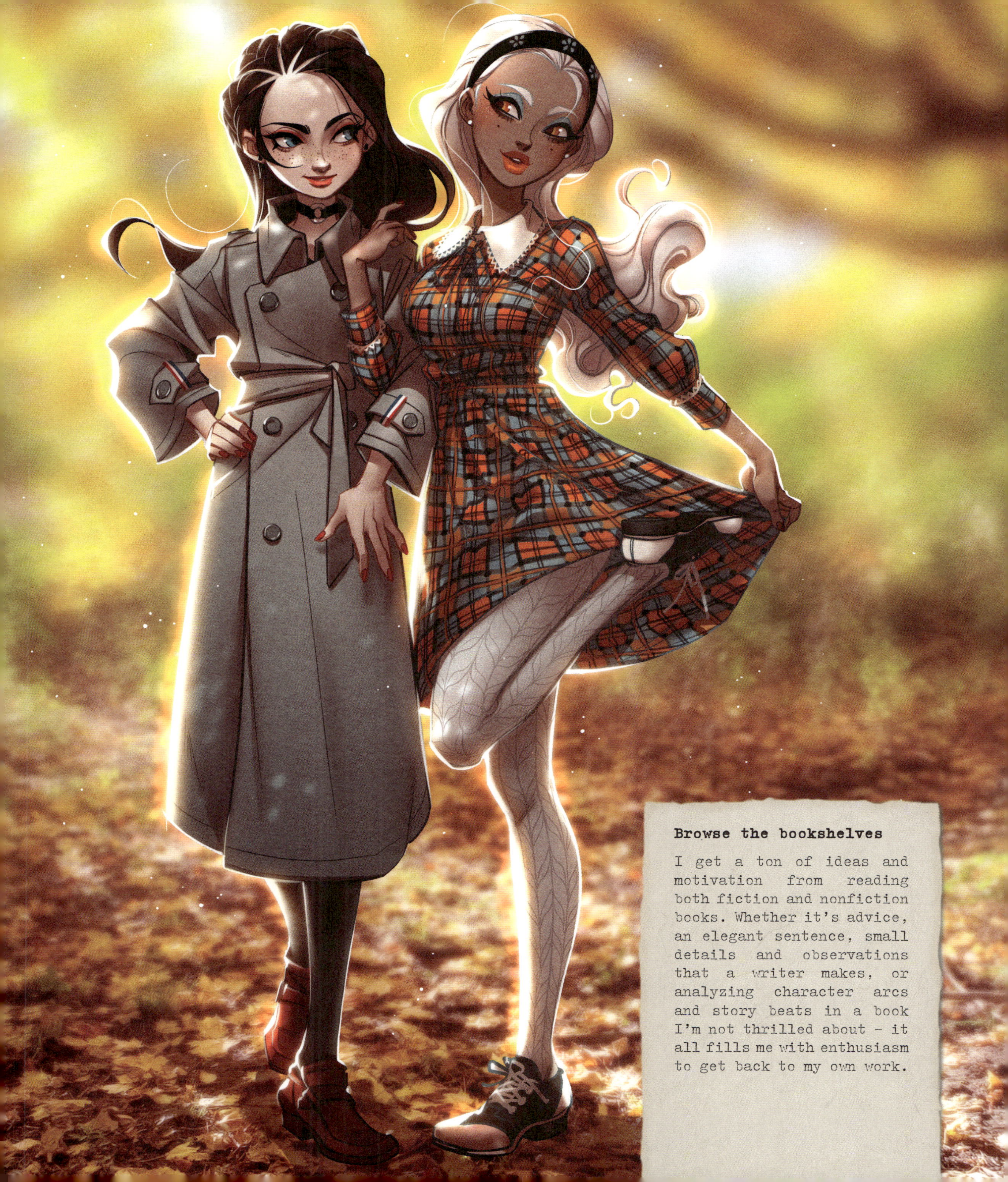

Browse the bookshelves

I get a ton of ideas and motivation from reading both fiction and nonfiction books. Whether it's advice, an elegant sentence, small details and observations that a writer makes, or analyzing character arcs and story beats in a book I'm not thrilled about – it all fills me with enthusiasm to get back to my own work.

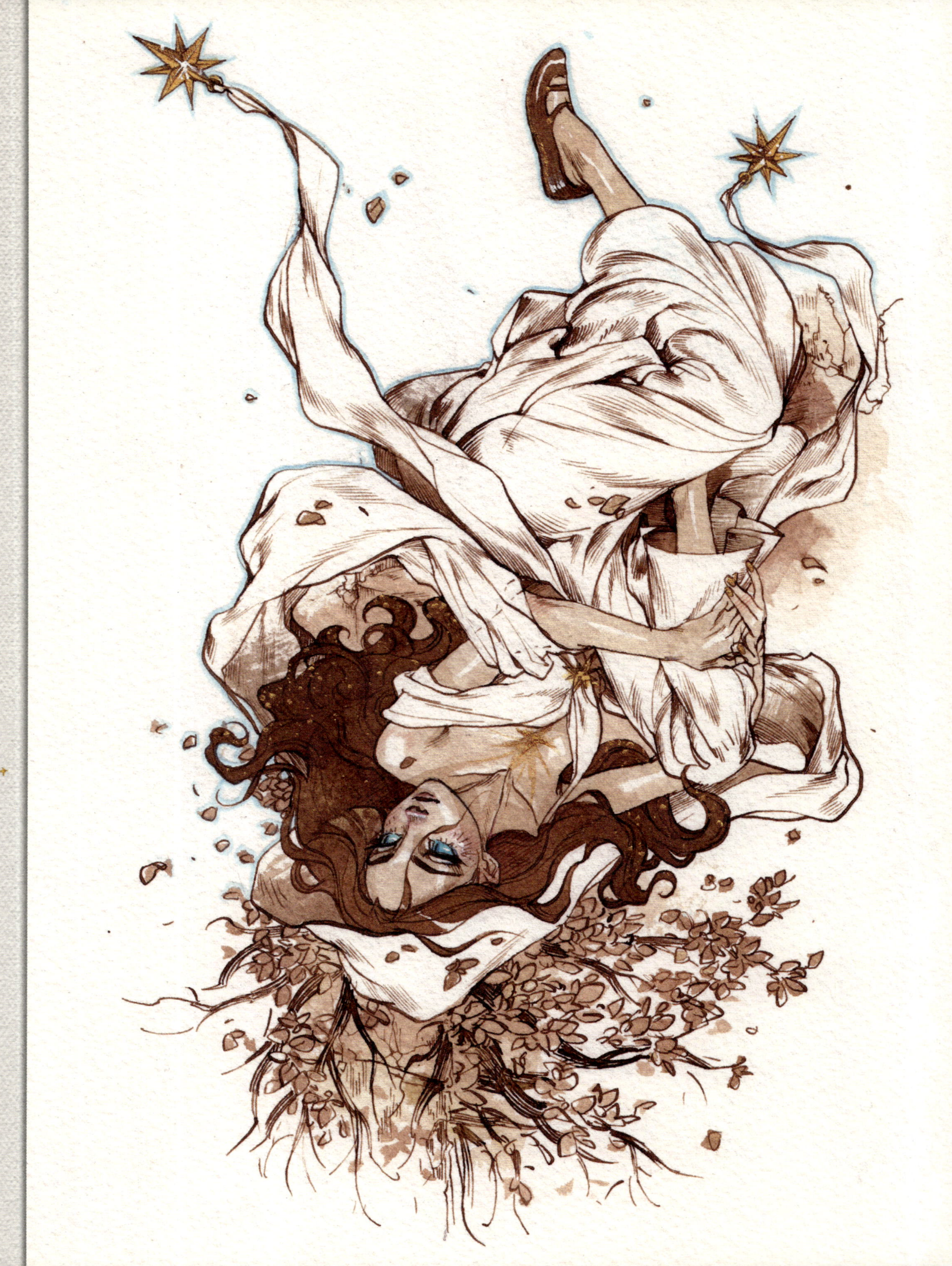

Dealing with criticism

I have always found illustration or one-off (non-sequential) artwork to be just non-specific enough that I never felt too vulnerable sharing it with the world. If somebody points out something I find embarrassing or too private about my work, I can claim it's been misinterpreted – right? Haha!

But jokes aside, a lot is up for interpretation. This is probably also because I no longer over-identify with the imagery I create. That being said, I think the fear of criticism is a big barrier that keeps me from fully committing to publishing my comic series, my story. The story itself is inevitably too close to me, and of course introducing a clear narrative would leave me feeling very exposed. It's like opening a door to my soul, my thoughts, my beliefs. The possibility of harsh criticism for that leaves me horrified.

They *must* know best...

Sometimes, counterproductive criticism can come from an authority figure or somebody who is technically supposed to help you. If this criticism doesn't sit right and feels insulting or derailing, it may be helpful to remember that the person dishing out the criticism doesn't necessarily aim to be helpful to you. They may not have your best interests in mind, even if it is their professional responsibility to help you. If this is the case, it's best to ignore what they have to say and not take it to heart. I've seen some college and university professors demolish their students in displays that I could only describe as public humiliation, and those are probably some of the worst examples of "critiques" I've had the misfortune to witness.

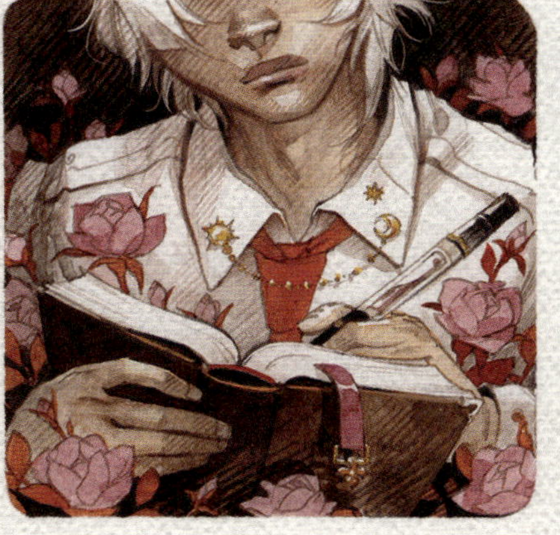

I have never been great at dealing with criticism and have unfortunately had to deal with a lot of it, especially early on in life. Thankfully, it has really dwindled over the years. Before I started to separate myself from my art, in a sense, I was extremely close to it. Too close. Any criticism of my art felt like a personal attack and caused me a lot of anguish, especially when it came from people whose validation mattered a great deal to me.

Over time, I learned that unsolicited criticism should just be ignored completely. I don't think all criticism is equal or valid, and not every person's opinion matters. In fact, depending on the context, nobody's opinion inherently matters. I also think that many people are simply unqualified to give meaningful feedback on topics they're clearly not familiar with, as harsh as that might sound. Don't get me wrong – I firmly believe that everybody has something of value to share with others, and new things can be learned from every single person. However, good advice about a specific topic is sometimes hard to come by. I should also mention that there's a big difference between criticism and advice being a simple suggestion for potential improvement – which can often be a good thing or at least worth considering.

But ignoring useless criticism isn't the same as believing you have no areas in need of improvement. If you're mostly unwilling to seek critique (which is how I've always been), you have to put on a "realist" hat from time to time. Being able to look at my work in a detached way and comparing it to the artists I look up to has always been an incredibly useful thing to do. It helps me set goals, learn to think analytically, and improve quickly. However, you can only do this without destroying your self-worth if you truly believe that you can and will reach any goal with hard work and commitment.

The importance of self-belief

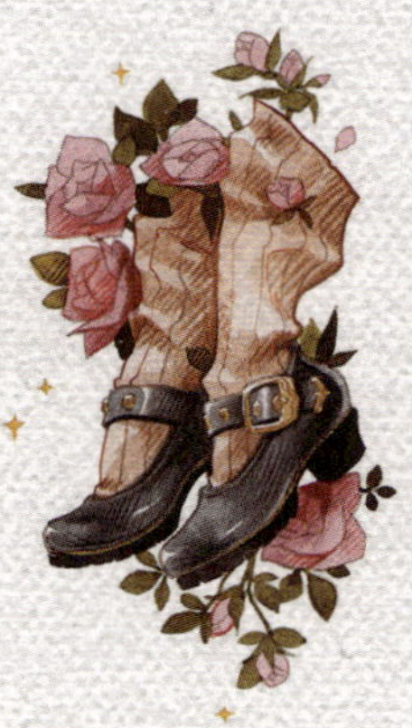

Everybody's art journey is very different, so it's tough to narrow down my experience to a single, appropriately useful piece of advice. As clichéd as it sounds though, I think the best advice really is to believe in yourself. That's right – just believe in yourself! I will elaborate on that: to put it bluntly, the number of internal and external struggles that arise from making your most precious hobby into a career are more than enough as it is, without also constantly doubting yourself. Self-doubt is a *huge* impediment. I don't think I would have made it to where I am now if plagued with doubts about my ability to improve my skills or succeed.

Ask the right questions

If you're doubting yourself and thinking along the lines of, "Will I be able to make art my career? Is it a good idea? Is it a risk I should take?", you should change that to, "I have to make this work, and there are no other options." I know this may sound excessively dramatic, but to me it was always either make it work or nothing at all. Interpret that as you will.

Self-doubt is a waste of your precious time – it's best to deal with that demon first and foremost, or it will harass you every step of the way. That's not to say I never doubt myself, but at least it is a very low-level self-doubt that produces questions like, "Will I get it together and finish today's workload without getting too distracted?" Much easier to deal with.

Value resilience

I think the most important belief to have is in your own potential and ability to grow with hard work and dedication, and your absolute right to pursue your highest calling.

Even if it seems like others are born lucky, more talented, or more successful, you never really know what their personal path looked like and what demons they had to face along the way. For this reason, it's best to leave self-pity and circumstance comparisons behind. The easiest and most self-destructive thing to do is to pretend that you've just been handed a bad deal and, as a result, hate life for it. On the other hand, one of the most difficult yet rewarding things is to see the barriers and limitations you face as something positive, because resilience and ingenuity are born from limitations, and are the most valuable tools.

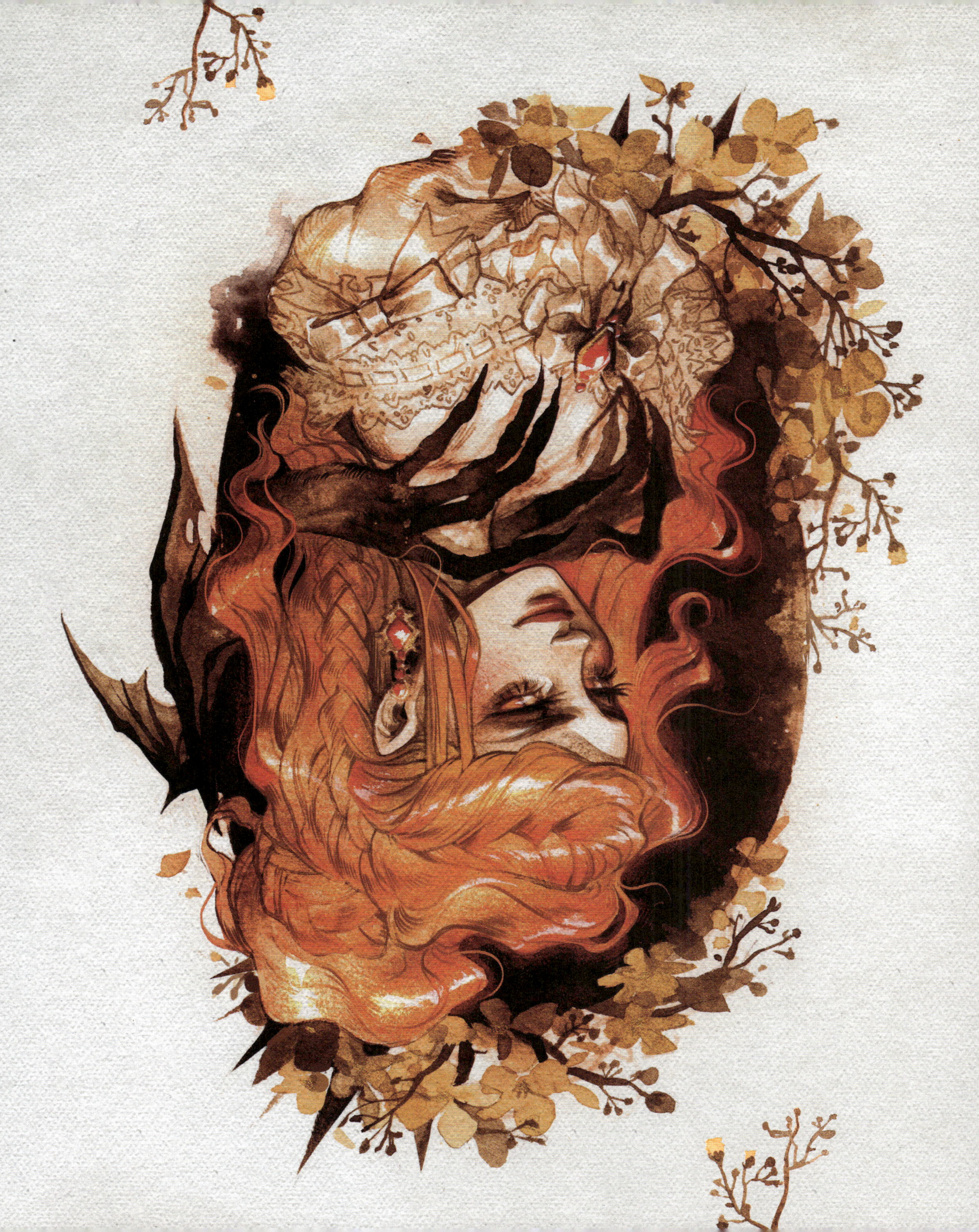

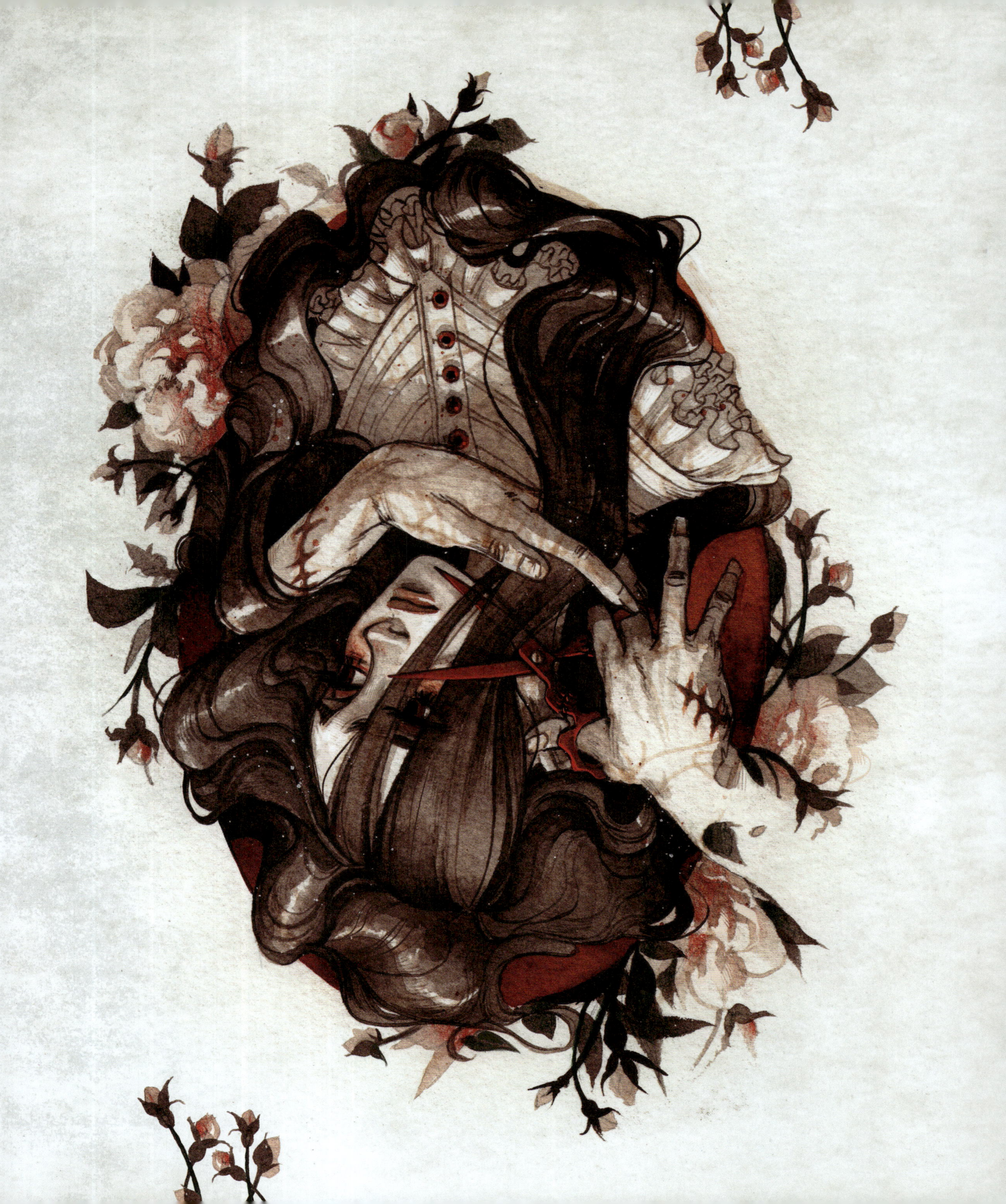

Develop a strategy

The great thing about making a career in art is that it's a huge and broad industry, and there are many corners of it that do not require you to compete with anybody. If you feel strongly enough about wanting to become an artist and manage to shed the self-doubt, you can start to strategize how to get there. This is where practicality and pragmatism really come in handy. It's extremely common for artistically inclined people to be sorely lacking in that department, but if you want to succeed and don't have a pragmatic and grounded person constantly by your side to balance you out, you must learn how to develop those qualities in yourself. You have to weigh out time versus money, effort versus reward, and so on, and always re-evaluate these things. I think being strict, schedule-oriented, organized, and driven is extremely important.

I personally am no different to most artists in this department, so it was very difficult to improve this weaker side of my personality. I still work hard to be organized and schedule-oriented. Although it feels like I'm failing most of the time in the end, I thankfully somehow still manage to get things done.

Keep the spark!

Lastly, it's very important not to let the workloads, frustrations, and dull reality rob you of the childlike spark of wonder that comes from creating. It can be hard to hold on to that, especially as you get older, and life gets busy and complicated. But with some effort, I think it's possible to bring it back.

I've always held on to my old artwork, and really enjoy looking back on it from time to time. It's not always a pleasant experience right away, but skill isn't everything and I don't linger too much on the mistakes and shortcomings when I look back on the things I drew as a kid. Since I have always drawn my characters and loved them so much, I can still feel that resonance from the old drawings. It's this pure feeling of being in love with the things you create, the idea of them, and that's what transcends lack of skill and feelings of inadequacy. This type of love for your imaginary creations is beyond ego. I think that's the spark that should be treasured.

"You have to weigh out time versus money, effort versus reward, and so on..."

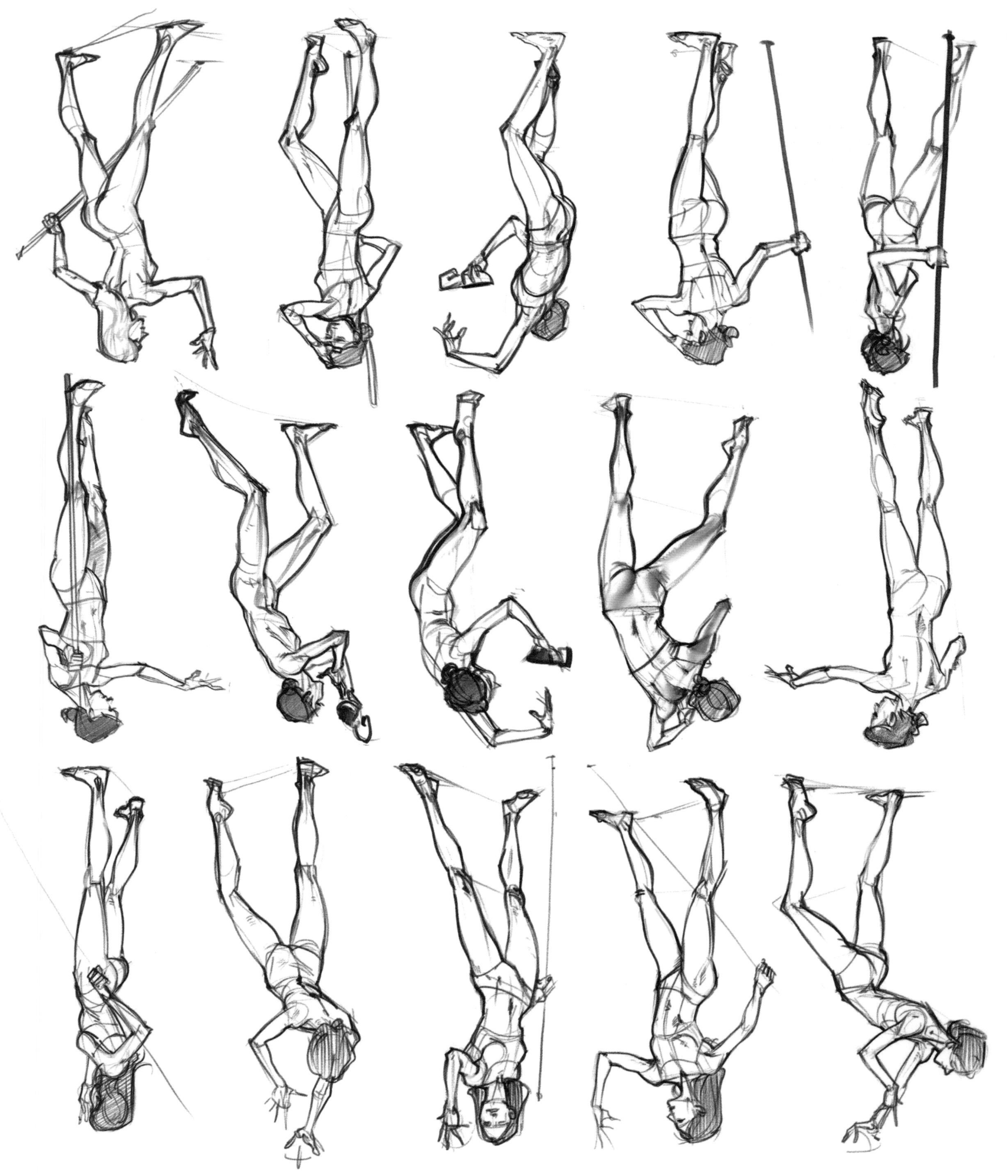

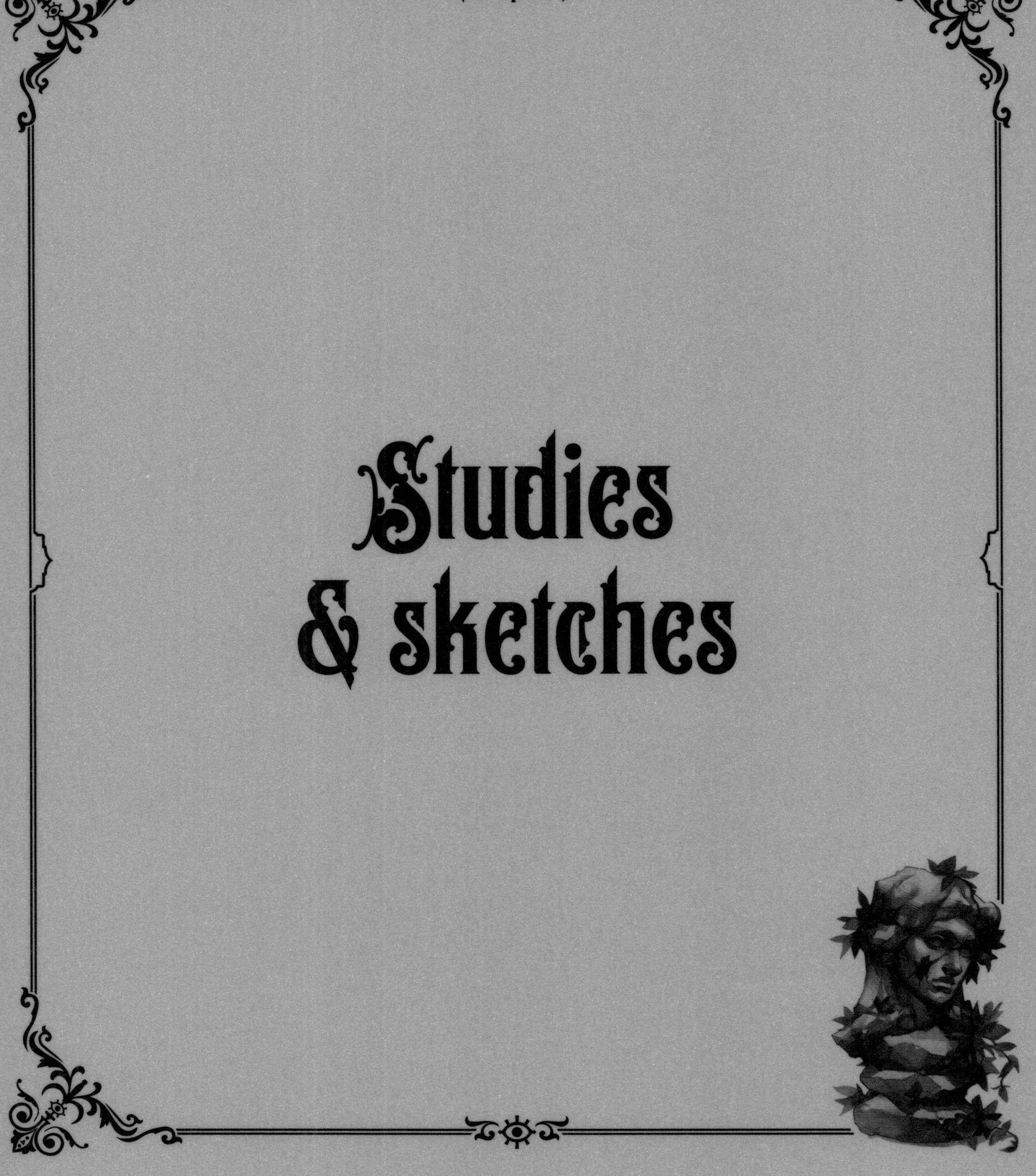

Studies & sketches

Studies
& sketches

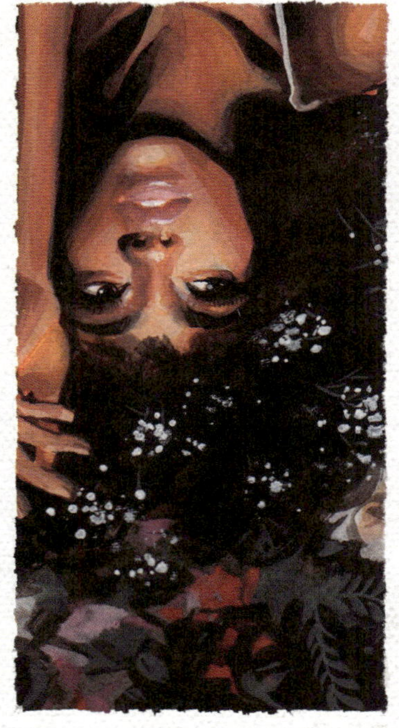
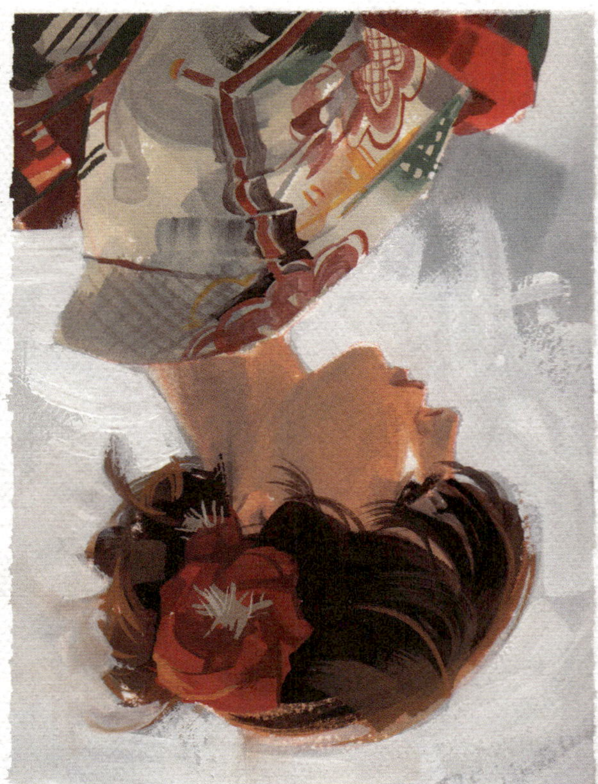
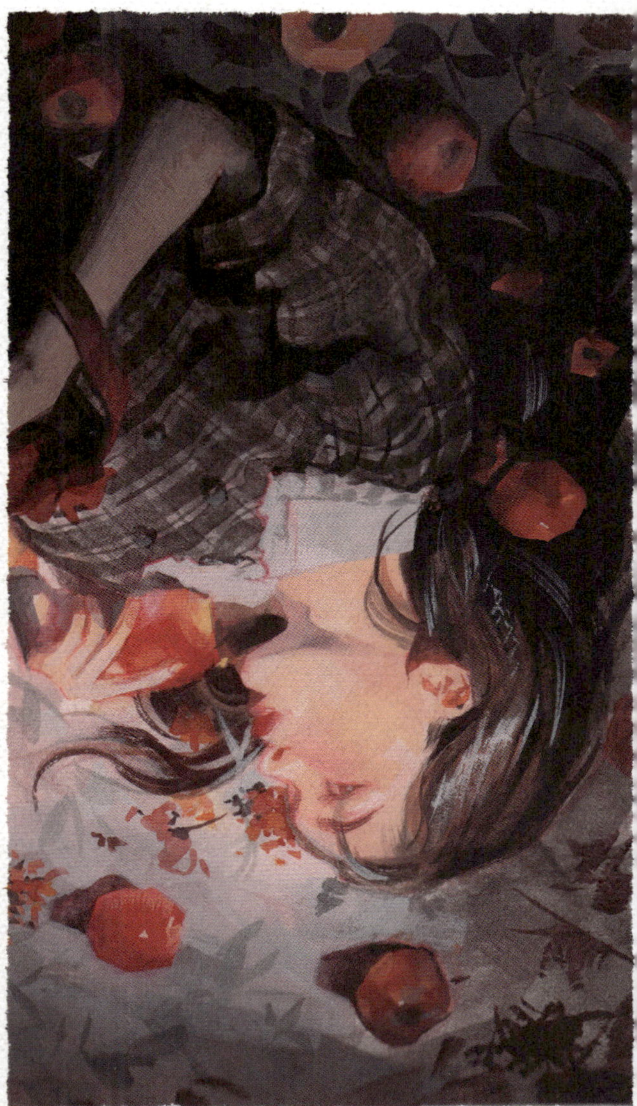
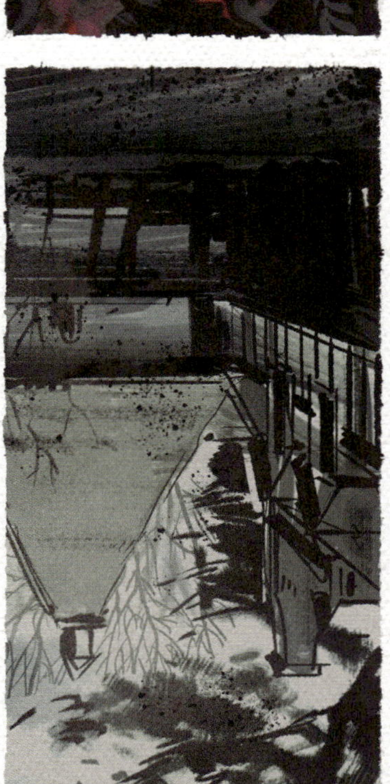
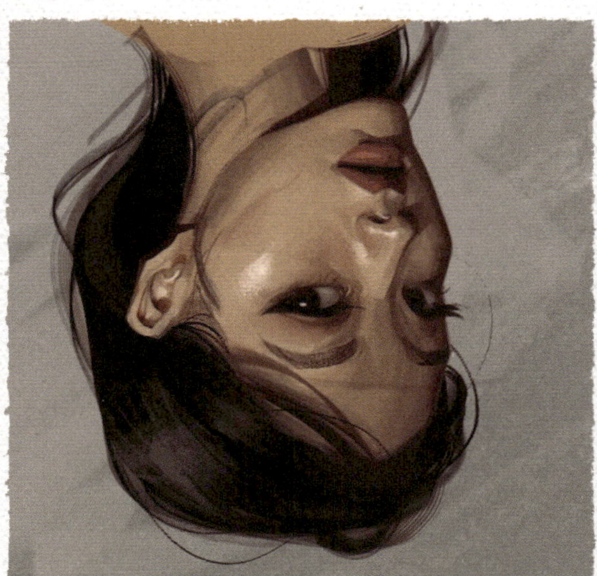
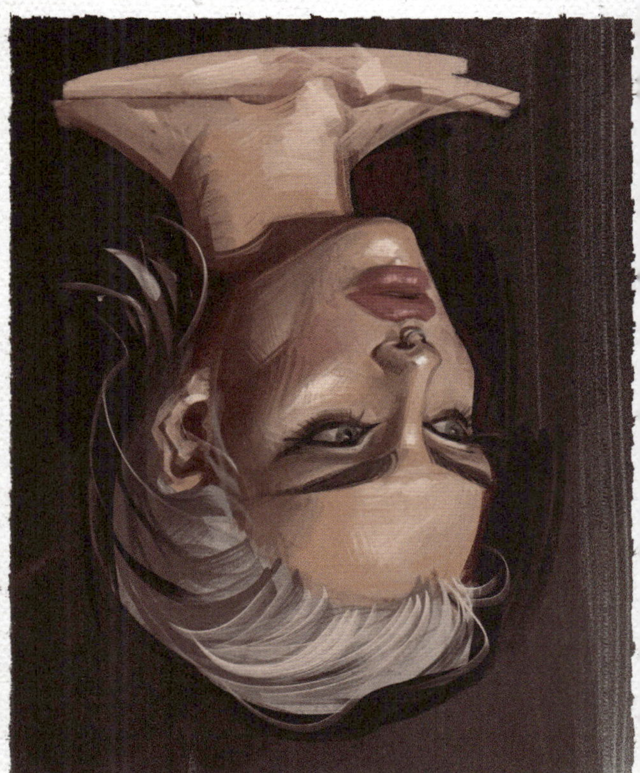
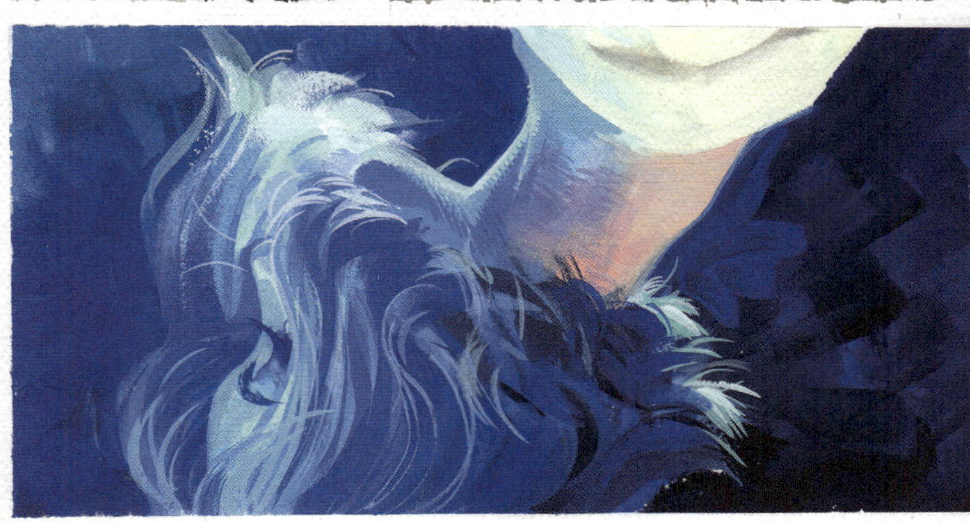

Figure drawing

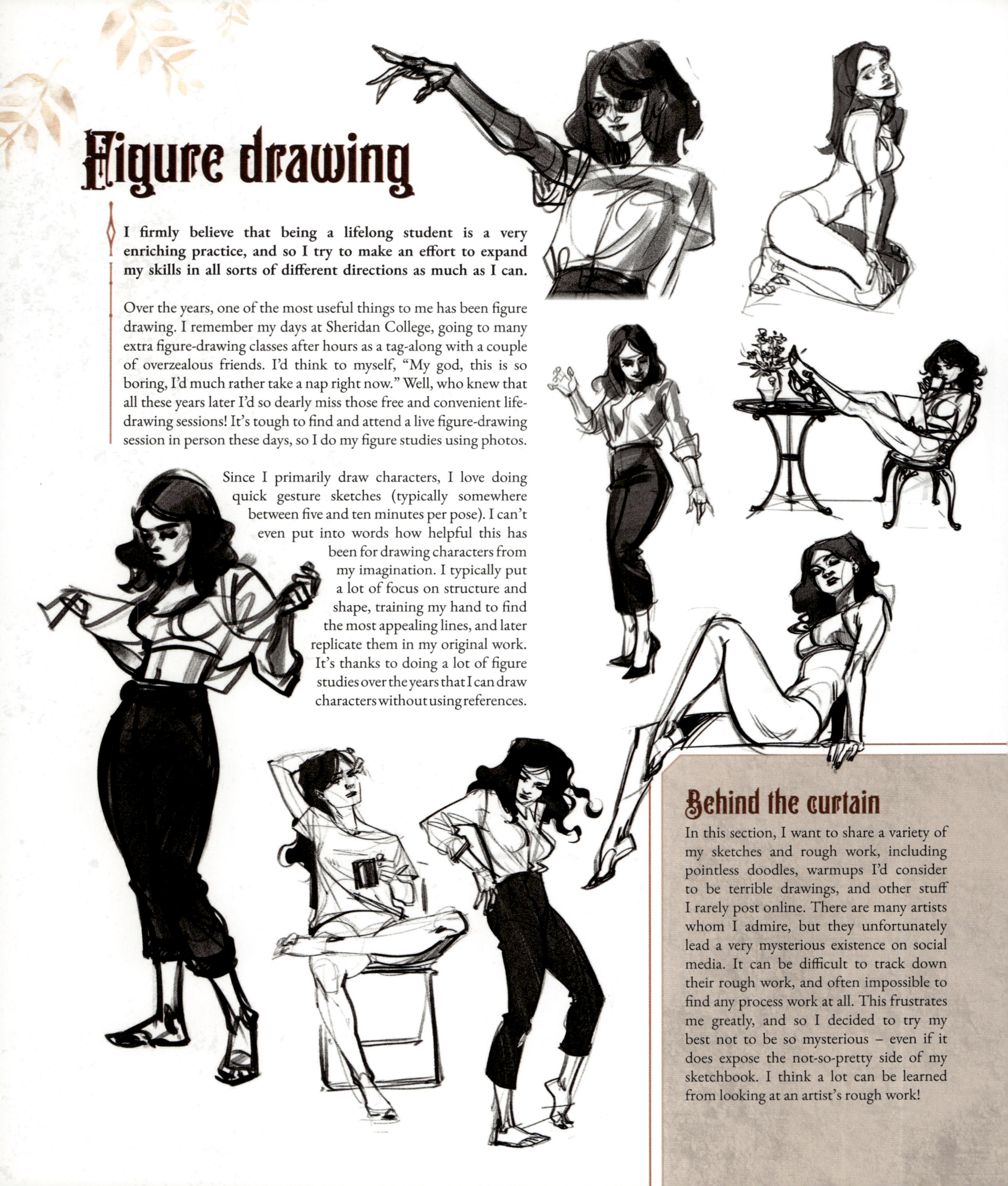

I firmly believe that being a lifelong student is a very enriching practice, and so I try to make an effort to expand my skills in all sorts of different directions as much as I can.

Over the years, one of the most useful things to me has been figure drawing. I remember my days at Sheridan College, going to many extra figure-drawing classes after hours as a tag-along with a couple of overzealous friends. I'd think to myself, "My god, this is so boring, I'd much rather take a nap right now." Well, who knew that all these years later I'd so dearly miss those free and convenient life-drawing sessions! It's tough to find and attend a live figure-drawing session in person these days, so I do my figure studies using photos.

Since I primarily draw characters, I love doing quick gesture sketches (typically somewhere between five and ten minutes per pose). I can't even put into words how helpful this has been for drawing characters from my imagination. I typically put a lot of focus on structure and shape, training my hand to find the most appealing lines, and later replicate them in my original work. It's thanks to doing a lot of figure studies over the years that I can draw characters without using references.

Behind the curtain

In this section, I want to share a variety of my sketches and rough work, including pointless doodles, warmups I'd consider to be terrible drawings, and other stuff I rarely post online. There are many artists whom I admire, but they unfortunately lead a very mysterious existence on social media. It can be difficult to track down their rough work, and often impossible to find any process work at all. This frustrates me greatly, and so I decided to try my best not to be so mysterious – even if it does expose the not-so-pretty side of my sketchbook. I think a lot can be learned from looking at an artist's rough work!

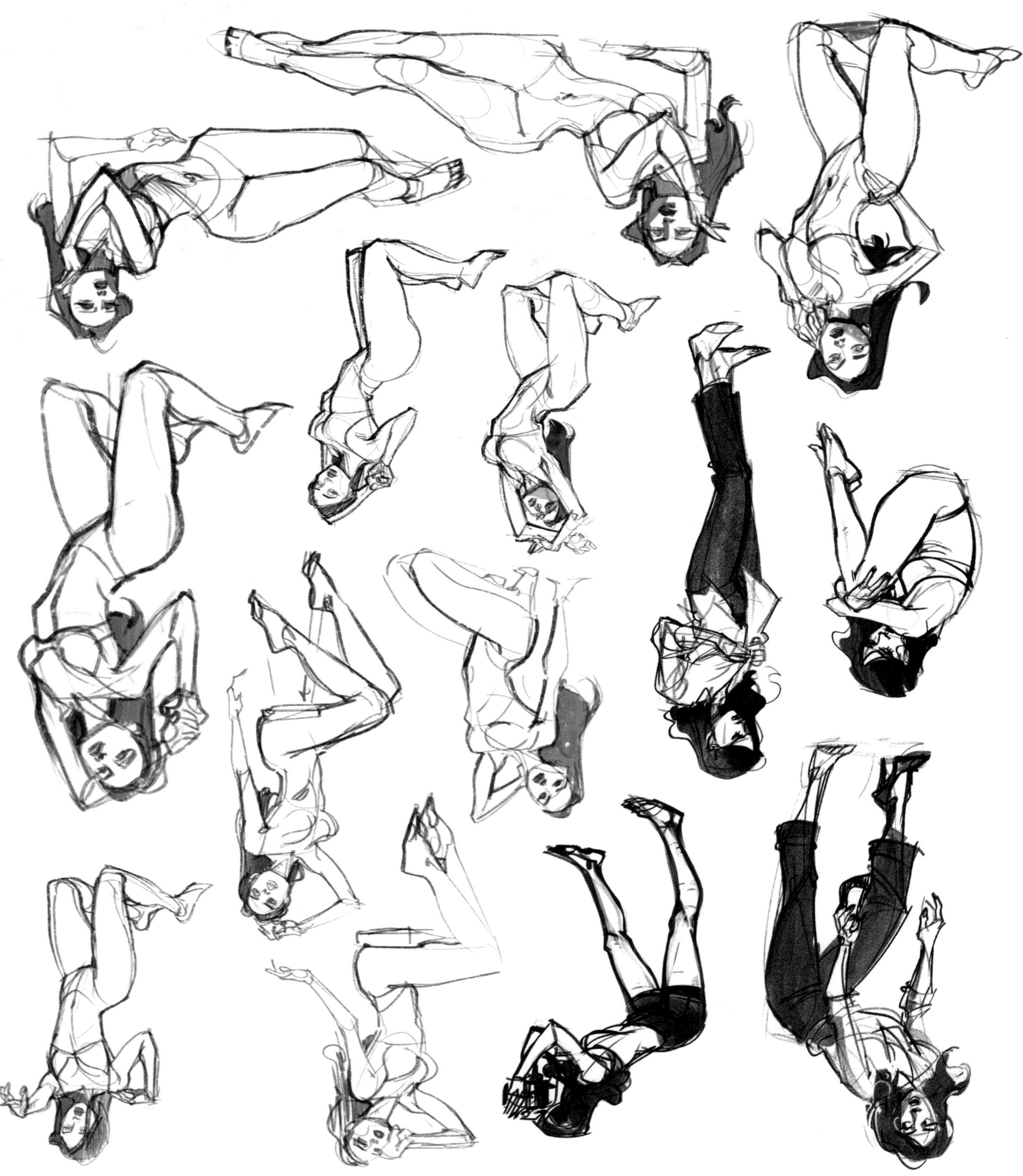

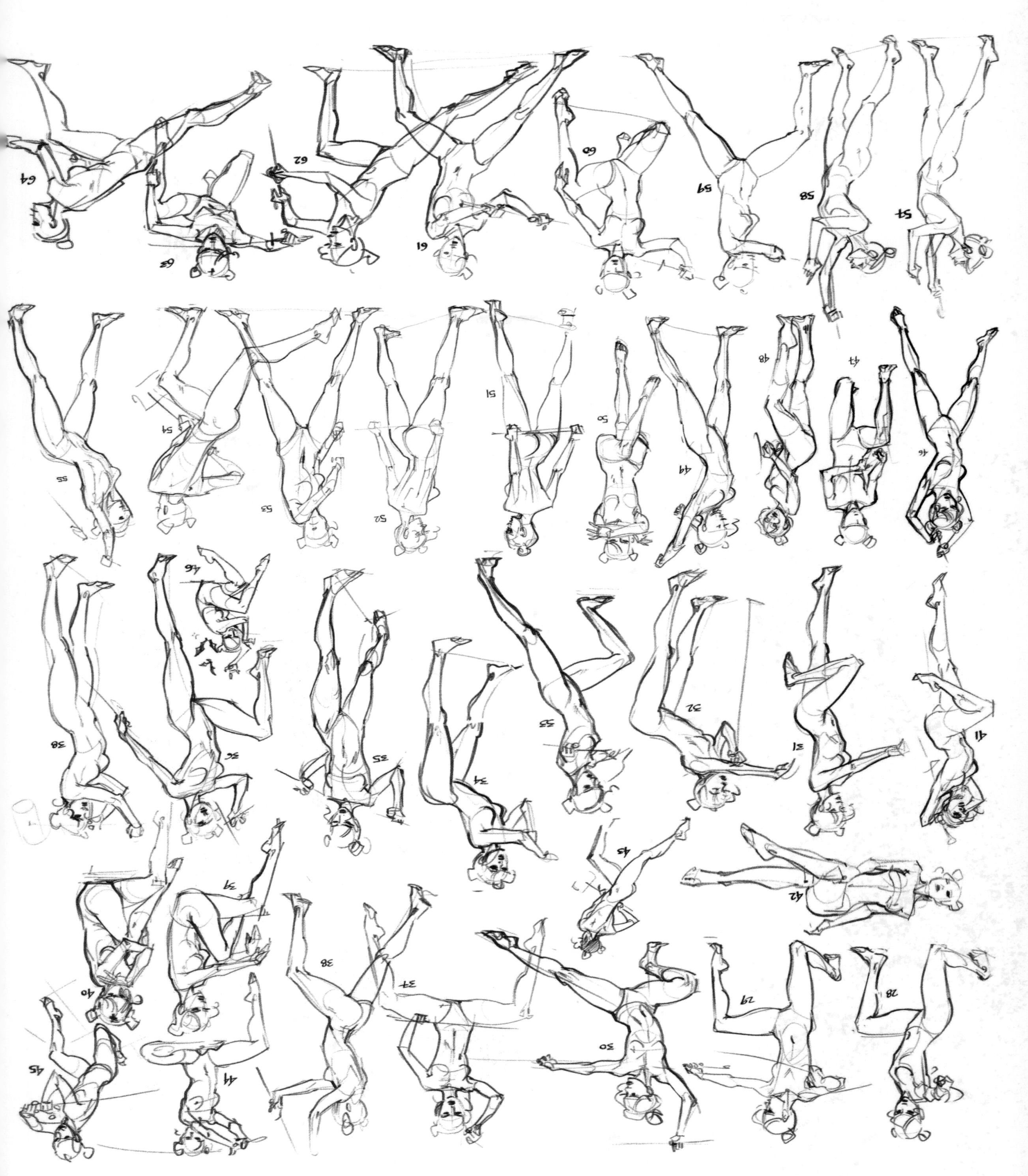

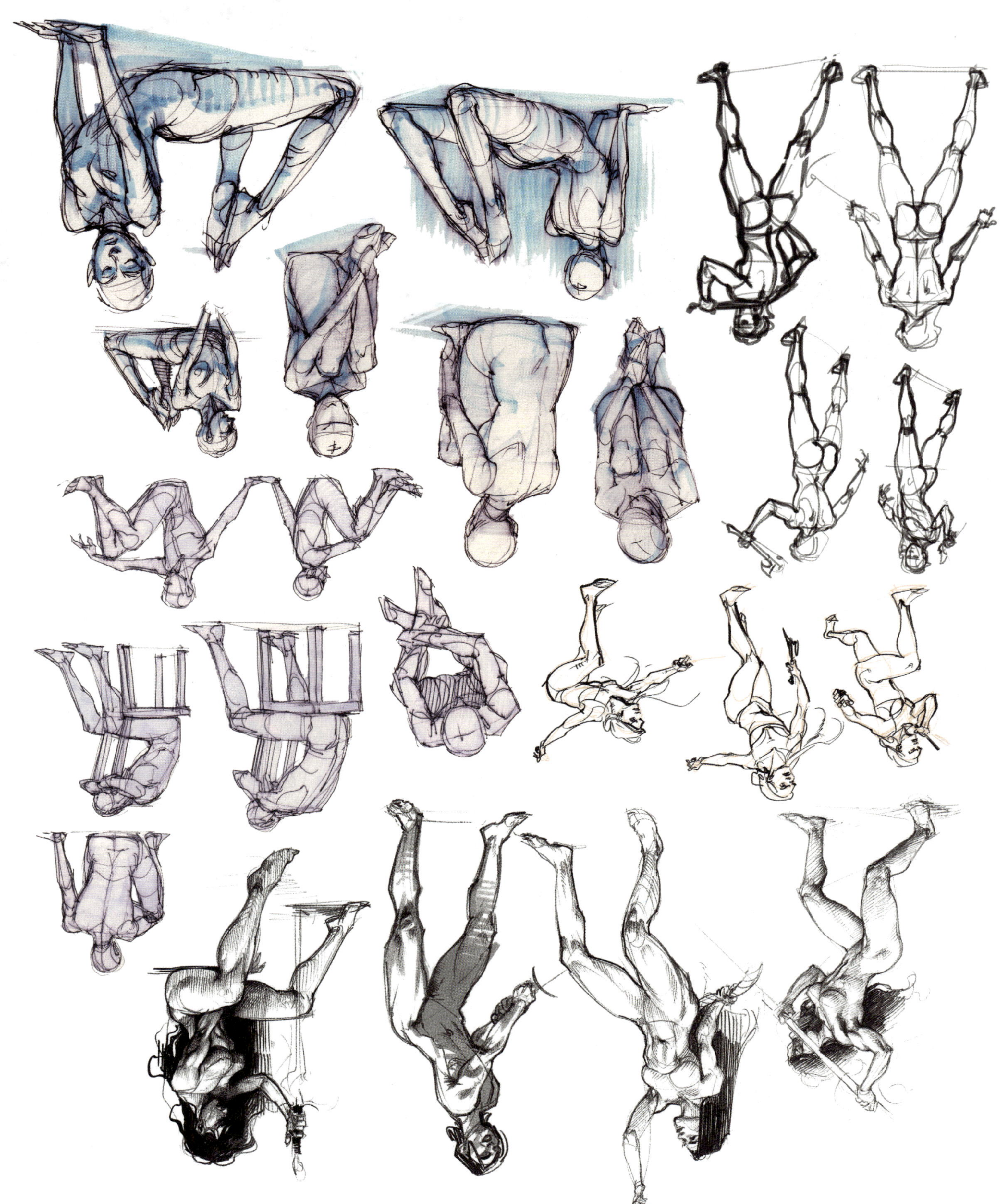

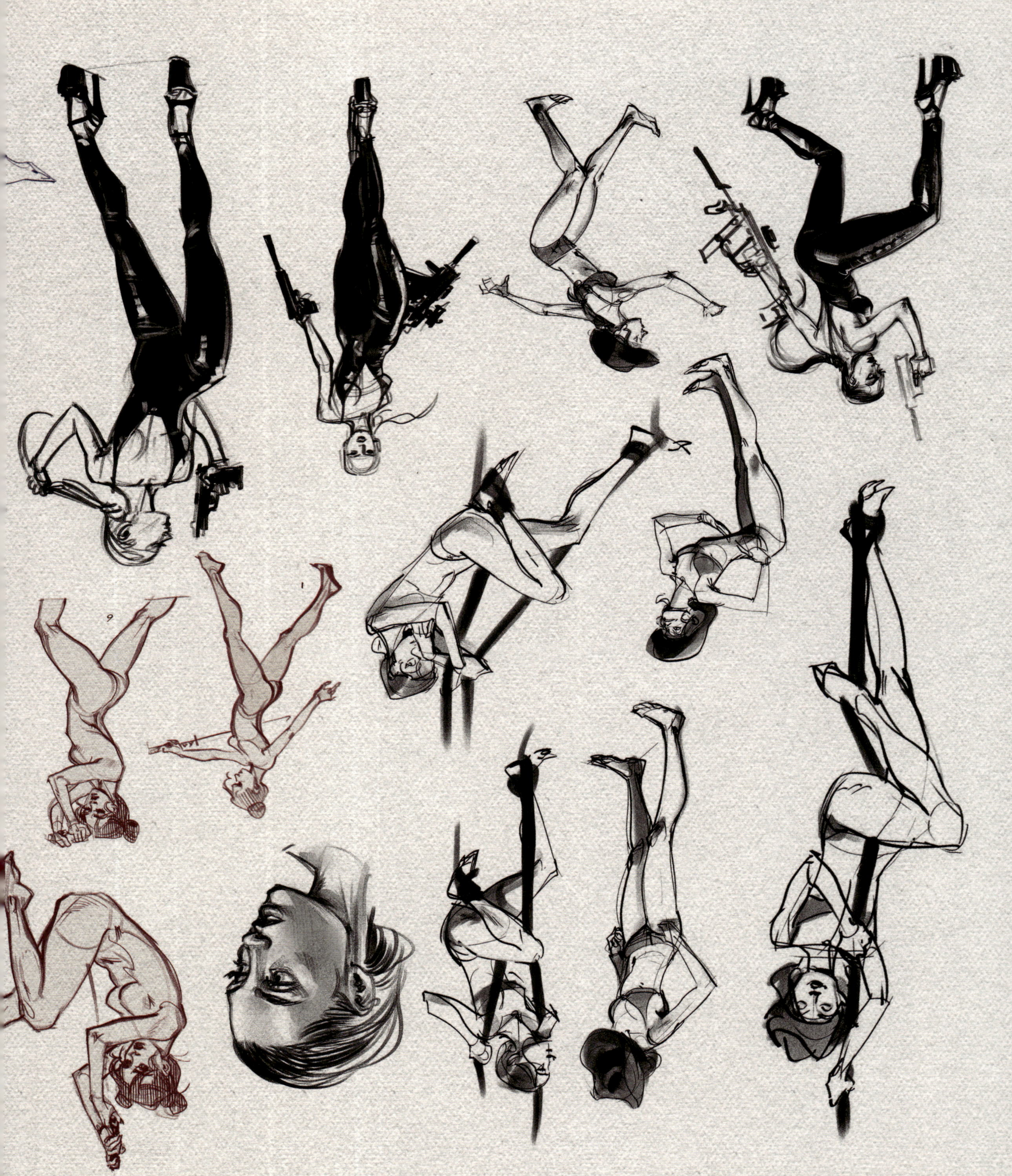

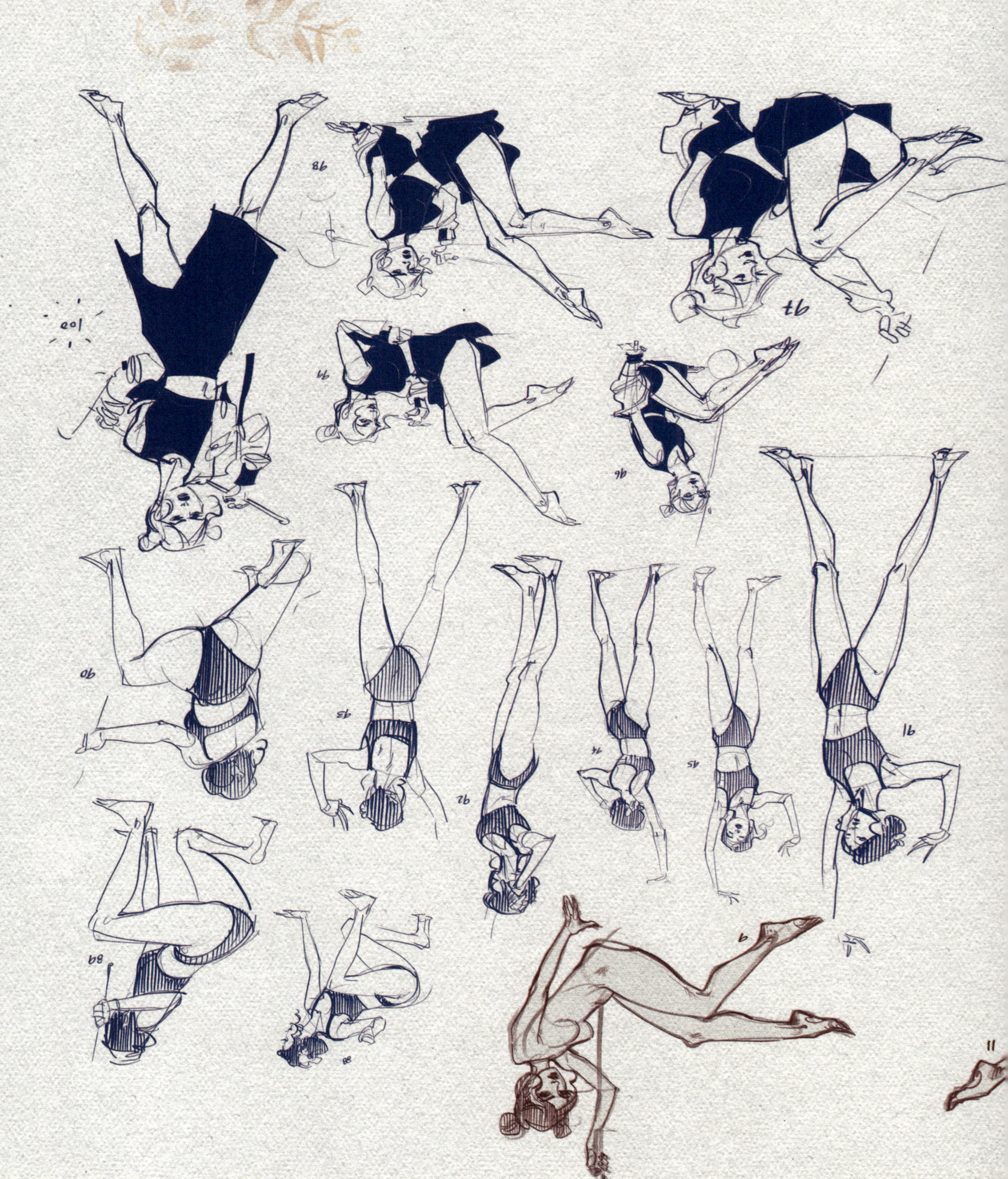

Sketchbook pages

On the next few pages, you'll find pages from my various sketchbooks, containing both roughs and more polished sketches.

I bounce between mediums now and then, but my favorite sketching tool over the years has been a thin ballpoint pen. I've always felt like there's no room for erasing when a sketch is just for warming up, and drawing with a ballpoint pen certainly helps with that. I do warm-up sketches for at least thirty minutes (up to an hour or more) before getting to work. I learned the hard way that trying to get straight to work frequently results in a lot of frustration and wasted effort, and I often spend at least thirty minutes just hacking away at a sketch anyway. It's best to do a bunch of quick, throw-away sketches instead – the actual work afterward feels like smooth sailing. It's not always that simple, but it does do the trick at least ninety percent of the time for me!

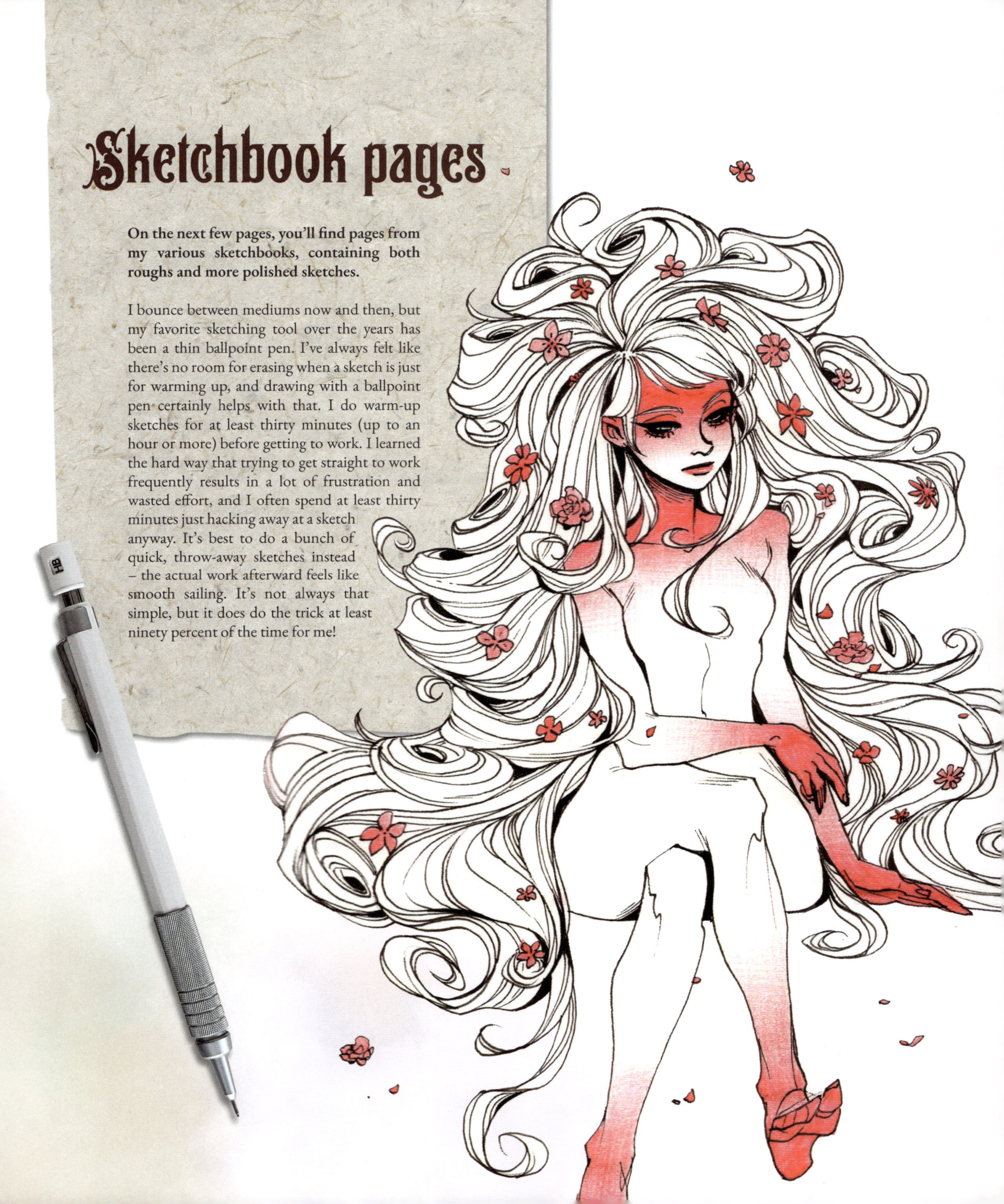

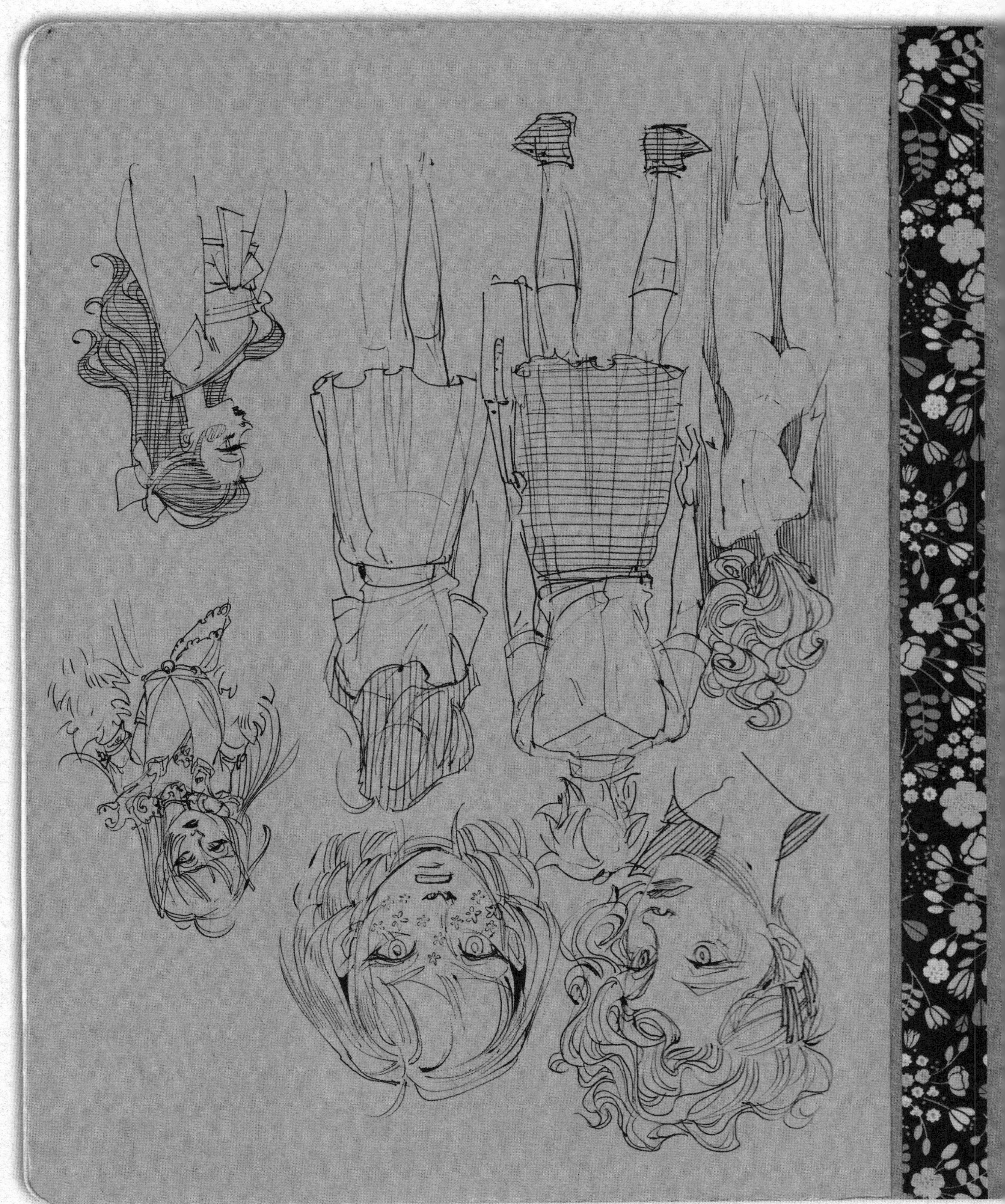

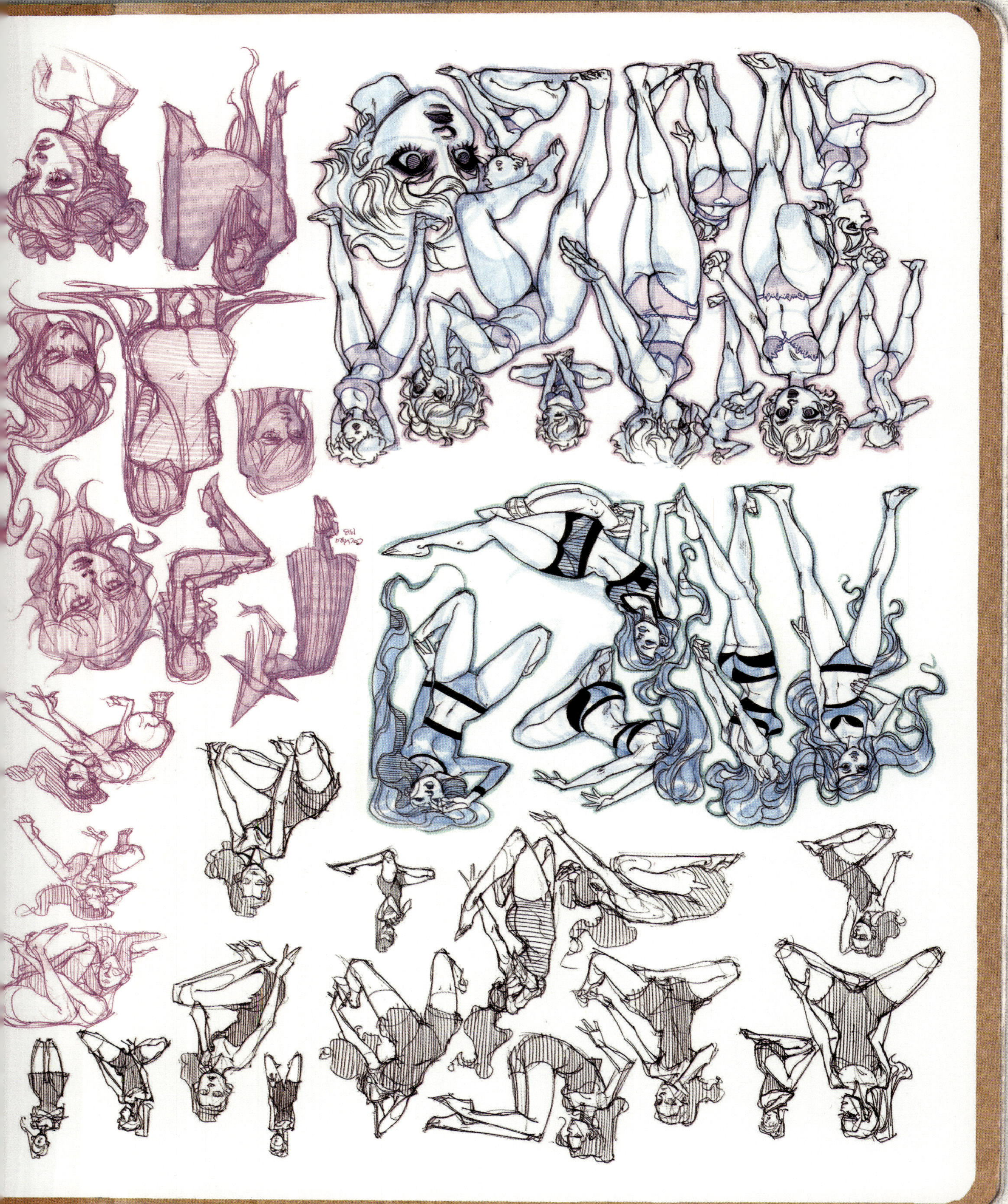

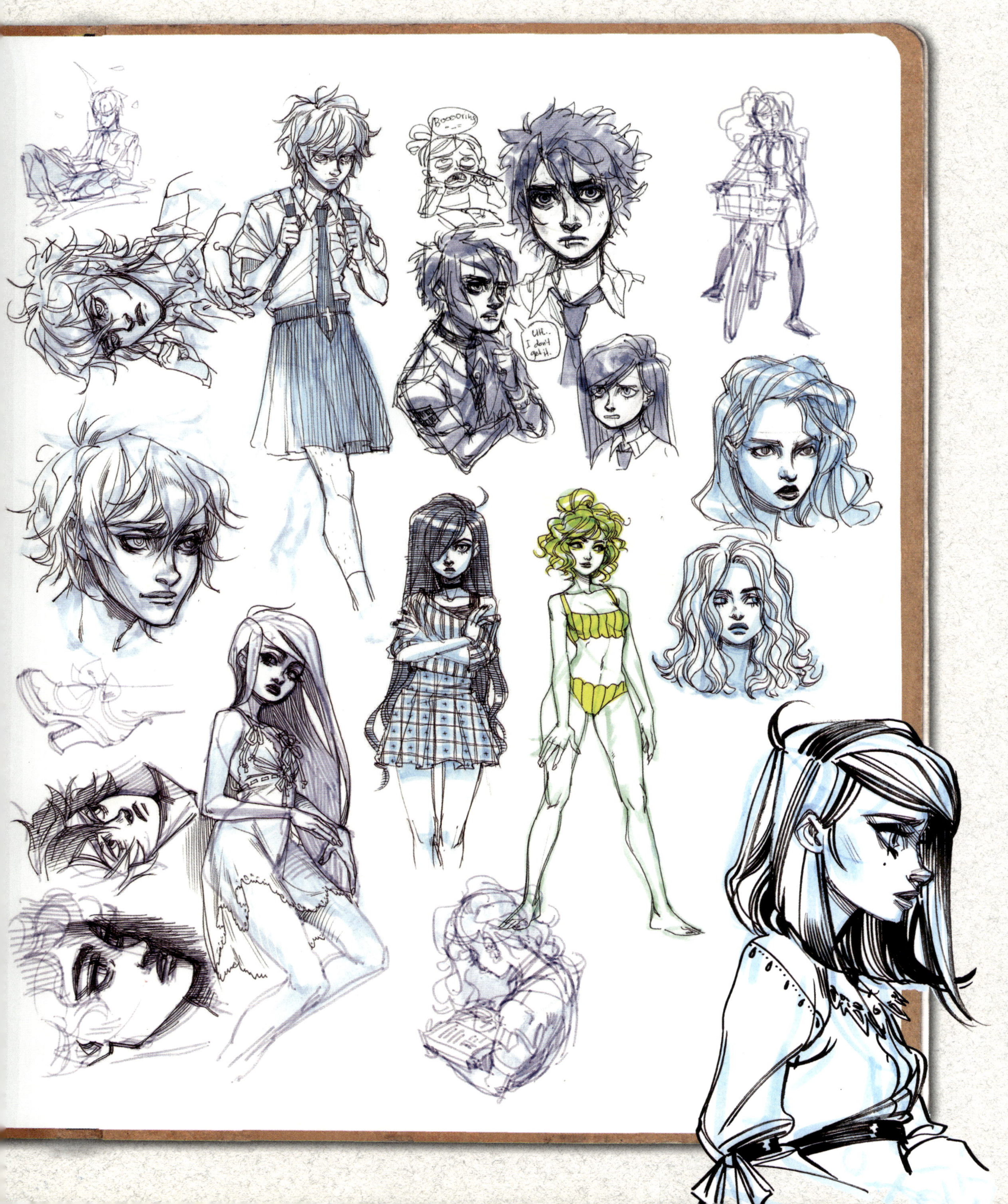
Booooring
-_-
Uh..
I don't
get it.

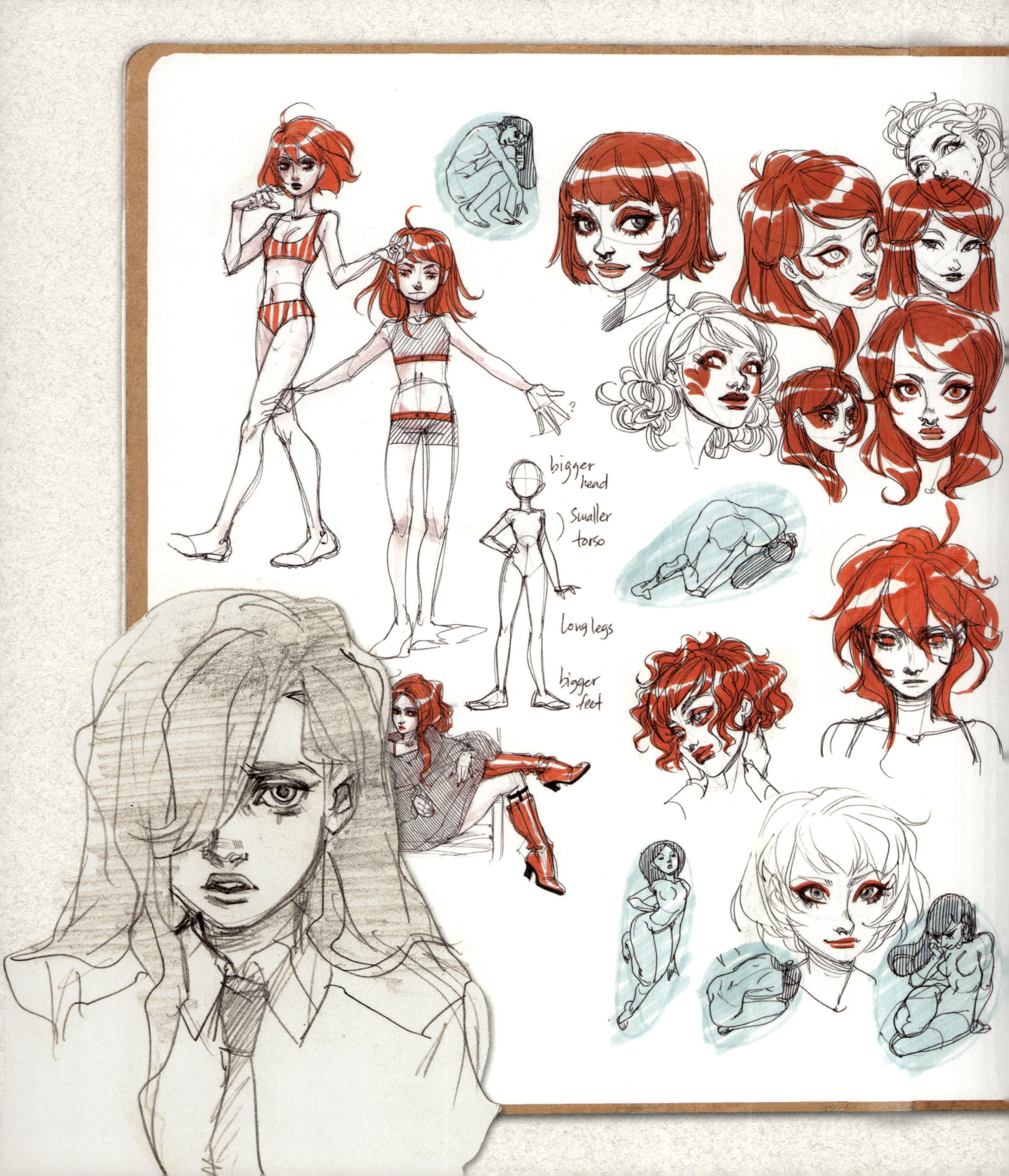
bigger head
smaller torso
long legs
bigger feet
?

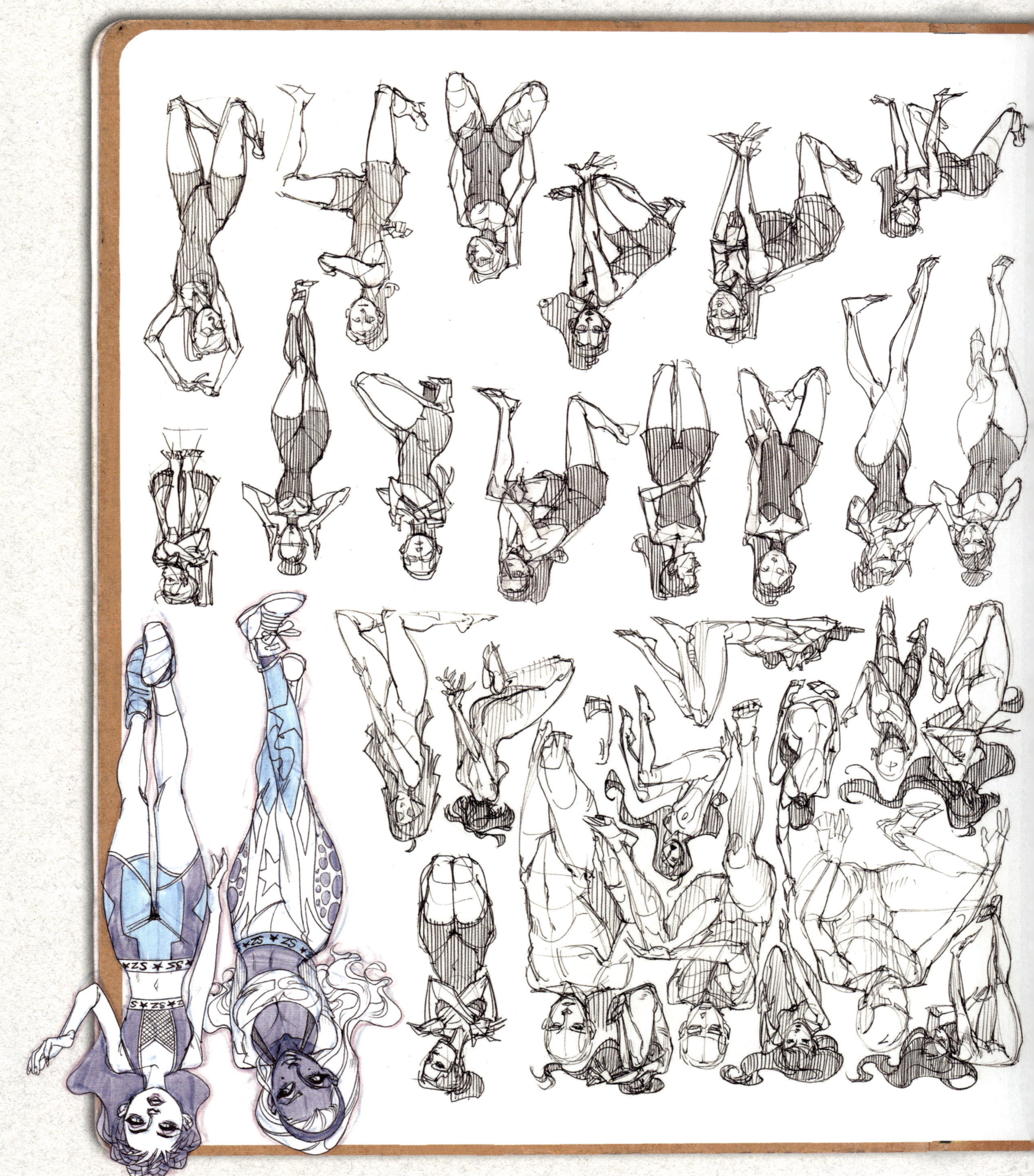

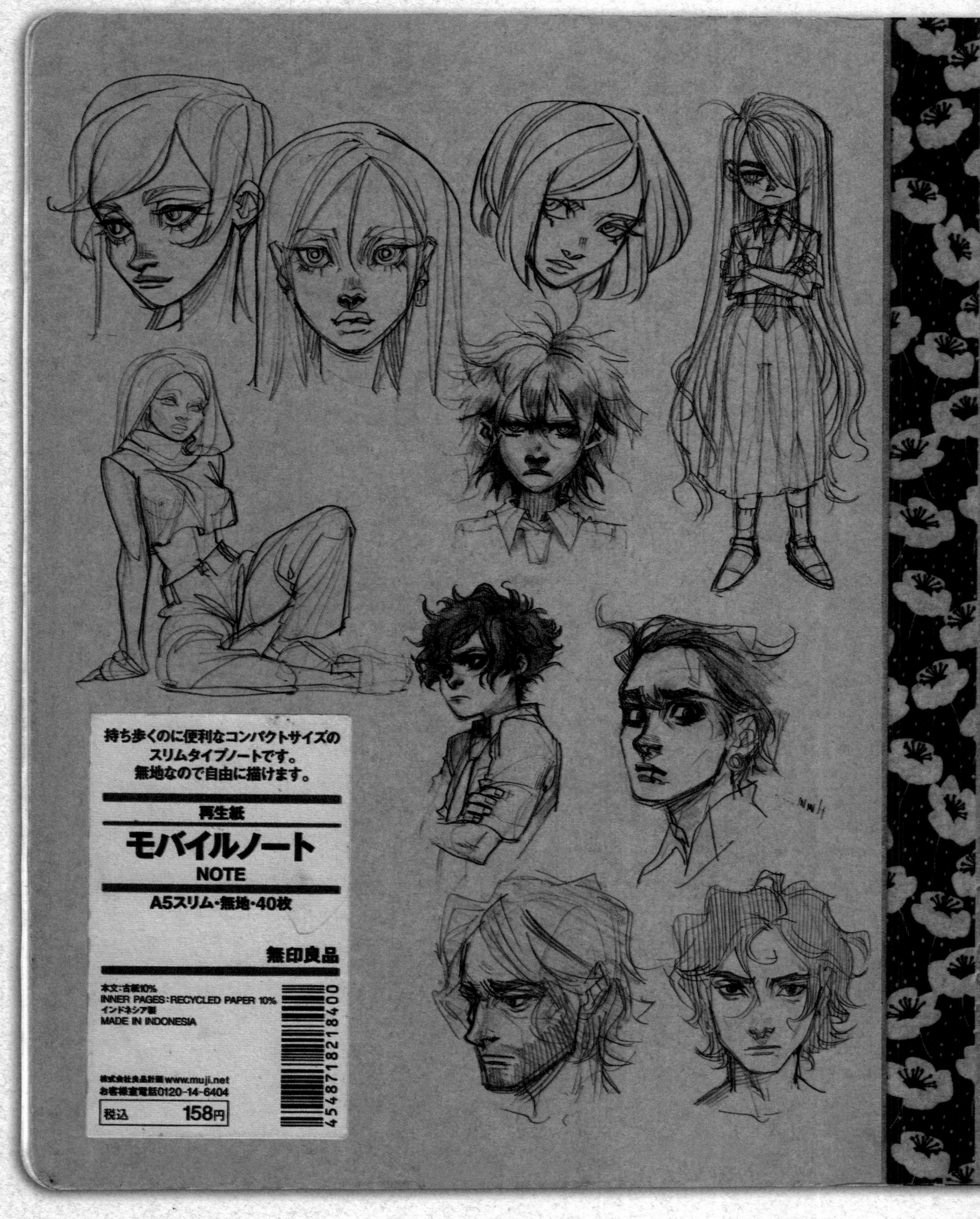
持ち歩くのに便利なコンパクトサイズの
スリムタイプノートです。
無地なので自由に描けます。
再生紙
モバイルノート
NOTE
A5スリム・無地・40枚
無印良品
本文：古紙10%
INNER PAGES：RECYCLED PAPER 10%
インドネシア製
MADE IN INDONESIA
株式会社良品計画 www.muji.net
お客様室電話0120-14-6404
税込 158円
4548718218400
NNH

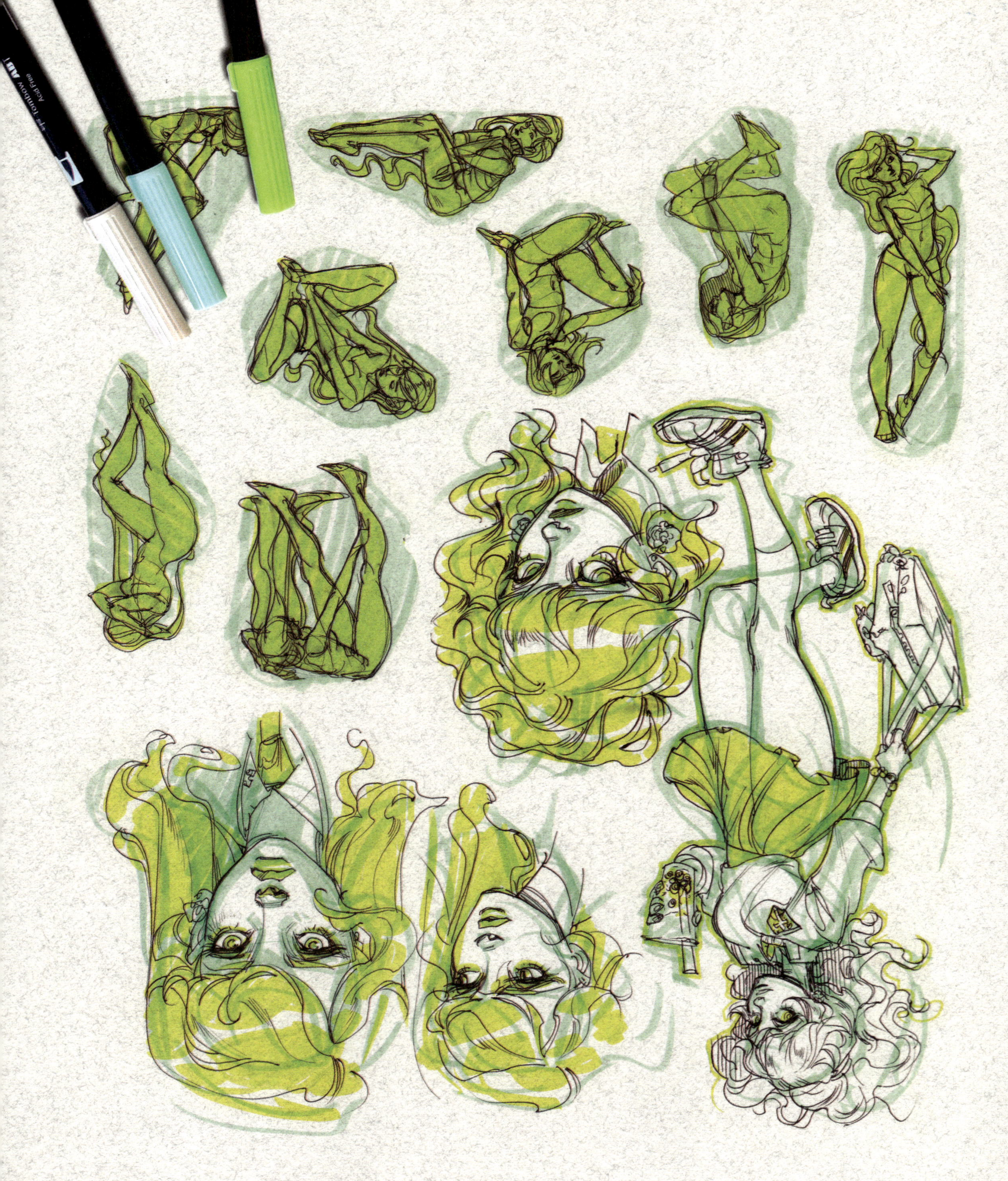

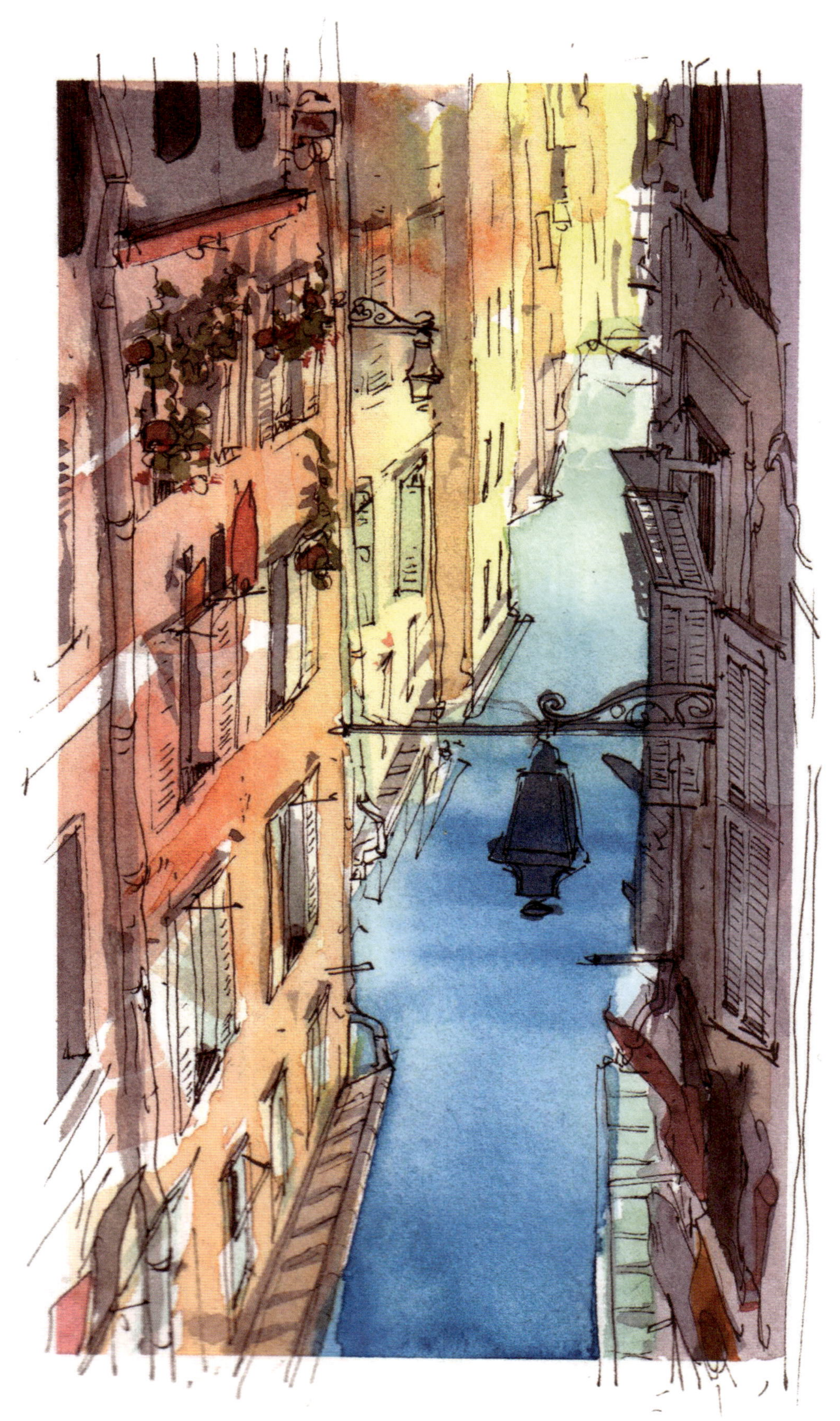

Materials & workflow

Materials & workflow

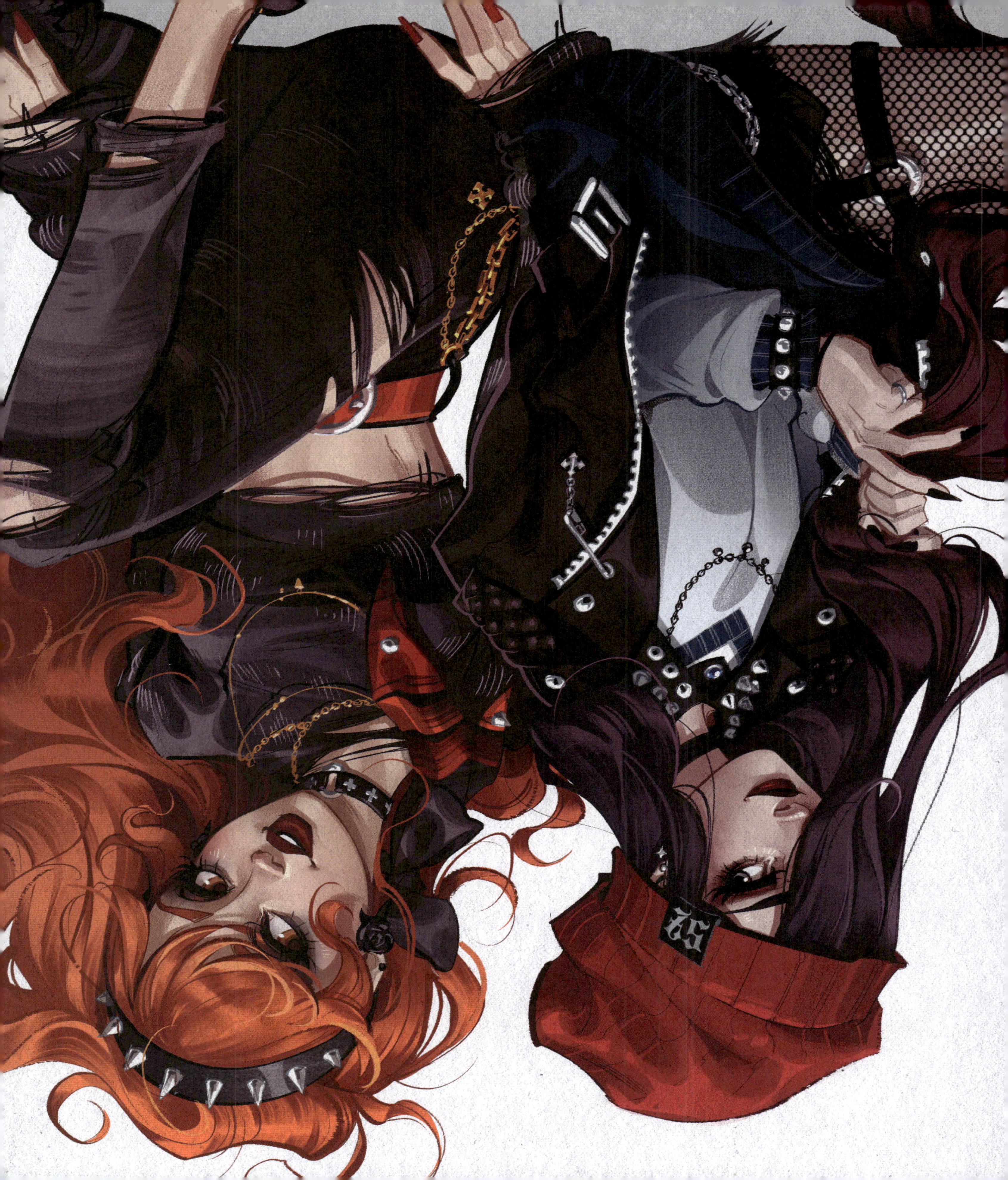

Traditional process

I'd like to take you through my traditional and digital illustration processes from start to finish, using very different types of media. We'll start with my favorite and most-trusted traditional tools and materials. I have a tendency to be experimental now and then, especially with mixing mediums and random tools I have on hand. However, over many years of experimentation, I've come to use certain materials very regularly, some of which I will share with you here and briefly explain why I like them so much.

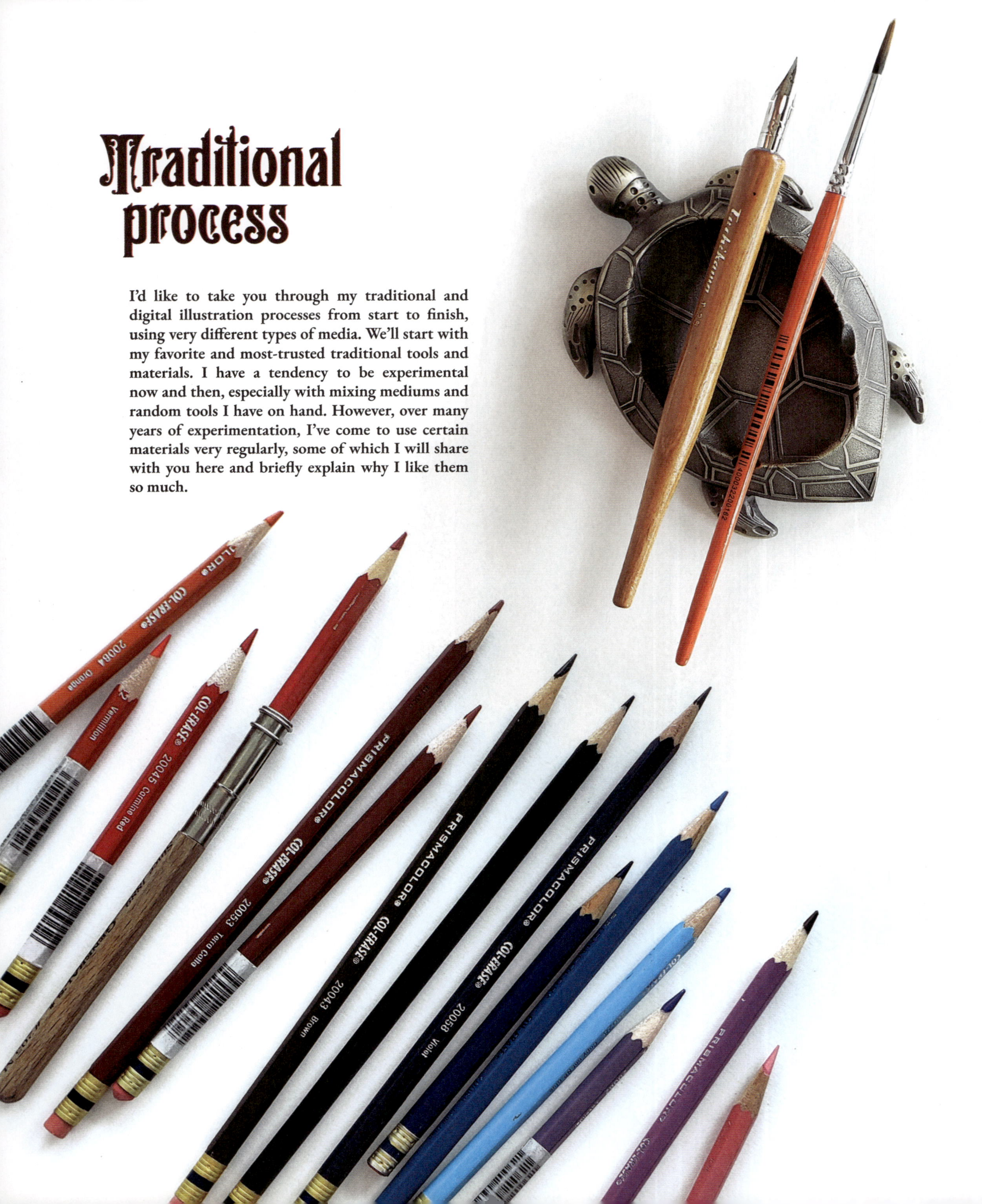

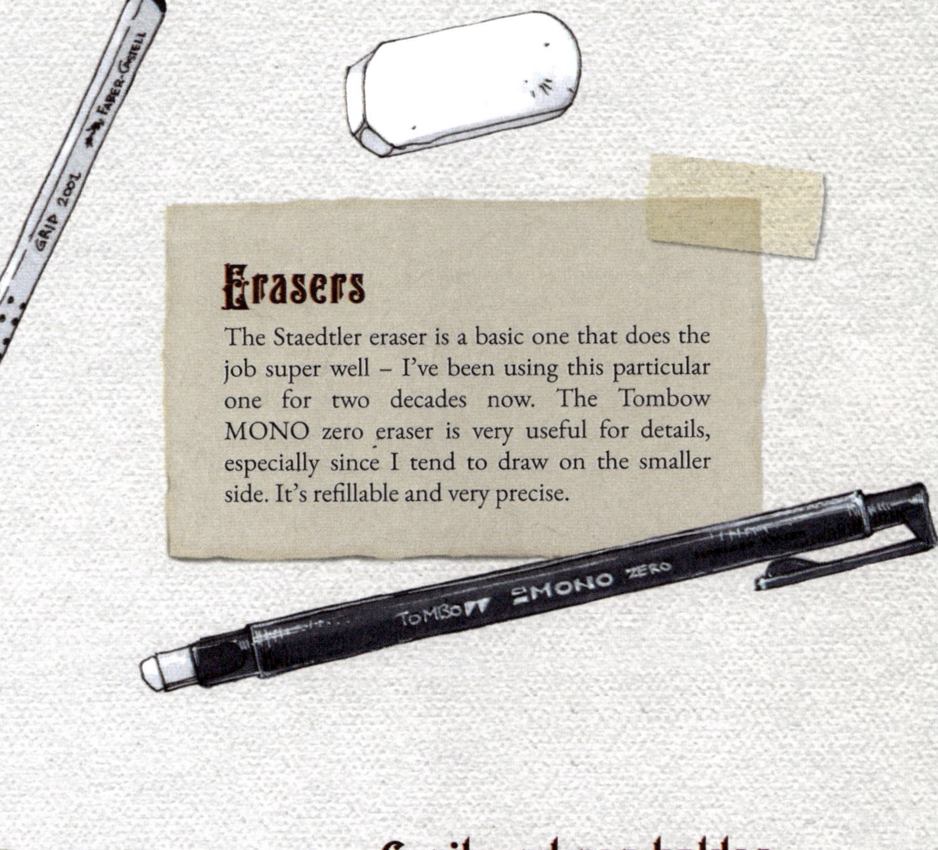

Hard pencil (H-3H)

The brand doesn't really matter too much – I use Faber-Castell, but other brands inlcude Lyra and Staedtler. But I want to focus on why I prefer H lead. I have a tendency to press very hard when I sketch on paper, so this type of graphite lead really helps me to control my pressure, because I can immediately see it making indents in the surface of the paper if I press too hard. This lead also tends to produce very clean results that don't smudge, unlike a softer HB or B pencil. This is my go-to choice for transferring a digital sketch onto watercolor paper using a lightbox.

Erasers

The Staedtler eraser is a basic one that does the job super well – I've been using this particular one for two decades now. The Tombow MONO zero eraser is very useful for details, especially since I tend to draw on the smaller side. It's refillable and very precise.

Synthetic brushes

I don't have a single brand I prefer, but I like the Betty Hayways set as well as ones from a local art store called Above Ground. I like the synthetic brushes because they're a bit firmer than real sable brushes, and thus easier to control. They're also relatively inexpensive and so I'm not too worried about ruining them somehow.

G-nib and pen holder

The G-nib has been an absolute favorite for many years now. I've tried out several other nibs, but always go back to this one – it has a very flexible tip which allows for a variety of line width and glides very easily. The Tachikawa pen holder is standard and I don't even remember where I got it from, but I've also had it for several years now.

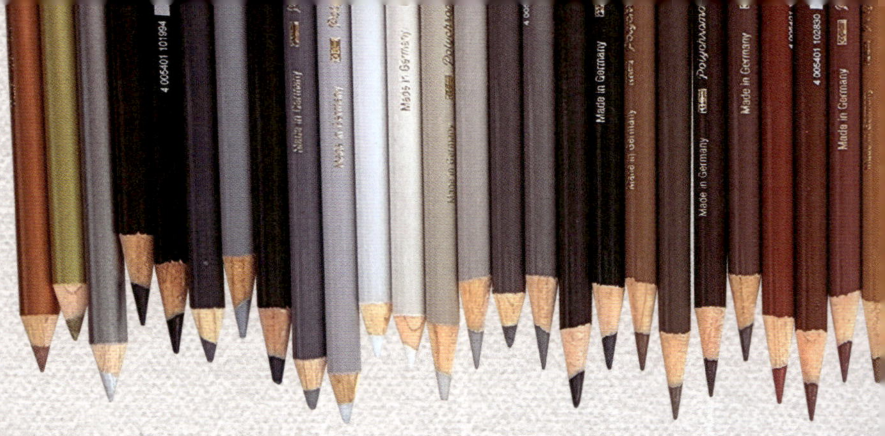

Colored pencils

The newest addition to my typical preferred tools, these Faber-Castell Polychromos pencils are great for layering on top of a watercolor or ink-based drawings. I've been using them for a few years now and love the mixed-media look.

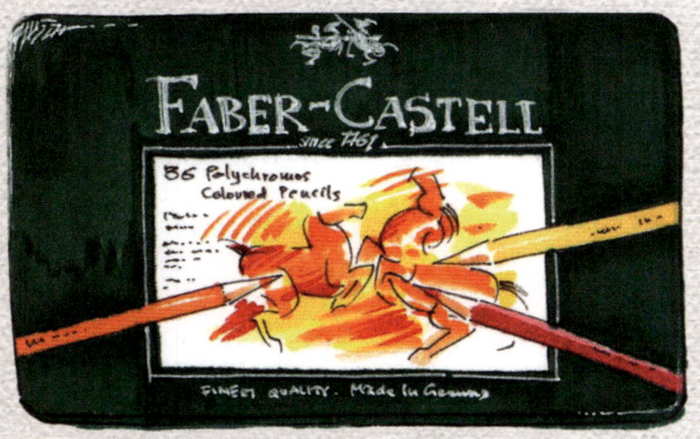

Porcelain palette

This may seem like an obvious choice, but it took me years to get a proper porcelain palette for some reason. I've spent many years cycling through various plastic and even metal palettes, and always had so much trouble with cleaning them and ended up throwing them all away in the end. This palette was a much-needed upgrade – even when using colored ink that dries quickly and is difficult to remove, I simply soak the palette in water for ten minutes or so and the ink peels right off without staining.

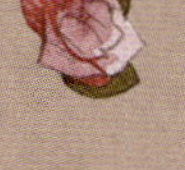

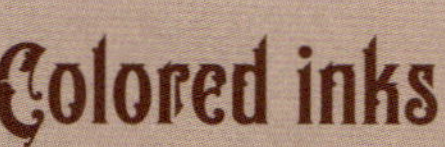

Colored inks

After discovering Rohrer & Klingner inks through the artist Heikala, they have become my go-to favorite material. I like the convenience of the small bottles and that they come in a variety of colors. I use other brands like Dr. Ph. Martin's as well, but these have been the ones I keep coming back to.

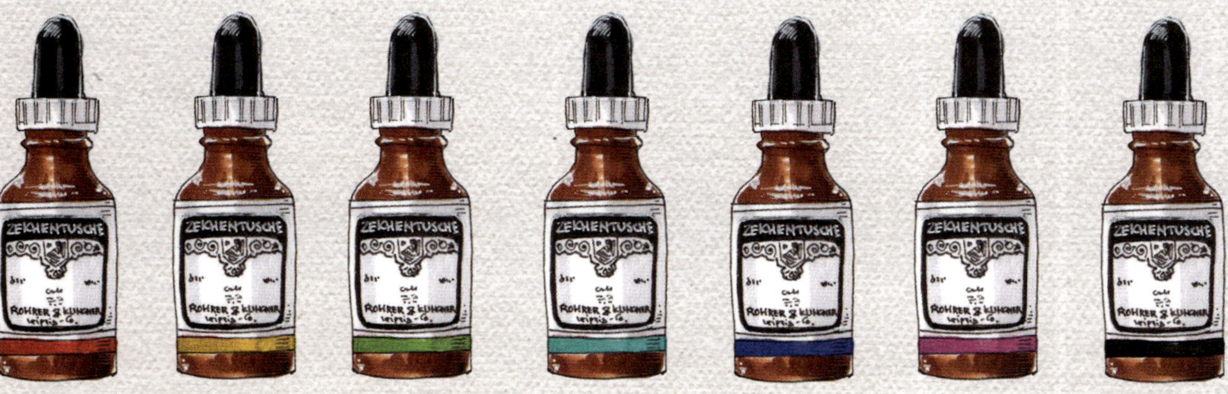

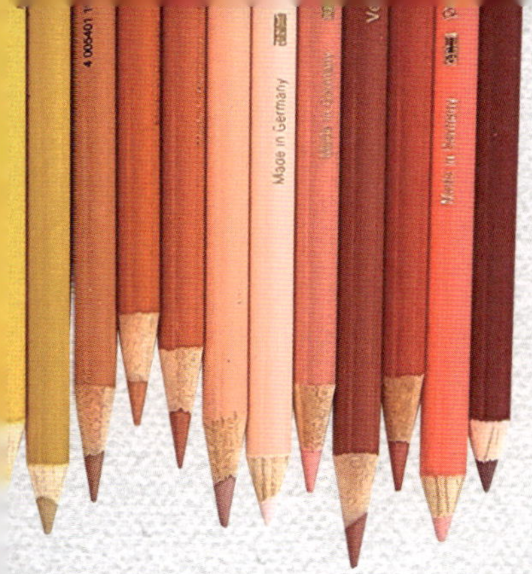

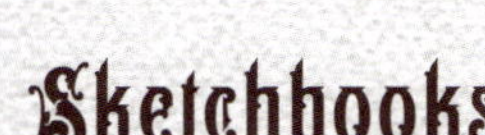

Sketchbooks

MUJI sketchbooks are super inexpensive and great for basic quick sketching or warmups. I've filled up quite a few of these over the years – I like the smoothness of the paper although it is very thin.

Now and then I use Strathmore 400 Series Mixed Media pads, and they're great for ink and watercolor art. There's not much texture to the paper, but it's heavy enough to take water-based media and is very easy to find at pretty much any art store I've ever been to.

Of the journals and sketchbooks I've tried, the Strathmore 500 Series Mixed Media journal is a particular favorite. The soft cover has a nice feel, and it's a great format. The paper has a nice texture and can handle a wet wash very well.

I really like Saunders Waterford cold-press watercolor paper of late – it's my current go-to paper for finished illustrations. I also discovered this brand through the works of Heikala!

Other materials

There are many other art materials that I use now and then, so I figured I'd mention a few here:

- Artograph LightPad for transferring digital sketches
- Sakura Pigma Micron fineliners
- Holbein Acryla Gouache
- Copic and Prismacolor alcohol markers
- Winsor & Newton Artist Gouache
- Kuretake Gold Mica calligraphy ink
- Dr. Ph. Martin's Synchromatic liquid watercolors
- Dr. Ph. Martin's India ink

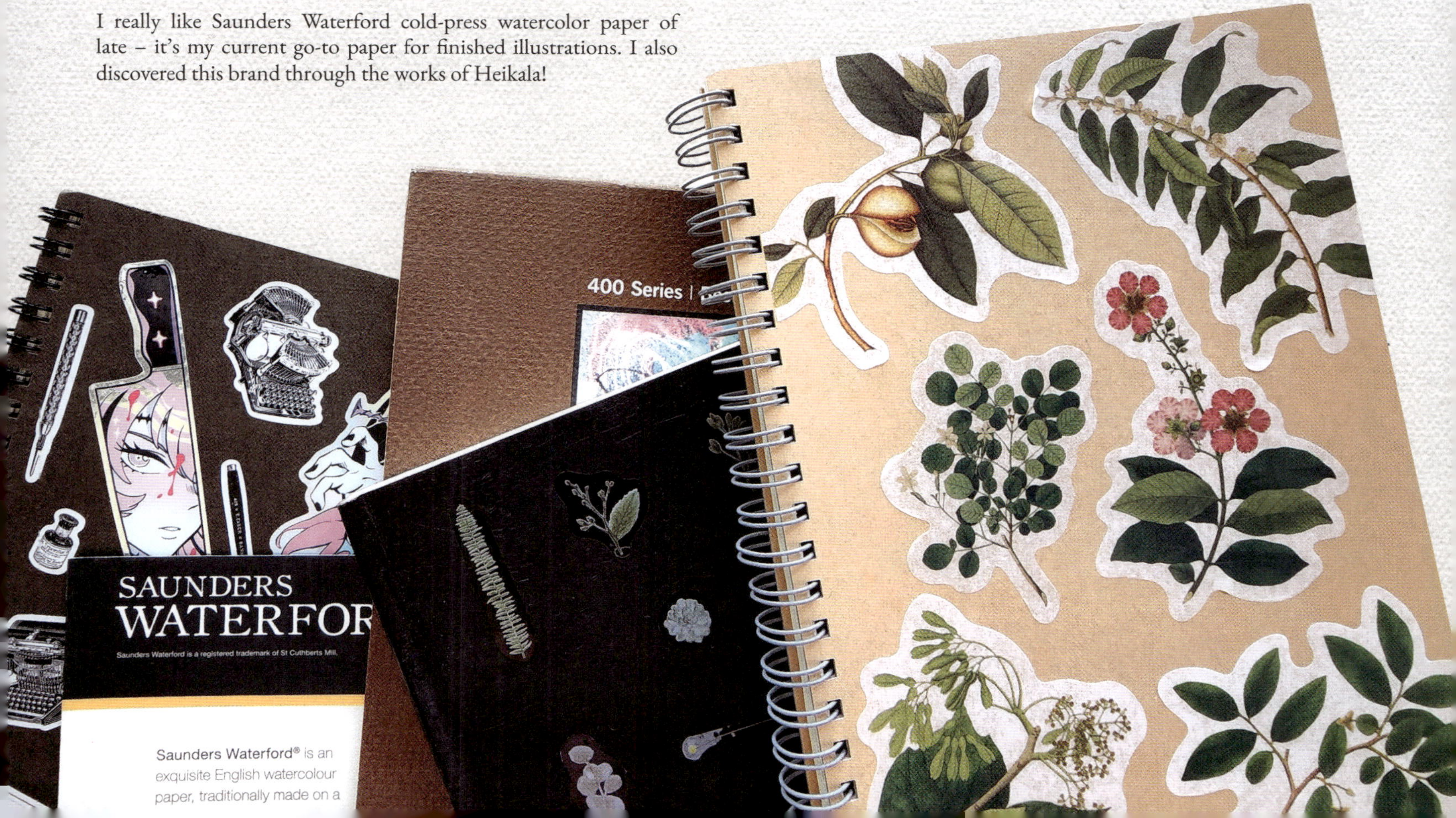

CREATING

Sweet Astronomer

I want to share my process for a very popular subject matter among artists: the character portrait. I love drawing character portraits like this and have done many in the past. I'm a big fan of decorative ornamental elements as well, and in this tutorial I will take you through my process of creating an ornate character portrait illustration using a digital sketch and colored ink, with a mix of other traditional media.

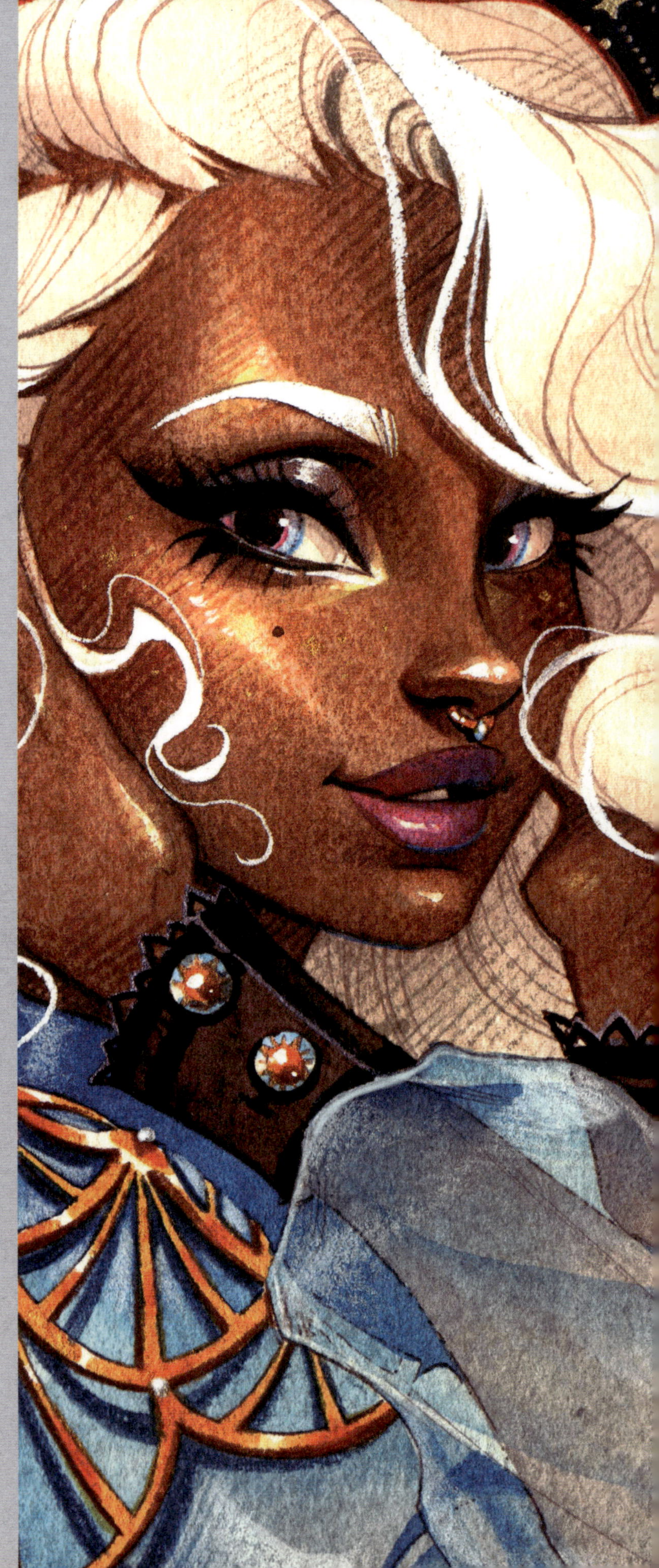

1 References and sketch

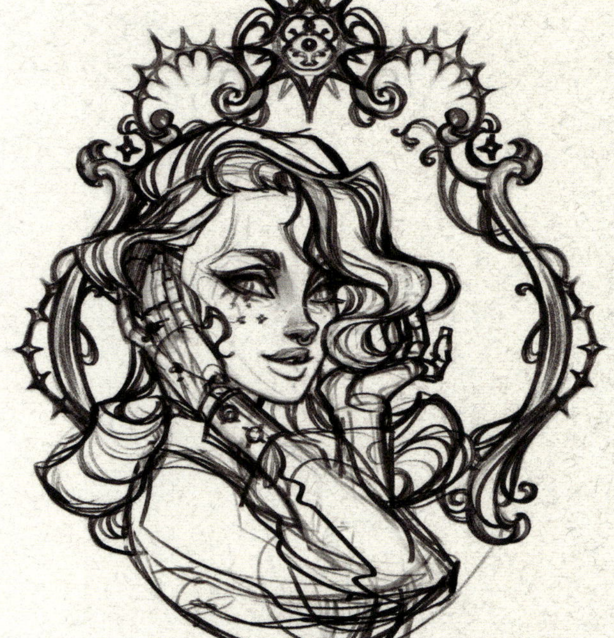

After deciding which character to draw, I pick a theme and gather digital references into an app (PureRef) on my desktop. This helps me set the mood and provides ideas for the ornamental elements. In this case, the theme is "astronomer," and I gather a lot of images to inform the potential color scheme from which to pull little details. I typically gather references either right before starting, or during, the sketching process. I prefer to sketch digitally for designs that have symmetrical and ornate elements like this one.

I drew the ornate frame first, using the Symmetry tool in Photoshop CC to keep it neat and symmetrical, and to save time. I prefer digital sketches for complex illustrations with overlapping elements because the tools can save a lot of time in the planning stages. Most notably: Layers, Symmetry Mode, Free Transform, Lasso selection, and Copy + Paste.

I use Photoshop CC for all my digital art, and have a go-to textured sketch brush (rough pastel), which helps imitate traditional sketching.

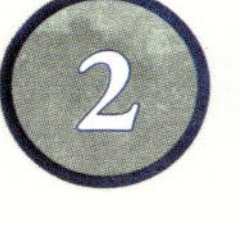

2 Transferring the sketch

Once the sketch is finished, I print it out as large as necessary for the size of the paper. In this case, I'm using a sheet of cold-press Saunders Waterford watercolor paper (9 × 12in), and a lightbox for tracing the sketch (Artograph LightPad).

This step is straightforward, but over the years I've introduced a subtle workflow tweak. My first instinct is always to go into a detailed sketch immediately, but a more efficient technique is to start with a very light, rough outline that places all the elements on paper as quickly as possible. Then, do a detailed pass after turning the lightbox off. It may seem like a regression from the digital sketch at first glance, but I see it as a chance to improve upon it.

Notice that the focus is mostly on large shapes – this creates a very solid base to add details to.

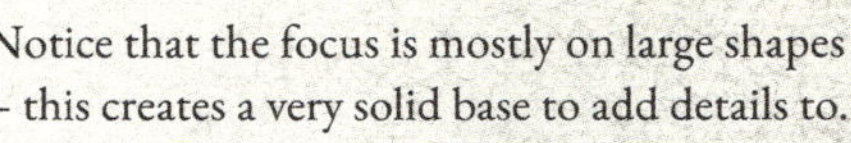

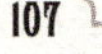

3 Finalizing the sketch

After turning off the lightbox, I reference the printed sketch on the side while finalizing my transferred sketch with a second pass. I take this opportunity to correct any shapes and add firm placement for small details and ornamental elements. The final sketch ends up being much cleaner and neater than the digital version, although the digital version served its purpose in initially helping me visualize the final product.

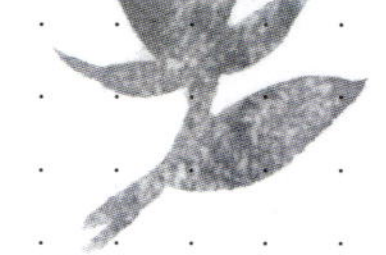

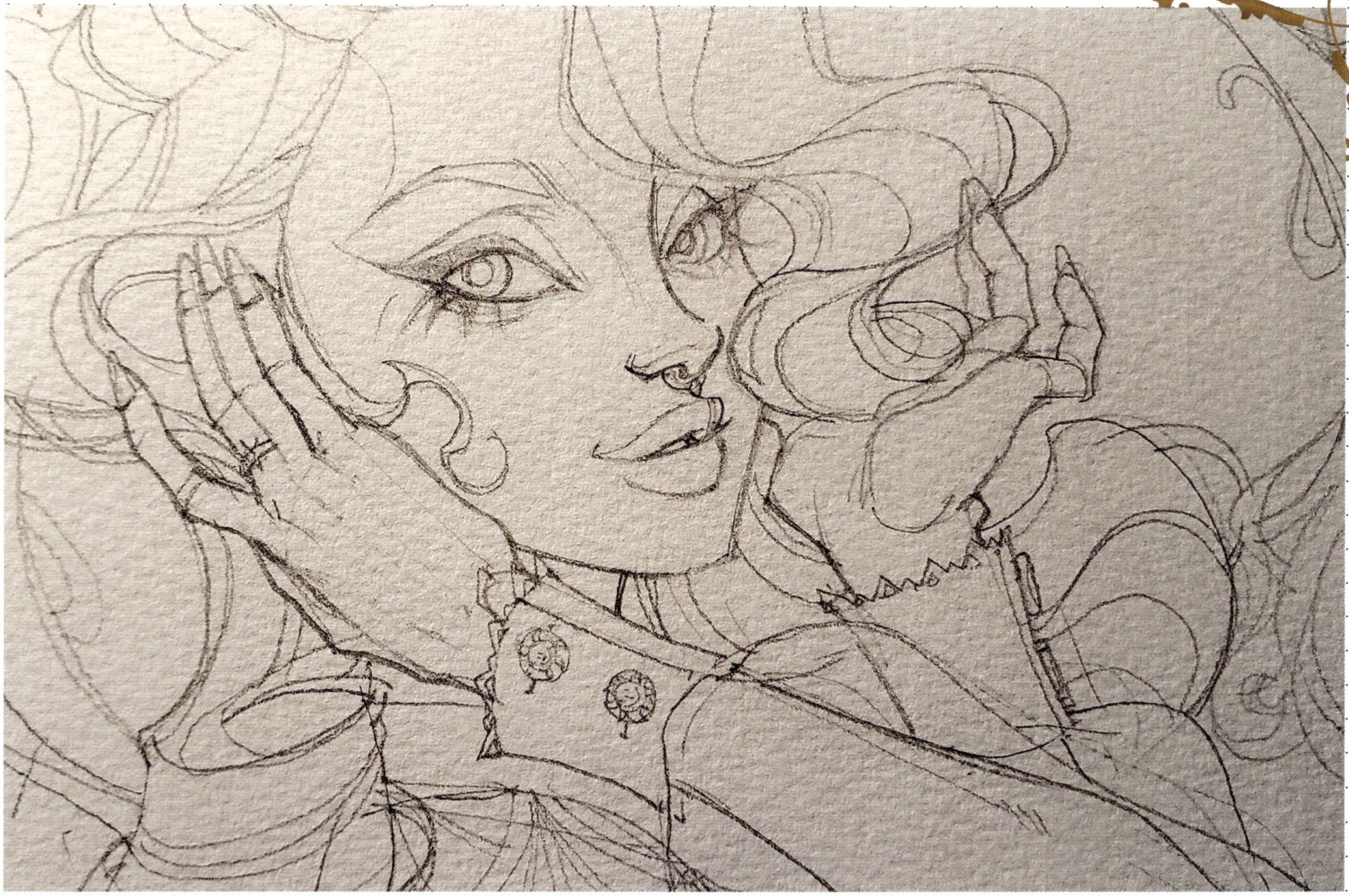

I keep the sketch as clean as possible to make the inking process faster.

Preparing the line-art ink

When the sketch is complete, I go back to the reference board and decide on a final color scheme, or at least pick a more specific direction. I say this because I often end up with something very different from what I set out to do, so never really land on a "final" scheme until the piece is finished. It comes together organically and I take a more spontaneous decision-making approach, which I enjoy.

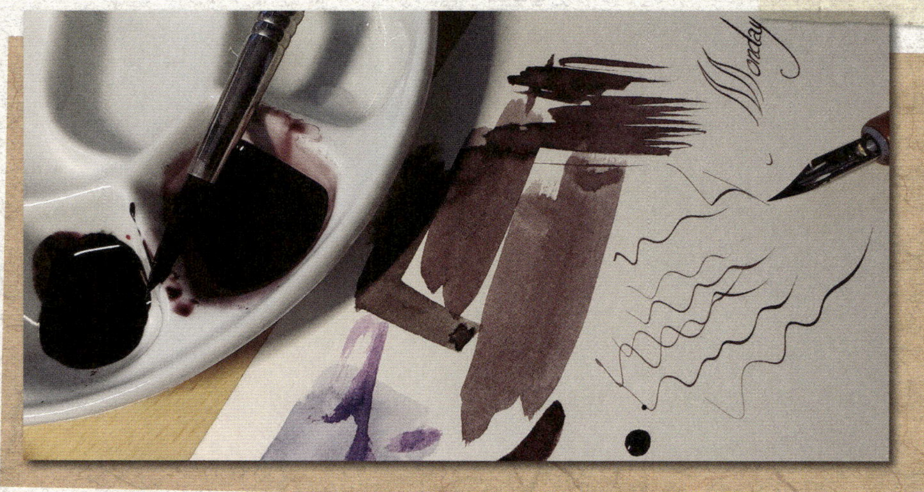

I used to have a lot of incidents in which my brush rolled away or made a mess when I kept it on the palette like this. I now have a brush rest (shown in Traditional Process), which is incredibly helpful for avoiding this kind of accident.

The important step here is to pick an appropriate tint for the line work and dilute a good amount of ink in my porcelain palette. This requires quite a bit of testing, which I do on paper similar to the type I use for the final illustration. I mix my go-to Rohrer & Klingner black ink with some red. Then, in a separate palette, take some of this mix and add a fair amount of water to it – sometimes I premix another even more diluted ink right away, creating a total of three tones. I don't have a specific mixing ratio and rely on eyeballing the amounts while testing frequently, and use the middle tone for the line work. Here, the mixture of black and cool red ink provides a harmonious undertone for my character's darker skin and the purple-blue background.

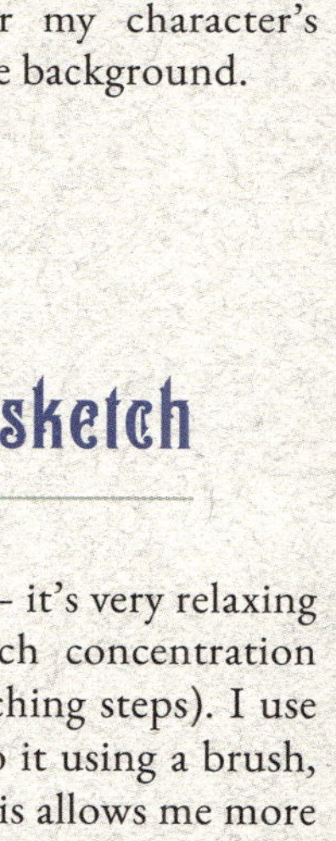

Inking the sketch

The inking step is my favorite – it's very relaxing and doesn't require too much concentration (unlike the planning and sketching steps). I use a nib, and prefer adding ink to it using a brush, instead of dipping the pen. This allows me more control over the amount of ink I add, and less chance of accidental drops. But unfortunately, this is bound to happen at least once during almost every single one of my ink illustrations, due to my lack of patience!

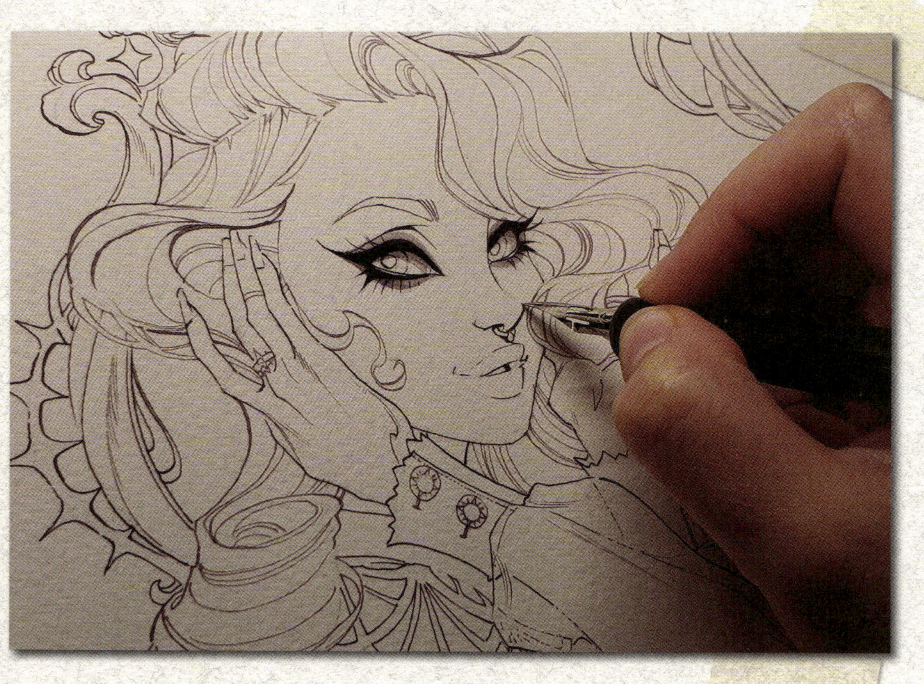

My favorite inking tool is a G-nib – its flexible nib and smooth flow allow for a wide range of line weights.

6 Tonal pass

Once the line work is clean and complete, I do a tonal pass. I migrated this step from my digital painting process. In my traditional process, I like this step for a few reasons. It allows me to establish the light/shadow scenario straight away, in one step. This in turn gives me a better idea of the tonal composition of the final image, and influences my color-picking decisions to some degree. It's easier for me to make decisions based on tones and not colors, which is probably why I do the tonal pass first.

I switch to a medium-sized brush (or a small brush if it's detail work), and use pre-mixed diluted inks to slowly add shadows. If necessary, I add more water to soften edges. A darker tonal pass with ink can get muddy if you're not careful, so I do this sparingly, knowing that I can go back in later and add darker tones if necessary. For that reason I don't add shadows to the border at this time.

The two-towel rule

I always keep two paper towels in close proximity! One is for wiping away excess ink or water from brushes and nibs. The other – the absolute lifesaver – is to dab away ink or water from the image if an accident occurs (which happens all the time). I keep the two towels separate because the brush-cleaning paper towel typically gets wet and dirty very quickly, so it's important to have a clean one handy for emergencies.

Notice that in addition to the tonal pass, I also fill in the darkest areas with a brush (cuffs, eyelashes, and eyeliner). I use the undiluted tinted ink color for this.

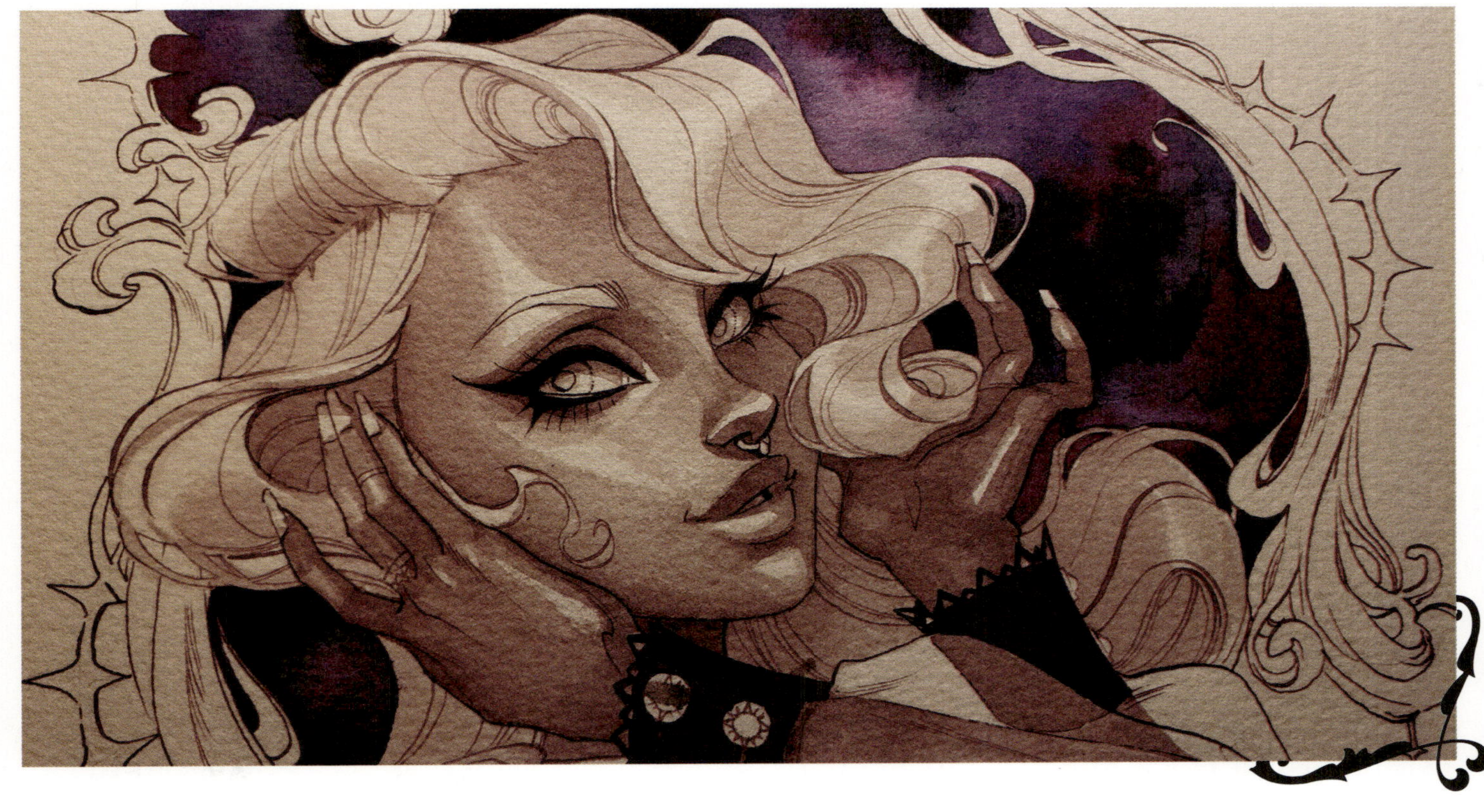

7 Local colors

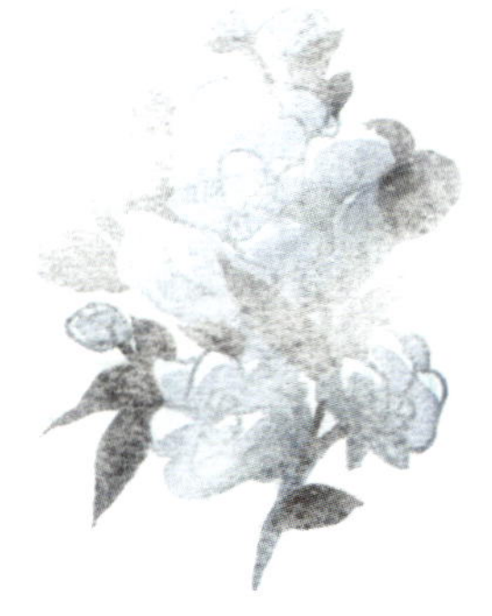

To me, adding local color is the most stressful step because I use colored ink, which is permanent when dry. With no chance of lifting it or making changes, I have to be careful. I put in the purple-blue background first – it will contrast nicely with the white hair, and is the only color pick I'm sure of at this stage. I use a wet-on-wet technique for the background which helps create the galaxy sky effect and shows the ink's beautiful natural property. This effect is difficult to replicate digitally in an organic way.

Next, I tackle Sweet's skin tone. I carefully fill sections of her face to get the smoothest flat tone, which I have difficulty with on darker skin. Thankfully it turned out well, and I choose a bright blue for her blouse to contrast with the rest of the image. The end of this step can look underwhelming; it's important to remind myself that a lot can be done in the next step. Even if I'm not happy with the piece straight after the local colors have been established, I need to just keep trucking!

For the final local color, I fill the frame with a vibrant warm yellow, which is a better choice than the more muted copper I was picturing initially.

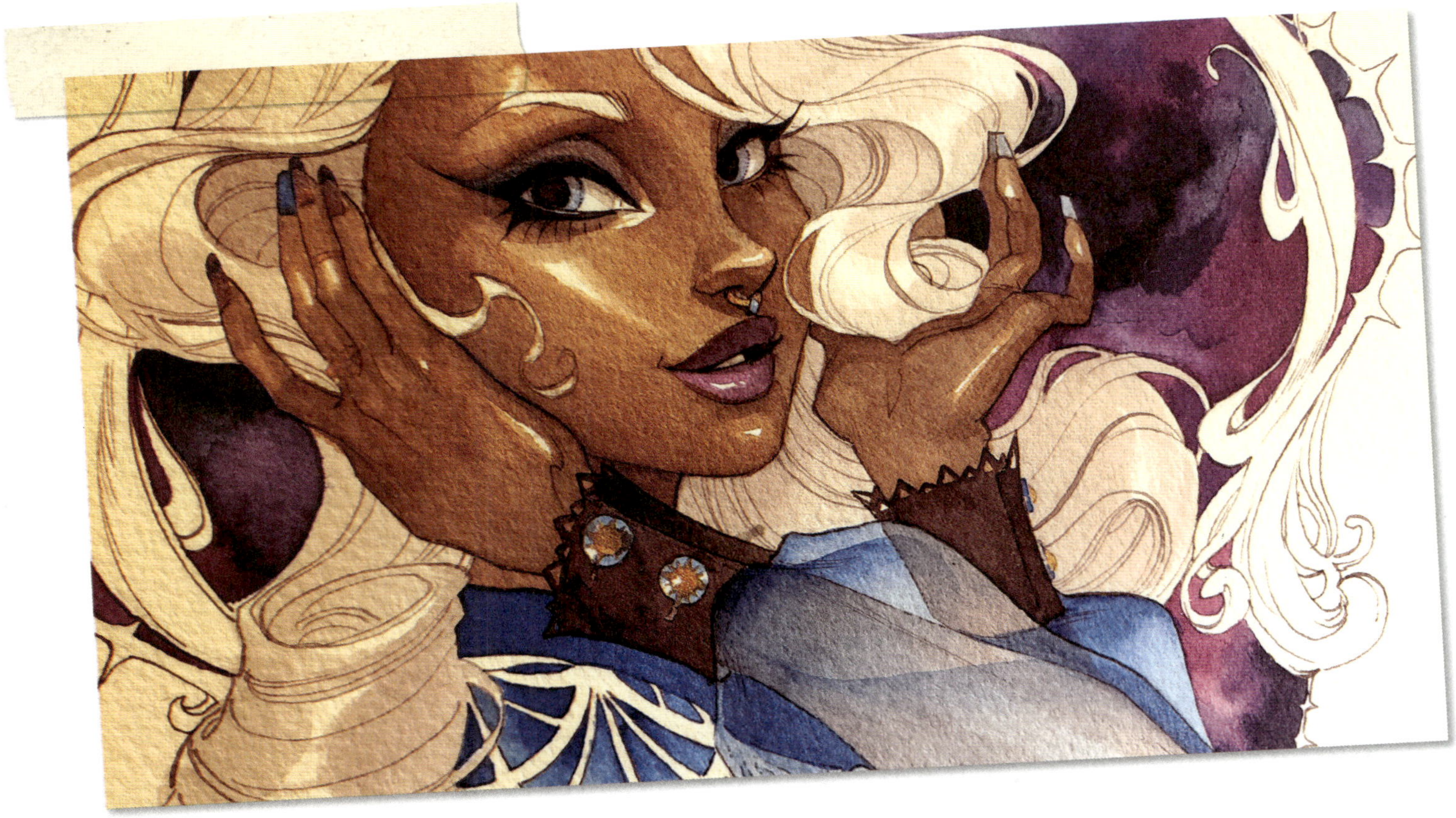

8 Colored pencil details

The most satisfying step of this workflow! I use a big set of Faber-Castell Polychromos colored pencils to pull the image together and add a texture. I typically pick colors that are slightly darker than the darkest parts of each local color area, and slowly enhance the shadows by making parallel strokes in one direction. It's a bit tough for me to ensure all the strokes adhere to that single direction, but I really love the effect it creates and thus take care to pause here and there to make sure they're lining up properly. I keep going darker and darker with the colors until I achieve a level of contrast and form that I'm satisfied with. I also decide to add thick color outlines to the two elements – the border, and the character within.

I also use an opaque silver ink to add the stars and constellations to the galaxy background.

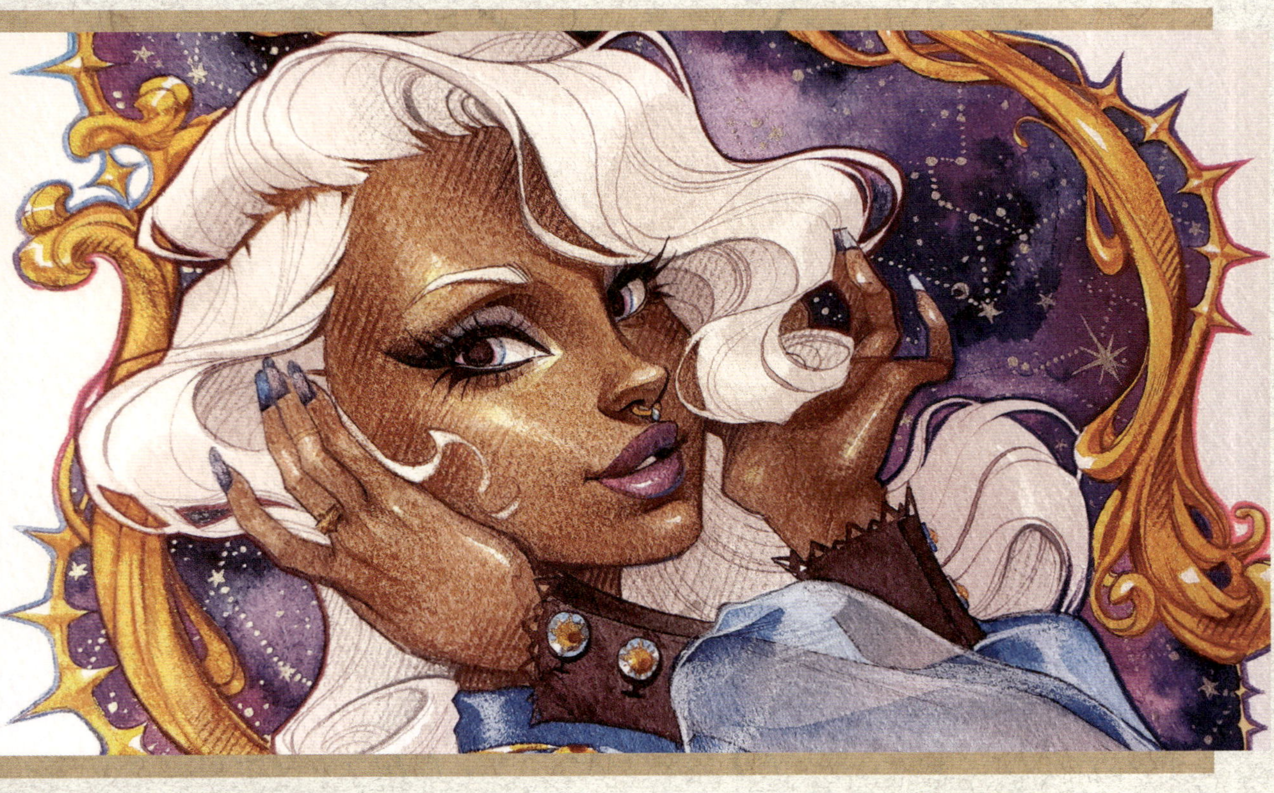

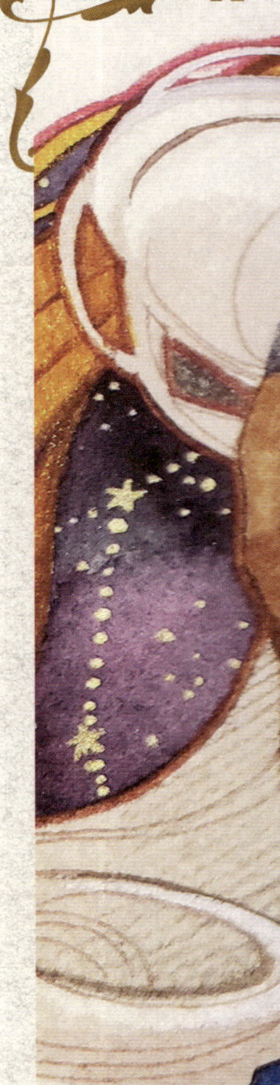

9 Finalizing with mixed media

Although the colored pencils do a lot to pull the image together, sometimes just a little more is needed at the end. I used to move straight to scanning, adding whatever I felt was missing in Photoshop, but in recent years I've decided to put more effort into finalizing my traditional pieces as far as possible before scanning them in. Relying less on digital aid increases the value of the original work. I use white and black acrylic gouache to add eye highlights, small hair strands, and darken Sweet's eyelashes and eyeliner. This may *seem* trivial, but it makes a huge difference. After I add these small finishing touches with opaque paint, I'm so happy with the result that I don't feel the need to fix or add anything digitally. This is a rare occurrence for me, so I think the years of practice and experimentation are finally starting to pay off.

I add gold sparkles to her cheeks using Kuretake Gold Mica calligraphy ink.

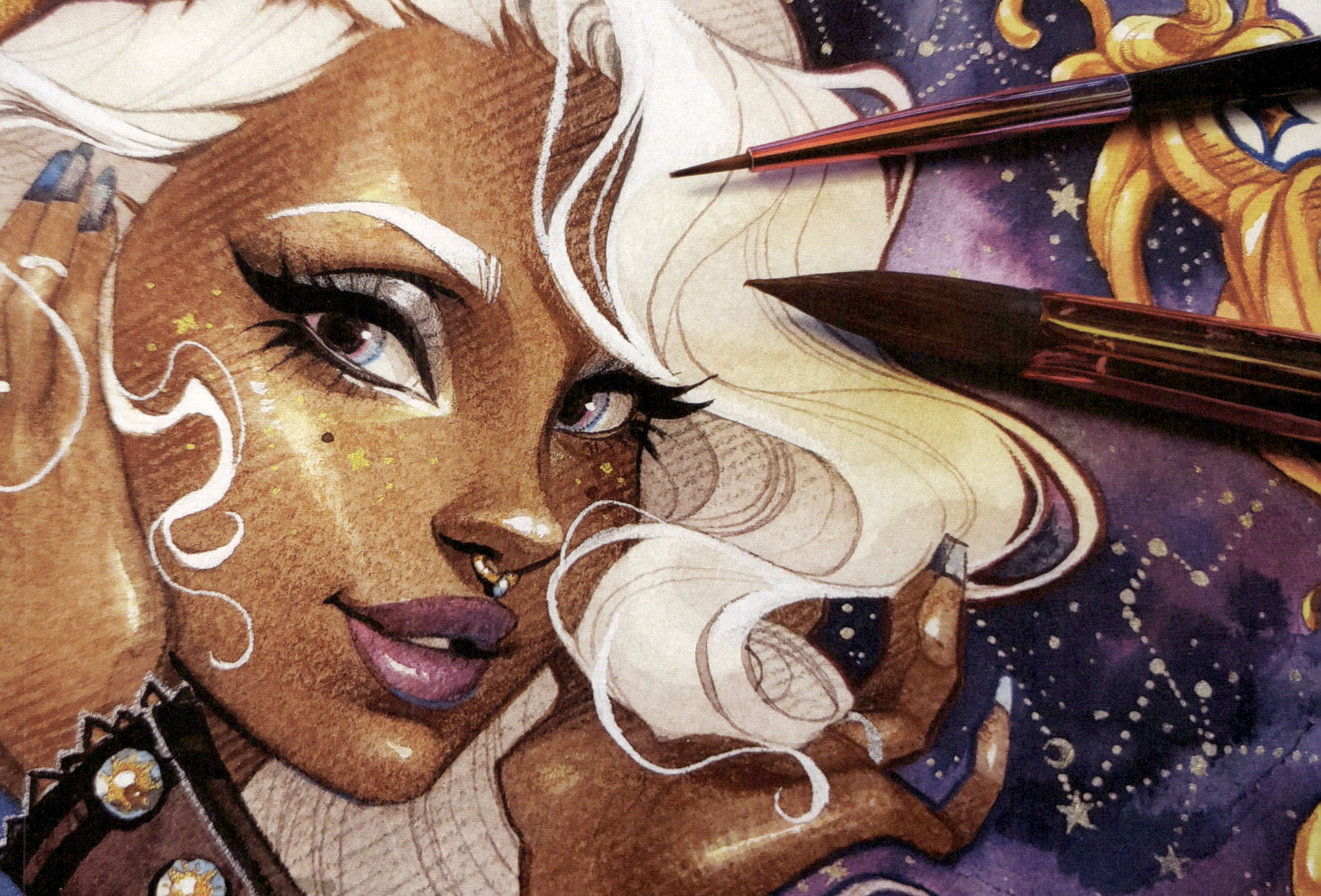

10 Digital cleanup

This step is often overlooked, but I wanted to include it. To make prints, the artwork needs to be scanned and cleaned up. I scan the image at 600dpi, sometimes in two parts, then use Photomerge in Photoshop CC to stitch the image back together (this tool is a lifesaver!). Then I adjust the levels, bumping up the darks and lights, so that the image looks cleaner and more crisp. This brings the image back to life, but be careful not to overexpose it with the highlights. Finally, I adjust the color balance slightly, usually adding a bit of red to the mid-tones, and sometimes tweaking the highlights and shadows. Here, I bump up the yellows in the highlights. After this basic editing, I paint over certain details for cleanup if necessary, but do this sparingly to keep the initial image as close to the original artwork as possible.

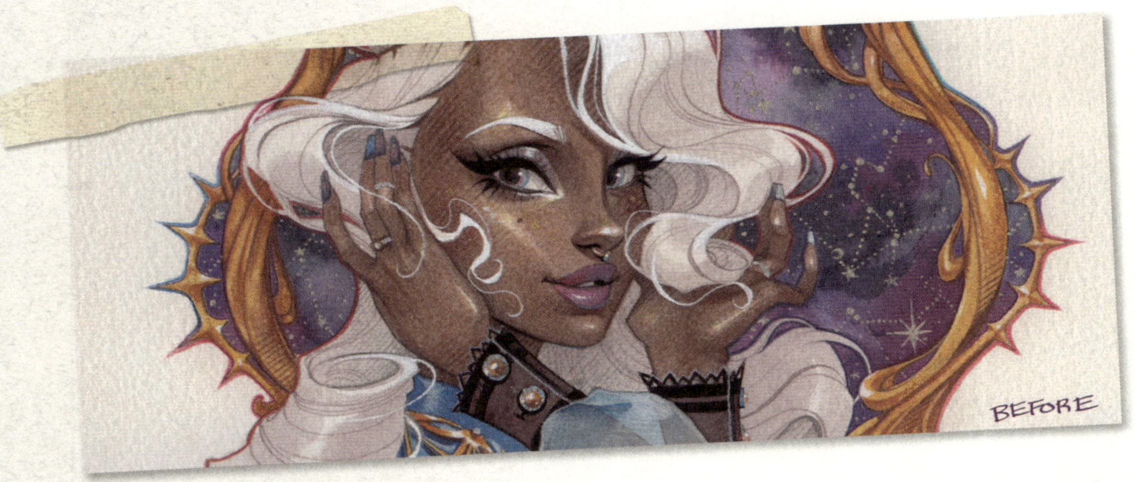

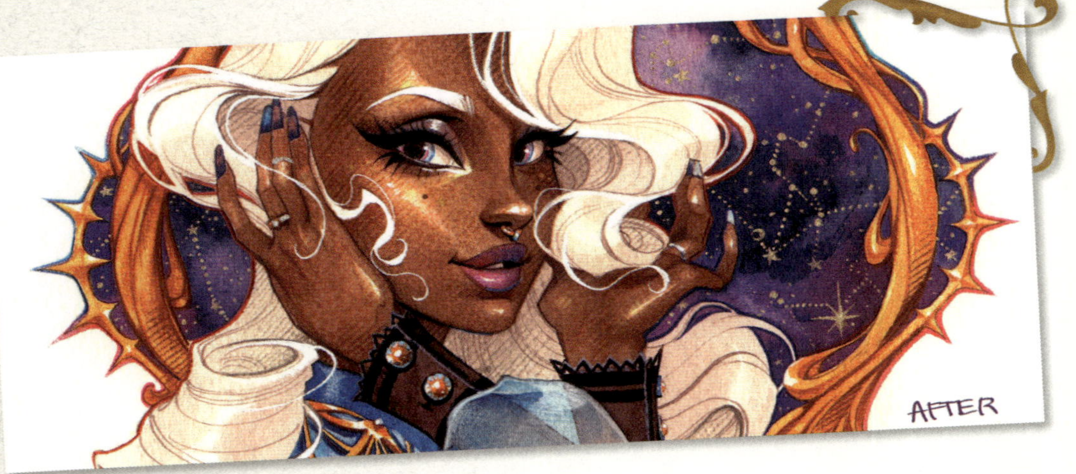

This image is actually incredibly neat compared to a lot of my other work, and I end up only spending two minutes drawing over a couple of hairs. Drawing larger really pays off!

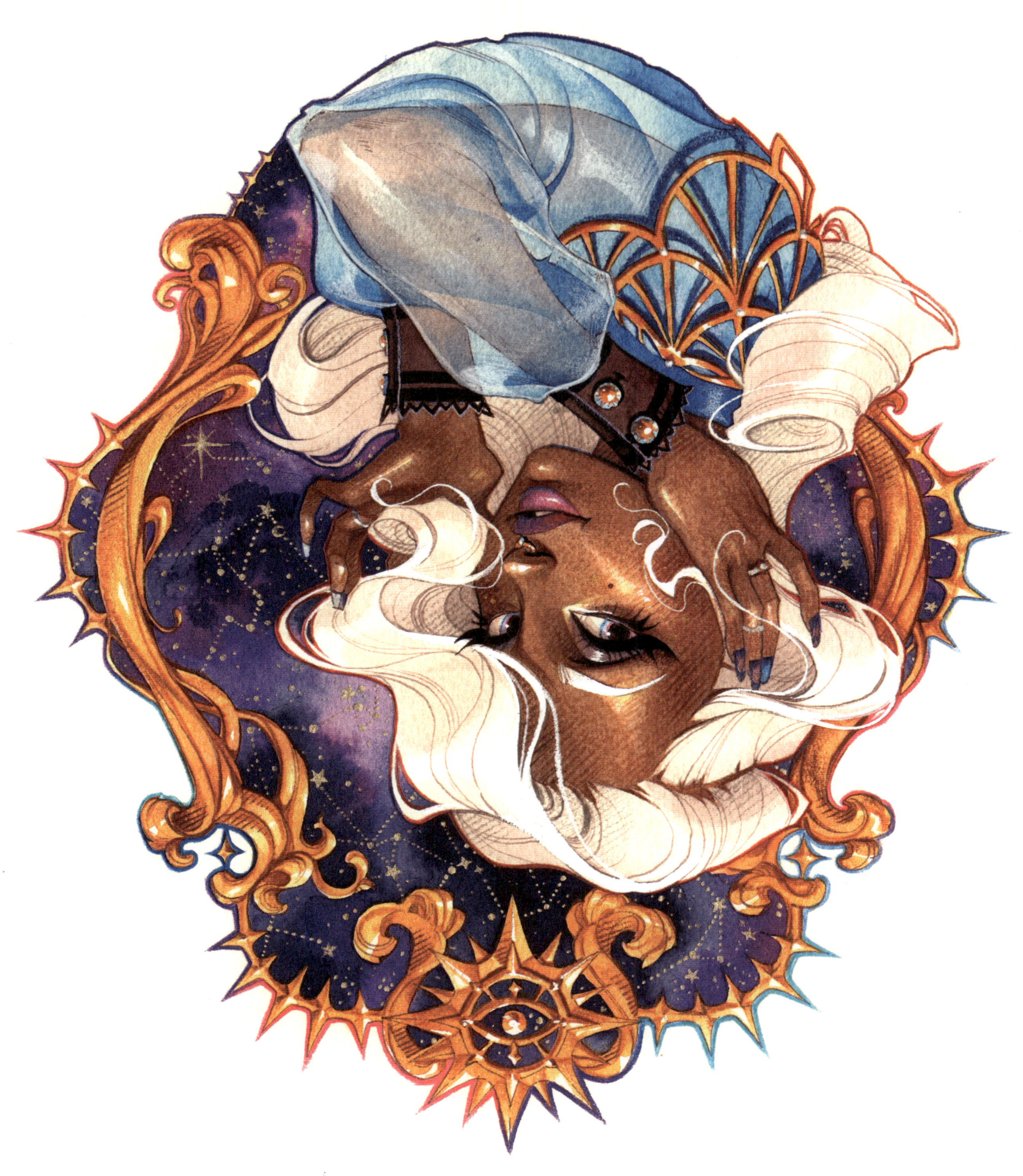

COMPOSING

the cover artwork

I thought it would be interesting to share the cover-creation process for this book! For weeks, I was mulling over ideas, trying to come up with something meaningful that would get me excited to work on the cover, and eventually arrived at this. Although there is a very specific narrative context for this image, I don't think it matters at all – there's so much room for personal interpretation.

This is one of the biggest and more time-consuming pieces I've had the pleasure to work on in several years. For it, I chose my favorite mediums: a mix of colored inks and Faber-Castell Polychromos colored pencils on cold-press watercolor paper. I wanted to create an image that has a vintage storybook feel: something timeless and cozy, like a favorite dark fairy-tale book you want to keep under your pillow.

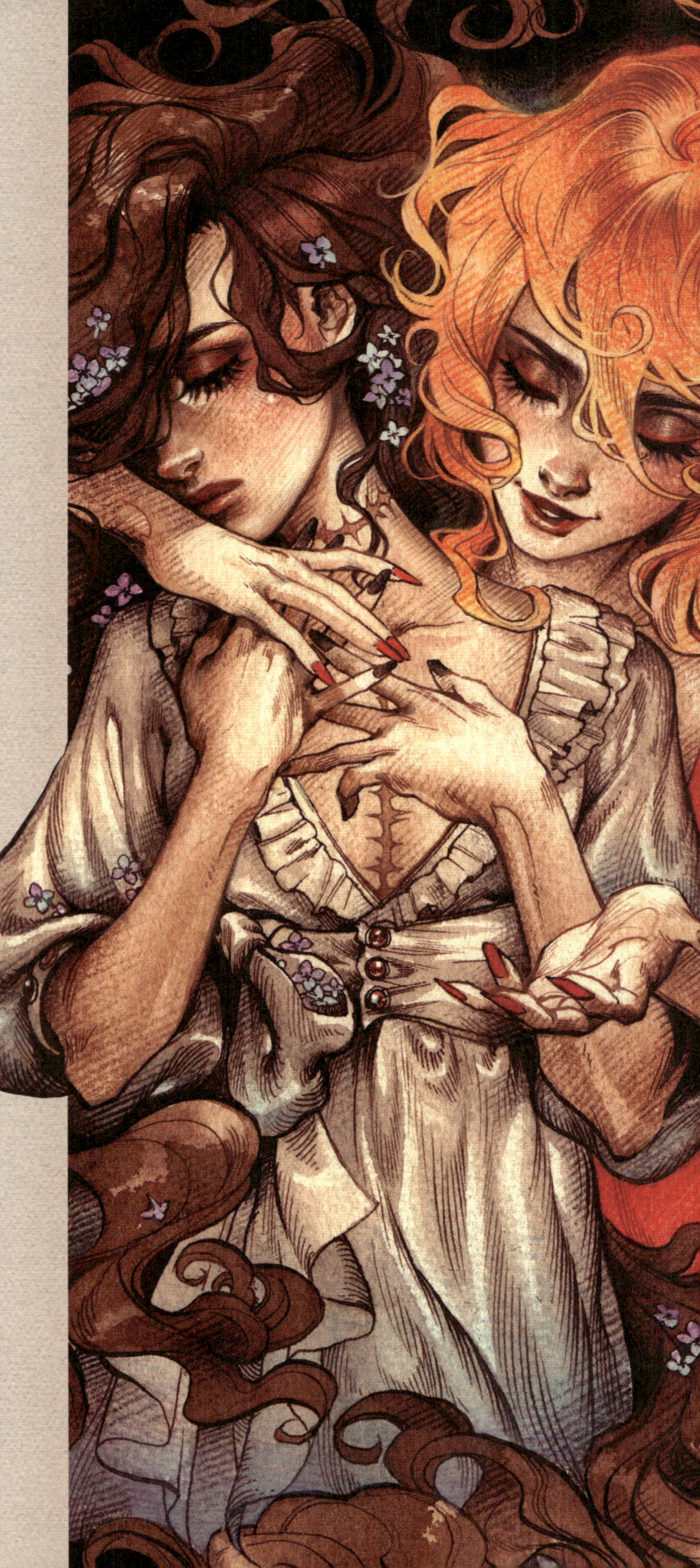

1 How I approach brainstorming

I always have the best luck coming up with ideas in transit, especially public transport, like a long bus or train ride. Typically, I'll be listening to favorite familiar music that strongly corresponds with the baseline mood of my artwork. Often, I don't even make a sketch or thumbnail during the initial brainstorming stage, but instead describe the image briefly in my phone notes. When I have a good idea of what I need to draw, I feel ready to make a very simple thumbnail sketch to figure out the general composition. I don't tend to worry about the quality of the sketch.

Despite the primitive nature of the thumbnail sketch, it is actually a perfectly accurate representation of the finished drawing!

If it doesn't feel authentic – toss it

At one point, the cover featured a close-up character portrait because I felt like a ton of artbooks I love have that in common. I created thumbnails trying to flesh this out, but in the end couldn't get excited about it. Because I really love expressing something through character interactions, I decided to go with that instead.

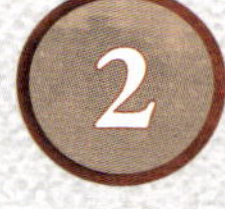

2 Digital rough sketch and mock-up

I choose to make a digital sketch to have as much freedom as possible when trying different versions of framing, lighting, cropping, and so on, before moving on to the final composition. In the initial rough sketch, I include a very rough treatment for the title as well, deciding what kind of finish I might want for it. This leads me to exclude the central prism element from the actual painting, since I want it to be some sort of foil stamp. I also want the cover to be quarter-bound, which will include a vertical strip of fabric-like material down the left-hand edge of the front cover, hence the red placeholder border. It's important to think about these things as early as possible in the process.

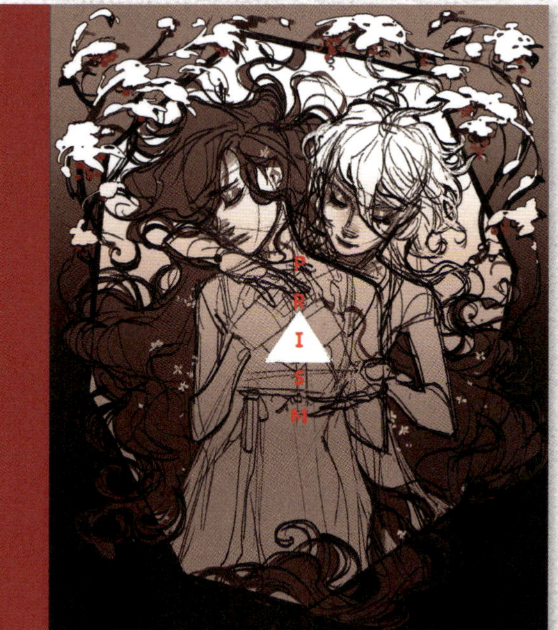

The sketch isn't particularly detailed and the hands are barely resolved. I consider it a waste of time to be more precise at this stage of the process – only the placement, flow, and composition are crucial.

3 Iterations and composition tweaks

After discussion and helpful suggestions, I try a more intimate, closer crop of the characters (i). I make a couple of small tweaks and iterations, and end up changing HaeJin's (the dark-haired character) attire in order to serve the composition better (ii). I also do a quick and simple color pass on Kima's hair, seeing how it would roughly look with its usual orange glow, and like the result (iii). The decision to include her on this cover is very meaningful to me; HaeJin has been alone on the cover of my two previous art books, and the addition of Kima and their interaction holds great personal significance.

i

ii

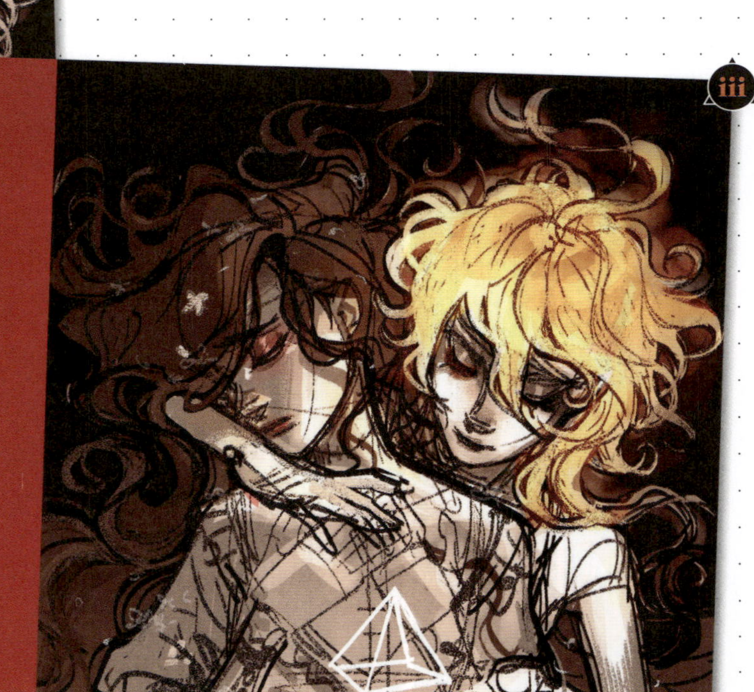

I don't want the lighting in this piece to be too dramatic, so I end up toning it down quite a bit in the final piece.

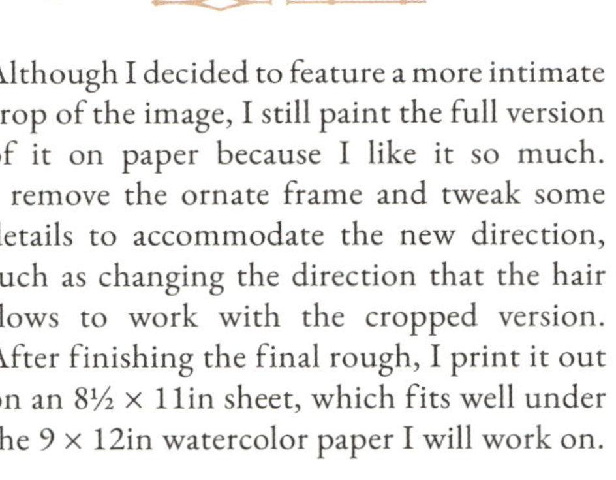

4 Final rough

Although I decided to feature a more intimate crop of the image, I still paint the full version of it on paper because I like it so much. I remove the ornate frame and tweak some details to accommodate the new direction, such as changing the direction that the hair flows to work with the cropped version. After finishing the final rough, I print it out on an 8½ × 11in sheet, which fits well under the 9 × 12in watercolor paper I will work on.

So far, 9 × 12in is the largest paper size I typically work with; perhaps one day soon I'll try something bigger!

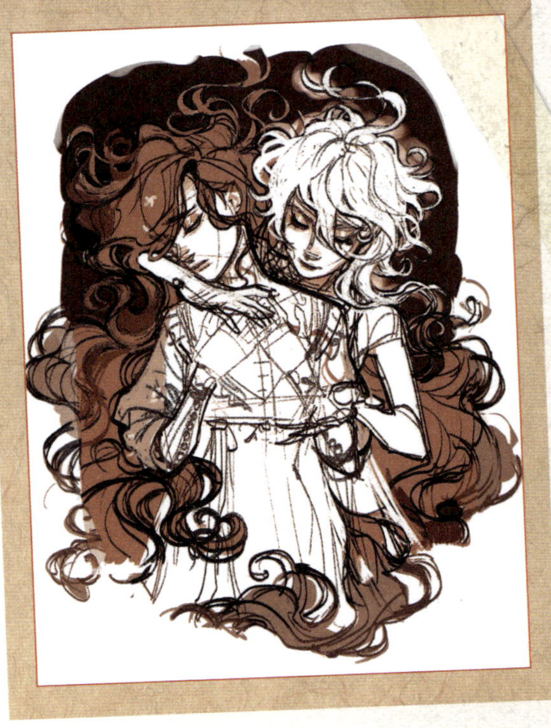

5 Transferring the sketch onto paper

As usual, I use my Artograph lightbox for this step – I lightly trace over the entire sketch to ensure the correct placement of all the objects, correcting some curves here and there. I like to get this step over with as quickly as possible and not get bogged down trying to replicate the sketch underneath exactly. In addition, the quick transfer means that I can do a more detailed pass afterwards without the glaring light in my eyes.

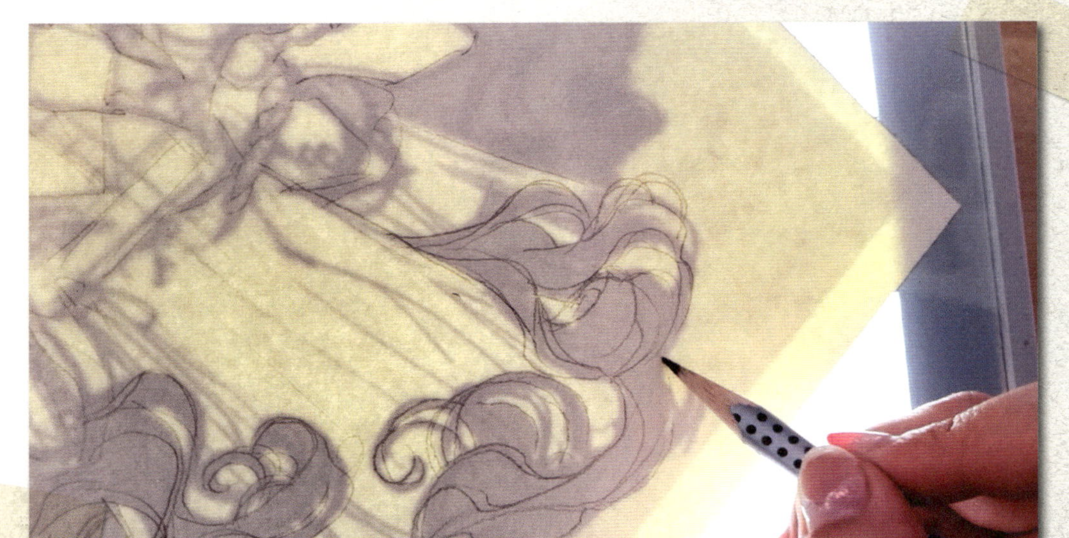

Thankfully the thickness of this particular watercolor paper (Saunders Waterford cold-press, 140lb) still allows me to see the printout underneath quite well.

Clean sketch and references

With the quick sketch now transferred, I go over it again with more focus and precision. I use photo references of my own hands to capture the exact gestures I am aiming for with a bit more subtlety. I typically don't put much more work into hair as it's something quite organic and I prefer to add detail in the inking stage. But for everything else, such as the faces, hands, and clothing folds, I like to elaborate the sketch as much as possible to get a solid and precise base for the inking. This step of the process can be relatively time consuming, especially if I use references as I do here. However it's really worthwhile to put in the due diligence at this point and not leave much up to chance when it comes to the next steps – ink is permanent and making corrections can be tricky.

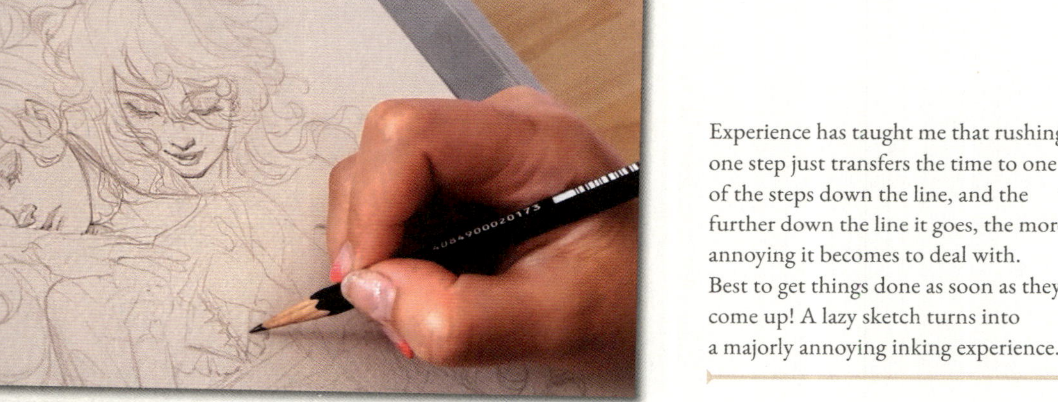

Experience has taught me that rushing one step just transfers the time to one of the steps down the line, and the further down the line it goes, the more annoying it becomes to deal with. Best to get things done as soon as they come up! A lazy sketch turns into a majorly annoying inking experience.

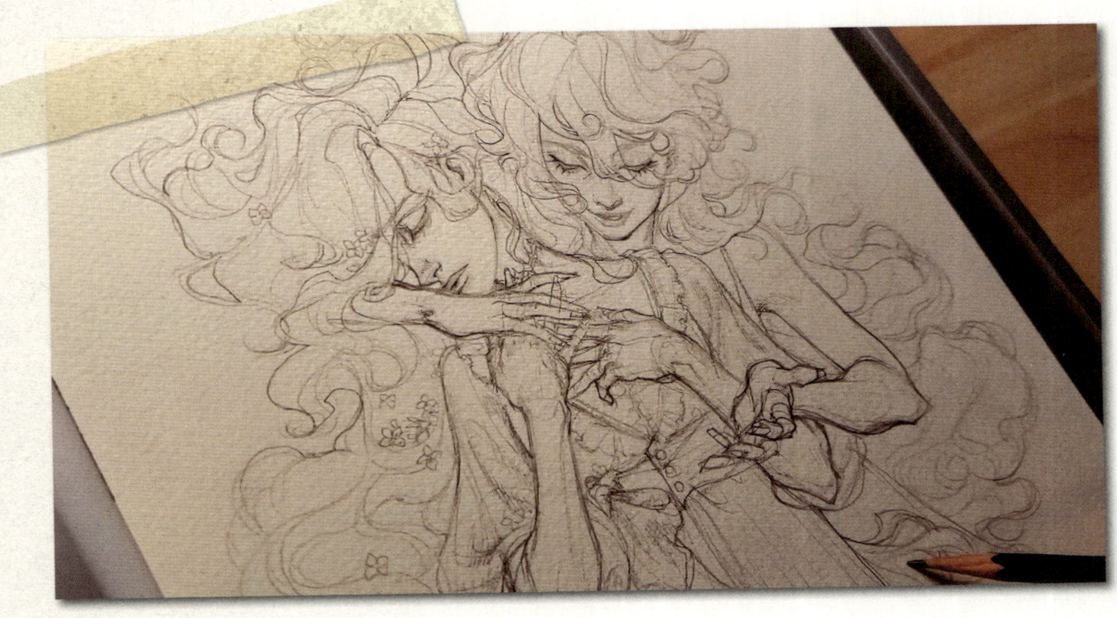

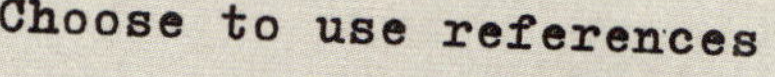

Choose to use references

With pieces like this – characters with no background – I rarely use references (maybe due to laziness). But here, I want to capture something delicate and more refined than my typical depiction of hands. The hands in this piece communicate a lot. I take photos of my own hands in the positions I want to capture. They help me to create the desired subtle specificity. Taking quick reference photos to aid a specific need is very useful!

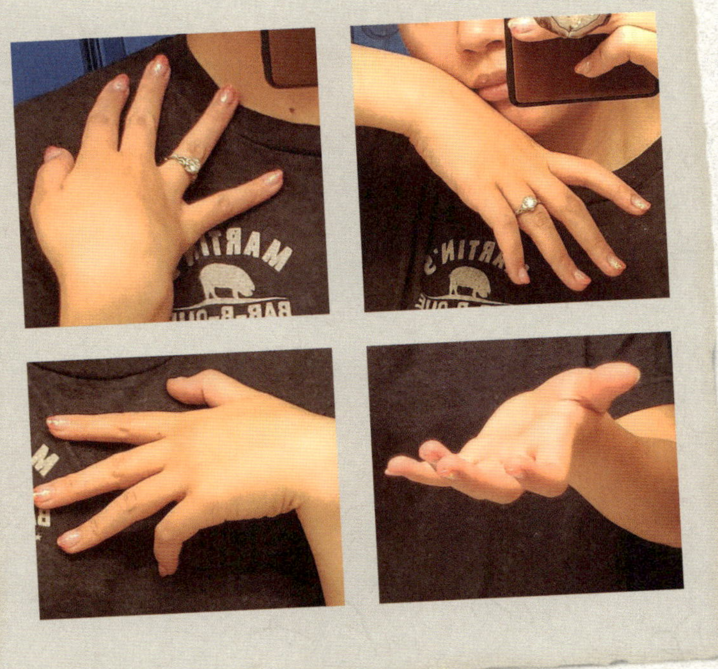

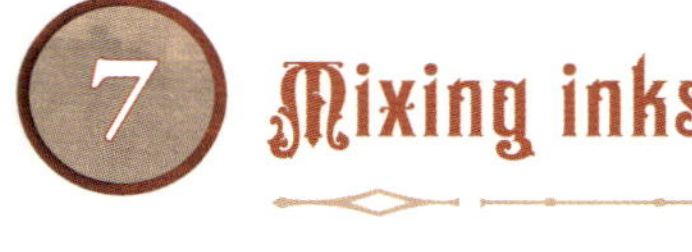

7 Mixing inks

Once the sketch is resolved and ready, but before inking, I sometimes clean it up a bit with a kneadable eraser before moving on to the inking stage. I always take time to mix the inks before jumping in, doing various tests on a separate piece of paper to make sure I have what I need and won't have to remix any mid-process. In this case, I want to get a bleeding effect with the line work, and this can sometimes be captured by mixing two different types of inks together. I don't know how acceptable this practice is among other artists, but I like to experiment with mixing inks all the time. I add a small amount of Writing Desk by Ferris Wheel Press into Rohrer & Klingner's Sepia or Umbra, typically used to get a vintage effect. The Ferris Wheel Press ink is easily revived with water and isn't permanent, so I figure it will bleed a bit once I move on to execute the next steps of the painting.

In the end, the bleeding effect doesn't come through very noticeably at all, either because I didn't add enough of the bleeding ink, or perhaps it just blended too seamlessly into the other layers of diluted ink – who knows! Experimentation is great, but doesn't always pan out the way you intend, which is just another part of the process.

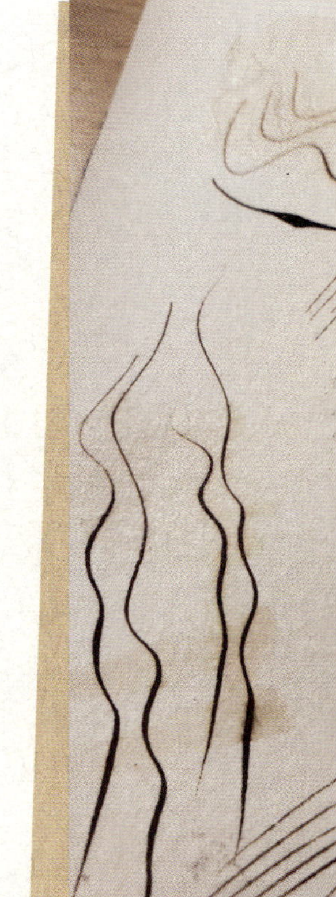

The effect seemed to show through on my test page, but for whatever reason it just isn't the same in the final execution.

8 Clean and detailed line work

This step is relatively straightforward and like my typical process. However, I decide to go much heavier on the line art and add a lot more directional and form hatching than is typical for me (i). This technique will capture that antiquated and vintage feel, reminiscent of Arthur Rackham's fairy-tale illustrations and Victorian ink illustrations. My favorite inking tool (a G-nib) is absolutely perfect for this stylistic approach (ii). Being very flexible, it makes beautiful lines that vary in thickness – you can see this effect in the hatching of the dress (iii).

Keeping mixed ink from drying

Sometimes it's tough to finish a piece in one day, and it has to be left overnight. Often, my ink would dry up and I'd have to remix it again the next day. A simple solution is simply to cover the palette with cling film – this has saved me a lot of trouble!

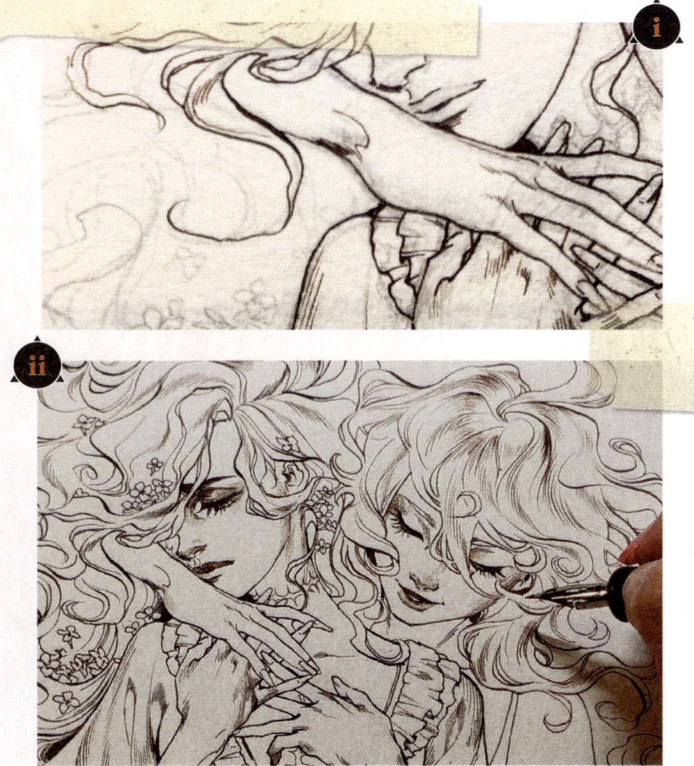

In retrospect, I think I would have liked the ink to be less saturated and more diluted like in most of my other illustrations. I think trying to achieve the bleeding-lines effect threw me off slightly, but at the end of the day I'm still happy with the result.

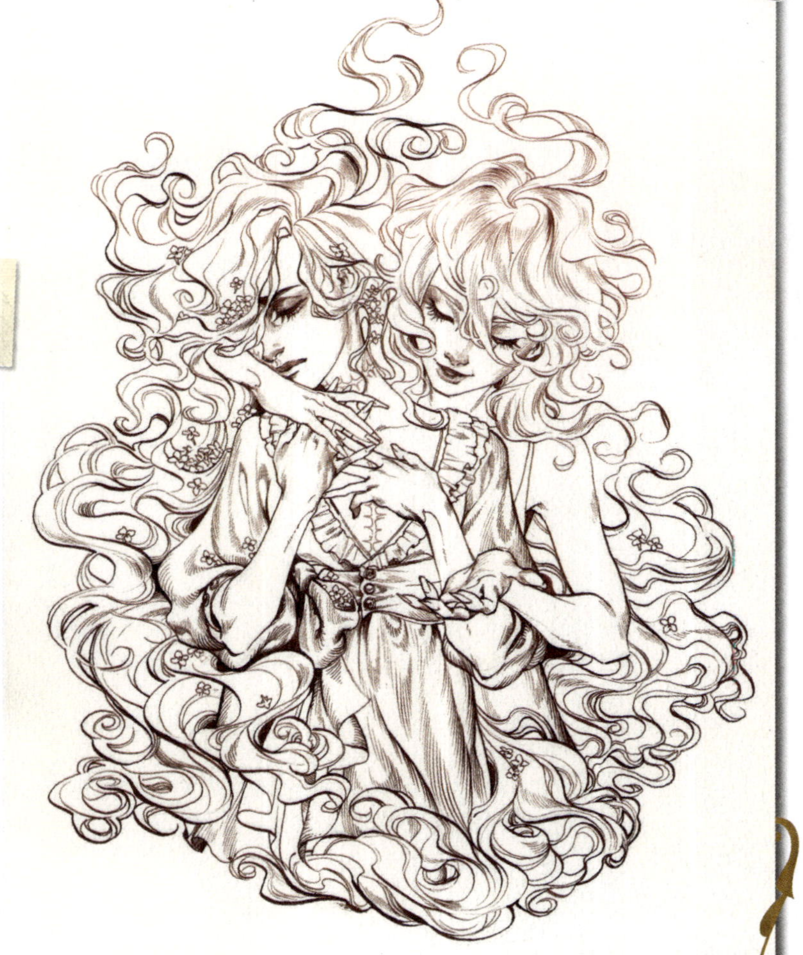

9 Background inkwash

After the line work is done, I usually take a second to decide what the next best step would be – in this case, it's tackling the background ink wash. I carefully outline the silhouette of the characters and fill in all the little gaps using a small brush and the darkest ink I have. Simultaneously, I use a wet-on-wet technique with a much larger brush to fan the darkness out toward the edges of the paper and introduce browns into the mix to create visual interest.

I do this step first because it creates a clean silhouette, making it easier to see the borders of certain visual elements (such as the hair). It also lets me fill the elements that border with the dark background a lot faster, since I don't have to be meticulous about staying within lines. Even if I go outside the edges, no ink will show on top of the black background.

I don't typically choose a flat black background – I see it as a missed opportunity to show the beauty of ink, so use the wet-on-wet technique to create texture.

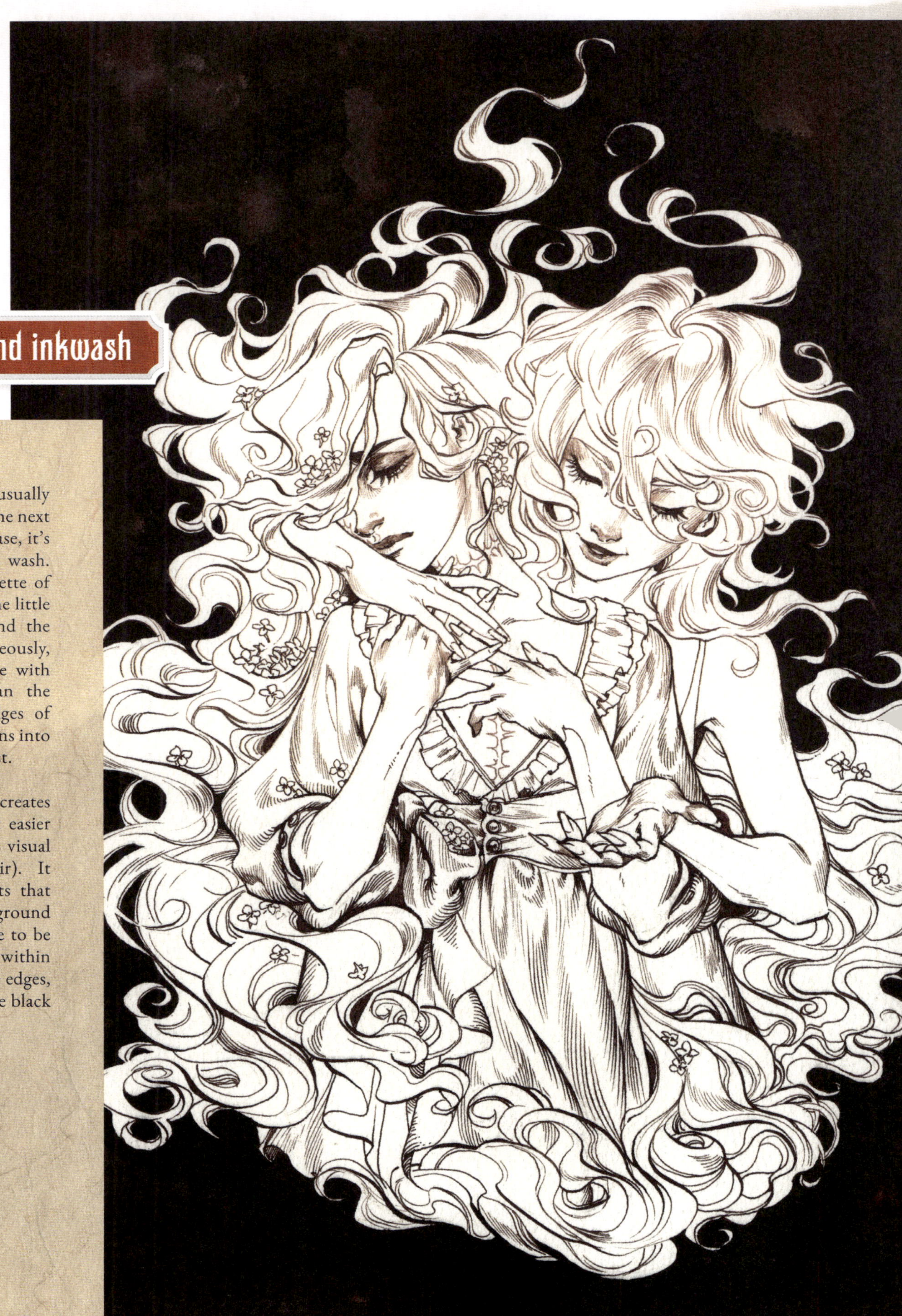

10 Painting in the local colors

When painting the local colors of each element, such as the hair, skin, and dress, I slightly vary my approach. For hair, I frequently like to use wet-on-wet and create as much texture as I can for the base layer of colors. I can elaborate on the tones afterward, and add shadows and details, but having an interesting and textured first layer can make a big difference in the end (i). I could have added a slightly different color and created a gradient to HaeJin's hair, but didn't think of that at the time. For the skin, I tend to be much more careful, starting with a very light wash, increasing the tonal intensity slowly, but keeping it light and simple. I don't have a particular color scheme in mind other than the vintage brown tone, and Kima's glowing orange hair. Once I finish with the basic elements, I decide that her dress should be red to reinforce the duality aspect of the drawing (ii).

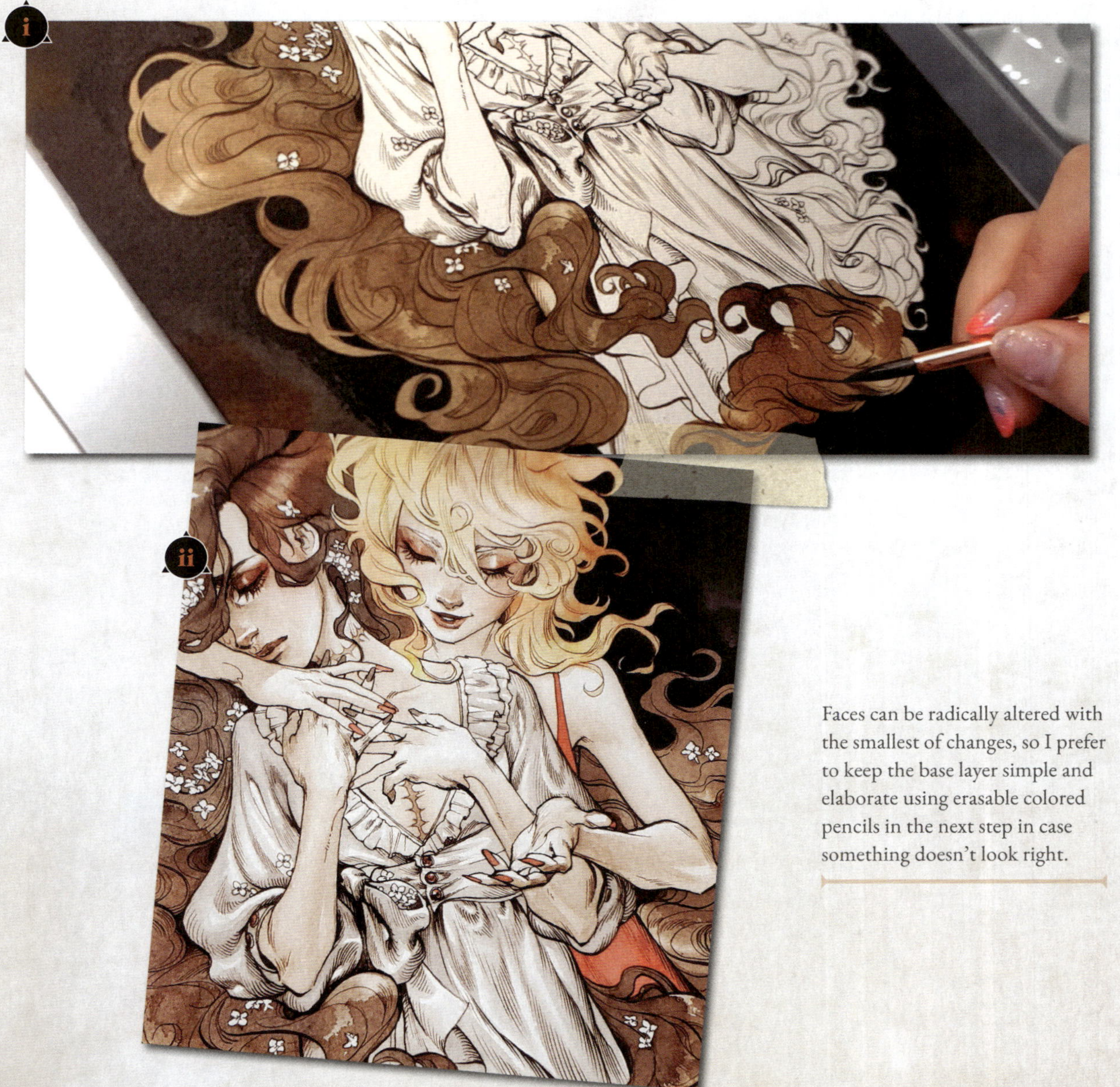

Faces can be radically altered with the smallest of changes, so I prefer to keep the base layer simple and elaborate using erasable colored pencils in the next step in case something doesn't look right.

Colored pencils: details and texture

This part of the process is very satisfying – colored pencils can make a huge difference to the piece in a relatively short amount of time. One of my current favorite techniques is using the pencils to add a single-direction hatch throughout the piece (i). This is something I've been doing for a couple of years now and I love the overall texture it creates. I typically start out by adding details to the hair, keeping them concentrated around the face. My natural habit is to spread details evenly all over, but I try to avoid this as much as I can – the result can be much more striking if the details are mostly concentrated around focal-point areas and the rest of the piece is left a bit more general. As you can probably see, this isn't something I'm very good at! It's a bit tough to have "looser" areas when my process is so strictly split into steps.

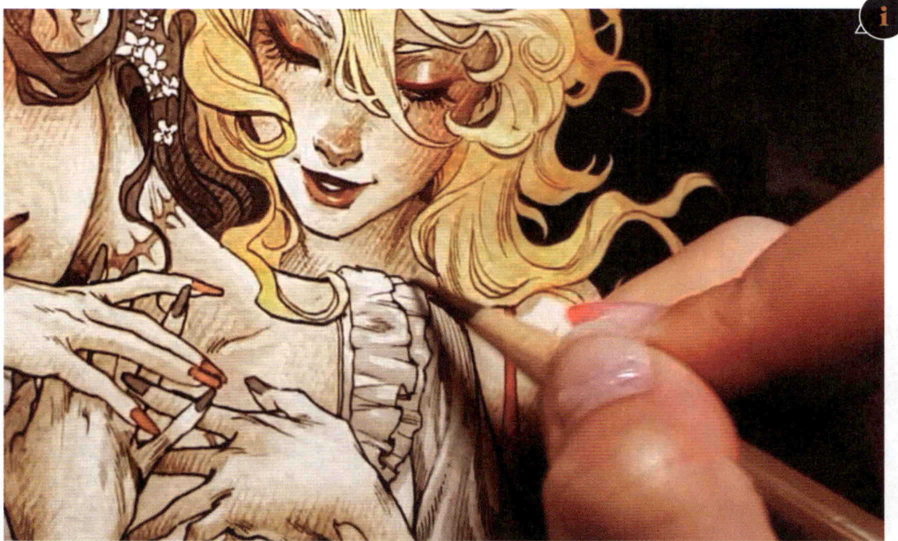

I spontaneously decide to add lilac and blue into HaeJin's dress, and flowers in her hair (ii). Originally, I was going to keep the flowers and dress white, but I thought introducing a cool color would be good. It also helps to harmonize the overall color scheme of the piece, because it was leaning a bit too heavily into the warm monochromatic color scheme of brown/orange and red.

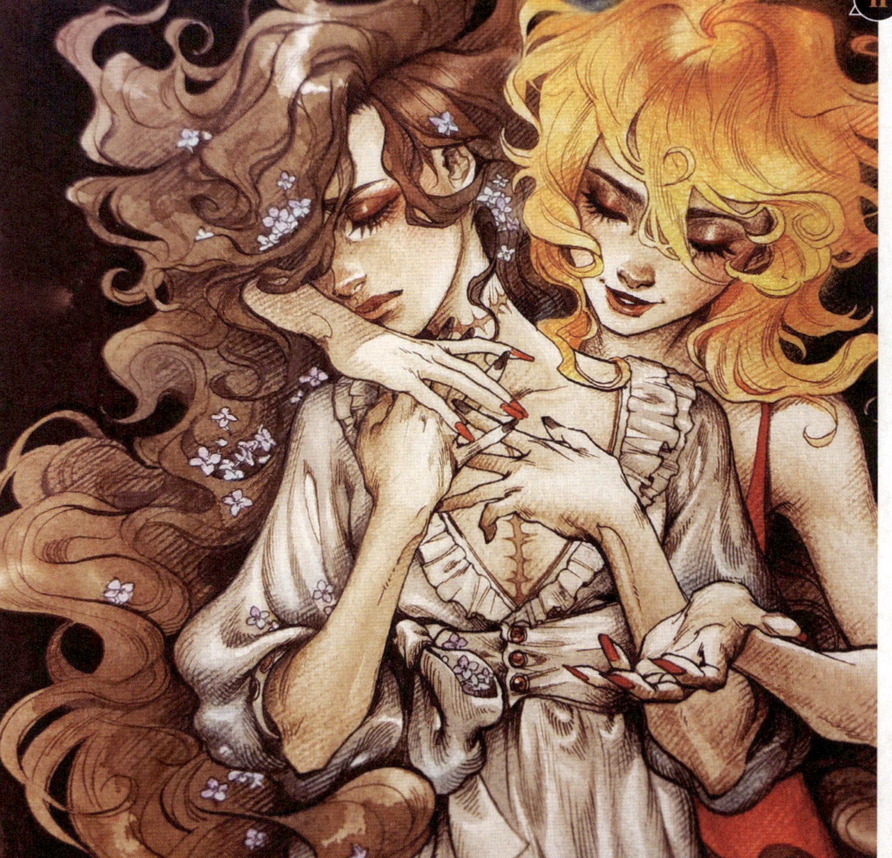

Sharpening the pencils frequently helps to keep the lines crisp and uniform.

Creating a soft glow and final touches

I chose to talk about this step separately from the previous one not only because it is the final step I take on paper, but also because I think the effect it achieves is so interesting. Here I take a bright orange pencil and start hatching little gradients, starting at the edges of Kima's hair and fanning out into the dark background. At some point while doing this, I decide that it might be interesting to introduce a rainbow glow where Kima's hair joins up with HaeJin's. This is a spontaneous decision, and a nice little touch to echo the "prism" concept. I always like to leave room for small spontaneous decisions, even when creating a thoroughly planned-out large piece like this. It keeps the process engaging and allows me to discover new things along the way.

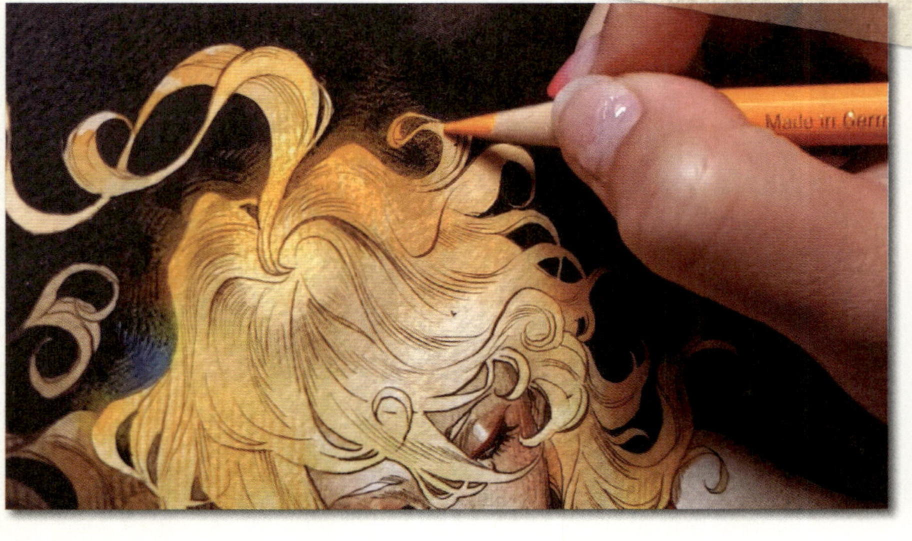

There are many ways to create a glowing effect with inks alone, but I think using a colored pencil allows for more control and vintage-looking results.

Scanning and cleanup in Photoshop

Once the image looks finished, I scan it using my little old CanoScan LiDE 35 scanner. The raw scan requires quite a few adjustments (including levels and color balance) in order to make it look alive again, but it also affords opportunities for tweaking the colors more to my liking. In this image, I put in a bit of extra work cleaning up the finer details digitally, such as the little lilac flowers in HaeJin's hair, and slightly softening the line work here and there. I mentioned in Step 8 that I wish I had mixed a more diluted brown for the inking – some of that can now be achieved using digital tools.

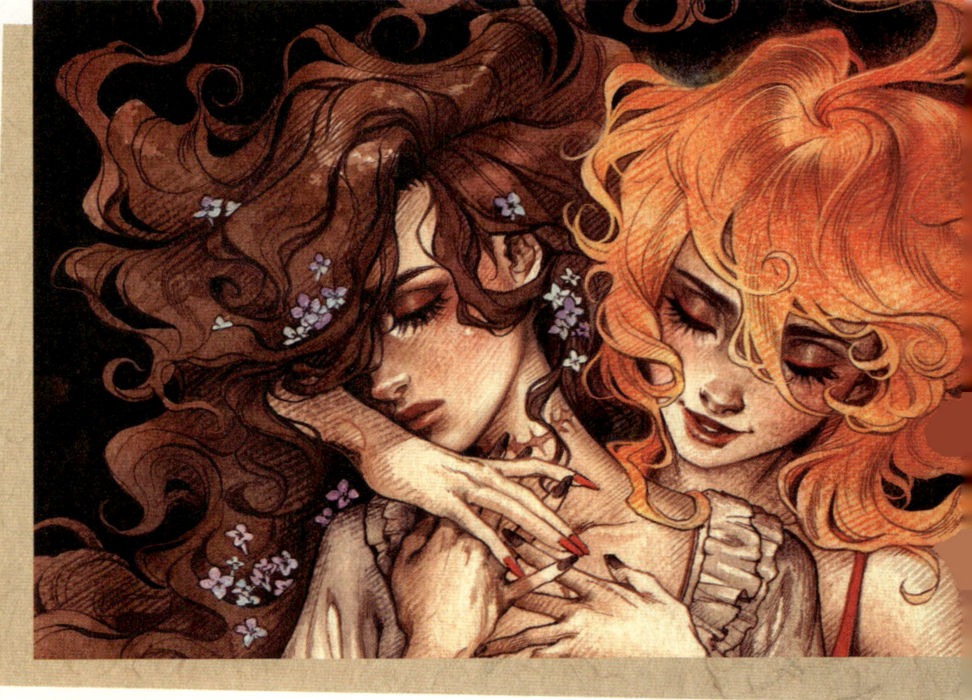

My scanner did a good enough job, but I have to scan the image in two parts, then stitch it together using Photomerge in Photoshop.

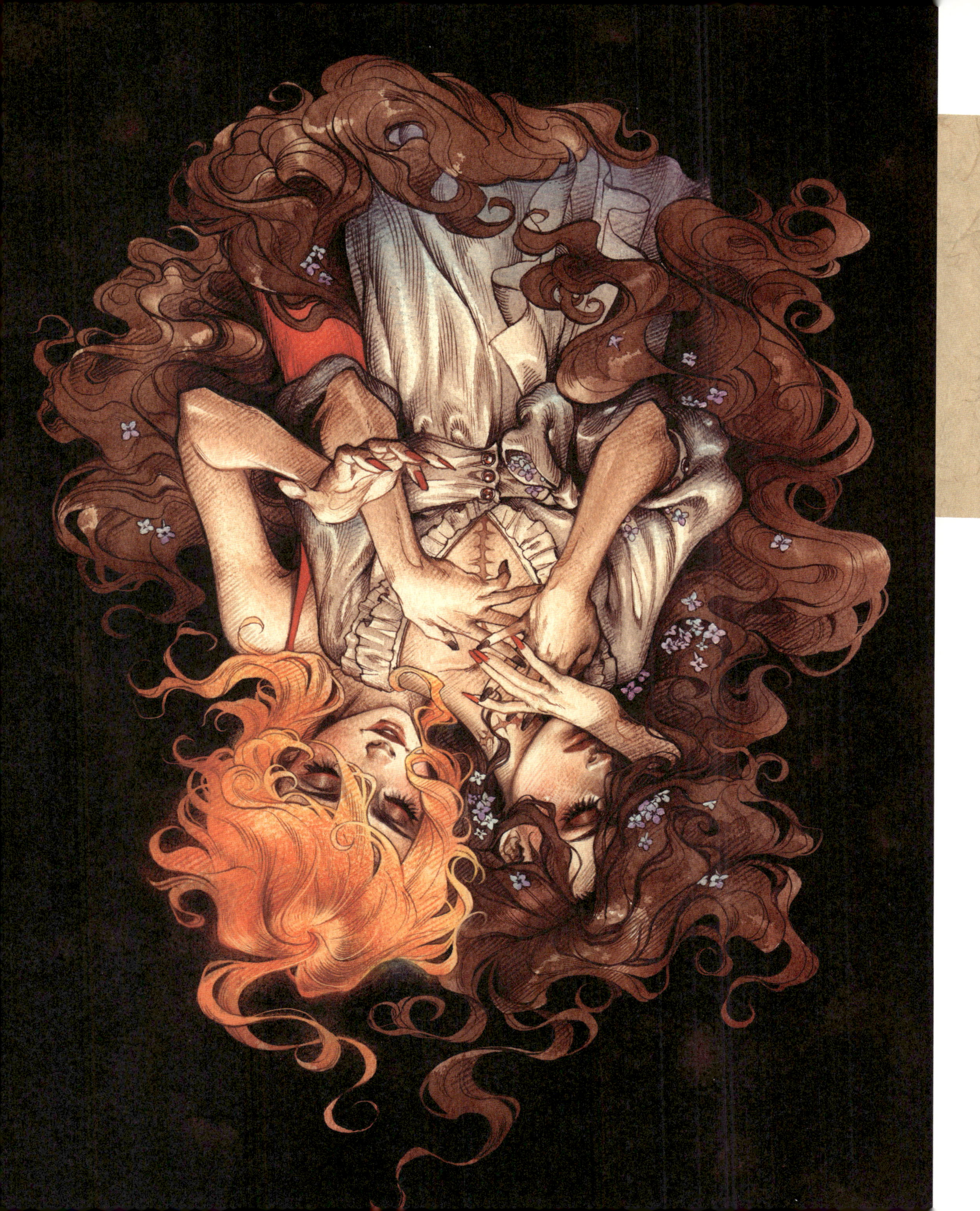

Digital process

My digital materials are very simple! I'm currently using a Wacom Cintiq 22 Pro, and have previously used only Wacom products. For working away from home, I use a Samsung Galaxy Book Pro 360, which also makes use of Wacom technology.

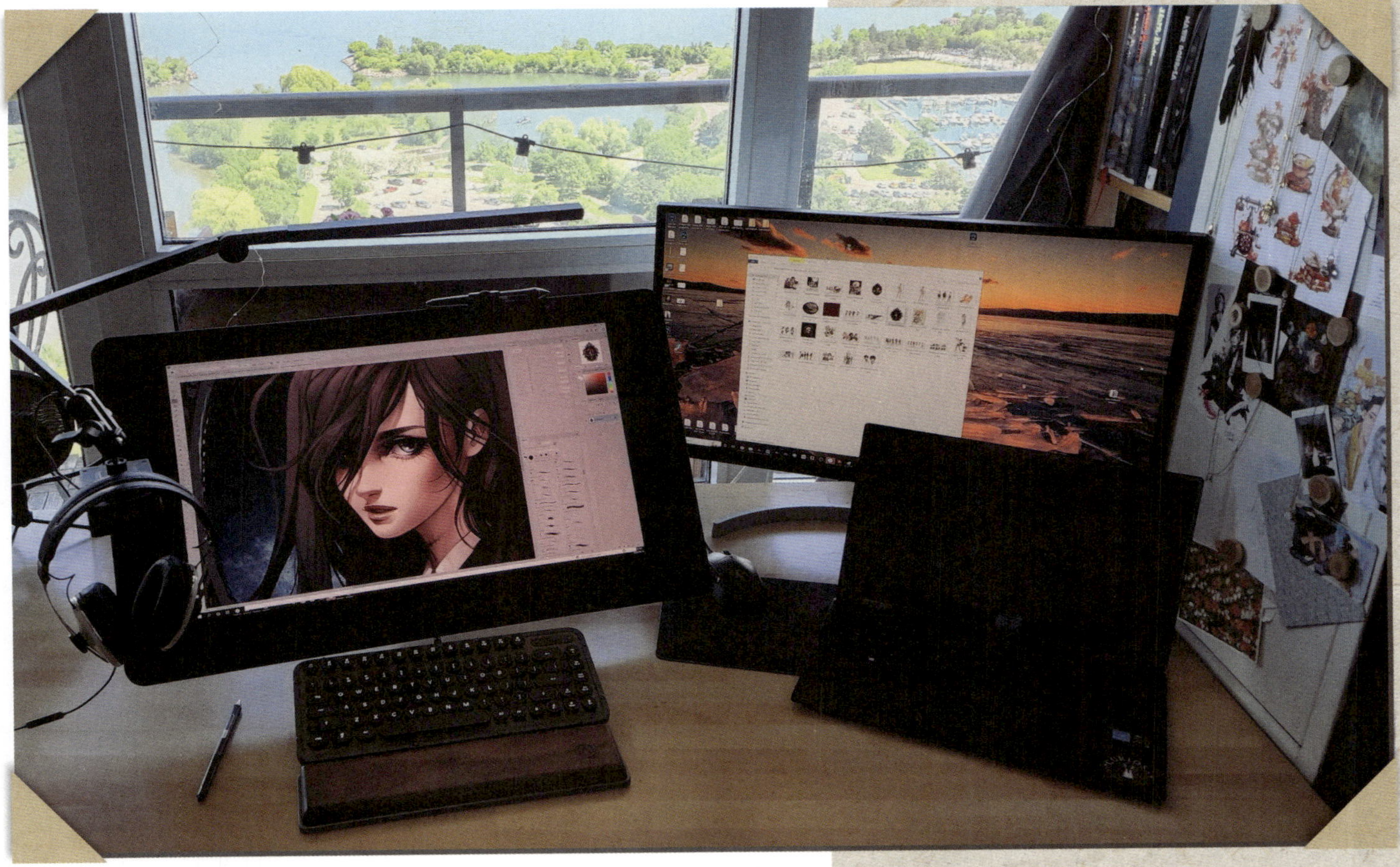

Software

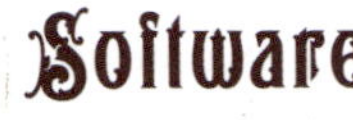

My preferred digital app/program has always been Adobe Photoshop CC, although Clip Studio Paint seems very useful and has comic-specific tools, so I want to try using it in the future.

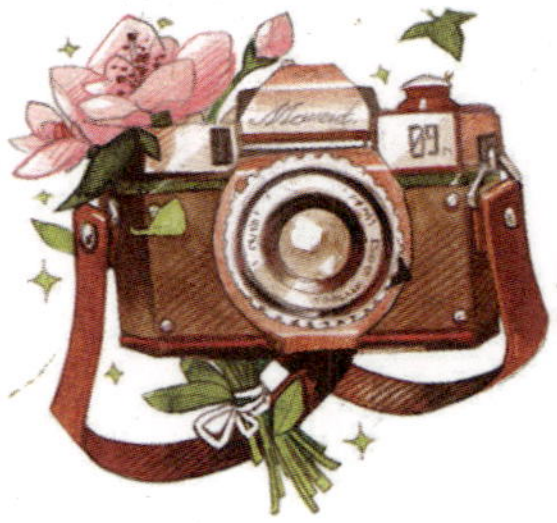

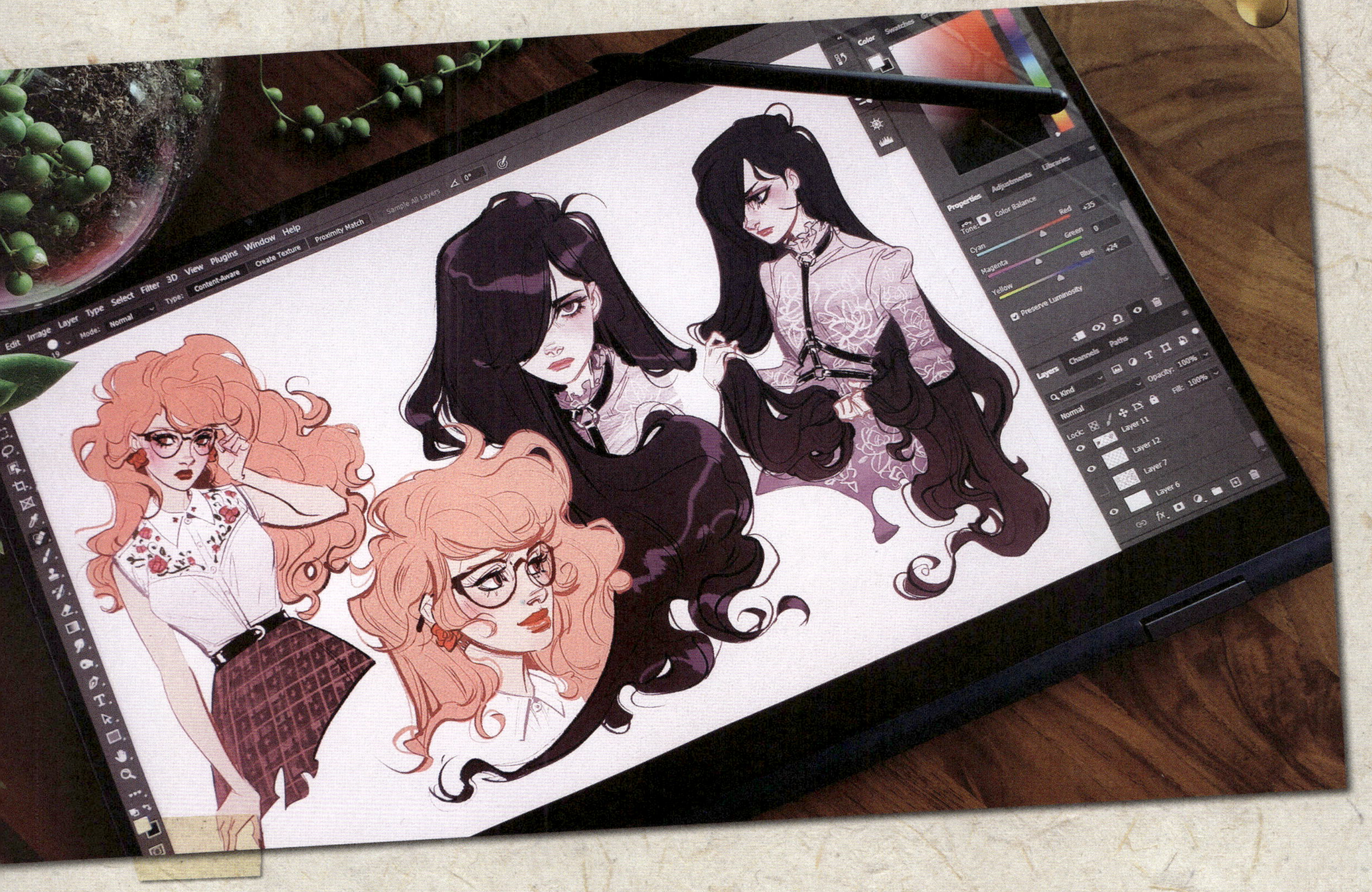

Brushes

In terms of digital brushes, I tend to switch around and use different brushes quite frequently, depending on my current illustration needs. It's good to experiment a lot and figure out how to achieve certain looks using digital techniques. This helped me to be a lot more flexible about using the brushes I have, tweaking their settings to suit my needs.

These are some of my favorite Photoshop brushes. I've collected and modified them over many years, and I'm not entirely sure where I got them at this point. As you can see, I prefer very textured brushes.

RENDERING

polished pin-up characters

In this digital tutorial, I'd like to give you an in-depth overview of my process for executing a detailed and polished character illustration. I typically use this process for most of my client work – it's a workflow that's relatively straightforward in terms of step division. This makes it a better choice for me than lineless digital painting, which requires a lot more back and forth, and is difficult to divide into coherent steps (it can go on forever!). The clean step division demonstrated in this tutorial makes it easy to plan out my workdays and estimate hourly completion time. As a freelance artist, this is incredibly useful. For my digital home setup, I use a Wacom Cintiq Pro 22, Windows PC, and Photoshop CC.

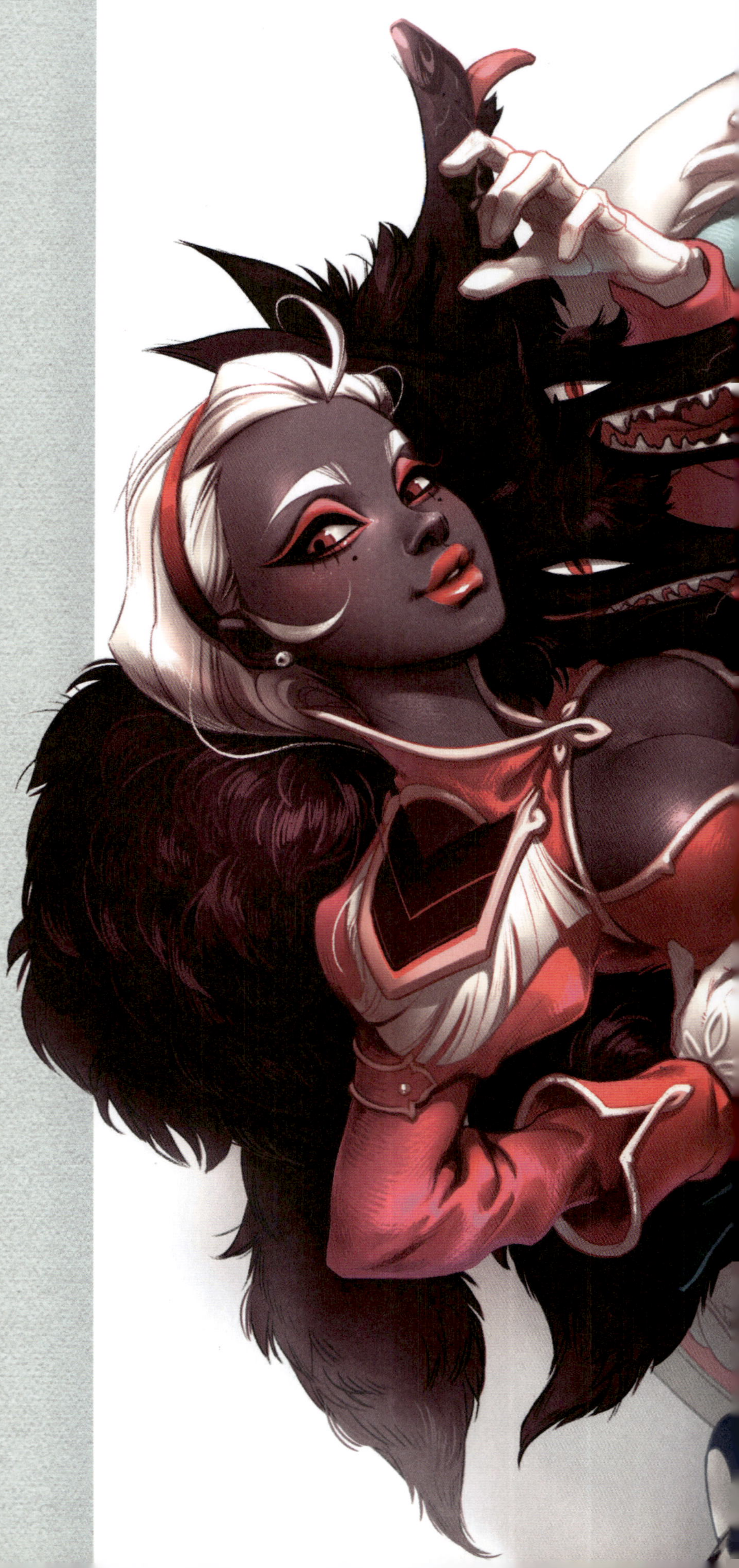

1 Thumbnails and pose exploration

Since the vast majority of my work prominently features characters, the most important aspect of the thumbnail is working out the composition. During this stage of the process, I do not use a reference – they're more of an idea hindrance in a situation where I know what kind of image I want to make, but am not too certain about which angle or poses I will use. The idea: a pin-up style illustration of my model characters (Sweet and Zero) posed on a Victorian-style couch. I start with a very simple generic couch shape, leaving the details for later – here I establish the base prop and the perspective – a down shot.

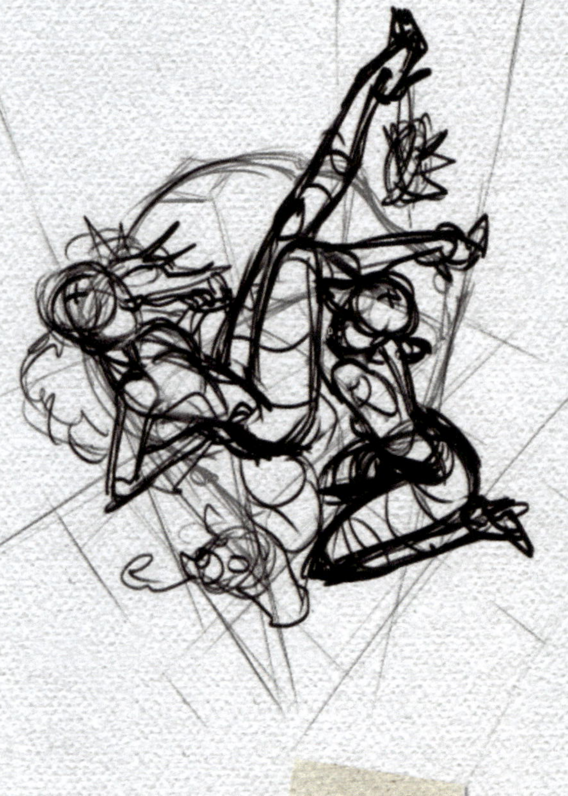

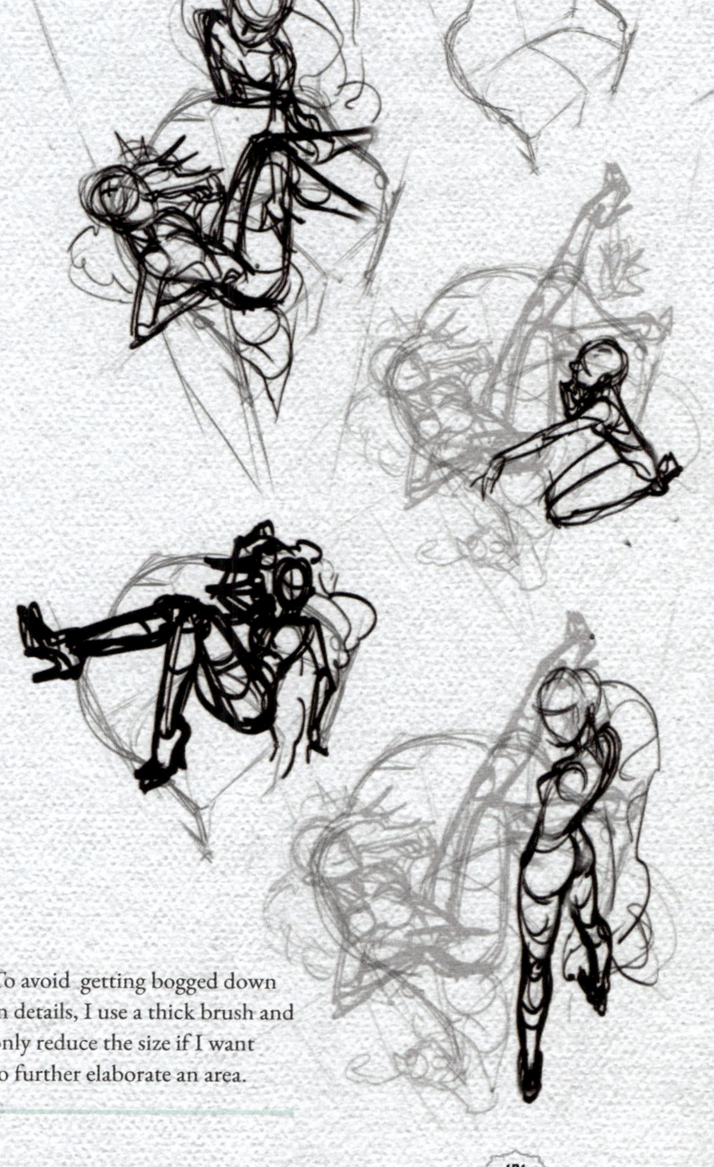

To avoid getting bogged down in details, I use a thick brush and only reduce the size if I want to further elaborate an area.

Use a floor grid

A rudimentary floor grid can go a long way to help with constructing the figures. Once the base is determined, I try out different poses for the characters – I didn't include all of them here, but this is the gist: I look for dynamic poses that are fun to look at and flow well in relation to each other. I love Sweet's pose from the second try, then try more until I find one I like for Zero. I draw these mannequin-like figures very quickly, so this process doesn't take particularly long – it's definitely a worthwhile venture to explore as many poses as possible.

2 Rough sketch

The rough sketch is basically the thumbnail enlarged to match the desired image size, and slightly elaborated to include all the very basic shapes of elements that will be included in the illustration. In this case I decide that I want to put my characters into their original outfits of Ringmaster and Jester, with their respective animal masks and Sweet's signature triple-headed fur cape, so I jot those things in. I also add more perspective lines to help make the next step easier.

I finish this step by setting this layer to a very low opacity so it functions as a guide for the clean sketch.

The thumbnail solidifies the biggest and most prominent shapes first and foremost, and I leave a lot of details to be worked out later in the sketching process.

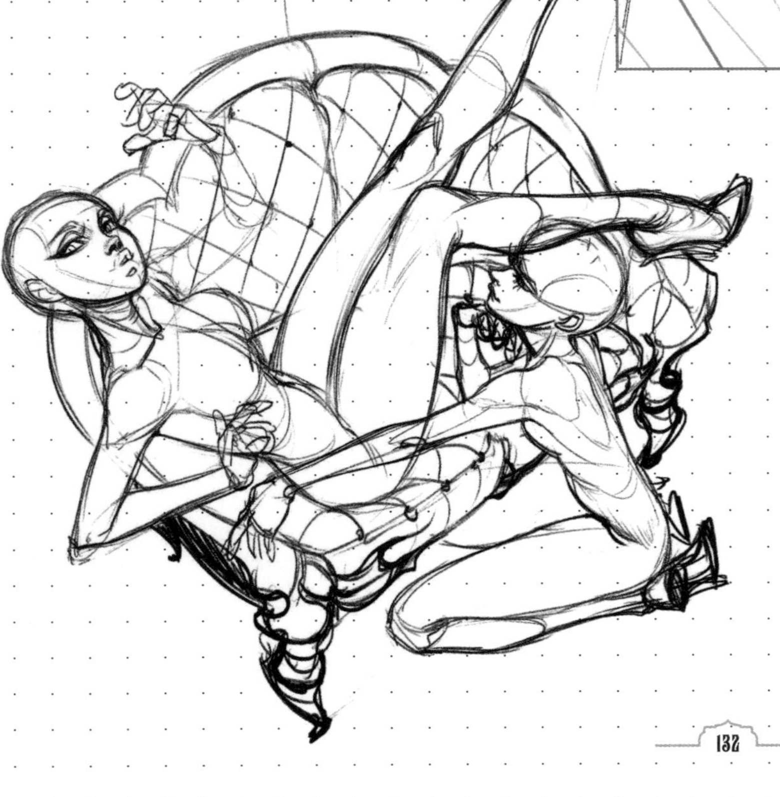

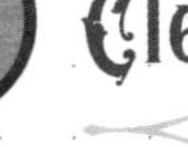

3 Clean sketch – base

For this step, I make the brush much smaller to achieve more precise and clean shapes with the thinner lines. I also work a bit of detail into the couch. The primary aim of this step is to finalize the anatomy, hand gestures, and facial expressions of the characters.

This step is for establishing a clean and solid shape base to be built on, so I still leave out clothing and hair details.

4 Clean sketch–details

This is where things get more fun – sketching in the fashion, hairstyles, and other smaller details. I designed these outfits previously, so use the original sketch as a reference image and make some small modifications. I also finalize the design of the couch, and once everything is established I am ready to move on to the inking step.

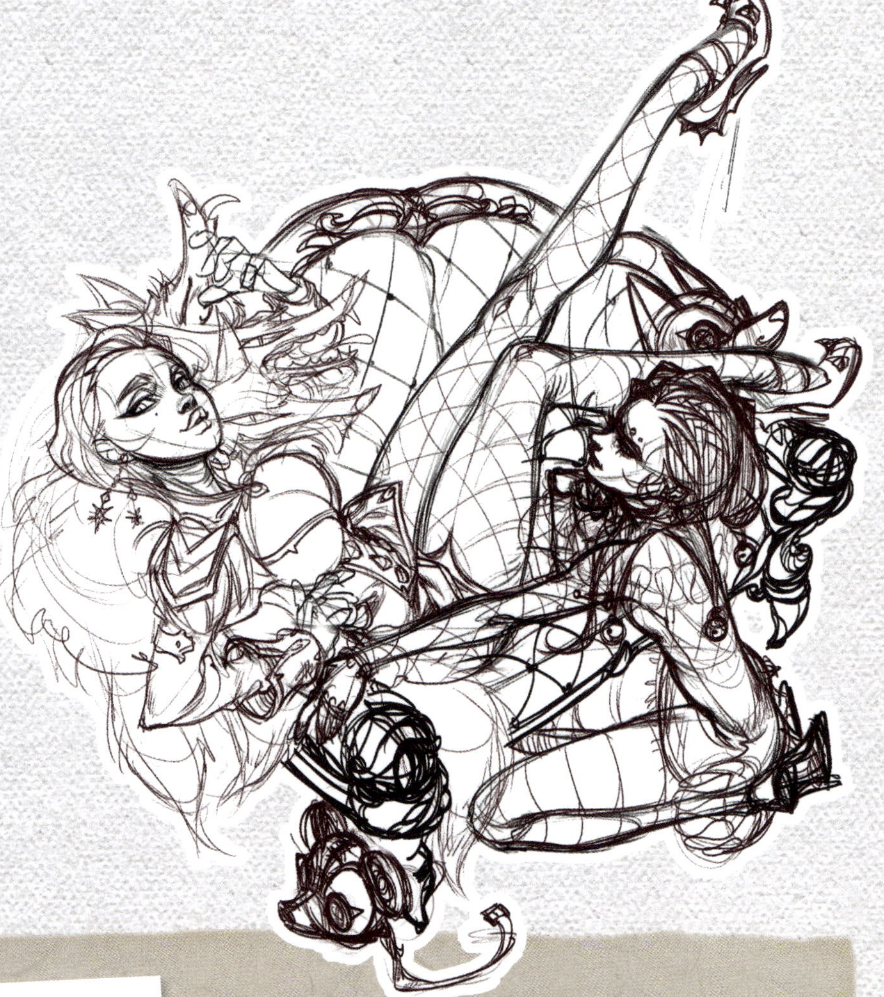

I use an even thinner brush to sketch in these details. This helps a little to keep the overall sketch clean, although here and there it gets a bit messy where a lot of elements overlap.

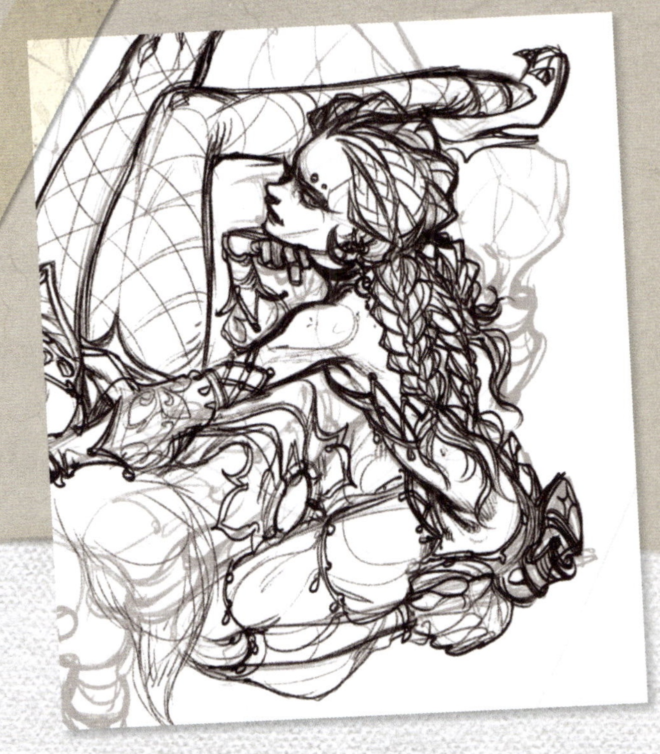

Zero's unused outfit and hair design

When elaborating on the clothes, I first decided that Zero's original Jester outfit may be too boring for this illustration, so I sketch out a new outfit with a different hairstyle. But I end up erasing it and going back to the Jester outfit, which makes more sense contextually. It's still fun to explore options!

5 Inking and cleanup

This step locks all the elements and their shapes into place. I do all the hard work in establishing shapes, details, overlapping elements, compositional flow, and so on first, then lock it in during this inking step. This is important because I don't have to attend to these things later. I do not make any major changes after the lines are in place, and this greatly reduces potential anxiety about leaving aspects unresolved or undetermined. I know some artists love a more exploratory process that involves a lot of big changes throughout the piece, but I'm definitely not one of those. I like a strict division between steps for efficiency.

In this illustration, I slightly reduce the texture of the brush I sketched with, and use it for inking. This is probably the thinnest brush size I've ever used for line work. As a general rule, the thinner the brush, the more difficult it is to make clean and accurate lines, and thus the longer it takes to get through this step. Most of the time I use a thicker brush in order to save time, although it does make a visual difference in the end.

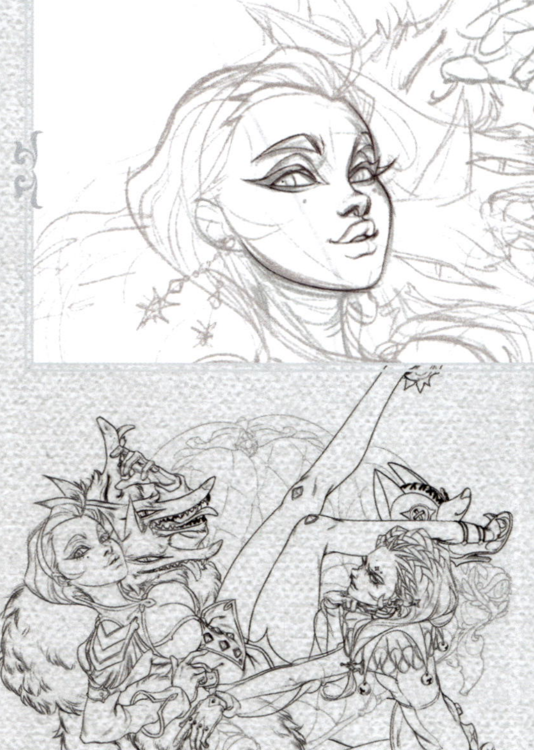

The name of the brush I used for sketching and inking this illustration is "rough pastel." I believe it comes with Photoshop CC.

6 Basic flat color

In this step, I fill every separate element with a random solid color, putting each color on a different layer. The logic: I fill the silhouette of each character separately, as well as the couch, lining of the couch, masks, and so on, to make it much easier to color in the details and do the shadow pass later. In Photoshop, you can select the pixels on any given layer (ctrl + left-click the desired layer). Keeping these silhouettes on separate layers will be extremely useful in multiple steps going forward. I can also use these ready silhouettes for the purpose of creating a clipping mask.

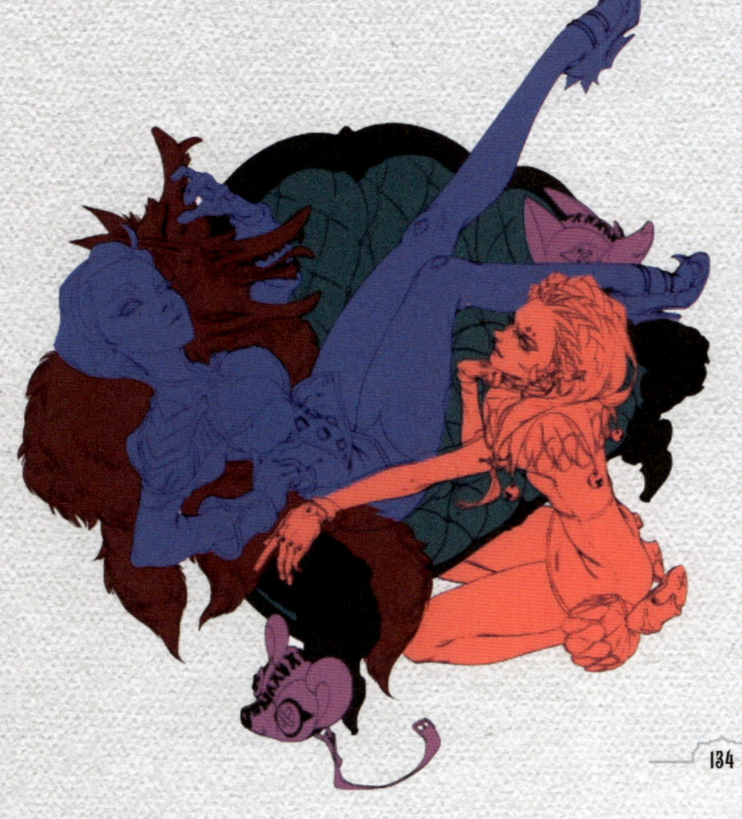

It doesn't look pretty, but this is a purely utilitarian step; the color choices here don't matter.

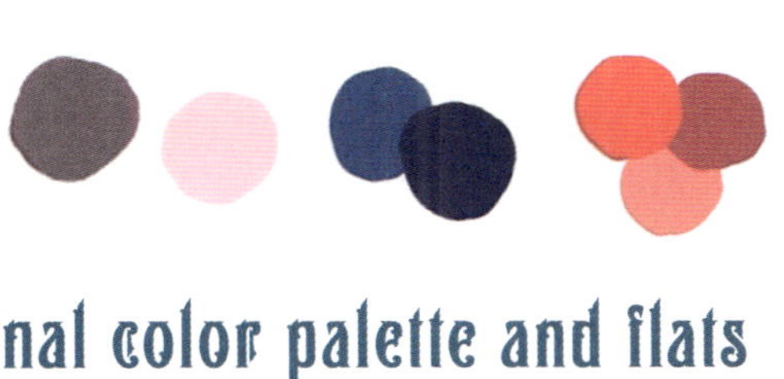

7 Final color palette and flats

With the line work complete and the masking done, I move on to deciding on the color palette and final flat colors. I pick two contrasting colors that are somewhat similar to the original colors that I assigned to Sweet and Zero's circus outfits: red and blue. I go with a coral-pink and mint-teal color scheme, and analogous colors like a cooler pink and a darker ocean-blue. Once I pick out all the approximate colors, I fill in all the areas with the local flat colors, utilizing the silhouette selection throughout the process.

It takes me a while to decide on the color of the couch, which I do after flatting both characters. At first I want to make the couch dark, but Sweet's furry cape blends into it, so I decide to make the couch lighter instead. I also add gradients all over during this step. The last part of flatting and finalizing the color scheme is changing the colors of the line work. To do this, I use the pixel lock/alpha lock layer option on all the line-work layers, and pick colors similar to the local color of the element but darker in tone and less saturated.

This step is meticulous and a bit boring, but I find the results very satisfying to look at.

8 Shadow pass

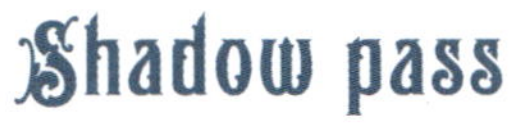

Before I move on to the shadow pass step, I duplicate and merge everything up to this point into a single layer (but without the white background) so that I can select out the entire silhouette in addition to the separate elements. Once again, having these silhouette masks ready to go makes the process of adding shadows much quicker than it would be otherwise. To add the shadows, I create a new layer on top of everything and set it to 55% opacity and Multiply layer mode. I always use a very dark reddish color (almost black, but not quite) for shadows, and then modify it later if necessary.

I add all the shadows on one layer, making use of an airbrush, hard brush and blender, and eraser. Selecting different elements while I add shadows to them helps a lot to keep everything neat. Since I didn't use references, the shadows are a guess on my part. My general rule is that as long as everything looks attractive and somewhat believable, it's fine!

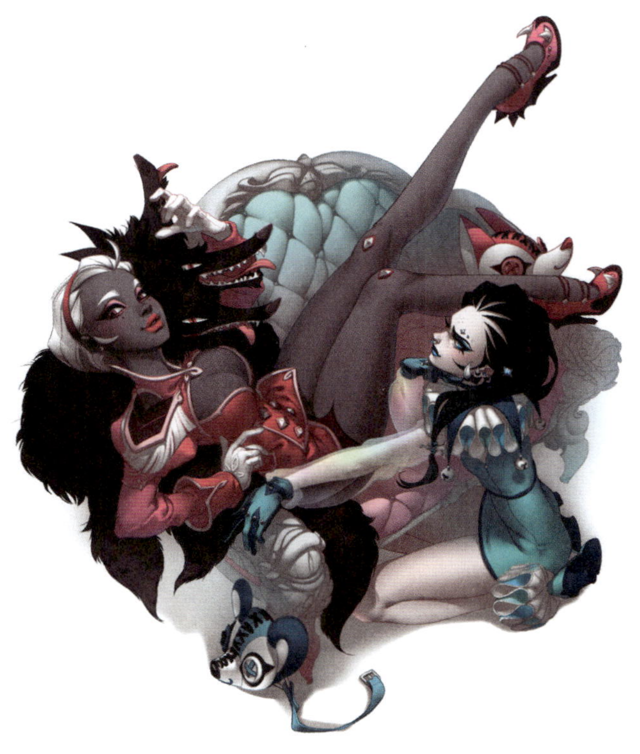

Adding shadows can kill the vibrancy of the flatted image, but this is temporary. Everything will come together in the end after the whole process is complete and all adjustments are made.

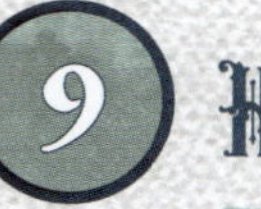

Highlights and details paintover

Once I finish the shadow pass, I make a new layer on top of the shadow layer on which I will add all the highlights and small details/paintover. In this step, I switch over to the same brush I used for the line work/sketching steps. I like to hatch and cross-hatch in order to retain an organic and textured look to the illustration – avoiding making everything too smooth and airbrushed. The shadows are easier to execute with the airbrush, but the highlights look great with a bit of texture. In this step I try to add more definition to forms and add some lively details such as stray hairs.

Sometimes I also paint over some line work, but not too much – my goal isn't to get rid of the line work completely. Putting too much effort into blending the lines into the render can make the image look overworked, in my opinion, and for this reason I even leave some small areas without elaborating much on the shadows either.

At this point, the image is almost complete and only requires some overall adjustments.

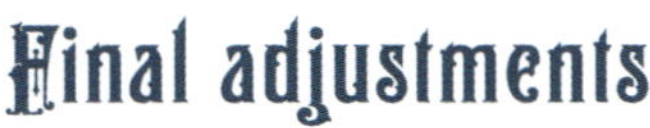

Final adjustments

In order to add final overall color and contrast adjustments to the image, I select all the layers and group them into a folder (typically naming it "RAW"). I then duplicate the folder, hide the original from view, and merge the top folder into a single layer. This way the entire image is on one layer and if I make adjustments to it, it affects everything. I do this instead of making an adjustment layer on top of everything because I prefer to adjust the levels, color balance, and so on, all on this single merged layer, rather than create lots of separate adjustment layers on top of everything else. It's mostly a visual layer-decluttering decision for me.

I bump up the reds and make the colors a bit more saturated, also adding fishnet tights to Sweet. I use the Dodge tool a bit as well, but very sparingly as it tends to give illustrations an overly digital look that I'm not a huge fan of. With these final adjustments, the illustration is complete!

I also fade out some outer elements of the composition in order to enhance the depth.

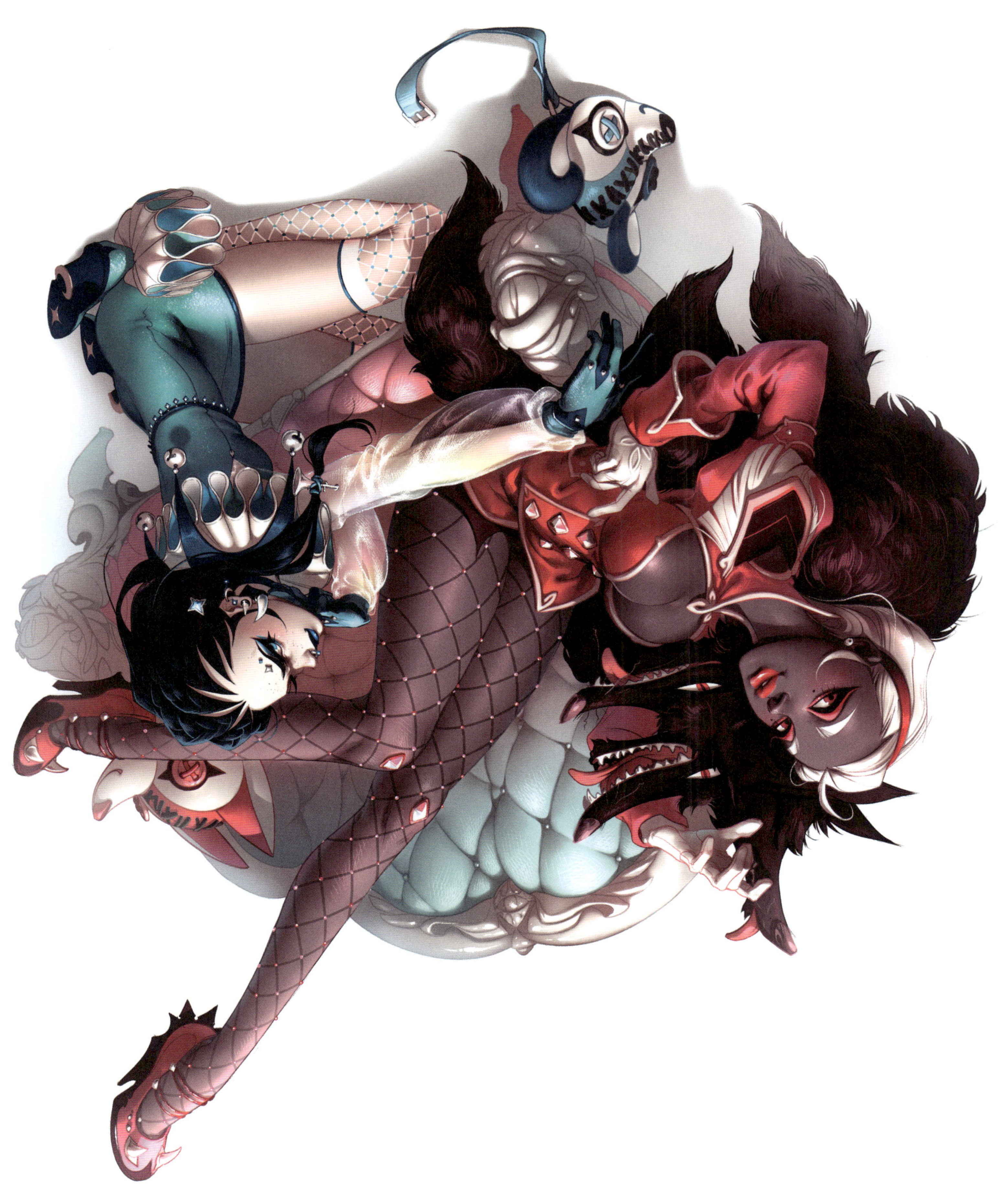

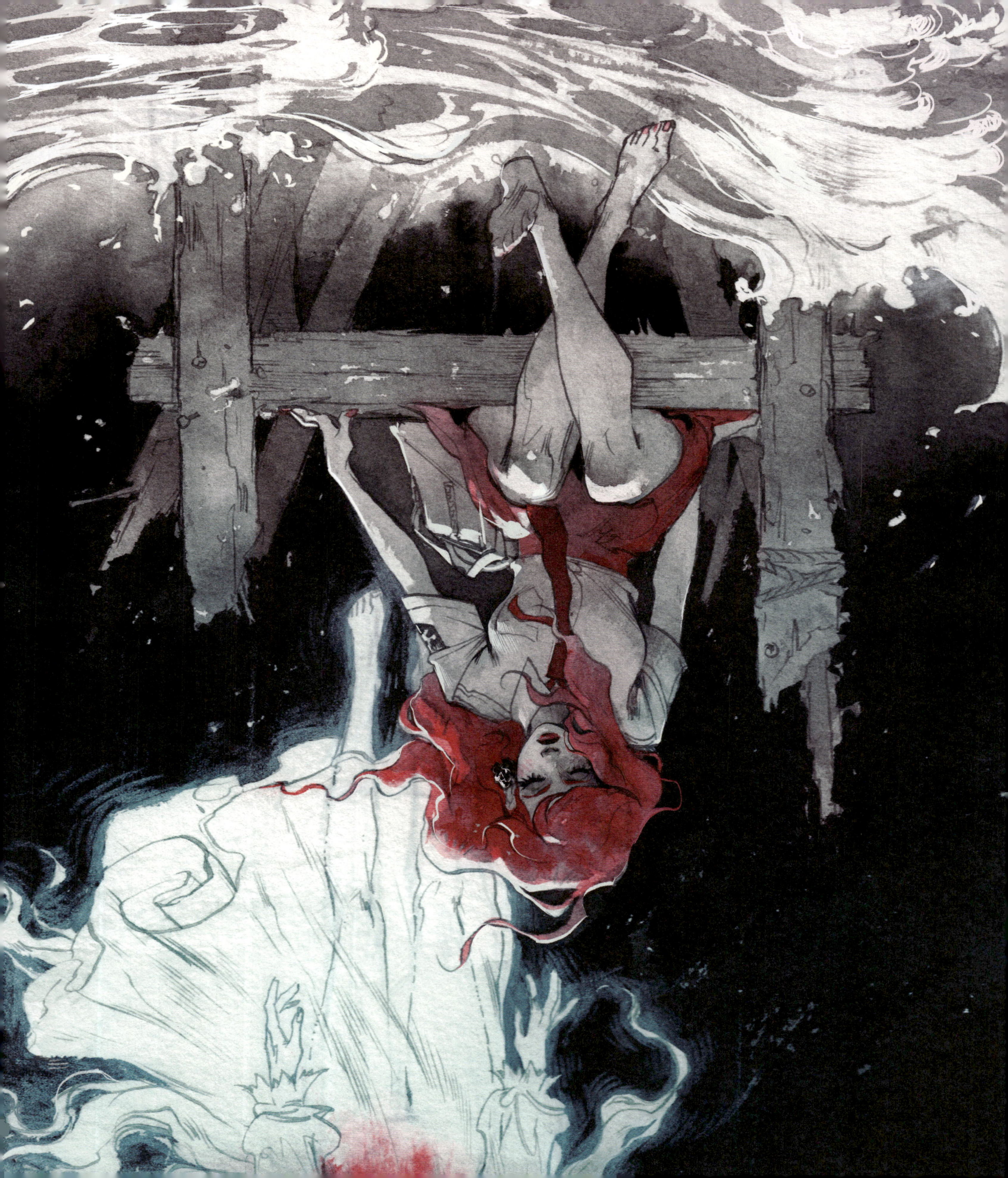

Plans for the future: Gloaminguale

Plans for the future: Gloamingvale

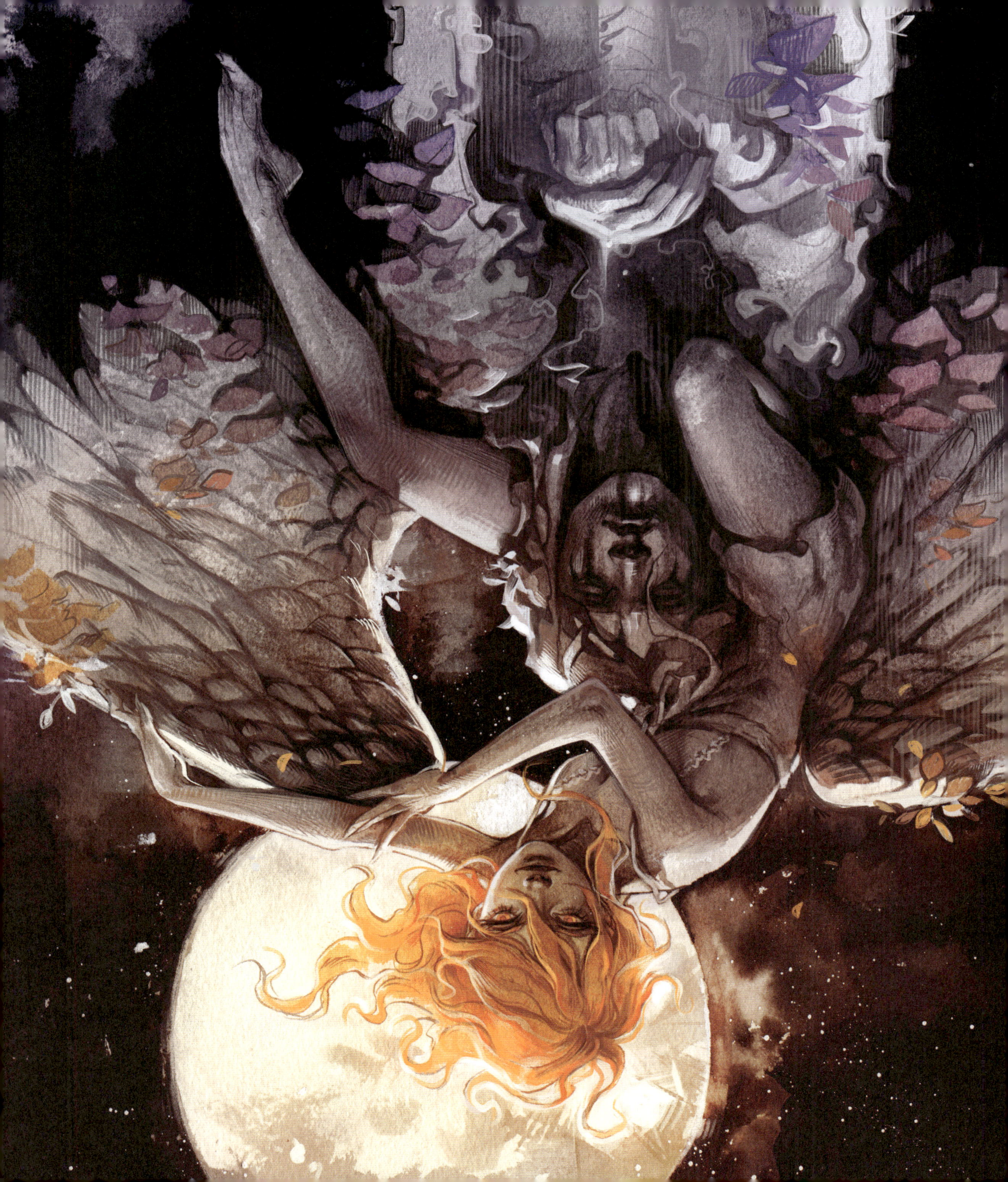

Welcome to the town of Gloaminguale

A remote little artisan town haunted by its secret history. The founding families have been slowly infiltrated by something sinister, and are on the brink of executing a century-long plot that may corrupt the town's citizens beyond repair.

Legend has it that the Shards of Aether will one day return to tip the scales back into a state of balance... but will they, ever? How many times will their broken vessels be dragged through the dark halls of the House of Three Sisters before they finally finish what they started so long ago? Perhaps it's just another Old Faith fairy tale, one of the many nonsensical chunks of their crumbling grand narrative. Aether is dead and their churches stand empty – the world has moved on.

Yes... but none of this really matters to Noelle, Fiona, or Sock. Not yet, anyway. They have too many immediate problems to care about what happens to their town at large, but especially HaeJin – nothing matters to her at all! Nothing but the sweet release of death – which appears to be horribly difficult to come by, due to her inconvenient state of unwanted immortality. At least that's what she keeps telling herself....

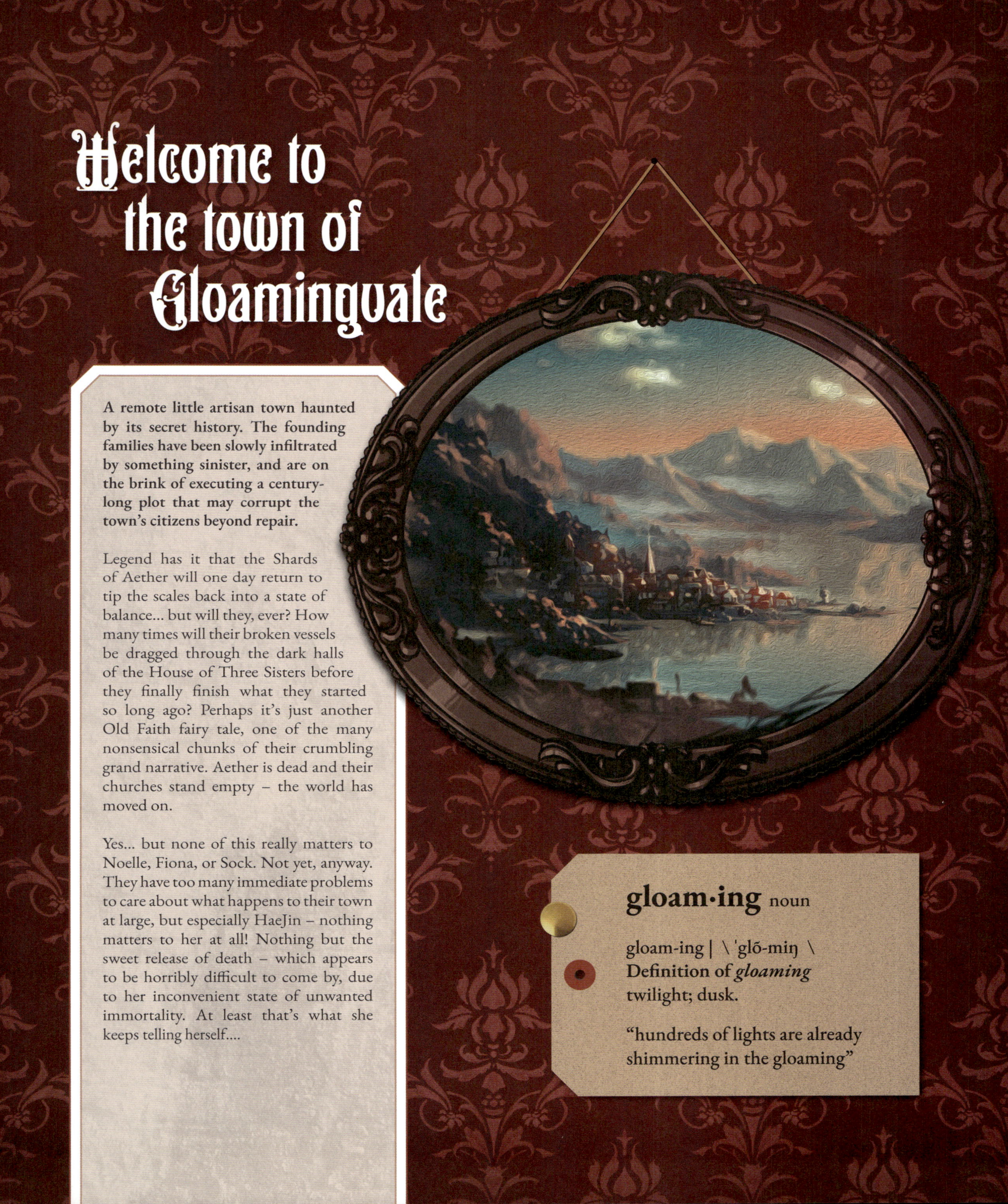

gloam·ing noun

gloam-ing | \ ˈglō-miŋ \
Definition of *gloaming*
twilight; dusk.

"hundreds of lights are already shimmering in the gloaming"

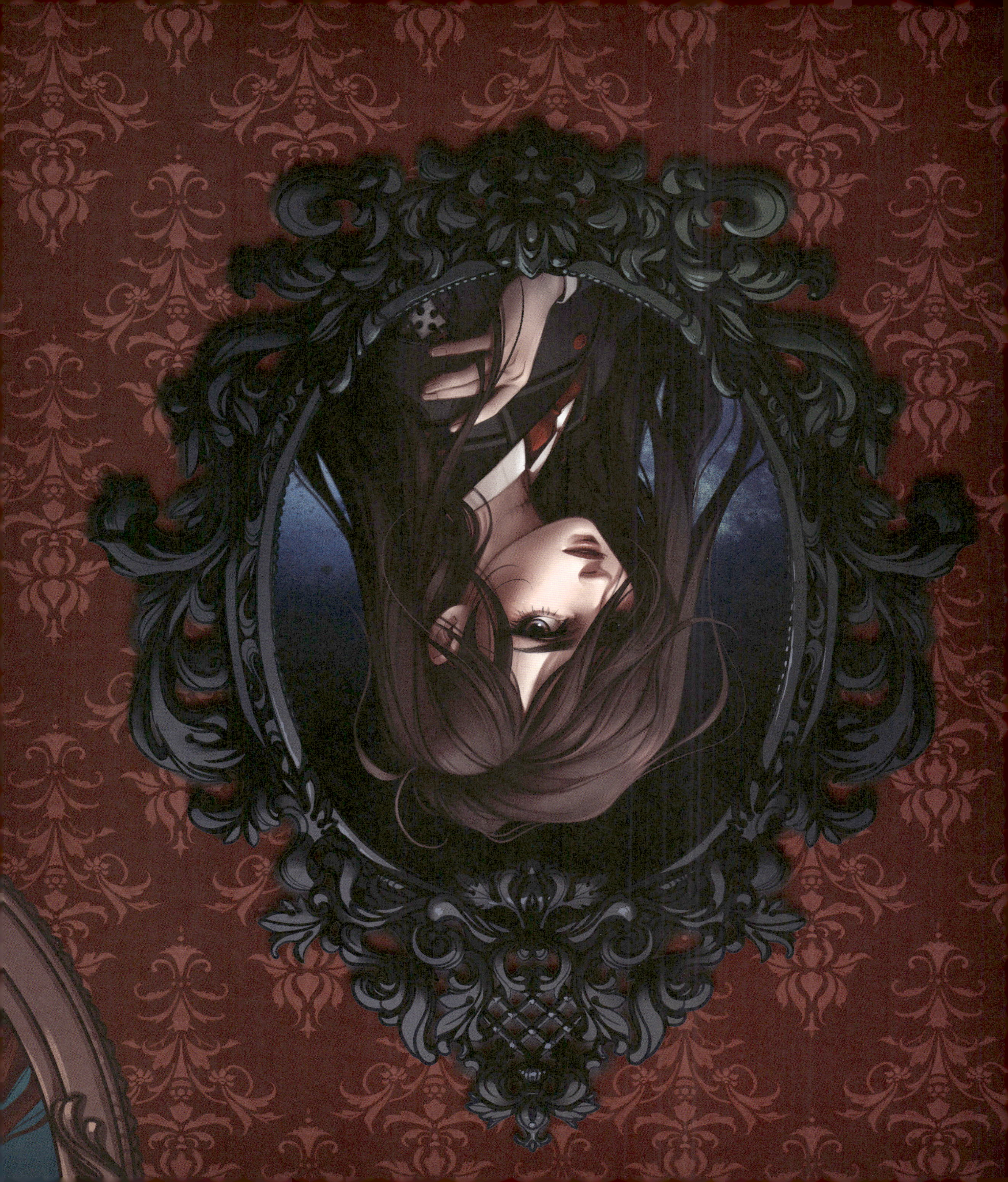

... AND SO THE STORY BEGINS

That was a purposefully cryptic gist of *Gloamingvale* – my ultimate personal project, my glittering dream, my carrot on a stick, if you will. I've spent the better part of the last sixteen years organizing my life around the desire to just happily work on this project in peace, but of course that's much easier said than done. I made about one-hundred pages over the span of four years, but I was too young. Then I was too depressed, then too unskilled, too broke, too busy... and the list went on and on – you get the idea. But I never stopped thinking about the project, not for a single day – it's like being hopelessly in love. I will try to give you a brief rundown of where it all started, and why it has gripped me so tightly.

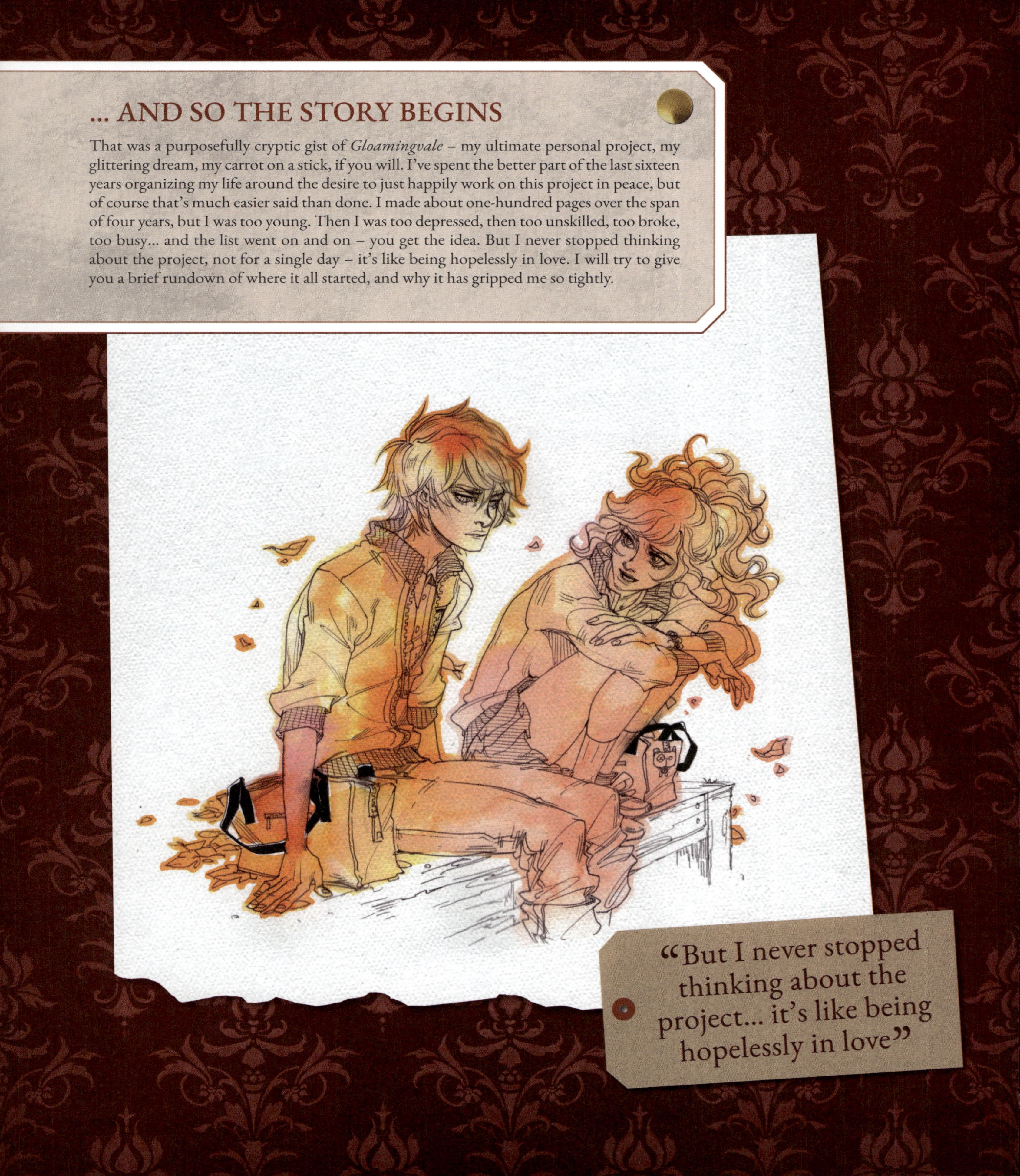

"But I never stopped thinking about the project... it's like being hopelessly in love"

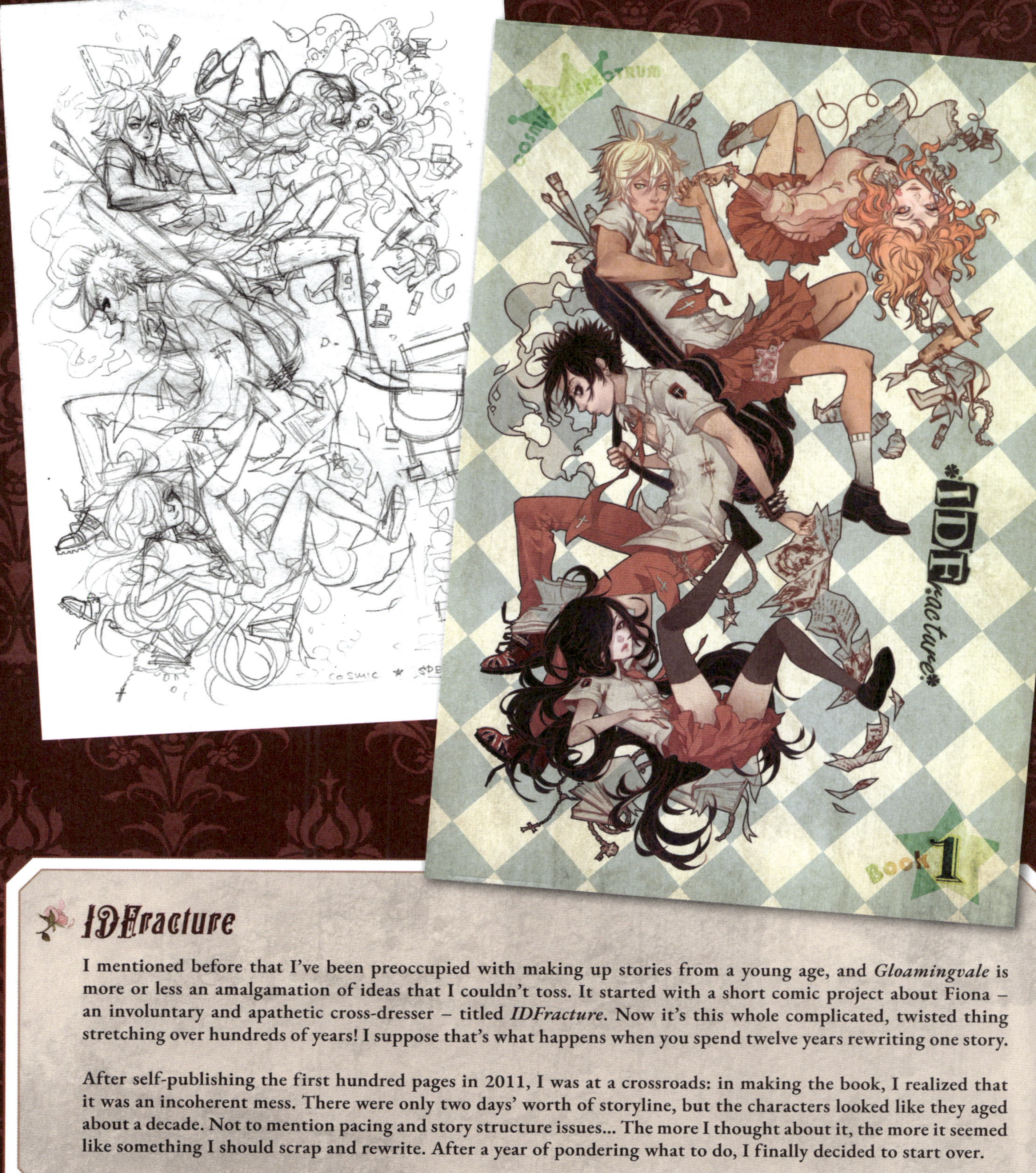

IDFracture

I mentioned before that I've been preoccupied with making up stories from a young age, and *Gloamingvale* is more or less an amalgamation of ideas that I couldn't toss. It started with a short comic project about Fiona – an involuntary and apathetic cross-dresser – titled *IDFracture*. Now it's this whole complicated, twisted thing stretching over hundreds of years! I suppose that's what happens when you spend twelve years rewriting one story.

After self-publishing the first hundred pages in 2011, I was at a crossroads: in making the book, I realized that it was an incoherent mess. There were only two days' worth of storyline, but the characters looked like they aged about a decade. Not to mention pacing and story structure issues... The more I thought about it, the more it seemed like something I should scrap and rewrite. After a year of pondering what to do, I finally decided to start over.

Character design and visual development

Although I try to cultivate an adequate amount of skill when it comes to all aspects of illustration and comics, my absolute favorite is character design.

I've been drawing and developing *Gloamingvale* characters for many years, but I've actually changed very little about them since the very start! I tend to approach character design for personal projects very differently from client work. Client work typically requires a lot of feedback, and back-and-forth changes. Many people are part of that process and the number of factors that need to be taken into consideration is vast. For my personal projects though, it's much simpler: I just aim to make characters that can be differentiated from each other, and feel "real" to me.

Who *is* this character?

I start character design with the "nature" versus "nurture" approach. Before I do any sort of visual development or character design, I do need to know some basic information – the character's name, role in the story, life circumstances, outward personality and habits, internal beliefs monologue, and attitude toward oneself. It may sound intense, but it's rather basic. Let's take Fiona here as an example:

Name
Fiona Morgan

Role
One of the main characters; the one that might have a corruption and redemption arc.

Life circumstances
Lives alone with an intrusive and controlling single mother, father out of the picture for the most part, has several older brothers that have all moved out, lives in a decrepit mansion because the family fortune was old and has been depleted almost completely by the previous generation. Is an involuntary cross-dresser.

Outward personality
Quietly suffering – deadpan/apathetic, doesn't like socializing at all, has virtually no friends with the exception of Noelle. Does not open up to people, is an observer. Likes to draw and is quite talented, although very secretive.

Internal beliefs monologue
"Life is pointless and I feel like crap most of the time; the only thing that matters is mom's happiness, she doesn't deserve all these terrible things that happened to her, and the least I can do is keep up the pretense that I'm a girl. It's fine if it makes her happy."

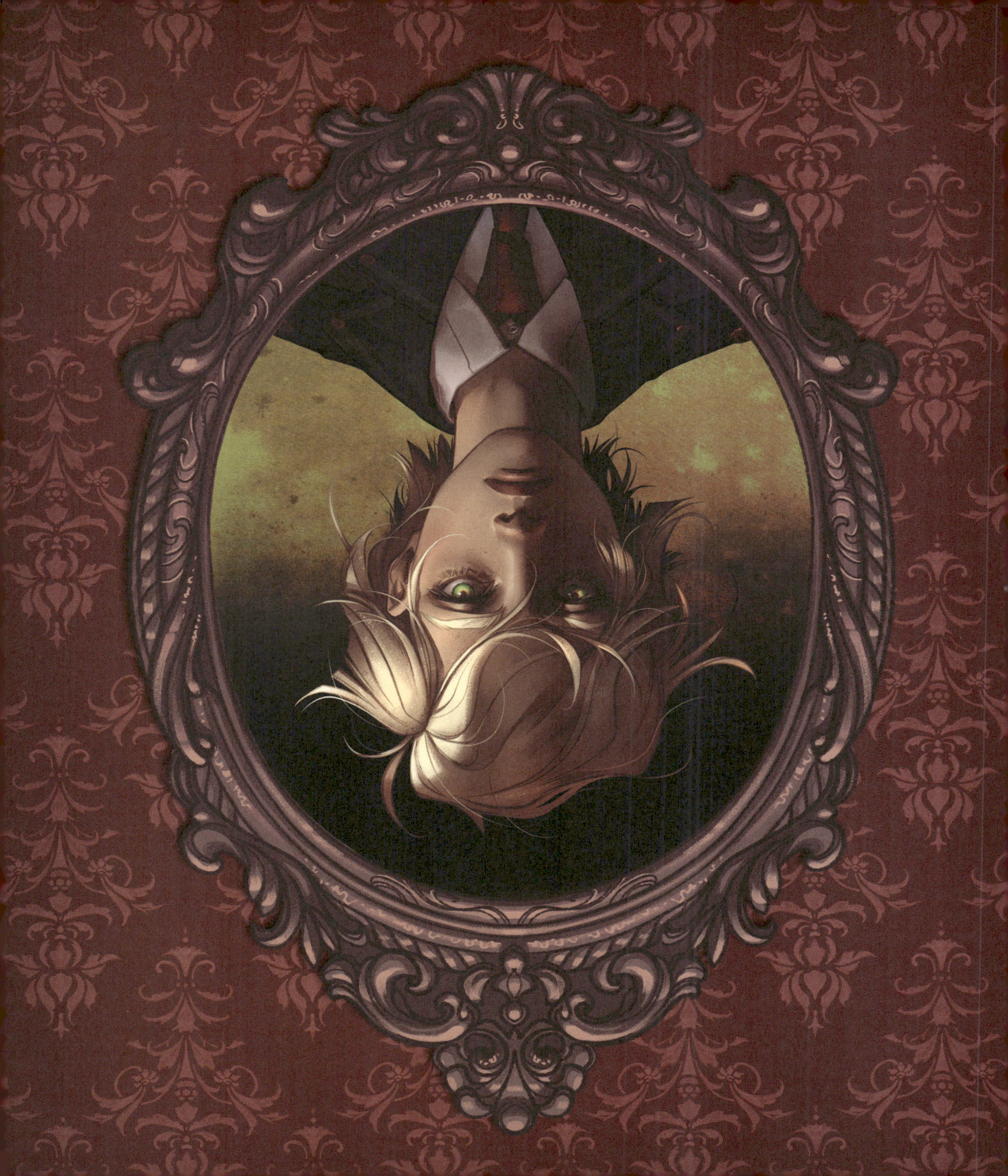

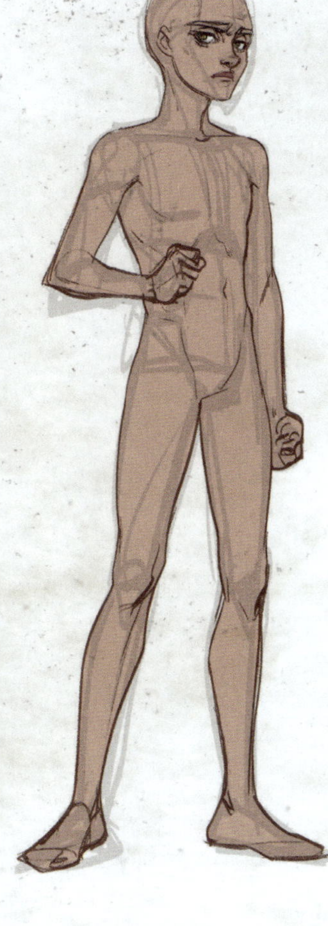

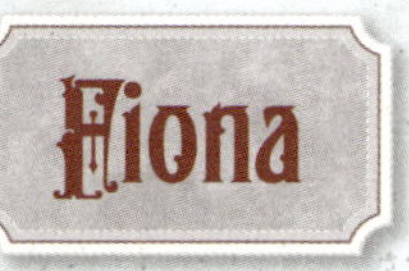

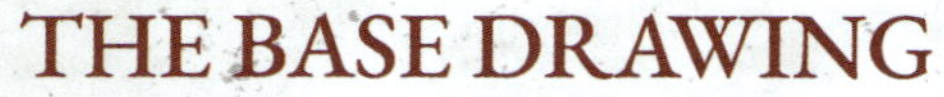

THE BASE DRAWING

Once I've established the basic information, I determine the "nature" qualities of the character. These are essentially biologically predetermined things like height, natural hair and eye color, gender, general body-type, and facial features.

The base drawing may look pretty boring, but it only gets more and more fun from here! Once I have a base like this, it's like playing dress-up with a doll. I start to consider the "nurture" factors – things that are visually apparent due to personal choice or circumstances. In this case, Fiona likes to cut his own hair, so it's roughly chopped and shaggy. He also likes plants and is minoring on the Botanist path at Gloamingvale Academy, thus the cacti boxers.

FASHION CHOICES

Next (and the most fun) is the character's fashion! In this story, I have the constraint of the academy uniform, which makes things extra fun – the character's personal choices really come through. Fiona pretends to be a girl, but is also rather prim and proper – or tries to be. He would wear super baggy everything, but is afraid that would look too sloppy and thus attract negative attention. So he wears the longest skirt available, but otherwise keeps the tie in its proper place and just opts for an oversized cardigan. Fiona also chooses the most covering options for the gym uniform – a baggy tracksuit. He needs some new gym shoes – his are getting too small and worn out. His bag is accidentally stylish – he actually found it, all dusty, up in the attic. It's a true vintage piece that probably belonged to his late grandfather.

Other characters

I'd like to share some other character designs and fashion options – I wonder what you can glean from them without any explanation?

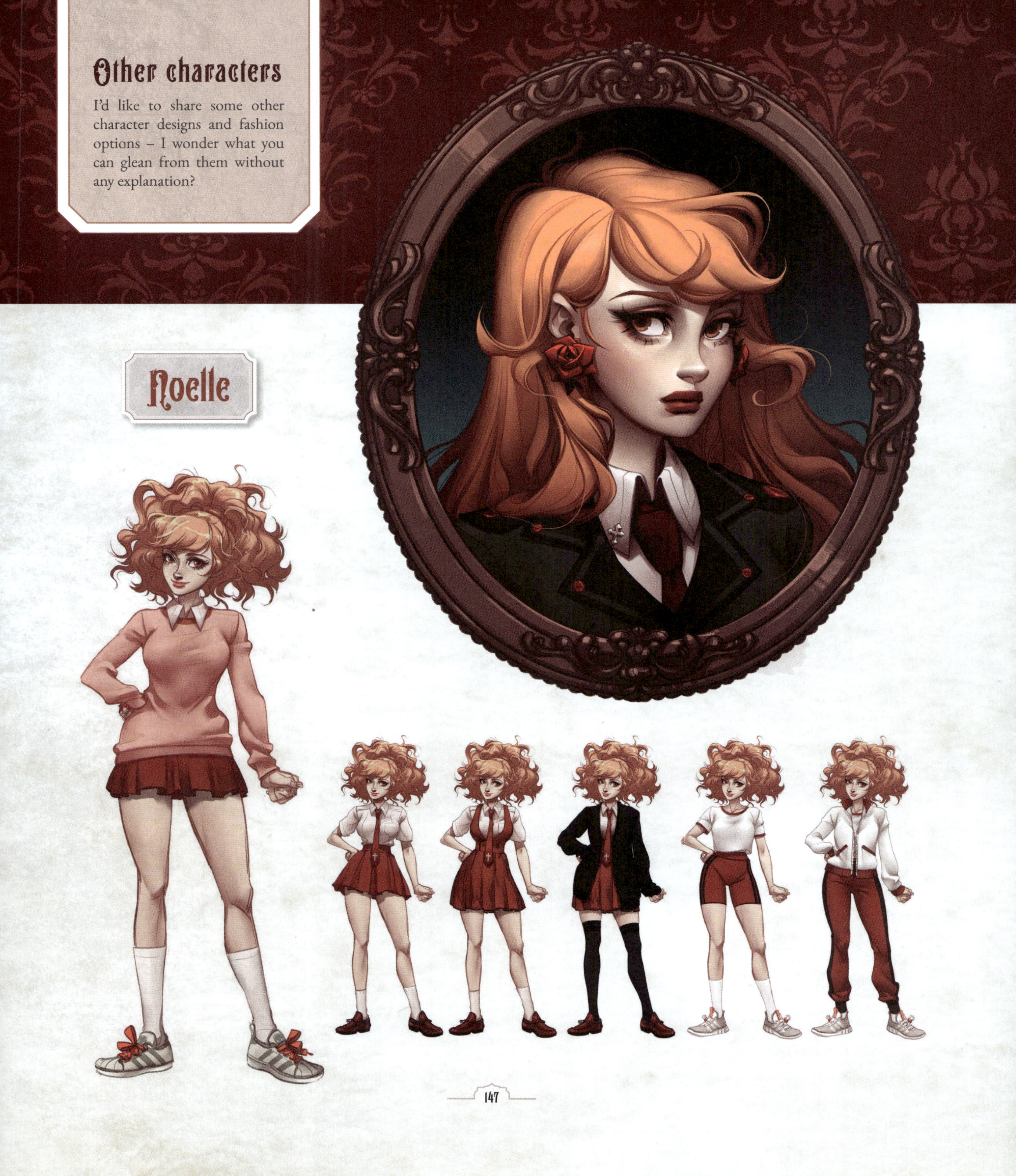

Noelle

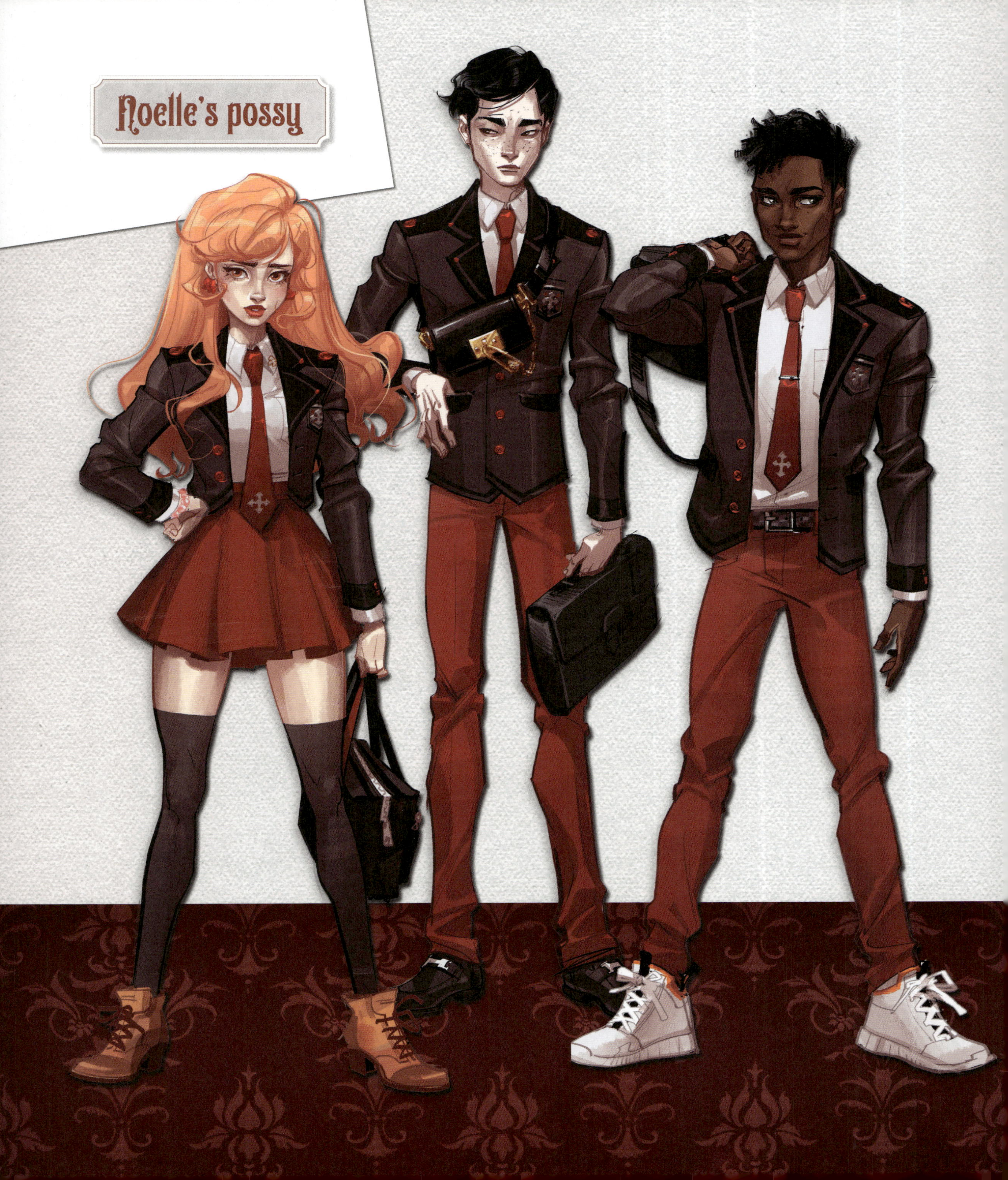
Noelle's possy

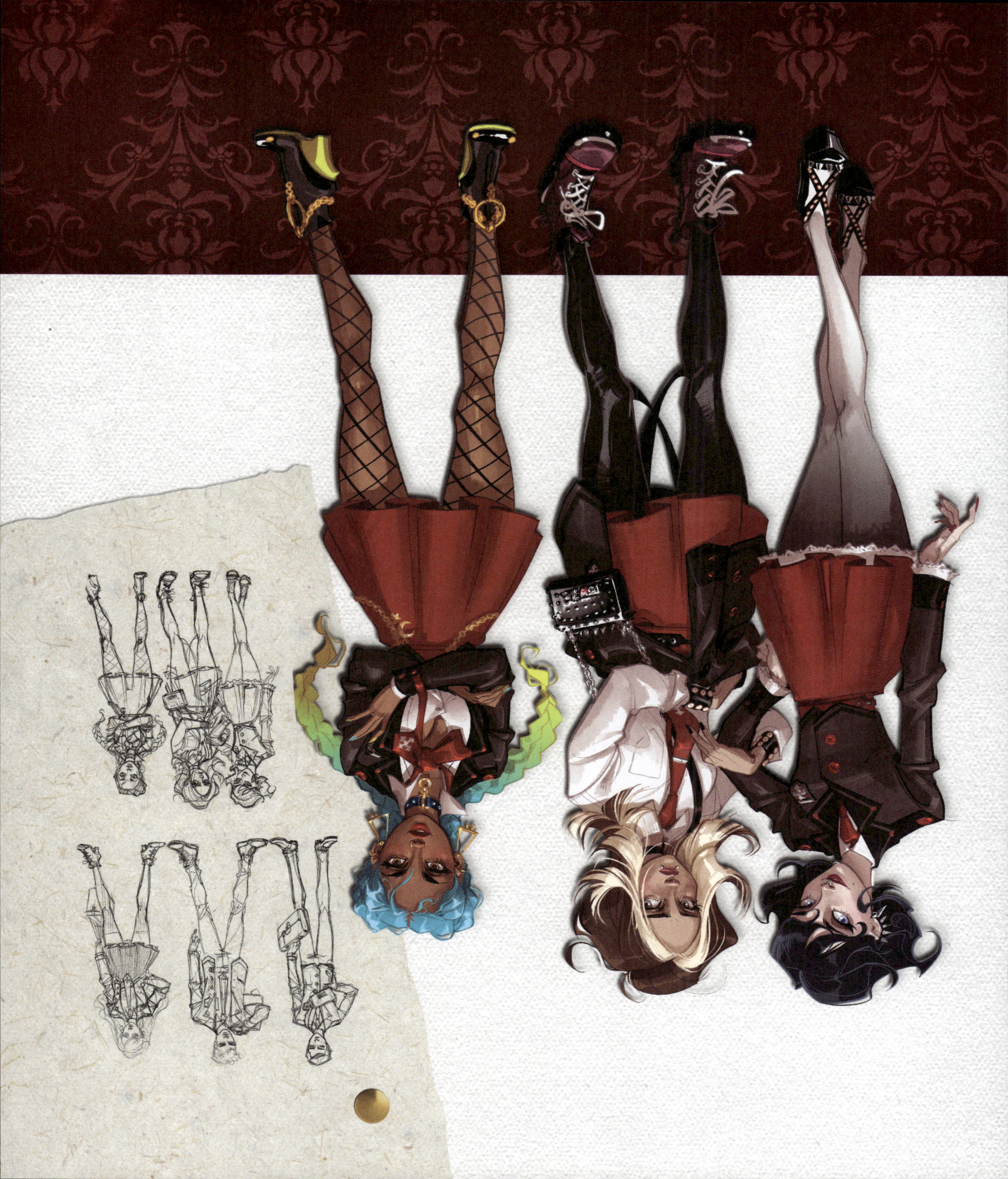

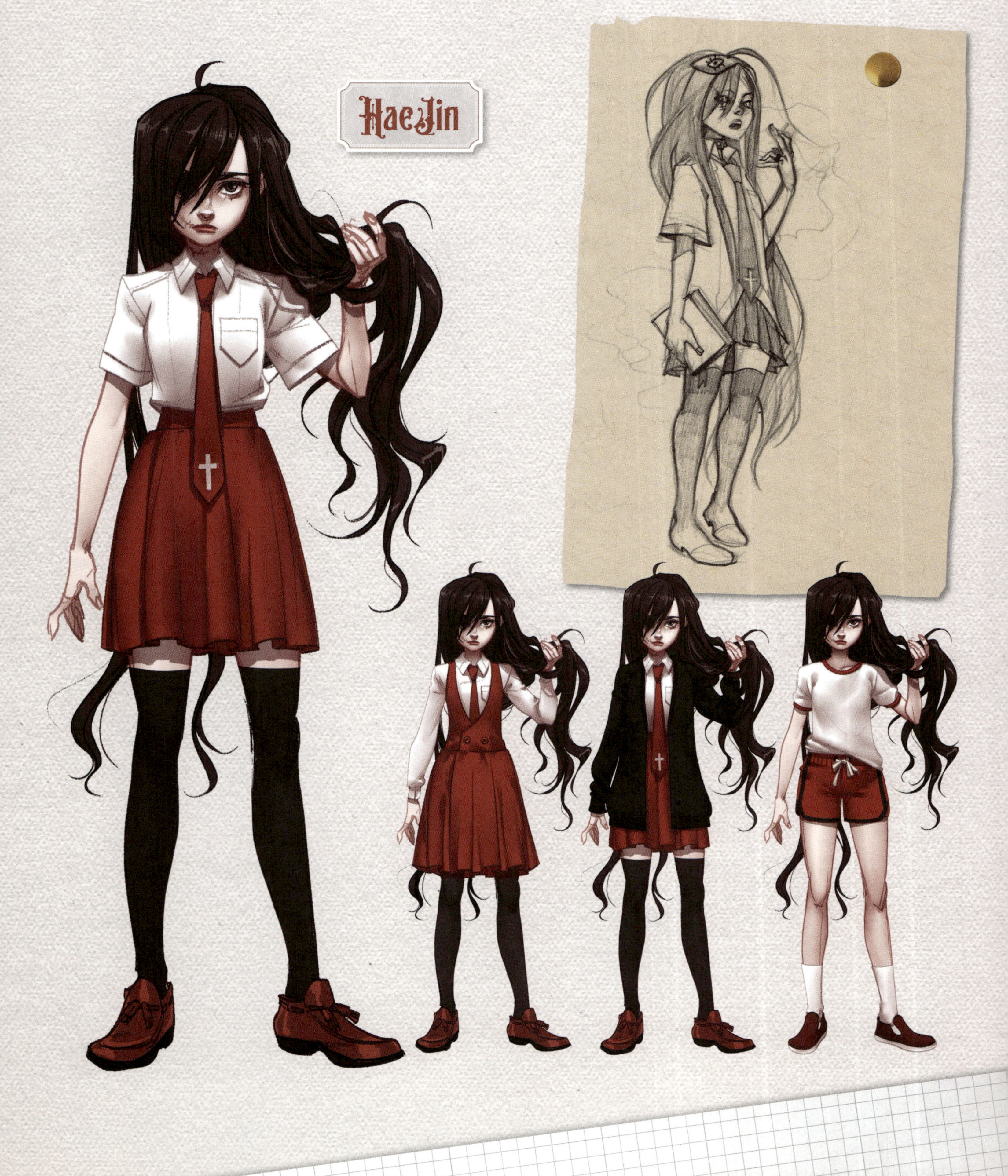
HaeJin

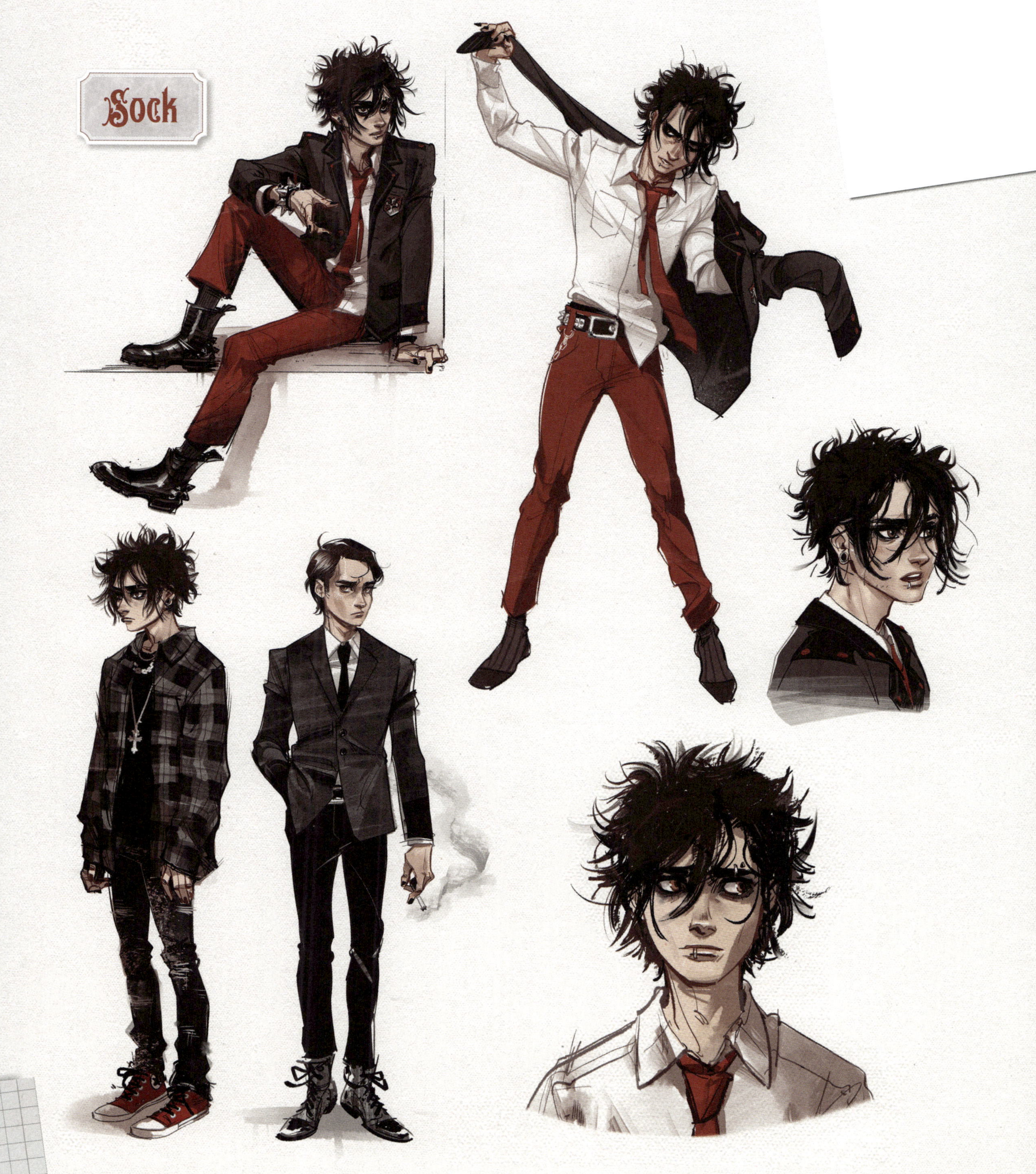
Sock

Worldbuilding

I like to take an organic approach toward worldbuilding, often elaborating on details and social structures as they become necessary and relevant to the characters and story. Most of what I know about *Gloamingvale* came about very slowly and in proportion to how much I planned out the story arcs of my characters

I typically do worldbuilding in written format, without much drawing, but I like to supplement written notes with random doodles of character interactions. Something I'd like to do more of is to make artwork that features settings and backgrounds more prominently. In my art journey timeline, I mentioned that one of the first personal projects I became very involved with was called *Hotel of Nightmares*. What ended up happening during my decade-long rewrite of *IDFracture* is that I merged *H.o.N.* into it completely. Miraculously, it fitted in like a missing puzzle piece. The whole process is still completely mysterious to me, and it actually gave me faith that the story will just work itself out as I chip away at it.

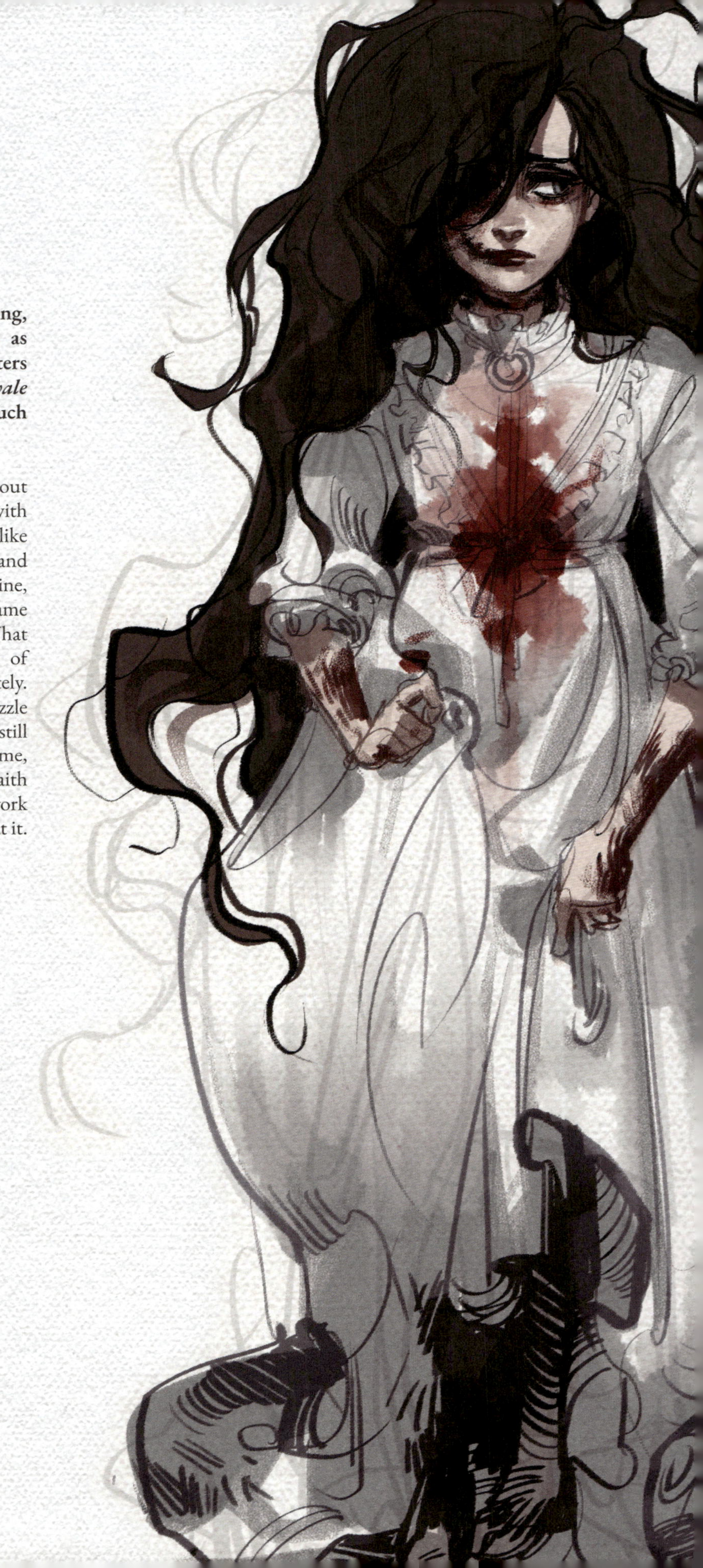

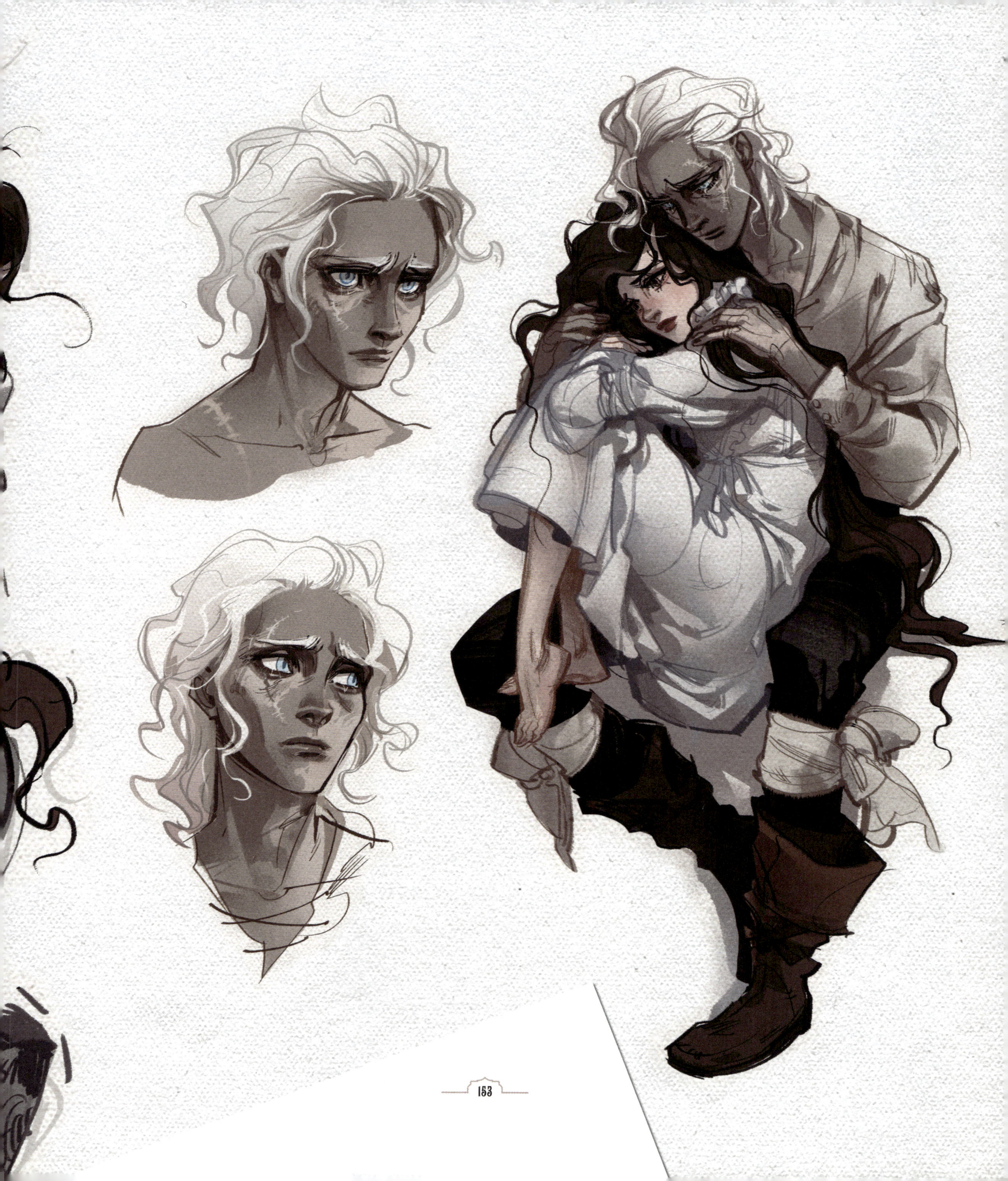

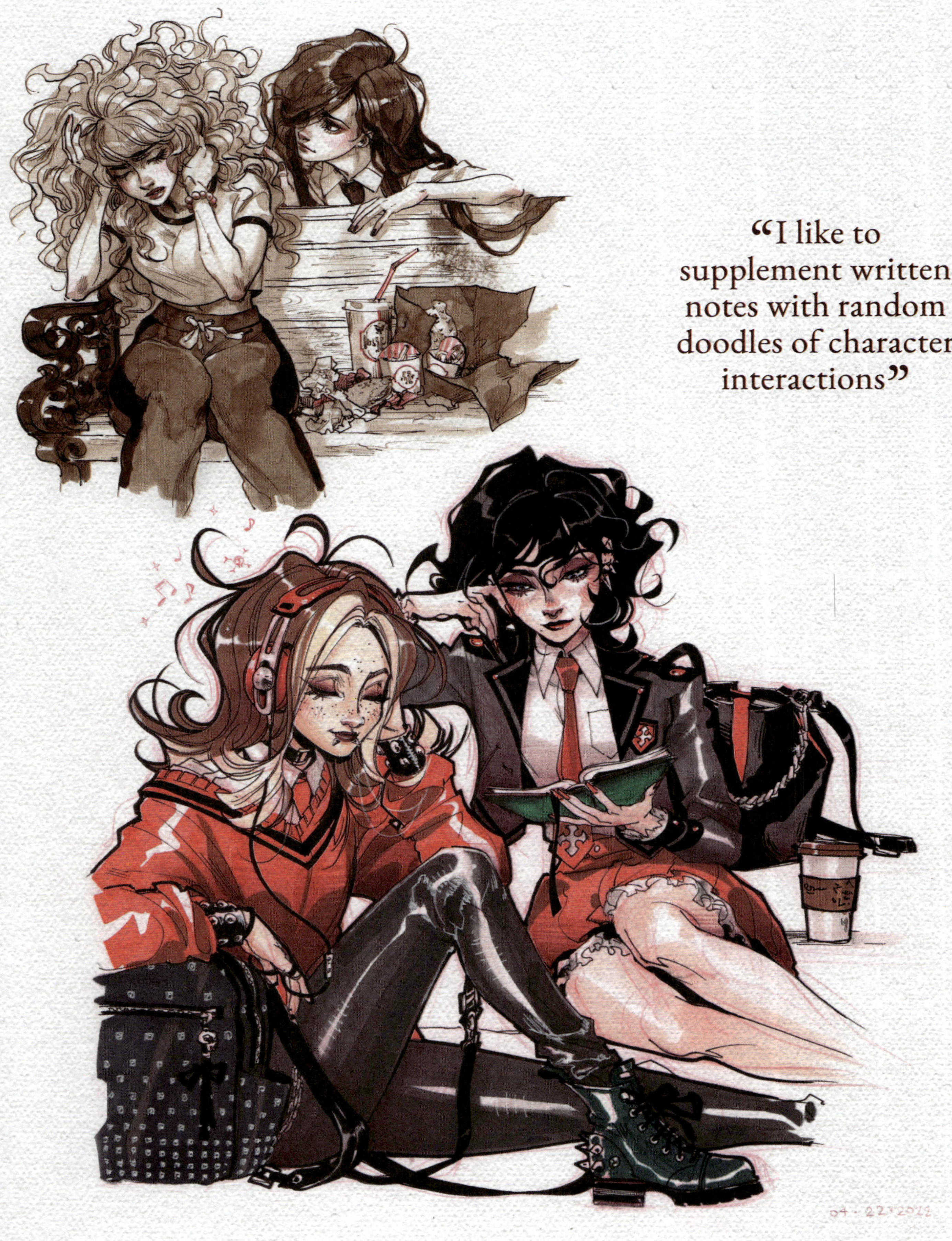

"I like to supplement written notes with random doodles of character interactions"

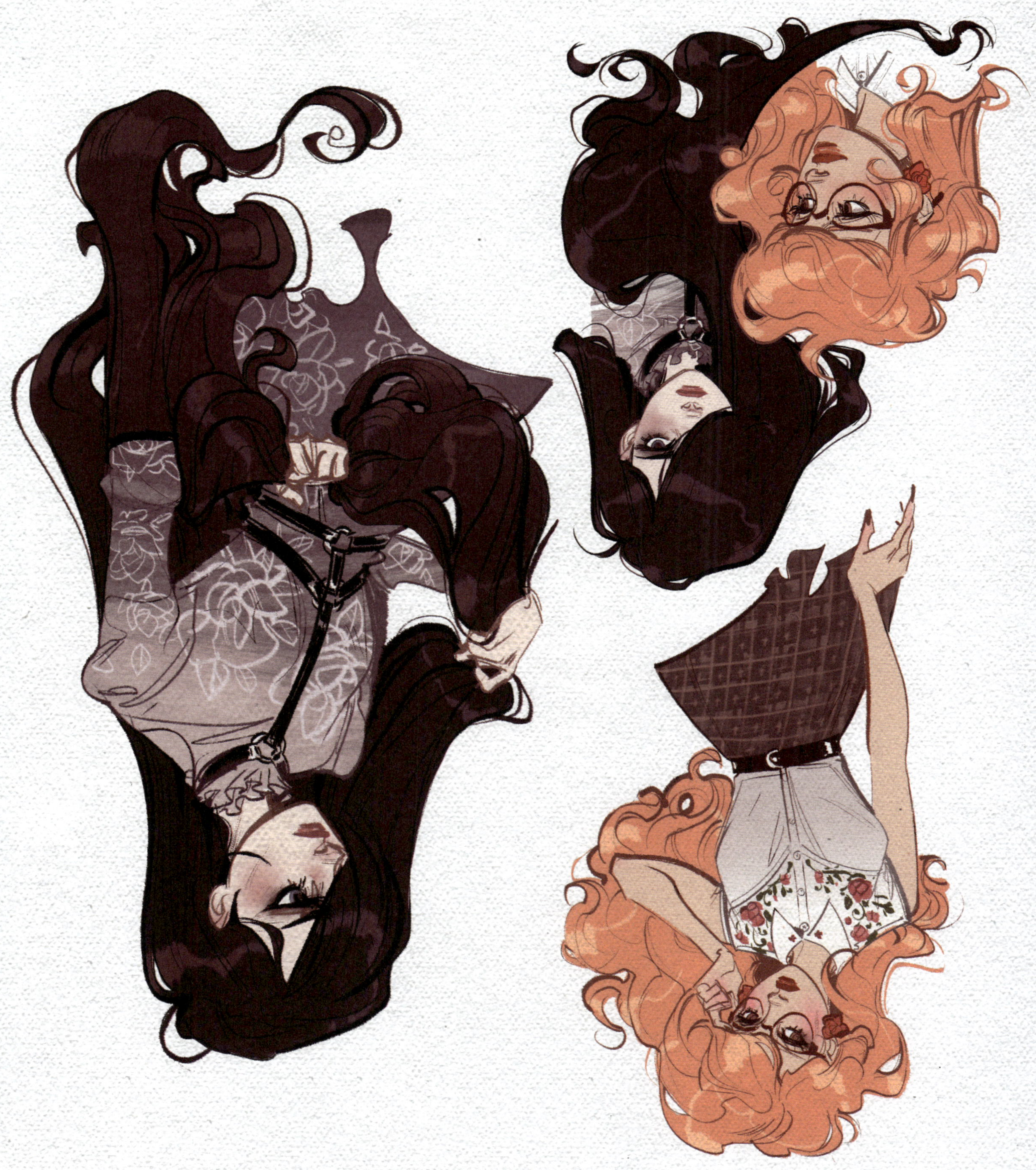

Meaning

It's been a decade since I decided to restart *IDFracture/Gloamingvale*, and although I lament the fact that I still haven't started executing the actual comic, I have managed to make a lot of progress.

I understand now that it had to take this long for me to figure out what kind of story I want to tell. I've kept tons of text documents with ideas on the characters and story over the years, but many of them devolved into heated rants about the fact that life endlessly frustrated me and I didn't have any answers. I always hit a dead end when trying to figure out where to take a character's arc because their perpetual state of depression and confusion merely mirrored my own; unfortunately, I had no solutions for that. I just felt I had nothing to offer, and writing my stories was a personal hidey-hole and nothing more. I wanted my stories to have meaning.

So, what's the answer?

The solutions only came in my late twenties, after I took a proverbial journey to hell and back. Some terrible things happened but I managed to get back on my feet, and after the dust settled, at long last I suddenly knew exactly what to do with my characters' story arcs. I finally figured out some solutions to my problems – and now my characters could too. You might be wondering what my problems were exactly… well. I'll just be honest – life was too disappointing, too sad, love felt covertly conditional and futile, and I felt profoundly alone; I've been plagued by this to various degrees of intensity since I was about thirteen. It felt like my existence was a boring and pointless fluke. I wasn't thrilled about it to say the least. The worst of it was that I had no "real" reason to feel that way at all, or at least that's how inexplicable depression seems when you only assess a few basic external circumstances.

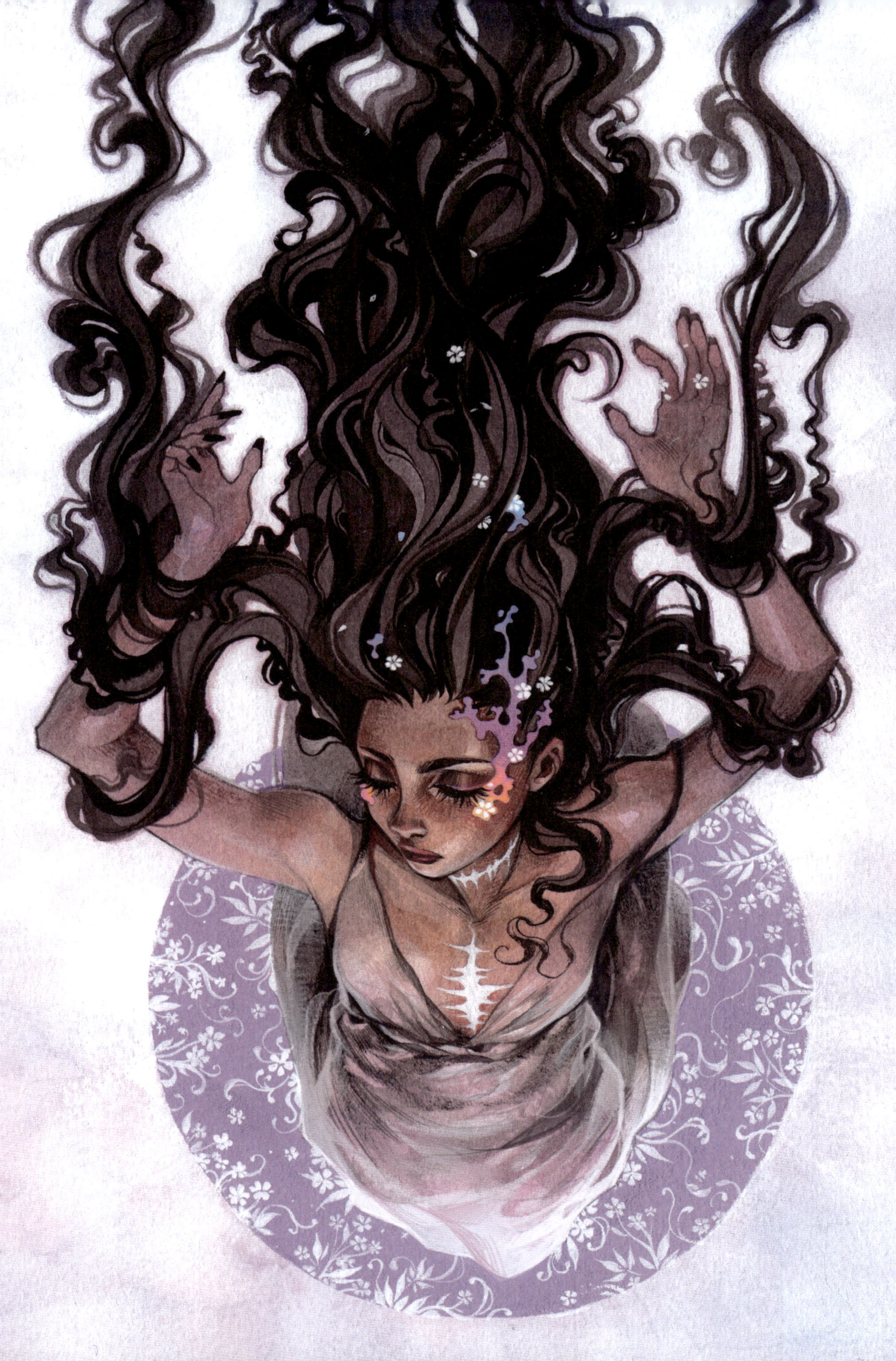

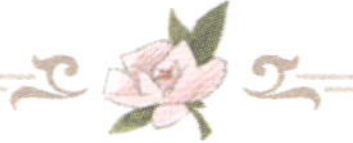

HERE'S WHAT I HAVE COME TO LEARN...

The world is just a reflection of your soul – it isn't any one way, and logic is an insufficient tool for understanding it. It isn't this or that, good or bad, terrible or beautiful – it's everything all at once; saying something like that invites any logician's warranted criticism, but it doesn't really matter – it's something you either understand or you don't, and people can live through their entire life either way.

The core of your soul reflects the world back at you. Self-worth isn't something that can be earned, given, or taken away, regardless of your current perception of it.

It's intrinsic – your actions don't change it, nothing changes it. A person's worth is equivalent to their potential, and potential is an infinite well.

You are a prism through which the world can see itself anew, and your mortality and separation from it is instrumental to that. You're both separate and as one with the world at all times, and it's not a contradiction.

And finally, the only life worth living is one committed to reflecting the good things about the world back to it.

I think that understanding these things properly allowed me to feel at ease with existing, and I'm no longer plagued by depression – I understand my place in this world. I haven't experienced any depression for four years now, which is nothing short of a miracle in my books. I realize that the statements I made sound like a collection of cryptic platitudes, and I could attempt to unpack them, but no. Thankfully, this book isn't (entirely) dedicated to my pseudo-philosophizing.

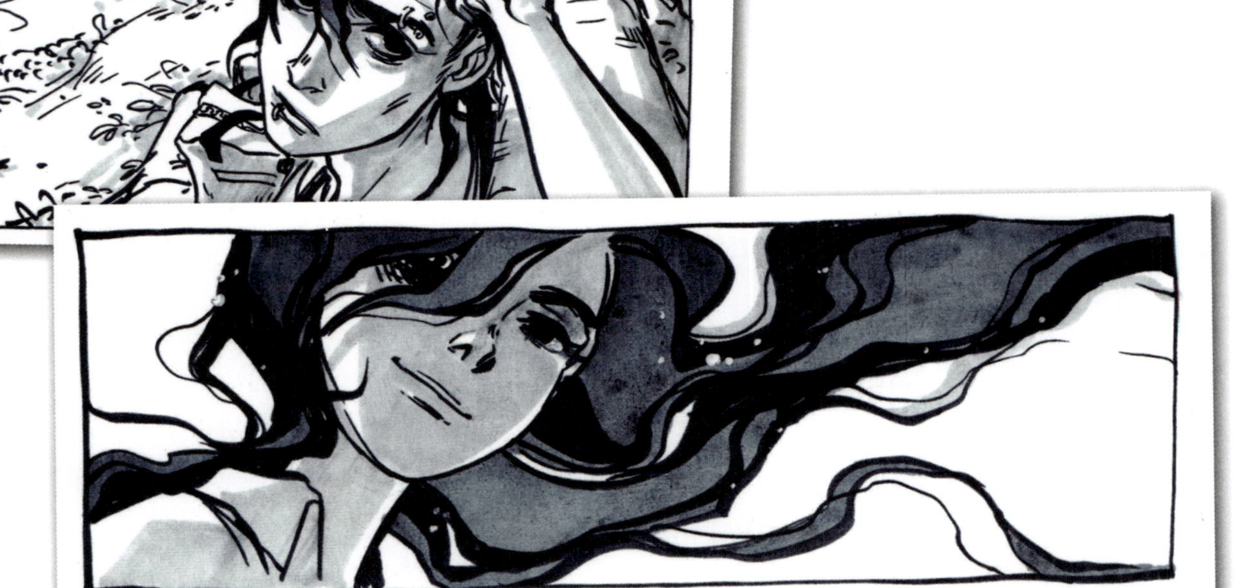

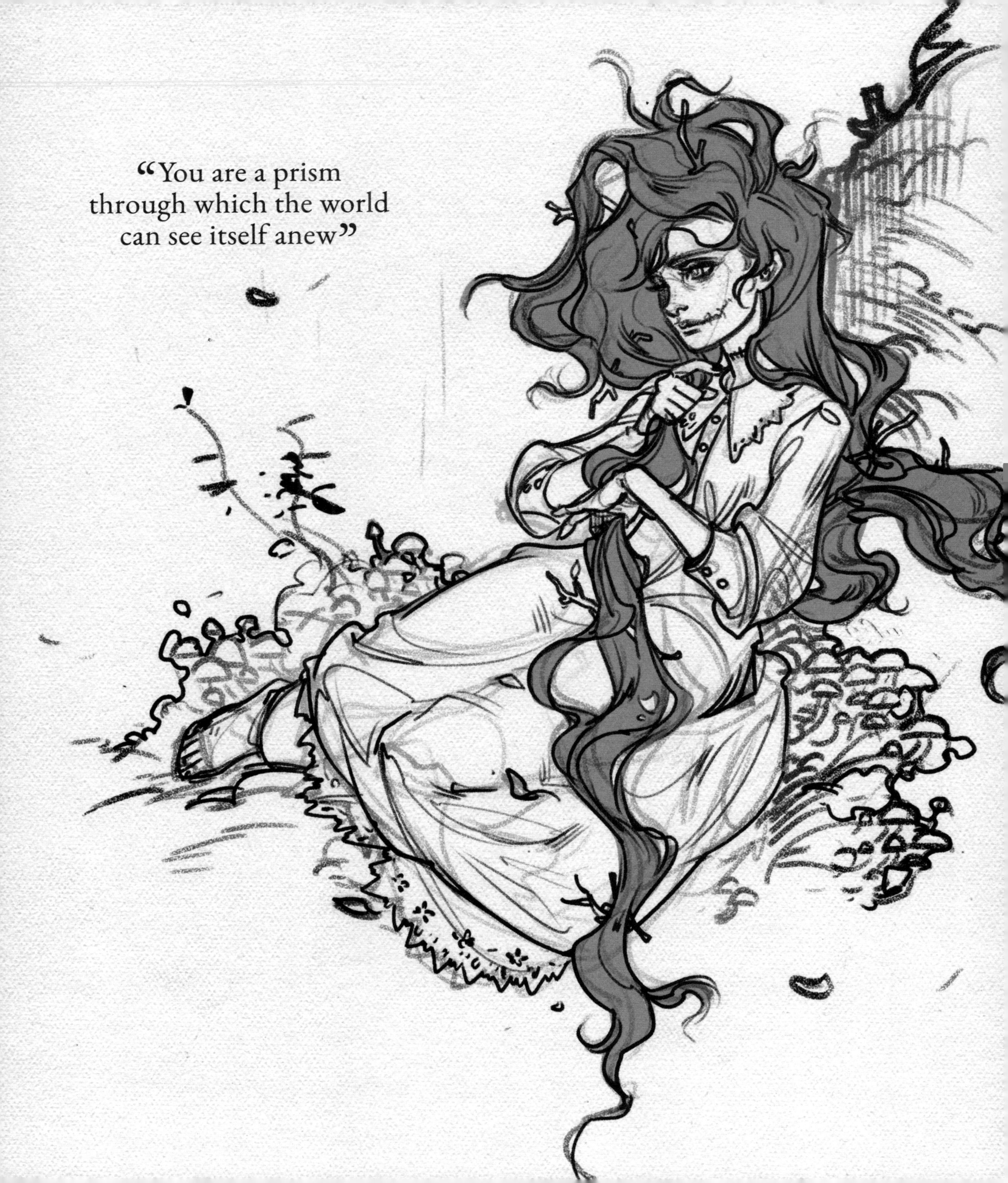
“You are a prism
through which the world
can see itself anew”

The "suffering artist" misconception

There's this idea floating around that meaningful artistic output is fueled by negative emotions such as depression and angst, and this has created a romanticized image of the suffering artist as the "true artist."

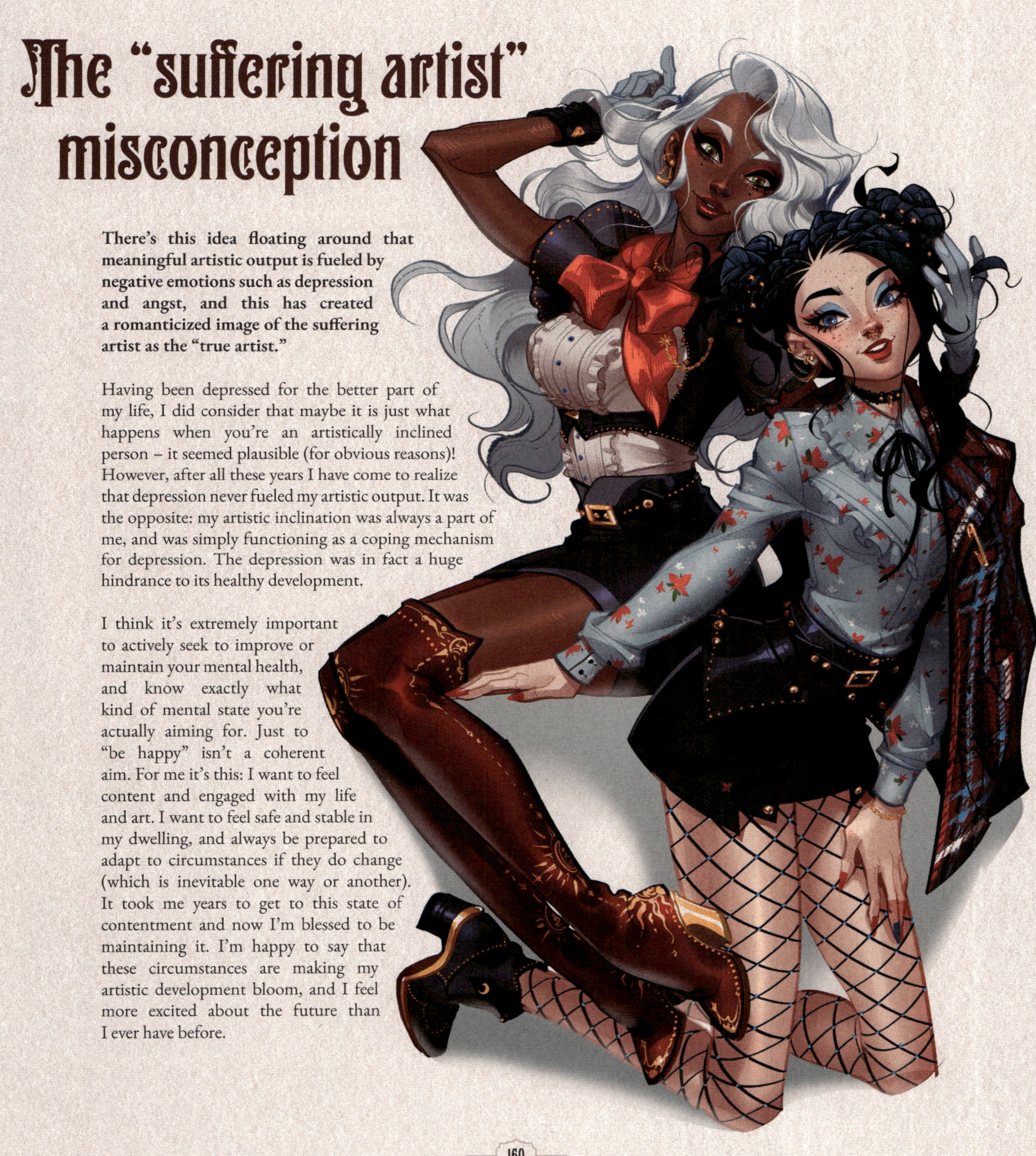

Having been depressed for the better part of my life, I did consider that maybe it is just what happens when you're an artistically inclined person – it seemed plausible (for obvious reasons)! However, after all these years I have come to realize that depression never fueled my artistic output. It was the opposite: my artistic inclination was always a part of me, and was simply functioning as a coping mechanism for depression. The depression was in fact a huge hindrance to its healthy development.

I think it's extremely important to actively seek to improve or maintain your mental health, and know exactly what kind of mental state you're actually aiming for. Just to "be happy" isn't a coherent aim. For me it's this: I want to feel content and engaged with my life and art. I want to feel safe and stable in my dwelling, and always be prepared to adapt to circumstances if they do change (which is inevitable one way or another). It took me years to get to this state of contentment and now I'm blessed to be maintaining it. I'm happy to say that these circumstances are making my artistic development bloom, and I feel more excited about the future than I ever have before.

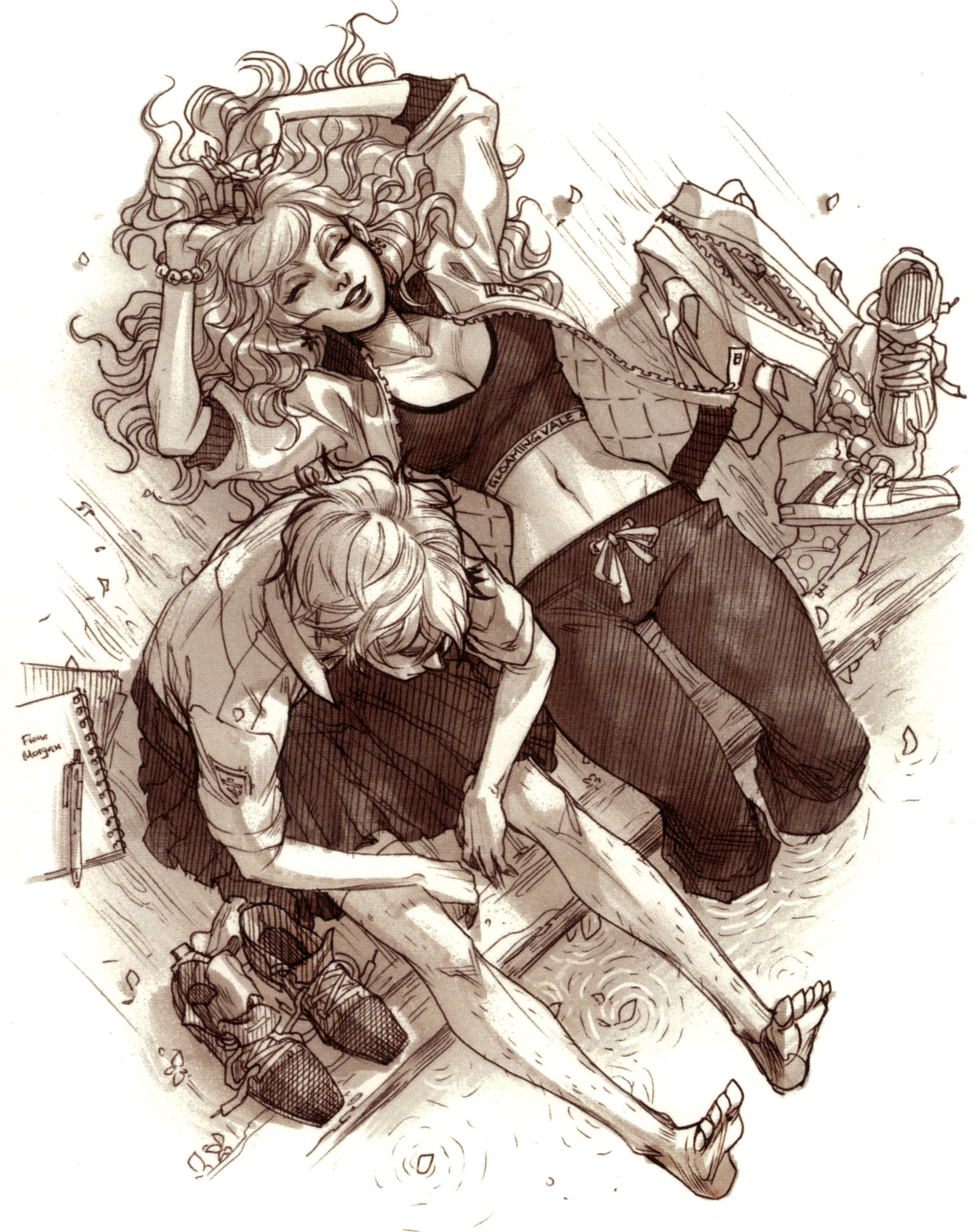
GLOAMING VALE
Fiona Morgan

What the future holds

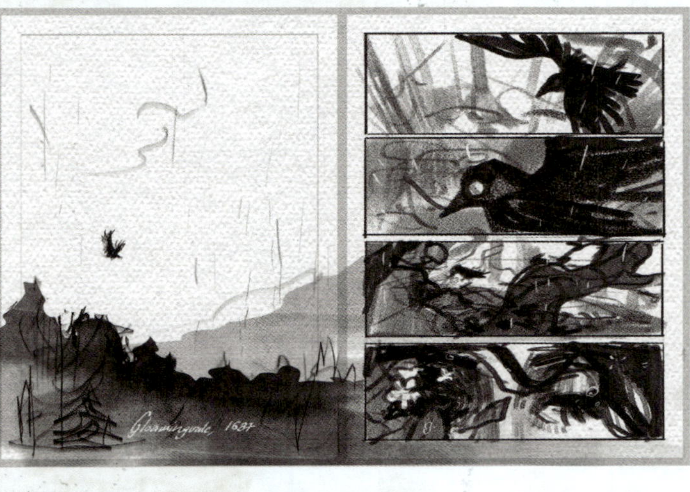

In late 2021, I had a sudden urge to drop all my work and start drawing thumbnails and layouts for the actual comic content of *Gloamingvale*. After all, for many months I'd been sitting on two fully scripted chapters that overall amount to something like a hundred and twenty comic pages.

I guess my frustration at putting it off did have some sort of limit! Those few weeks were absolute artistic bliss – I planned the layouts for the prologue, and started working on missing character designs in accordance with the script. Since all I ever do is obstruct myself from doing this type of work, when I actually get to it now and again, the euphoria that floods in during the process makes me almost want to cry (haha)... I don't know why I do this to myself.

Picking a good starting point for *Gloamingvale* is very difficult, and I'm still not a hundred percent sure that this will be it. I have plans for a non-linear story structure, and since the story takes place over a period of hundreds of years, I feel an enormous amount of pressure about the first piece of information that I choose to disclose. I am very insecure about my abilities as a writer, but I still want to give it my best shot and continue studying the craft.

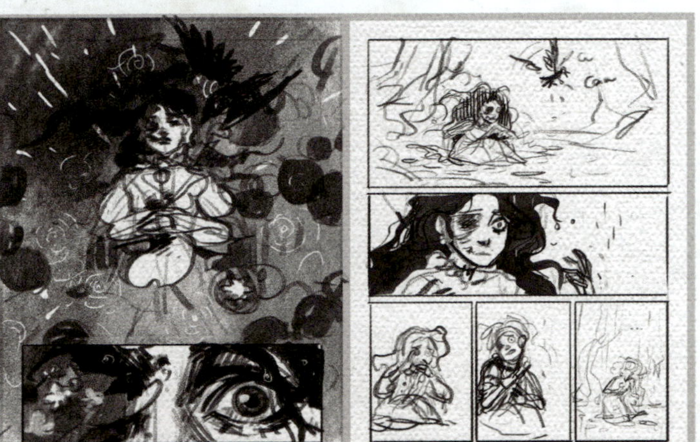

Here are the layouts! My hope is that by the time this book is printed I will have finished executing these pages and shared them online, fingers crossed.

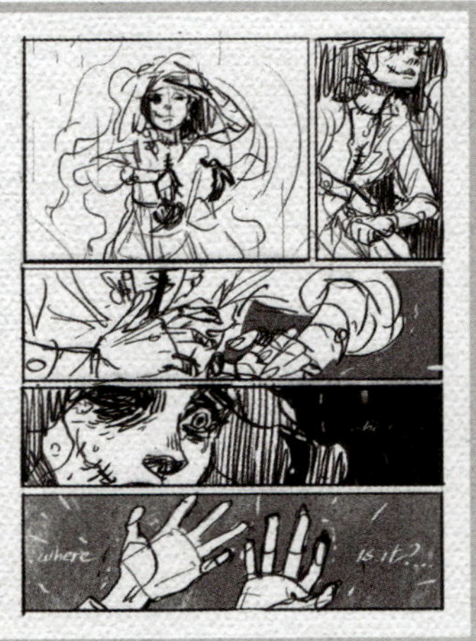

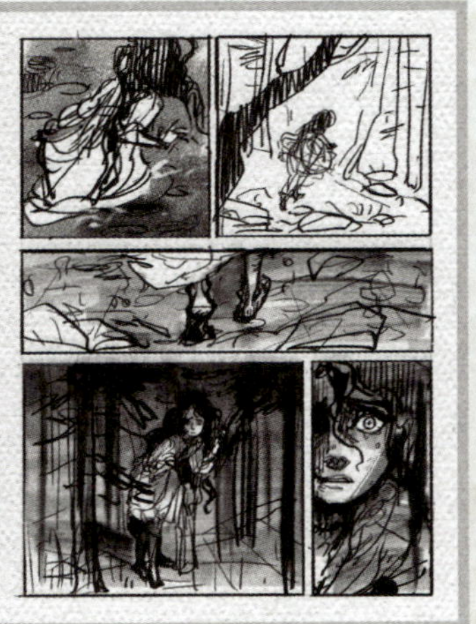

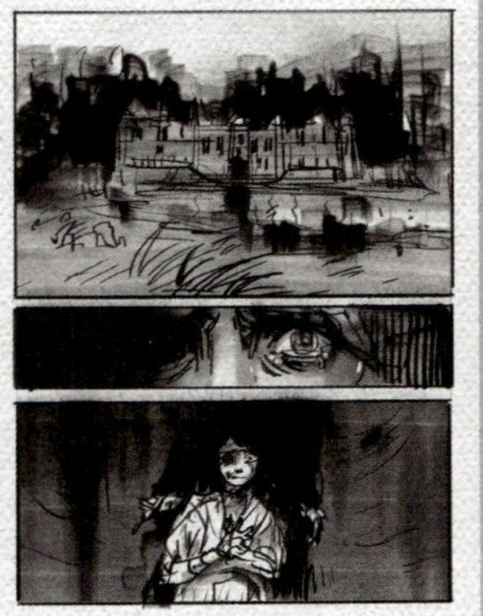

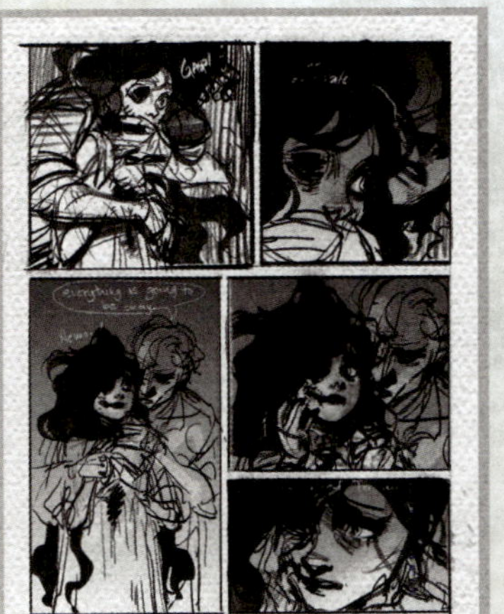

My plan for the immediate future is to wrap up whatever freelance work I have left, and schedule at least three days per week that I can dedicate solely to the development and production of *Gloamingvale*. One of the numerous fears that hold me back is that I will mess up the story like I did last time, and have to start all over again – but I understand that this is an irrational fear.

There is such a thing as being too "prepared" – it's called pre-production purgatory, and I'm currently in it. I'm letting go of the fear of the unknown and choosing to trust the process. The story will sort itself out, and even if it turns into a mess, I'd much rather do my best to make it work now than have my tombstone say, "In the end, she never did manage to start her comic."

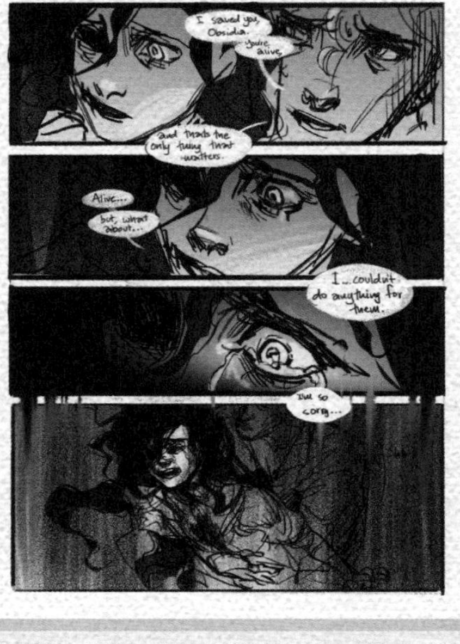
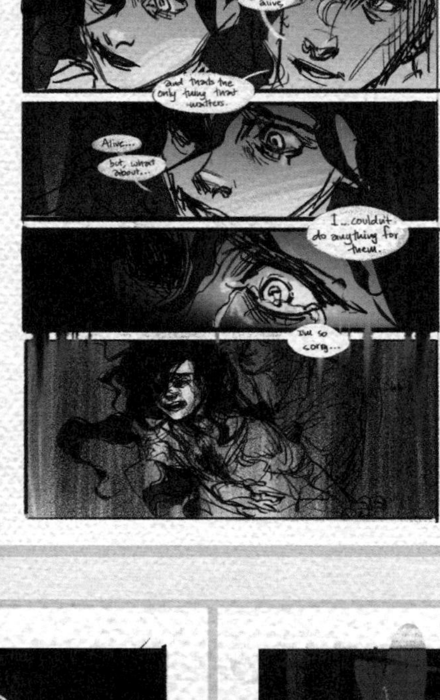

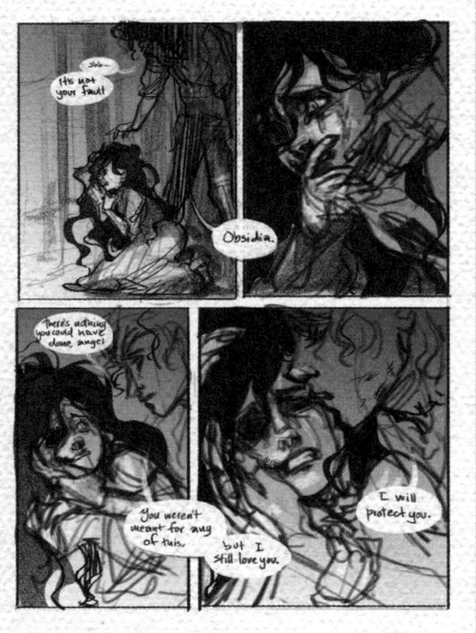

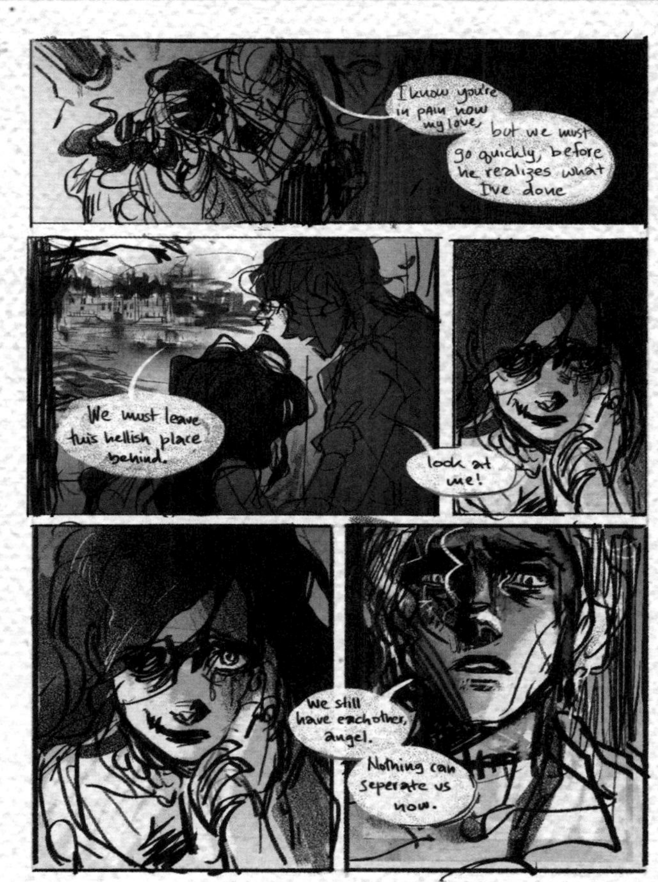

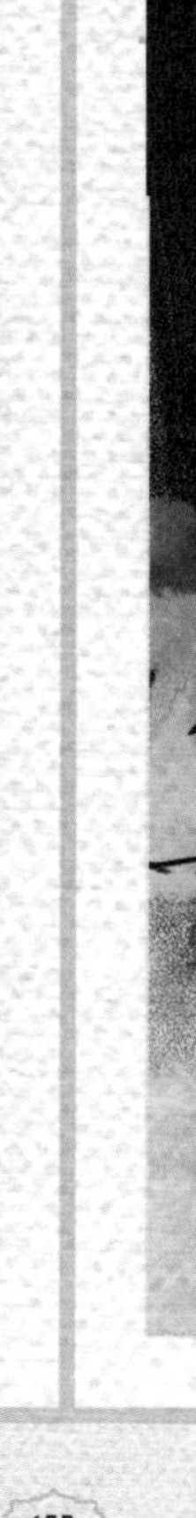

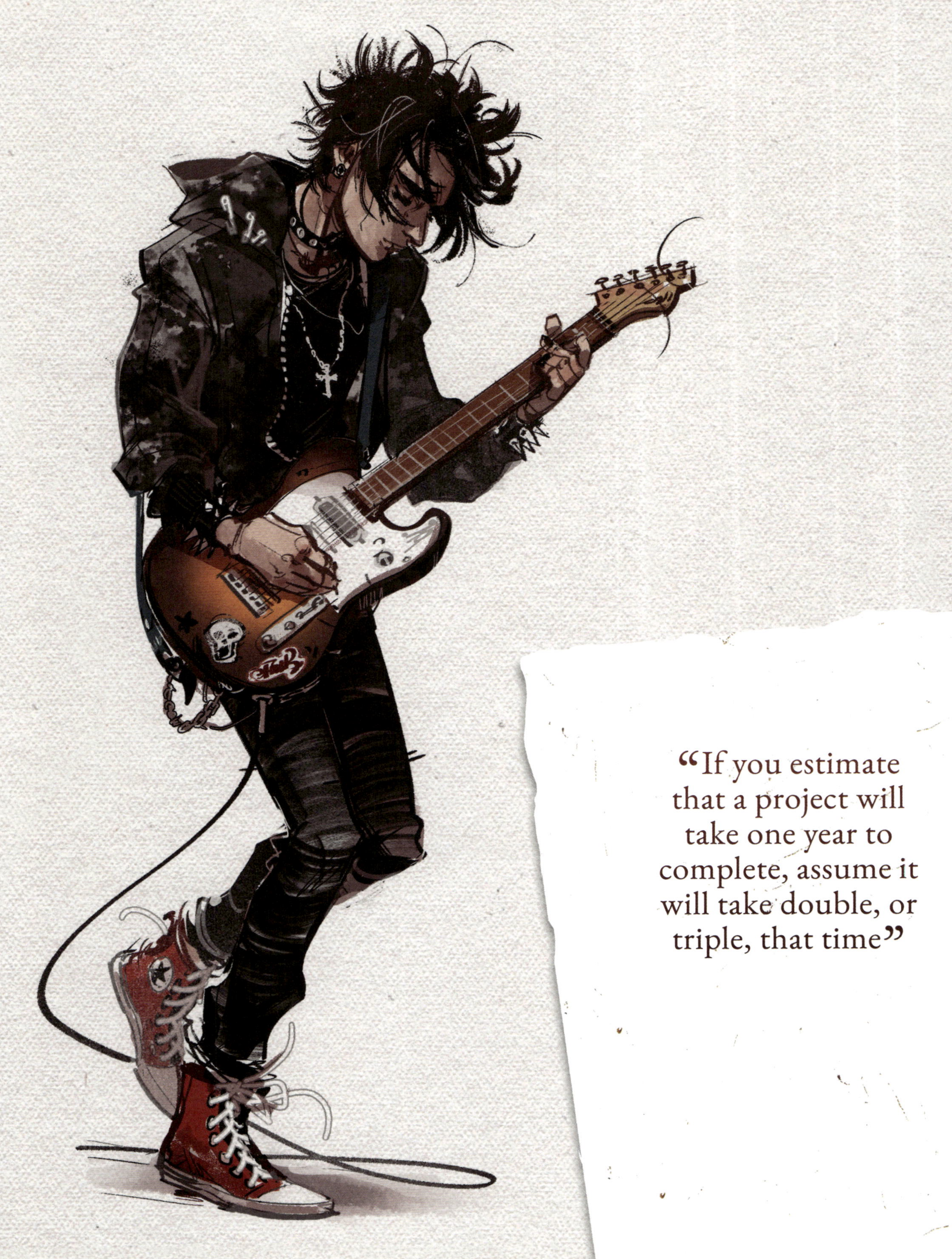

"If you estimate that a project will take one year to complete, assume it will take double, or triple, that time"

Words of wisdom

If I had to boil down all my experiences as a professional artist down to one single takeaway, it would be this – **personal responsibility**. After doing a lot of personal reflection and assessing the projects I have undertaken so far, I was able to glean some golden nuggets. This is the advice I would offer my past self:

1 Know your worth

Never accept less than **living wage**, especially for a long-term project. No amount of hypothetical exposure or experience is worth the constant stress of financial troubles.

2 Schedule realistically

If you estimate that a project will take one year to complete, assume it will take double, or triple, that time. This is a **realistic estimate**, taking unforeseen circumstances into consideration. Do the liveable wage math in accordance with a realistic time estimate.

3 Value your time

Ask yourself, **"Will this project be the best use of your time?"** What is the absolute worst potential outcome of the project? Would you be content with the time spent and wages earned in the worst-case scenario? If the answer is no, do not accept the project.

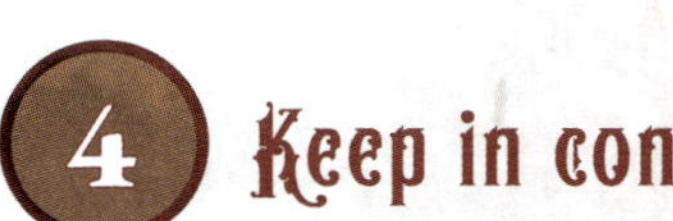

4 Keep in contact

Be in frequent communication about a project's progress with the entire team. Always ask questions as soon as they arise – no question or concern should be left unaddressed, even if it seems trivial. **If it's a point of stress for you – it isn't trivial**.

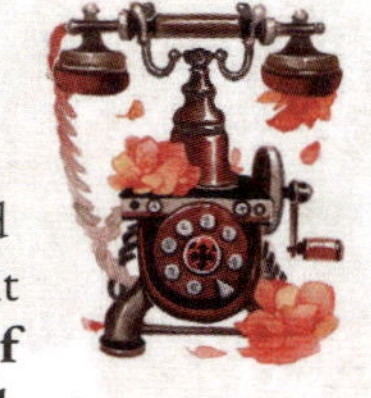

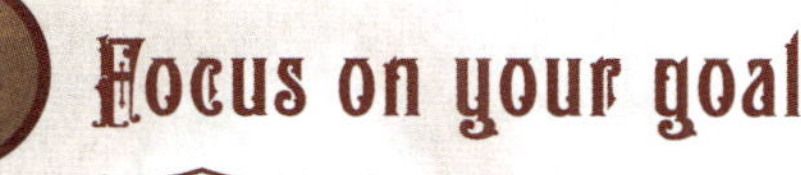

5 Focus on your goal

Finally – make a career plan and work **consciously** toward your goal. **Outline your ultimate goal in great detail**. Framing every potential opportunity in the context of the ultimate goal (whether it will serve or distract from it) is a good strategy for assessment. Do not assume that you can simply stumble your way toward it.

Thank you

I really hope my art journey was as fun to experience through these pages as they were to put together. I'm so thankful for the opportunity to be able to create yet another art book, but above all, I'm incredibly grateful to you – dear reader – for adding this book to your shelf and supporting my work. Whether you stumbled upon it in a bookstore, online, or generously contributed to the Kickstarter campaign in order to make it possible, I thank you from the bottom of my heart. I wouldn't be where I am today without my wonderful audience and feel truly blessed to have been born in a time that allows me to so easily connect with so many people around the world.

A huge thank you is in order to the amazing 3dtotal Publishing team for making this book beyond anything I could have imagined. I'm so grateful and proud to have been able to create *Prism* together, and it couldn't have been done without the careful input and support from Jenny and Sophie, the gorgeous and creative layouts from Joe, the ideas and guidance from Simon, and of course the valuable contribution of everybody else who had a hand in this project. Thank you all so much for believing in my work and giving me this amazing opportunity to join the long list of wonderful artists whose works you have published.

Lastly, I'd like to thank my close friends and colleagues for always encouraging my creative pursuits and giving me their honest feedback, and my wonderful husband for always supporting me and steering me back on the right path when I stumble. I'm excited for what the future holds, and hope to dedicate more and more time to bringing my stories to life, and making beautiful books.

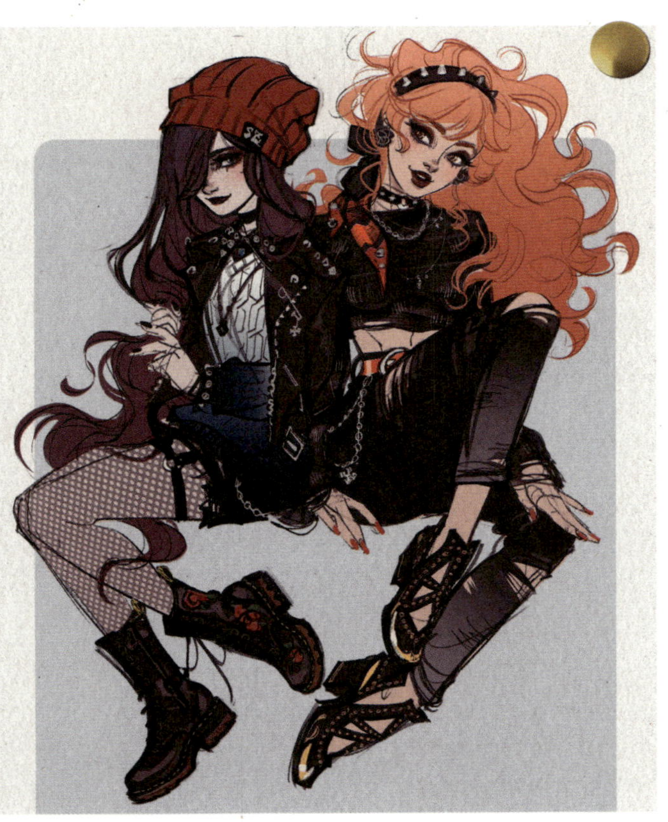

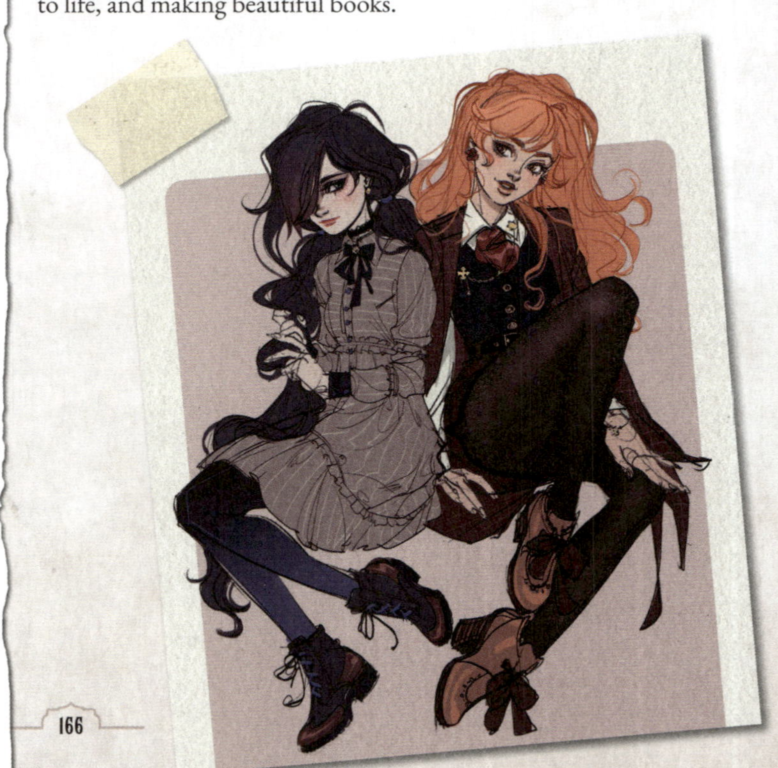

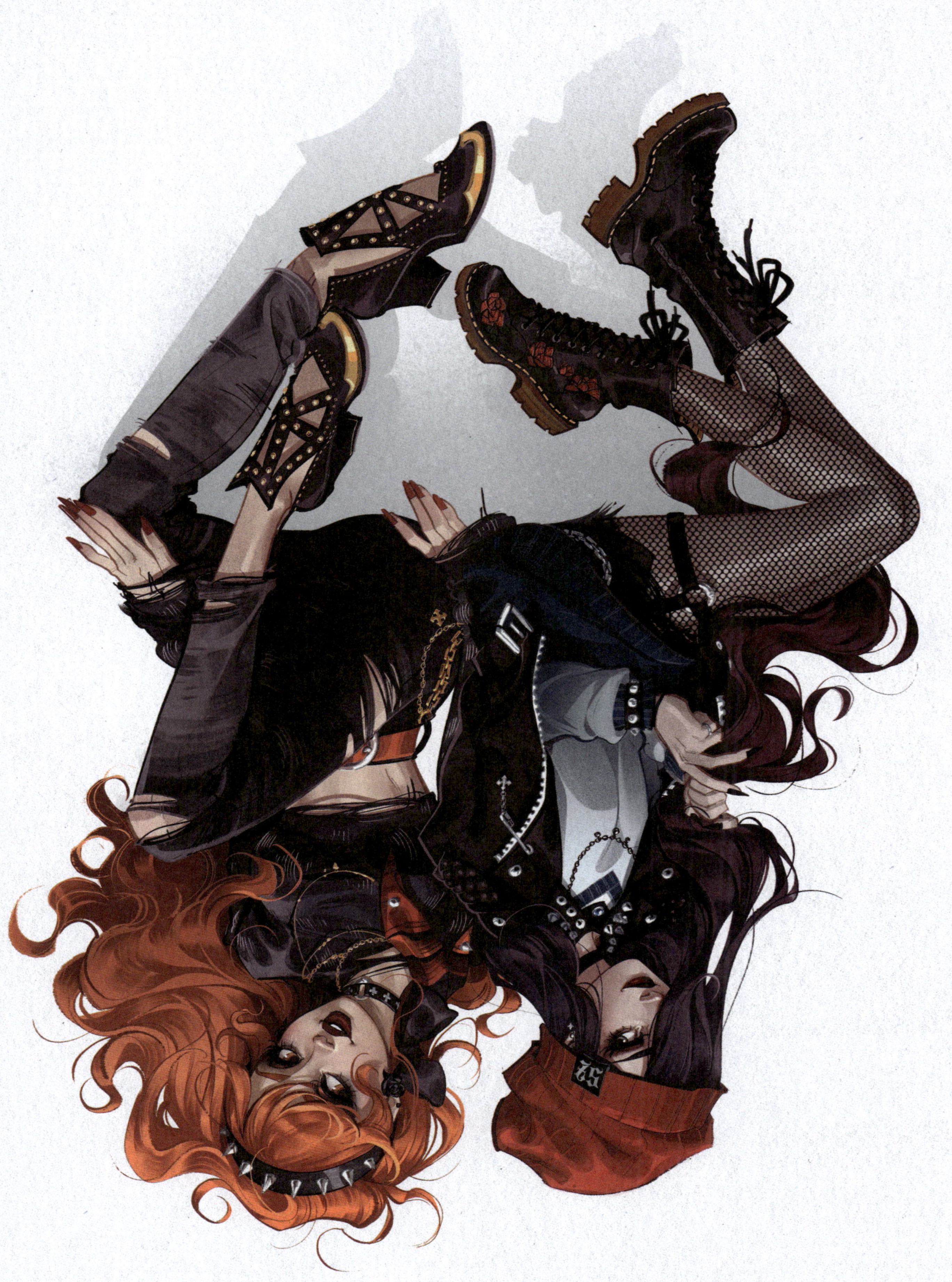

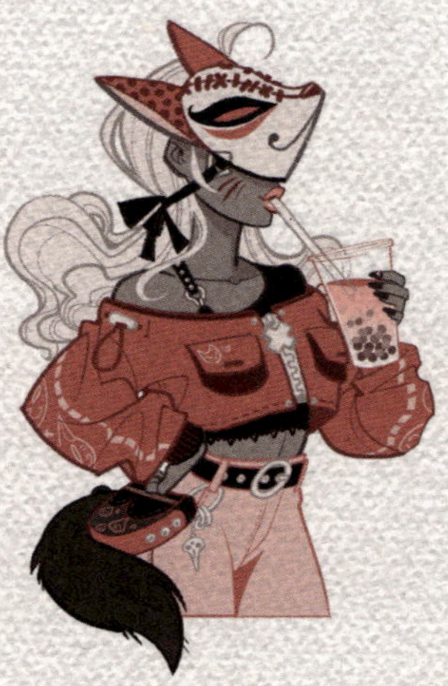

3dtotalPublishing

3dtotal Publishing is a trailblazing, creative publisher specializing in inspirational and educational resources for artists.

Our titles feature top industry professionals from around the globe who share their experience in skillfully written step-by-step tutorials and fascinating, detailed guides. Illustrated throughout with stunning artwork, these best-selling publications offer creative insight, expert advice, and essential motivation. Fans of digital art will enjoy our comprehensive volumes covering Adobe Photoshop, Procreate, and Blender, as well as our superb titles based around character design, including *Fundamentals of Character Design* and *Creating Characters for the Entertainment Industry*. The dedicated, high-quality blend of instruction and inspiration also extends to traditional art. Titles covering a range of techniques, genres, and abilities allow your creativity to flourish while building essential skills.

Well-established within the industry, we now offer over 100 titles and counting, many of which have been translated into multiple languages around the world. With something for every artist, we are proud to say that our books offer the 3dtotal package:

LEARN • CREATE • SHARE